About the Author

Patrick Whitworth is an accomplished author of early church history and of an important survey of English Christianity from 200 AD to 2020 called, *And Did Those Feet: The Story and Character of the English Church AD 200–2020* (Sacristy Press 2021). He was a parish priest in York, London and Bath for forty years but managed to travel extensively in that period. Now living in west Berkshire, he is married to Olivia and has four married children and seven grandchildren. He loves to read, write and travel, and meet people from many backgrounds and countries.

A Witness of Struggle: Telling Tales of a Rambling Rector

Patrick Whitworth

A Witness of Struggle: Telling Tales of a Rambling Rector

Olympia Publishers
London

www.olympiapublishers.com
OLYMPIA PAPERBACK EDITION

A CIP catalogue record for this title is
available from the British Library.

ISBN: 978-1-80074-443-1

First Published in 2023

Olympia Publishers
Tallis House
2 Tallis Street
London
EC4Y 0AB

Printed in Great Britain

Dedication

I dedicate this book to my wife Olivia who had the goodness to let me travel and, even better, accompany me on some trips!

Contents

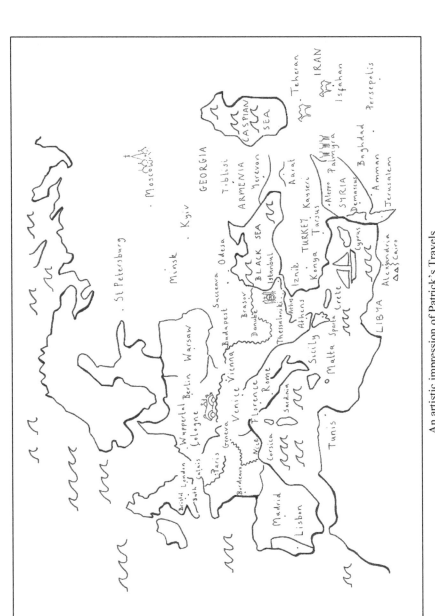

An artistic impression of Patrick's Travels

Preface

In many ways travel has become more difficult now than at any point since 1989 and the collapse of the Berlin Wall. The Middle East has been riven by war in recent years, with the implosion of Syria, Iraq and Afghanistan. Terrorism has become much more of a threat. Russia and China and their dependent territories have become more hostile to the western traveller, notably since the unprovoked attack on Ukraine by Russia. The reality of climate change may further curtail travel in the future. And of course, the pandemic has frozen travel and we have yet to see how things will be when borders re-open and the travel industry gears up again. Looking back, the years between 1989 and 2020 may turn out to be golden years of travel. If so, I have been more than fortunate to fit in much of my travelling in that period and indeed the years before that when the world was emerging from the immediate post war era. And so, in some ways this is a travel record of that period.

What follows in this book is an account of a number of journeys taken by myself and various companions over the last seventy years, when time has allowed and my family and work have generously permitted. Most, but not all of these, were undertaken when I was a Rector of three parishes outside Bath. For the most part they were short journeys of a week, except for two or three that were longer. They resulted from an interest in the classical world, spurred by a book on the Roman Empire which I still have and read when I was ten years old, and then later, from the need to research the growth and struggles of the church in its earliest centuries in order to write about them. I have been drawn to places where, like the earth's tectonic plates, there is or has been friction or conflict. Just as movement in the planet's tectonic plates create earthquakes or tsunamis, there are human fault lines in the world's communities, and they too create tension and explosions. These fault lines exist in the Balkans, in the near Middle East or the Levant, in Palestine, in Northern Iraq, in the Caucuses, in Kashmir and in the Hindu

Kush, in Afghanistan, in Ireland, and on the borders of Russia and Belarus with the Ukraine and Poland, and no doubt elsewhere also. The fault lines are constructed by the proximity of ethnic differences, historical grievances, land claims, religious rivalries or hatreds, and frequently great economic disparity. These fault lines have deeply affected, or are now affecting, millions of our fellow human beings, generating hatred and the displacement of peoples who are seeking sanctuary outside their borders.

Alongside those deeper reasons for travel—to help with an understanding and appreciation of history as well as past or present grievances—there are precious lighter moments: meetings, conversations, mishaps, surprises, scenery, changing cultures, architecture, customs, meals, food, wine, beauty, women, men and children and unforgettable memories. It was Robert Louis Stevenson who famously said, "to travel hopefully is a better thing than to arrive", but why should one want to travel at all, forsaking the comfort and certainty of one's own home for the uncertainty and mild discomfort of something unknown? The answer for me is found in this book.

I would like to thank all those who have travelled with me over the years. At the outset it was Mark Wrightson, Charles Higgins, my brother Charles and sister Teresa. More recently there have been quite a number of stimulating and faithful travel companions: Michael Fowler, Paul Bright, Tom Peryer, Richard and Sarah Parry, Geoff Hudson and, of course, Olivia. I would like to thank Wiola Hola-Peryer for sharing details of her mother's extraordinary journey during WWII from the borders of Russia to Nazareth with General Anders. I would like to thank William Close for giving me the idea of writing this book and Kitty Willis for helpful comments on chapter nineteen on Romania, which she knows well and also Richard Dannatt, Jocey Hurndall and Tom Peryer for their generous comments. I would like to thank the Parishes of All Saints Bath Weston, Langridge and North Stoke and Christ Church Gipsy Hill for supporting and being interested in my travels, turning out for yet another talk by the Rambling Rector!

Finally, I would like to thank all those who have helped in the production of this book, my parents Rex and June who encouraged travel and exploration, the team at Olympia—especially Kristina, and our daughter Louisa Mulvaney who drew the map. It has been a pleasure to write and I hope it has opened a few windows onto our extraordinary and fragile world. I had plenty of time to complete as it was done in "lockdown" which provided an excuse to travel-in-the-mind to all these places, and recall diverse and rich experiences through diaries and photos, scarcely looked at in fifty years.

Patrick Whitworth
March 2022

Chapter I
European Beginnings

I was born in the British Military Hospital in Wuppertal, Germany, in March 1951. The hospital was part of the British Army of the Rhine. Although initially an army of liberation, the Army of the Rhine soon became the main defensive contribution of Britain to NATO in the event of a Soviet attack across the North German Plain. It lasted as long as the Cold War: it was there in defence of freedom. It comprised some fifty thousand troops, and remained in place until 1994, when, at the end of the collapse of the Iron Curtain in 1989, the peace dividend meant the gradual return of the troops to the United Kingdom, mostly to Catterick and Tidworth—considerably less exotic than Berlin, Aden and Hong Kong, where forces were once stationed.

My parents had married right after the end of the war in 1946 at Holy Trinity Brompton, having fulfilled residency rules entitling a person to be married in a particular parish by leaving a suitcase overnight in a local hotel! My father, then a Major in the Grenadier Guards, was married in military uniform. My parents had met before the war through my Aunt Ursula, who later married Roddy Thesiger, captured at Arnhem and a younger brother of the great explorer, Wilfred Thesiger. My mother had gone with Aunt Ursula at the end of the war to Naples in the Autumn of 1945, where my father was based at Caserta, the Neapolitan Palace, taken over by the Allies as the Allied Supreme Command Head Quarters. My father, Rex, had moved there with British and American troops from North Africa through Sicily to mainland Italy, and was then an Intelligence Officer with Guards 24 Brigade, and then later at the divisional Headquarters at Caserta, before being moved to Trieste.

My mother, June, had lost a beloved older brother, Bill, in Tunisia in March 1943. He was buried in the Military Cemetery at Sfax, Tunisia. During the last part of the war she worked in Baker Street, London, with the FANYs (The First Aid Nursing Yeomanry) founded in 1907. It was involved with nursing and intelligence work. Latterly, it worked with the SOE (Special Operations Executive) and one of its bravest members was Violette Szabo who was captured in France and was executed in Ravensbruck aged twenty-six. She is commemorated with a bust outside Lambeth Palace on the Embankment. My mother prepared special forces to be dropped behind enemy lines in a building in Baker Street, London. She would check their kit to ensure there was nothing incriminating, such as tags saying bought in the Army and Navy Stores, Regent Street! Having sworn the Official Secrets Act, she never subsequently spoke about the work. She wore a military uniform at the time, looking smart in a tie and beret, and appears to have been trained at Roydon in Norfolk, near her home at Hardingham, with a group of companions who became good friends. Being a free spirit, and up for a bit of adventure and romance, she travelled with Ursula, my father's sister, to Naples in September 1945 just four months after VE Day. They were met on the quayside by my father!

Ursula and June had travelled on a troop ship, and were going to work in an officer's canteen at Caserta, and then in Trieste. My mother kept the menu from the canteen on board the ship: black pudding and eggs for breakfast; sauté of rabbit and ham, followed by plums and custard for lunch; and chicken marengo, roast loin of pork and lemon meringue tart for dinner. It sounded better than the severe rationing then applying in England. Once arrived, there were plenty of eligible officers to meet, all of them relieved to be alive at the end of the war. Geoffrey Dicker, a Norfolk friend; Madron Seligman—later an Olympic skier, friend of Ted Heath at Balliol and a European politician; Ian Hunter, the arts impresario and founder of many music festivals in Britain, including the Edinburgh Festival; and David Erskine, the historian. Some would be lifelong friends. Undoubtedly, theirs was a unique fellowship born of war.

These were some of the officers, all in battledress, in my mother's wartime photo album. Several had come through the fierce fighting at Anzio and Monte Casino and now could enjoy a breathing space. And in those few months, at the end of 1945, there was skiing north of Trieste, horse-riding and even sight-seeing in Rome to enjoy, with a hotel reserved for officers. My mother had a beagle who appears in some of her photographs. Out of all these officers, my father was the fortunate one, and they were married in June 1946, less than a year later. In 1949 my older brother Charles was born, and in 1951 the family was moved to Germany and the Army of the Rhine, where I entered the world.

Of the first twelve years of my life, at least seven were spent in Germany and France. Like many military families in those days, considerable time was spent abroad. The years following the war necessitated large troop deployments, not so much to hold down a defeated Germany as to deter Soviet aggression in central Europe. There were also large deployments of forces east of Suez.

In August 1950, our family had moved to No 117 *Hutten Allee* in Krefeld, close to the Rhine, and a little north of Dusseldorf. Our quarters were a spacious suburban house with a large garden, with plenty of room for children's parties. At least one summer beach holiday was taken at Sharbeutz, a big sandy beach north east of Hamburg on the Baltic. There were picnics by the Rhine and trips to Holland. Then, in 1953, we were back in England. My father was now an army instructor at the Staff College at Camberley, and during this time my sister Teresa was born.

In many ways it was an idyllic childhood. There were trips to my grandparents' farm at Hardingham in Norfolk, where we were spoilt by my grandmother with cakes galore, and had fields to run in and could "help" with the harvest and watch my grandfather's cows being milked. There were tractors to ride. Cousins were being born. For my fourth birthday I was especially thrilled by a policeman's uniform. But it was soon time for my parents to take their three young children to the next army posting back in Germany. This time we were away from England for four years, on two consecutive postings.

By July 1955 we were back in Germany. This time we lived in Haus Glasmacher in Hubbelrath, east of the Rhine and nearer to Wuppertal, my birthplace. My father had been promoted to Lieutenant Colonel and was now commanding his regiment, the 1st Battalion Grenadier Guards. This was always a significant moment in the career of a soldier, and one of genuine honour. Once again, living in Germany gave easy access to beauty spots like Winterberg, east of Dusseldorf, which was a ski resort in winter (as its name suggests). In 1956 we even tried skiing at Kitzbuhl, no doubt driving there and back. In fact, we seemed to be driving to and from England or around Germany much of the time. German place names were becoming familiar, not that I knew where they were, but the adults kept talking about them: Osnabruck, Bielefeld, Luneburg, Hannover and the splendid sounding Monchengladbach, which sounded like a place of permanent happy eating! In reality, they were all towns in the British sector where troops were quartered or where military exercises took place. They became part of the background to our life in Germany, familiar but at the same time, to a small child, unknown.

It was in Hubbelrath that I first went to school. It was a British army school run by the British Forces Education Service (B.F.E.S). I have only one report from there, issued for Class IV in April 1957. In fact, I think it was probably my best report in twelve years of schooling—they were to go downhill from then on. Joan Stanbury, the class teacher, whom I don't remember, wrote "Patrick has made very good progress this term. He is happy and enters into his work with zest, and takes a keen interest in all school activities. He is popular and very co-operative in all group activities". They really did go downhill after that, and in any case in 1957 we moved to France, so there was no chance of either disappointing expectations, or building on this success!

My father had a new job after relinquishing command of his battalion. We were to go to France. He was to be a Senior Staff Officer at Supreme Headquarters Allied Powers Europe (SHAPE) based near Versailles. We were on the move again. We lived in a small French village in a rather delightful house that had an orchard behind it and shutters at the windows. Although the village of Milon-la-Chapelle was quiet, it was not far from Versailles or Paris. When visitors came, there were trips to both. The Eiffel Tower, Arc de Triomphe and Notre Dame were regularly on the agenda. I remember being temporarily lost in the Louvre, aged eight, separated from my parents. It seemed like the eyes of the portraits of the Old Masters swirled around me, following my predicament with a nightmarish stare, but it was not too long before we were re-united.

I went to an international school. I can't remember much of what we learnt, but I do remember that most break times we played marbles in the school yard, a kind of mini boules. The marbles, made of glass, had delicious swirls of reds, greens and blues in flowing patterns and were a highly desirable commodity to trade with.

More important things were afoot in France than playing marbles (although for a seven-year-old boy that was what really mattered). General de Gaulle was about to be re-summoned to government. Algeria had brought the Fourth Republic to its knees with the right wing violently opposed to Algerian independence, these extremists were threatening an invasion of France by French Algerian forces. The sixty-seven-year-old De Gaulle said that he was willing to serve again, having been defeated in the polls in 1946. Like Churchill in England, the war-time leader had been rejected by France, just as Churchill had been in Britain in 1945, as both countries sought new trajectories for the future. De Gaulle was voted back into office in June 1958. There had been riots in Paris, an invasion of Corsica by far-right Algerian French troops, and civil war threatened. A new constitution was voted for in a referendum in September 1958, and the Fifth Republic was ushered in with De Gaulle as President. He remained President until 1968, the "year of revolutions" in France and elsewhere. France's commitment to NATO and SHAPE, however, came under increasing strain, as the country under De Gaulle sought greater military independence, and in particular, independence from the Americans and the British. In the end De Gaulle removed French forces from the NATO command structure, and ejected SHAPE from French soil, which was typical of him.

Meanwhile, as these great events shaped up, I was invited to go to the SHAPE HQ to meet an important British soldier. Suitably dressed, my brother and I reported for this occasion at my father's office. The high-ranking officer came in. That he was important was obvious from the number of medal ribbons he had on his chest and the deferential staff who accompanied him. We all stood up and were presented to Field Marshal Bernard Montgomery of Alamein. He asked my father how discipline in the family was! My father replied that he thought it was adequate for the task! Montgomery swept out again, satisfied, hopefully, that this family unit was playing its part in those tempestuous Gallic times!

In 1960, after two years near Versailles, it was time for another posting. This time we were back in England with me attending a school in Camberley, but soon we were back in Europe again. My father had been promoted, aged forty-five, to become the Brigade Commander in Berlin from August 1961. By then I had started at a preparatory boarding school called Sunningdale, and the next two years, in terms of values being laid down, were to be among the most significant of my life.

Berlin 1961–1963

I don't remember exactly what the first day in Berlin was like when we moved there in August 1961, but my clear impressions were of the house we were to live in and of my father's very nice staff car, a Mercedes, which had a flag on the front with a star, when he was in it.

The house was very unusual, and, like the name of an excellent book about life in Berlin post–1900, was also *A House on the Lake*. The lake was the Havel, and the house was just above it. It had been requisitioned by the British, presumably soon after the end of the war. The house was on *Am Rupenhorn*, a street leading off a main thoroughfare called Heerstrasse, which eventually led to the Brandenburg Gate. It had been designed in 1928 by an important architect of the Bauhaus period, and was his home. His name was Eric Mendelsohn (1887–1953), and he was of Jewish family, a friend of Chaim Weizmann—the first President of Israel. He had fled the Nazi government in 1933 and worked in England, and then Israel. His architecture was known for its dynamic functionalism. And our house was certainly like that.

On one side and overlooking the street there were no windows, just a long wall rendered in cement. On the other side was a huge single window the size of a wall that opened out onto a terrace overlooking the lake that stretched away. The window would move up and down into its casing, operated by a single button. Imagine the power and excitement of pressing the button, and watching the whole wall disappear into its casing below, and stepping out onto the terrace. Mendelsohn probably never realised when he designed the house that its occupants could, if so inclined, hone their tennis skills for hours on end on the blank roadside-wall. In the basement was a metal horse that was operated electrically and which could walk, trot or canter as you sat astride it—exercise, of sorts, in those long winter nights. It was fun to entertain and get to know other families like the Holmers, including Julie and Sarah, the

Thistlethwaites and a Danish family called the Pratts.

There was a disconnect, of course, between the simple fascinations of a ten-year-old boy and the tragedy that had engulfed, and was engulfing Berlin in 1961. When we arrived in Berlin it was barely sixteen years since the end of the Second World War. Berlin had witnessed a terrible final conflagration between the allies and what remained of German forces, stubborn to the last. Over several years the Allies had bombed the city night after night to break the will and resistance of the Reich. Many of Bomber Command's flight crews had perished, and much of Berlin was turned to rubble. There was a Commonwealth War Grave cemetery a short distance from our house in *am Rupenhorn* at Friedhof where many airmen were buried.

Many signs of the war in the city could not but impress a boy: there were large gaps where there were no buildings at all, the rubble had been cleared but no new buildings begun. There were the symbolic remains of the Kaiser Wilhelm Memorial Church with its jagged tower bereft of its aisles, and called "the hollow tooth" by Berliners. The free-standing modern belfry and new octagonal church were still to be completed. Not far from where we lived there was the Olympic Stadium built for the Nazi Olympic Games in 1936 and the feats of the black athlete Jesse Owens, who won four golds much to the disgust of Hitler. It was there that the British military Headquarters resided, and my father worked. I remember in his office, at the top of the main entrance stairs, he had a chart entitled "Morale of the Brigade", with a graph beneath it. How one measured morale, I wasn't quite sure, but it appeared good. Generally, there was the overall sense of a city emerging from a catastrophe and beginning to live again, at least in its western half, although now confronted by a new and painful challenge in the Berlin Wall and separation from the East.

If the stones spoke bleakly of war and destruction, there were also human shadows around many corners. Hitler's bunker, where he committed suicide, had been erased and forgotten; but the curious wondered where it was. One survivor of the Reich, Rudolf Hess, lived on in imprisonment in West Berlin, in Spandau Gaol. Responsible for the Nuremberg Laws which stripped Jews of their civilian rights, he had been a senior member of Hitler's cabinet. He was captured by the British after a bizarre peace mission in 1941, in which he flew solo to Scotland to negotiate peace terms, as Hess hoped, with the Duke of Hamilton. Captured and kept in prison for the remainder of the war, Hess was prosecuted at Nuremberg at the end of the war and then imprisoned in Berlin. He was given a life sentence in prison and the Allies took it in turns, a month at a time, to guard him in Spandau Gaol until his eventual death in 1987, aged 93.

Another Berlin gaol, still open for visits at that time, told a more harrowing but more noble tale. This was Plötzensee Prison in Charlottenburg where Adam von Trott zu Solz and many of the co-conspirators against Hitler in 1944 were hung with piano wire—to make their deaths more excruciating.[1] They were filmed as they died and the film was hurried to Hitler so he could gloat over their deaths. I can still remember the room in the gaol where the executions took place. In all, some 5,764 were executed in different parts of Germany following the conspiracy to kill Hitler.[2] Von Trott's secretary and the author of *Berlin Diaries* 1940–1945, Marie (Missie) Vassiltchikov, recalled with elegance and courage the trials and dangers met by her circle during those years. In a visit to Berlin in 1987, to follow the publication of Missie's diary, her brother George recalled that the Tiergarten—the beautiful park and surrounding mansions in the centre of Berlin—" was itself a wasteland and along it still ran the infamous Berlin Wall".[3]

If the city contained ghosts from the past and the evidence of a terrible war, in 1961 it was ruthlessly divided. Berlin lay well inside East Germany, or, as it was misnamed, the German Democratic Republic, there was nothing democratic about it. It was a satellite of Moscow and ruled by its communist leader Walter Ulbricht with the help of countless secret police called *Stasi*. As late as June 1961, Ulbricht had said: "No one intends to put up a wall". Yet in the end the haemorrhaging of hard-pressed East Germans to the West through a comparatively open border in Berlin and the exaggerated fear of infiltration of the East by western spies, prompted the communist authorities to erect a wall to keep its

---

[1] Marie "Missie" Vassiltchikov, *Berlin Diaries* 1940–1945 (London: Pimlico, 1999), p. 223.
[2] Vassiltchikov, *Berlin Diaries*, p. 234
[3] Vassiltchikov, *Berlin Diaries*, p. 315.

citizens firmly under its communist dictatorship.

As Kennedy would remark in his famous Berlin speech of June 1963, "No western government had ever had to resort to putting up a wall to keep its citizens in." Over the night of 12–13 August 1961, the permanent barrier of a wall was erected through the centre of the city and a border of barbed wire, no man's land, dogs and watch towers encircled the city. The city was both divided and encircled. Berlin became the cockpit of the Cold War. With memories of the Berlin Airlift of 1948 and the Soviet desire to strangle the city, it also became the pressure point of Europe.

In the coming months there would be a number of crises in the city, but none more protracted than the awful division of families, lovers, colleagues and communities by the barrier of the wall, which lasted for nearly thirty years. One flashpoint occurred at "Check Point Charlie," the famous crossing point between West and East Berlin. On one occasion, when an American diplomat and officers were refused entry to the East, a build-up of tanks on both sides ensued until President Kennedy and Nikita Khrushchev dialled down the heat, removing the tanks one by one.

More serious was the Cuba Crisis of October 1962 when many thought the price of removing the nuclear missiles, stationed in Cuba and pointing at American cities, would be concessions over Berlin. The Allies remained calm and firm both in Washington and Berlin, and space was given for a climb-down by the Russians in the context of resolute action by Kennedy in placing an exclusion zone around Cuba until there was resolution of the crisis. Alongside these moments of great international tension were the ongoing personal tragedies of East Germans being shot by the East German border guards, called *Vopos,* which happened particularly across waterways such as the Tettow Canal and Bernauer Strasse, where apartments formed part of the "wall". Sometimes my father would return home at night downcast with news of another shooting and fatality. At the height of the Cuba Crisis my parents went on entertaining German civilian officials including the Mayor Willy Brandy, assuring them of the Allies commitment to the city under Russian pressure.

With so much at stake and with garrisons of French, American and British troops in West Berlin, it was no surprise, but still heartening to

Berliners, that leading statesmen called to see for themselves. Alec Douglas-Home came as British Foreign Secretary in 1962, but most significant was John Kennedy's visit in June 1963. He was invited by the Berlin Mayor Willy Brandt and the West German Chancellor Adenauer. As the Brandenburg Gate was across the wall from the British Sector, my father, as the Brigade commander and a good guide, showed Kennedy "the sights" from a specially constructed rostrum. Kennedy's speech later that day has echoed down the years. "Just as the proudest boast", he said, "of the ancient world was *Civis Romanus sum*, so the proudest boast of all free people was *Ich bin ein Berliner*". Despite the linguistic slip—as a *Berliner* meant a doughnut—the speech was full of conviction, humour and charm. Kennedy received rapturous applause from hundreds of thousands of Berliners.[4] They were assured of American support, itself a guarantee of freedom from Soviet communism. It was an unspeakable tragedy that less than six months later Kennedy was assassinated in Dallas, but his words and presence were never forgotten in Berlin. My father wrote to me at school, describing the assassination as a "catastrophe" for the Western Alliance.

Away from these heady moments of international significance, life for my family and I was full of interest. Travel to and from Berlin, since I was now at a boarding school in England, was always adventurous: sometimes we flew into Tempelhof Airport; occasionally we went by train along the rail corridor through East Germany into Berlin, where East German guards boarded the train until we arrived in West Berlin. And once we went by car. I can remember that car journey, as it was in winter and we travelled through snow, ice and darkness. My parents had hired a maths tutor, called Gary Williams, to help me brush up my maths for Common Entrance. The winter of 1962/3 was the coldest on record in England since 1895, and there were frequent stops to de-ice the car, or assist in clearing snow. In Berlin temperatures plummeted to $-20°$ C, and to touch metal with a bare hand was to risk injury, while the dry cold produced high levels of static electricity in our house.

The Havel Lake was a place of continual amusement through the seasons. My brother and I both had canoes. We could paddle across to the other side and visit the family of the most senior British officer, the

---

[4] The entire speech can be seen on YouTube and lasts just nine minutes.

General Officer Commanding, at Villa Lemm, with its gracious lawns which went down to the water's edge. In winter the Havel froze; sledging, skating, or fishing through a hole in the ice, were commonplace. Berliners would take a chair and sit by their fishing hole waiting and hoping for a catch. At night I could see from my bedroom window the lights of the barges that went through the Havel waterway system. Like carriages in a train the barges were linked together, and made their sedate way via the Havel and the river Elbe to Hamburg.

When visitors came, we would go through "Check Point Charlie" to visit East Berlin. The contrast could not have been greater between the sheer drabness of the East and the growing prosperity of the West, as the city was rebuilt. Later it reminded me of some words by Simone Weil, who wrote, "No desert is so dreary, monotonous and boring as evil". [5] This pretty much summed up the effect of communism on the lifestyle and architecture of East Berlin. The authorities made out there was something virtuous about it—a kind of puritanism compared with the corrupt West, but it was simply the absence of joy.

The museum district of Berlin was in the East and contained many treasures. The Pergamum Museum contained the Pergamum Altar taken from Turkey; the Ishtar Gate constructed in Babylon during the reign of Nebuchadnezzar II, the destroyer of Jerusalem, in c.580 BC, with its wonderful blue colour on which are placed, in decorated tiles, golden heraldic beasts and the interior of a rich merchant's home from Aleppo, which surely would have been destroyed in recent years if left in Aleppo.

Not far away in the *Neues Museum*, on Berlin's Museum Island, is the head of Nefertiti, the wife of Akhenaten and step-mother of Tutankhamun, one of the most beautiful artefacts to come out of Egypt. My parents had befriended the Knauer family, whose parents worked as academics in the museum although living in West Berlin, and their son Lawrence had lessons with my sister at our house.

These trips into East Berlin to see these treasures, and sometimes to see the vast cemeteries of the Russian war dead in communal graves of thousands, were carefully timed. Details of the visit had to be filed with BRIXMIS—a liaison mission that operated behind the Iron Curtain in

---

[5] Malcolm Muggeridge, *Chronicles of Wasted Time Vol II* (London: Fontana, 1975), p. 145.

the Cold War. It was only possible to go with their permission, and details of the visit had to be approved, and times adhered to. A list of permissions was filed at "Check Point Charlie", where we were checked out and checked back in.

Little did I realise the extent of it then, but Berlin was also a city of spies: the capital of the Cold War, where the great powers confronted each other in the context of a confined city, surrounded by barbed wire and watchtowers. As John Le Carré wrote in his novel, *A Perfect Spy*:

Berlin. What a garrison of spies, Tom! What a cabinet full of useless, liquid secrets, what a playground for every alchemist, miracle worker and rat-piper that ever took up the cloak and turned his face from the unpalatable constraints of political reality! In Berlin the Firm (UK Intelligence) had agents of influence, agents of disruption, subversion, sabotage and disinformation. We had tunnellers and smugglers, listeners and forgers, trainers and recruiters and talent spotters and couriers and watchers and seducers, assassins and balloonists, lip-readers and disguise artists. But whatever the Brits had; the Americans had more, and whatever the Americans had the East Germans had five of it and the Russians ten of it.[6]

As if to bear all this out, an exchange of spies was made on the Glienicke Bridge in February 1962, involving the U.S. spy plane pilot, Francis Gary Powers and the Russian Colonel Rudolf Abel.[7] The bridge was known as "The Bridge of Spies", with one side in the East and the other in the West, and it gave its name, reconstructing that event, to a film starring Tom Hanks and Mark Rylance. Berlin was indeed the spy capital of the world.

All this was exciting for a twelve-year-old boy, but in the summer of 1963 my father's appointment came to an end. It was time to return to England. In fact, there would be no more overseas appointments for him, and therefore no further possibility of experiencing another part of the world that way. Of the first twelve years of my life, seven had been spent in post War Europe as the Cold War reached its height and the western powers worked out their responses to a series of crises, with the threat of

---

[6] John le Carré, *A Perfect Spy* (London: Hodder, 1987), p. 563.
[7] Nina Willner, *Forty Autumns* (London: Abacus 2016), p. 274.

a nuclear war never far away. To have spent seven formative years in Germany and France at the start of my life left their mark: abroad was familiar. There were lessons I was learning: that interdependence was needed against a common threat; that strength came from unity; that reconciliation rather than recrimination was the way forward; that the past should not be a strait jacket, but a springboard for the future. Past failures must be acknowledged, but must not prevent common cause for the future. And perhaps most important of all, I learnt that freedom, freedom to pursue your life guaranteed by equality before the law, was what people craved above all, and would go to any lengths to obtain, as they regularly did in crossing the Berlin Wall. All these were good and important lessons, but alongside them came the conviction that going to places, seeing the sights, meeting people, reflecting *in situ* on what had been discovered and known in such places was fuel for understanding better the predicaments, aspirations, tragedies and achievements of the human family.

For the next five years I would travel no further than the beautiful north-west coast of Scotland to Loch Hourn, opposite the Isle of Skye on the Scottish mainland for summer holidays. Then, in 1968 overseas travel would resume again. Later I was to discover that there were others in my family, antecedents, who had been inveterate travellers, but in a different age and for largely different reasons. We will hear more of them in the last chapter.

Chapter II
Early Travels 1

From 1963, and for the next five years, all my holidays were taken in the British Isles, mostly in Scotland. In 1964 I had moved from Sunningdale School to Eton College, where my father had been an outstanding schoolboy. My family had a long association with the school. My grandfather, Aymer Whitworth, having been a boy there, had swiftly returned as a master (or a "beak" in Eton parlance). He was Master of College from 1908, before having a house of his own. His brightest pupil, he said, was Lord Hailsham, later Lord Chancellor and Tory politician. And for a year, from 1916, the more rebellious George Orwell (Eric Blair) was a pupil of his in college, before Aymer's tenure ended. The background to those years was the Great War. There was a growing roll call of the dead in Chapel: of the 5,687 Etonians who served in the Great War, 1,160 were killed and 1,467 wounded. (Bernard Crick George Orwell p 53 Secker and Warburg 1980)

Holidays in Scotland were mostly at Loch Hourn, as my family were close friends of the Birkbecks, whose extended family owned a property there. Mary Birkbeck was a prodigious organiser, and her husband, Bill, a banker with Barclays, was an artistic and reflective countryman. They were generous hosts, filling their house with families and young people over the summer months. The lodge was remote, accessed by a single-tracked unmade road many miles long. Of a summer evening we would be blessed with long, lingering sunsets over the sea with the Isle of Skye to the west. The lodge had no electricity, and after dark, light was provided by oil lamps. An elderly caretaker called Lena lived there the year round. Outdoor activities were the order of the day: walks, picnics, fishing on the sea loch, usually with numbers of other teenagers: children who were staying with their parents at the house.

One other holiday during this period was to the Scilly Isles in 1965 which gave me a taste for exploration. A school friend, Andrew

Thompson—later a Land Agent—and I travelled there and back by train and boat on our own. We were fourteen years old, and we stayed with another friend, Robert Dorrien Smith, whose family were 999-year tenants of the Duchy of Cornwall living at Tresco Abbey. Our stay had more than a touch of *Swallows and Amazons* about it—freedom to roam and enjoy the extraordinary island of Tresco, its coastline and the exotic and famous gardens, by sail or by foot. It was an adventure. The adult house party seemed to have had a kind of parallel existence, including matrimonial intrigues of which I was completely unaware. Tresco Abbey certainly had a more free-spirited atmosphere than the organised excursions at Loch Hourn.

Meanwhile school progressed towards its inevitable watershed of exams: O levels and then A levels. I was at Eton for a little over four years, leaving while still seventeen, having taken the Oxbridge University entrance examination in the winter term (half) of 1968. My academic record in the lower part of the school was very mediocre and I did not really progress until my specialist years of A levels. Meanwhile, my father kept me in touch with events in the wider world through his regular letters.

One week in February 1965, in between home news, he told me of the state funeral of Winston Churchill, which he had attended as an usher. He wrote, "I was most of the day at Winston Churchill's funeral, where I had the awe-inspiring honour of escorting Lady Churchill to and from her seat by the Queen, and opposite General de Gaulle". It was a moment to remember.

Following A Levels, I was eager to go on my first "solo" trip and my parents gamely allowed me to undertake a continental journey, which was to start a trend. My first foray in "solo travelling" (i.e., without parents) was with a school friend, Mark Wrightson who also lived nearby when my father served as GOC Northumbrian District, based at Catterick. While living there we made many Yorkshire friends and enjoyed their "sporting" lifestyle. Mark and I decided to hitch-hike to Madrid in the last summer holidays whilst still at school, during the summer of 1968. The idea was that we would take a ferry to France and then hitch to Madrid where Mark's sister Penelope lived. She was to have the pleasure of putting us up for a few days before we returned home the same way.

Hitch-hiking or "thumbing a lift" had become widespread in the mid '60s; it was part of the revolution that was sweeping the world. I remember my mother frequently giving people lifts in England. Many a young man would stand by the road, often with his girlfriend, feeling entitled to a place in one's car. To drive past with empty seats in the car was to court guilt at one's hardness of heart! Cars were community property now, and I am sure many of the more revolutionary types would have approved of Proudhon's dictum that all "property is theft".

We thought it would be plain sailing in France, but it was not. If there was just a trickle of lifts in France, in Spain there were virtually none. Perhaps this was an indicator that Spain was even more conservative than General de Gaulle's France. In 1968 Spain was still governed by Franco, although he was verging on his dotage. Progress to Madrid was thus very slow, with plenty of time for sitting by the roadside throwing pebbles and discussing the fate of nations, which in 1968 was a prominent conversation piece, given the revolutionary vibe of that year. Indeed, the ferment of politics in Europe in 1968 was such that most seventeen-year-olds would concur with Wordsworth's initial reaction to the French Revolution that, "Bliss was it then to be alive, but to be young was very Heaven!". In time we would come to appreciate instead Edmund Burke's *Reflections on the French Revolution*, and his warnings against precipitate, violent change.

We persevered with hitchhiking through France, camping by the side of the road and taking it in turns to persuade drivers with our pleading thumbs. We managed to get lifts down to the Pyrenees, where we stayed for a few days in a house belonging to some friends of Mark's family in a village called Lescun, south of Pau. We were over the watershed into the drier part of the Pyrenees. We did some desultory rock climbing, and prepared ourselves for Spain by reading Hemingway's *Death in the Afternoon* and discussing bull fighting. Pamplona, where bulls are released in the streets during the Bull Running of the San Fermin Festival each year in July, was not far away, and was a hot topic of conversation.

After a short break in Lescun we continued to Madrid, but virtually no lifts were forthcoming. Spanish drivers either thought hitch-hiking a decadent pastime, or news of this new form of travel had not filtered that far south. We resorted instead to the trains and travelled through countryside worthy of any wild west film. The weather by now was very hot, and to create a cooling draught we sat on the footplates of the carriages. In Madrid, Penelope made us welcome, made sure we washed, and continued to call me Anthony until I wrote an obituary for Anthony, who was naturally run over by a lorry whilst hitch-hiking, on our return journey, which I sent to her as a thank you note!

Apart from the heat in Madrid, my memories are of a very quick visit to the Prado, in no way doing justice to Spanish art, and a lot of late-night eating when it was a bit cooler washed down by copious quantities of sangria. We decided to train back to Paris, not relishing further interminable waits for drivers to have compassion on two ill-deserving youths. In Paris we emerged from a metro into a full-scale student street protest. This was *not* the demonstration by students and trades unionists against the French government that had occurred earlier in the year in May. The reason for this protest was that the day before, on 21 August 1968, the Russians and Warsaw Pact forces had suppressed the Prague Spring led by Alexander Dubcek. The Prague Spring had offered a glimmer of hope for liberty in the midst of communist repression. We joined in the march of thousands, but French riot police—already well prepared after the earlier student riots led by the German student Cohen Bendit in May, had little difficulty preventing us from reaching the presumed destination of the marchers: the Russian Embassy.

So, we detached ourselves from the protest and made our way back to England. Still only a few months over seventeen we returned for a final term (half) at school and the Oxbridge University Entrance.

As mentioned earlier, academic success at Eton had been slow in coming. My early years were spent in a fairly indolent way, taking part in sport, but not especially shining, doing my work, but with little obvious success. My reports ranged from calling me a "scallywag", to saying I had the occasional good idea, but expressed it in cumbersome and stilted prose. There was much to be desired. Compared with my father, who won almost all the accolades available at the same establishment—President of the Eton Society (Pop), Keeper of the Field (the Eton football game), a member of the VI Form (the top division in the school) the editor of the Eton Chronicle—I was a laggard. Yet looking back through all my letters from my parents whilst at school, I find not a word of reproach for what must have been a disappointing performance at times—surely a lesson in unconditional love and acceptance. By contrast my brother accrued distinctions in his Trials (Annual Exams) like confetti and A Levels in the way some people collect matchboxes. In that final term at school, with just the single focus of the Oxbridge University entrance exam, there was time for further reading and listening. I read Albert Camus, *The Outsider,* Franz Kafka, and Arthur Koestler's *Darkness at Noon*: suggesting a pretentious teenager, or perhaps an exploratory one. And I listened, almost daily, to Bob Dylan and Beethoven in alternate draughts.

Something had kicked in in terms of motivation, however, and aged seventeen, I made a real effort in self-improvement and showed some ambition to succeed. At the end of the summer term, I read *War and Peace* by Leo Tolstoy, revelling in the prose, characters and narrative. Then, in the autumn term, with no other purpose than the Oxbridge Exam in Modern History I worked hard, even rising early to read. I was given an interview at Christ Church, Oxford, which I thought went disastrously badly. The interview panel was chaired by Charles Stuart, who had interrogated captured Germans for MI6 in the war. When he asked if I had read my father's book on the eighteenth-century Huguenot Commander of British Forces in the Seven Years War, Field Marshal Lord Ligonier, I had to admit that I had not. I thought that was it: an interesting experience, a brief glimpse of the dreaming spires, but nothing more. Surprisingly I was awarded an Exhibition to read Modern History at Christ Church. My house master at Eton, Bobby Bourne, a classics teacher who had a difficult war as a prisoner and was a renowned oarsman, was kind in his assessment. One of his final reports read, "he enjoys life here and I am sure he's one of my most valuable protégés; he's been cheerfully charming and could, I fancy, get away with murder". Michael Kidson, who was to gain notoriety after a few more years at the school as a highly effective and eccentric history teacher, counting David Cameron as one of his pupils, wrote, "he shows above average perception and his style is clear and thoroughly sensible". Perhaps these were straws in the wind. Nevertheless, I left school in December 1968 and by February 1969, was heading to the United States for seven months of adventure.

Once Upon a Time in America

Gap years were in their infancy in 1969. The idea of spending six months to a year travelling or volunteering was gaining ground. National Service had finished in 1960 and there was a case for young people using the months between school and university to broaden their horizons. VSO (Voluntary Service Overseas) as a way of using time before university was well under way. My brother had already gone to Kenya to volunteer as a teacher in a school near Kisumu, and had used the time there to travel the country: climbing Mount Kenya and exploring the game parks. I decided to travel by myself around the States for seven months till late August, but to make the most of this time I needed some kind of structure and preparation.

This was because of one very good restriction, which imposed some kind of discipline on the trip, and that was you could take only take £50 in travellers' cheques with you, and £15 in cash. This was a government edict to counter our balance of payments deficit. I still have my passport from that year and it has in it the entry that the bearer was taking £50 currency with him.

Although £50 was worth considerably more then, than now, in no way was it sufficient for seven months' travel. This meant I would have to earn money. I was able to buy a Greyhound season bus ticket—something like a European Rail Card—before leaving. The Greyhound Bus Company International had an office in Lower Regent Street and they gave me a quote for four months' travel on their buses of $198.00 or £82.10. The exchange rate was then $2.40 to the £1. And there was something reassuringly solid and American about Sales Manager Stan Williams's letter, which concluded, "Your interest in Greyhound is very much appreciated". Long hours would be spent on their buses travelling, as I estimated in a note compiling statistics of the trip, 10,392 miles. It was and is still the longest road trip I have made.

To make a success of the trip I needed people with whom I might stay or who would give me work, so I asked all my parents' friends for names of people I might contact once in the States. These were forthcoming. My godfather, John Bury, told me of his step-parents Mr and Mrs Jack Wheelock who lived in New York, my first destination, on

East 57th Street. He said: "they are quite old (about eighty)". Sadly, I never met them as they were out of town. This was disappointing because Jack Wheelock was a poet, and according to my godfather, "belongs to a certain old-fashioned American type which I greatly admire but which is becoming quite rare". My godmother's husband, Anthony McCormick, had contacts in the American Tobacco Industry and told me of Charles D. Sands of the Export Leaf Tobacco Company in Richmond, Virginia who might be able to employ me. The tobacco industry is hardly kosher, but it accounted for much of Virginia's economy. I did get in touch with him, once in the States, and he gave me a job as a gardener. I also applied to an organisation called SERVAS, which provided lists of hosts across the States with whom I might stay.

The people who came up with the best contacts were army connections of my father, in particular his ADC, Charles Cordle, who wrote to me a long letter in December 1968 from Sharjah on the Gulf, detailing his contacts. Of one he said, "they are fairly unpleasant relations of mine", so I gave them a wide berth, but I did contact Allan C. Emery, who worked as the local franchiser of ServiceMaster, a cleaning company in Boston. This sounded promising. I wrote to him and he promised me employment when I came. So, with this offer in my pocket and the prospect of a very cheap flight on an army plane from Brize Norton, which left on Fridays, I waited for the call that there was a spare seat on the plane to JFK, New York. I left on the last Friday in February 1968, still only seventeen, and my parents saw me off. A few tears were shed (by my mother), and suddenly I was away from all that was familiar. I had the promise of work, £50 in travellers' cheques and an additional £15 in sterling. There is no doubt it was a unique moment in this young person's life, and a time for growing up.

For the duration of the trip, I kept a diary and my parents kept all the letters I wrote on those flimsy blue aerogrammes which predated emails. As far as I remember, I never rang once, but one or two telegrams were sent both ways. How different communication was! On the flight over I sat next to "a rather tweedy lady" who was on her way to Denver. On hearing of my need for money, she said if worst came to worst, I could always sell my blood! I had also made some brass rubbings from a nearby parish church at Childrey Berkshire, hearing that Americans would pay silly money for them; unfortunately, I left the rubbings on the luggage rack on the bus from the airport to the city. Selling blood was now my only fall-back option!

New York was overwhelming: its size and pace, the endless skyscrapers, the straight streets, and the subway system. My plan was stay in the YMCA and explore the city. I stayed for four days—basically a long weekend; I met a contact called Rupert Gosling for lunch one day, and I went to the Metropolitan Museum of Art where there was a photographic exhibition called *Harlem on my Mind,* and the Museum of Modern Art, where I saw an exhibition of American Folk Art by Grandma Moses (1860–1961) and the Canadian artist Philip Aziz. I met others at the YMCA: a jeweller from Rio de Janeiro, BOAC air stewardesses and plenty of young Americans. The food was good, and as always in the States, plentiful. A complete breakfast with lashings of bacon, waffles and orange juice was just 99c. But when a stranger (male) shoved a note under my door asking to meet, I was less at ease! I suspected his motives, and left pretty swiftly on the day I intended, taking a bus to Boston, although not yet activating my four-month Greyhound season ticket. I worked out that in the four days in New York I had spent $37, about $9 a day. Not much by today's standards, but it was time to start earning.

I arrived in Boston to a dump of snow of over four feet, and the city shutting up early. I went directly to the offices of ServiceMaster at 267 Summer Street, a long street of many commercial offices near the Inner Harbour. The Emery family had for generations imported wool for their textile business, on which they built their family fortune. When the textile industry changed, they moved into contract cleaning instead. That afternoon, when I reached their offices, they had closed early because of the snow. So, I found the YMCA and booked in for $6 a night. The next day I returned to Summer Street and met Mr Emery: an unpretentious, warm-hearted, honest, enthusiastic and charming Bostonian. The sense that I had immediately was of a hardworking organisation characterised with good humour, matched by high standards. After a warm welcome by Allan Emery and his charming secretary, Miss Gordon, I was taken by his son Arthur Emery Jnr, to get a Social Security number so that I could be employed. I still have it: No 249782. And, not having found any long-term accommodation, I was taken that night to Mr Emery's home, which was on the outskirts of the town, with a magnificent view over the city and built in the style of George Washington's home, Mt Vernon.

Mrs Emery was a cosy, devout American, hospitable, and a fine cook in the traditional "apple-pie" American way. We had cranberry juice, steak, and vegetables followed by ice-cream. It was good home cooking after the adventures of the flight and the days in New York. We talked a lot about the Royal Family, and to make me feel at home Mrs Emery even played the National Anthem at the end of the meal! I wondered for a moment if George III might be wheeled out for a toast. They loved teasing me about the American War of Independence, and would have loved the modern-day caricature of George III in the hit rap-musical, Hamilton. There were lots of soft furnishings, lace and cushions. They knew how to make themselves comfortable in an honest American way. The following day I started work at seven a.m., and it wasn't looking as if I was going to have to sell blood for money!

My job was to clean floors in the Parkway Hospital as part of the contract cleaning team of ServiceMaster. I mopped floors for eight hours a day with two coffee breaks and a lunch break. My supervisor at the outset was John Bates and he, like many of the staff, was fascinated by my accent, the prevalence of smog in London (as he supposed) and the mini-skirt, about which he spoke much. He obviously didn't think that the prevalence of the former would prevent sightings of the latter. Along with the American War of Independence, these were recurring subjects! I was a mini celebrity with the mop, with plenty of the nurses stopping for a chat, and in time I progressed to a buffing machine. Once you got over the problem of it running away with you, it was satisfying to manage the machine. The process entailed re-waxing floors, having stripped off the existing finish, and then buffing them with the machine until they shone like glass. Having started at the Parkway Hospital I was moved to Arlington Hospital, where ServiceMaster needed to make a good impression, and perhaps they thought my polishing skills, or my accent, would help!

After an initial three nights with the Emerys and a temporary stay at the company apartment, I found lodgings at 59 Beals Street, Brookline, near Coolidge Corner (Coolidge was an American President from Boston between 1923 and 1929). Just fifteen minutes' walk from the hospital, the neighbourhood was interesting. It was strongly Jewish, and had a synagogue on the corner. President Kennedy, I discovered, had been born in the street. I rented a room from a Jewish landlady, one Mrs Schultz. It was an airy room with shared kitchen and bathroom, and cost $20 a week. There were a number of other lodgers. One of them, Walter, insisted on bringing into the house two older women who were living on the cold street, producing an altercation with Mrs Schultz, who called the police to remove them. Another resident was a large Jewish girl, and there was also a man who smoked a good deal of marijuana, and wrote poetry and plays which he said had been presented to the Professor of English at Boston University. He was a strong civil rights protestor, once a Catholic, of Scottish descent, and much-admired Mary Queen of Scots! You know the type! Together we made up the party of lodgers, at least for the coming month; a more unlikely group of people you could not imagine. I enjoyed the strange diversity, however it certainly made a change from school.

In between this life of buffing floors in the hospital and being entertained by my fellow lodgers, I had some almost surreal experiences, by way of contrast, with another part of Boston society. I had two contacts from my parent's friends. Ian Hunter, the British Music Festival Director and Impresario with Harold Holt, and wartime friend of my parents, gave me the address of Mr Tod Perry, the Manager of the Boston Symphony Orchestra. He could not offer me work (I am not a musician), but he invited me to a concert, which included pieces from Rossini, Brahms and Carl Nielsen. The Symphony Hall was built around 1900, heavily gilded and stately; Mr Perry gave me coffee in the interval—a moment of cultural pleasure before returning to my bedsit. The other contact was Mr and Mrs Kellogg, no relation to the cereal empire, I don't think, for Mr Kellogg was an attorney. He invited me to a dinner party at which there were quite a few Bostonian intellectuals, including one woman who had driven around Germany on a motor bike. Boston was full of surprises. It was said to be run by the Roman Catholic Church and the Mafia, but was rapidly becoming a highly developed electronic and computing centre, with Harvard University and MIT close by.

In 1969 the United States was facing significant challenges. In November 1963 Kennedy had been assassinated, and Lyndon Johnson had succeeded him as President. A very different character, Johnson was a rugged Texan with strong reformist, Democrat ideals. He took America deeper into the Vietnam war and faced both increasing American casualties and the fallout from the morally-suspect bombing campaign. There was also increasing civil unrest at home from the Civil Rights movement and students. Two further assassinations were to rock the United States in 1968. In April, Martin Luther King was killed and likewise Bobby Kennedy was shot and killed while seeking the Democratic nomination in June the same year. In November, Richard Nixon was elected President for the Republican Party. This was a sign of the unease in conservative America at the progress of the war and the civil unrest at home. America had been, and was being rocked. Meanwhile on 13 March I had my eighteenth birthday, celebrated with an avocado and omelette in Beals Street. On 17 March, St Patrick's Day, all of Boston seemed to wear green and shamrock, such is the size of the Irish community there. I definitely had the right name. By April the students were out in force on Boston or Cambridge Common in the spring sunshine, smoking hash, playing guitars, listening to Hendrix, the Grateful Dead, Dylan, and Otis Reading. It was not two years since the *Summer of Love* in 1967 and the Woodstock Festival would follow in just a few months in Vermont. At Harvard University in nearby Cambridge the students had a sit-in, and the President controversially called in the police to disperse them. By contrast, Allan Emery held a weekly Bible Club in his beautiful house to which I would go along. There were perhaps forty young people there. On at least one occasion a young GI back on leave from the Vietnam war spoke of his experiences. There were songs led from the piano, a talk given by Mr Emery, and a light-hearted and good-humoured fellowship. Boston Common with its students, and Mr Emery's gracious sitting room presented contrasting images: both were America in uneasy juxtaposition in the late 60s. There would be time on the long bus journeys to think about where I fitted into the deep issues of the time.

By mid-April my time in Boston was coming to an end. I had enjoyed the city, its life and citizens, in all its variety and with its strong cultural life. When not polishing floors, I enjoyed weekend trips to Cape Cod with its wonderful sweep of sand dunes and the great Atlantic Ocean crashing onto those American shores.

There was one further surprise in store at the hospital. I was at that time working in Symmes Hospital, Arlington, in the north of the city, now a block of luxury flats. One day I went into room 100, a kind of janitors' store room where I normally emptied buckets of dirty water in the sink. That day there were two trolleys with sheets pulled over the top. I wondered what they were doing there, and being curious, lifted the sheet on one of them. On the trolley lay a middle-aged woman dressed in a smart checked sports jacket. She was dead. I quickly left and told a colleague what had happened. I am afraid we joked at my surprise, but it was the first time I had seen a dead person. The reality of it was something else to ponder: the incongruity of a body—someone's loved one, wearing a checked jacket, and lying in the janitors' cleaning store, a temporary resting place.

It was time to leave Boston with all its experiences and welcome. I had earned $414:85 and had paid $90.37 in tax. I was told I would be repaid most of the tax at the end of the year through ServiceMaster. I now had more money than I had come out with. America was undoubtedly a higher wage economy than our own. I activated my Greyhound Season Bus Pass in late April and first went to Montreal, leaving at eight thirty and arriving five thirty p.m., and once again booked into the YMCA for three nights for $12 Canadian. I enjoyed the city with its French culture; the recent and highly successful World Exhibition called Expo '67, and I even saw the new English Film on Henry II and Eleanor of Aquitaine (somehow fitting in Montreal) called *The Lion in Winter,* with Peter O'Toole, Katherine Hepburn and Anthony Hopkins. Hepburn was great as Eleanor of Aquitaine. Much later I would visit the tombs of Henry II and Eleanor in Fontevraud Abbey near Chinon, where they rest in monastic simplicity. A stormy couple, with dysfunctional children, they restlessly ruled an empire from Hadrian's Wall to the Pyrenees.

From Montreal it was a Greyhound to Buffalo, New York, from where it was possible to visit the Niagara Falls. Buffalo was then a town as seedy as the Niagara Falls were majestic. The YMCA was booked up, so I stayed in a cheap hotel where the cistern wheezed all night, and an old man loitered in the foyer, wheezing all day. The Falls were magnificent in their power; and years later I would recall how the tightrope walker, Blondin, crossed a section of the Falls pushing a boy in a wheel-barrow along a wire. I felt the boy in the barrow presented a supreme example of faith! From Buffalo, it was south through Pittsburgh, a declining steel town, and then to Indiana, Pennsylvania, where I stayed with a SERVAS family called the Carrs, who taught at the University. Mrs Carr was still breast feeding her nine-month year old daughter. I attended several of the lectures at the university, on American sociology and class structure! And from there I took a Greyhound to Washington.

The South: Dixie

Once again, the army kicked in with a contact in Washington. By now it was early May, and the temperature had soared to 26°C, the dogwood and cherry blossom were a wonderful pink colour against the white stone and marble of central Washington. My host for three days was Colonel Turner, part of the British Army Staff based in Washington as a kind of adjunct to the Embassy and Military Attaché. His family: his wife and two daughters, were out of town, so he was both cook and guide. On the first day of my stay the Colonel dropped me off at Gettysburg on the way to a meeting in Carlisle.

The Battle of Gettysburg was one of the principal battles of the American Civil War fought over 1–3 July 1863. There were heavy casualties on both sides but the Union forces (the North) halted the advance of the Confederate troops commanded by the charismatic General Robert E. Lee. Pickett's Charge was the *denouement* of the Confederate offensive, turning the confident Confederate army into a wounded and bleeding force. The battlefield is a hallowed site, not only because of the loss of life and the issues at stake, but also because of Lincoln's famous address. His immortal words honouring the dead of *both* sides, and seeking to unify the nation still resonate: "We resolve that these dead shall not have died in vain (and) this nation, under God, shall have a new birth of freedom—and that government of the people, by the people, for the people shall not perish from the earth".

If England's battlefields from the Wars of the Roses or the Civil War have long since returned to ordinary fields, it was not so in America. In 1969, I counted twelve separate visitor centres and a vivid cyclorama of

Picketts Charge at Gettysburg. Indeed, the site of Runnymede and the issuing of Magna Carta would have no memorial at all were it not for the commemoration, in a classical form, by the American Bar Association. What is left to the imagination or forgotten in England—with a nonchalance perhaps born of an embarrassment of riches when it comes to historic battlefields, is manicured and burnished in the States as a crucible of the nation.

The following day, Saturday, I was treated to the Colonel's "Instant Tour of Washington". It was breathless and included: the White House, then the residence of the Nixon administration; the Capitol, including the Senate and Congress which were connected by an underground railway; the space capsule, in which Glenn orbited the earth in 1962; the Wright Brothers' first aircraft; Kennedy's grave and eternal flame; the Arlington Cemetery and the Jeffersonian and Lincoln Memorials; Mount Vernon, George Washington's home; the Potomac; and the Pentagon. It needed to be pretty much an instant tour to crowd so much in! The impression was of a vibrant, powerful, confident, can-do nation in which the sky is *not* the limit. Already the earth had been orbited, and while I was in the States, a bid to overtake the Russians succeeded on 21 July, when the Space Programme, initiated by Kennedy, would bear fruit and place Neil Armstrong on the surface of the moon with "his giant leap for mankind".

The next day, Sunday, I am glad to say was quieter: a visit to the National Museum of Art and Smithsonian, and then tea at the extraordinarily spacious and gracious British Embassy with Colonel Turner. I was told that the Embassy employed six hundred people, and that day the Ambassador was entertaining the Labour Cabinet Minister, Roy Jenkins. The following day I left for Richmond Virginia, and for my second job, this time as a gardener to a Mr and Mrs Sands.

Richmond Virginia is the state capital, a tobacco town, and an important city in the South. There was still ample evidence of the segregation that resulted from slavery, which had only ended a hundred years before. I needed a haircut and went into a barber's shop only to discover it was blacks-only (or negroes only as it openly stated then, in a time before the term Afro-American took over all terms). In the barber shop they were uncomfortable about my presence, so I left to find a "whites-only" barber instead. It was indicative of where the States were on race at the time. Once again, I stayed for the best part of a fortnight in the YMCA, and was employed as a gardener by Charles Sands and his wife. Mr Sands worked in the Export Leaf Tobacco Company based in West Leigh, Virginia. The gardening was hardly back breaking and consisted in trimming hedges, weeding the "yard" and painting a small outhouse. A car was sent to pick me up in the morning and Mrs Sands made me a sandwich at lunch time!

At weekends I explored the area, met other Virginians and visited Thomas Jefferson's famous house at Moniticello, which showed the inventiveness and sheer intellectual range of this scholarly lawyer-farmer and polymath. He was the principal author of the American Declaration of Independence, committing the then thirteen States of America to the "self-evident" truths "that all men are created equal, that they are endowed by the Creator with certain inalienable rights, that among these are life, liberty and the pursuit of happiness". Clearly there was still much work to be done in realising this goal. Jefferson's task was only enlarged when he bought from Napoleon in 1803 what was called the Louisiana Purchase. It was agreed by Napoleon in the bath, and at a stroke, the purchase doubled the size of the United States. It was a snip at the equivalent of 2.6 billion dollars and consisted of most of the central part of the United Sates and New Orleans.

After two weeks in Richmond, and even better off for the gardening, I took a Greyhound to Greenville South Carolina where I was going to stay with another SERVAS family called the Rowlands. Gil Rowland worked for the *Greenville News*, and asked me on arrival if I would like to go to along with him to a meeting in a city church where Ralph Abernathy was speaking and which he was going to cover. After the assassination of Martin Luther King, Abernathy had become the main leader of the Civil Rights movement. Although lacking the charisma of King, and his extraordinary oratorical power, Abernathy would address the United Nations on Civil Rights in 1970. Gil and I made our way to the church, where we sat in seats reserved for the press. There were about five hundred there and soon Abernathy spoke. He had led civil rights marches from Selma to Montgomery when they were opposed by white segregationists. Amazingly, in 1965 Afro-American minorities did not have the right to vote; it was a right they only gained with the Voting

Rights Act of August 1965. The American Civil War had ended nearly a hundred years before. The Fourteenth Amendment, campaigned for by Abraham Lincoln, had placed on the statute book the right of emancipated slaves to equality with all American citizens, and yet a hundred years later, this had barely happened.

On this occasion Abernathy was speaking in support of striking hospital workers in Charleston. They wanted higher wages and the right to join a union. More broadly, he made the point that the white state administration discriminated against black citizens on the grounds of "law and order". Any protest was considered an infringement of law and order and was to be opposed, with force if necessary. It is a familiar position taken by repressive regimes, and has been their cry down the ages (as is still the case in Hong Kong).

Being in an almost entirely black congregation, who showed their support volubly for every sentence Abernathy uttered, was a new and unique experience. It was electric, and not like Eton College Chapel where verbally to endorse a preacher's point ("oh yes man or hallelujah") was probably a punishable offence! It was also quite probable that the grandparents of the older members of the church that day would themselves have been slaves. Slavery in the South was a living memory, a raw wound in need of healing. It was a reminder that it was one thing to pass a law putting the equality of all people on the statute book, as in 1865; it was another to change the hearts and minds of people long accustomed to thinking ill of their fellow Americans.

From Greenville I would travel south to New Orleans, the steamy centre of Creole America, a mix of Spanish, French, and American culture, and from there strike west. From New Orleans I took the bus in the early morning to nearby Texas and a small town called Navasota— still only 7,000 inhabitants—where my host in the SERVAS programme was Bob Whittaker, who owned the *Navasota Examiner* and the local radio station. He made me "work my passage" by doing a radio interview about my travels and then write an article for the Examiner. I suppose in a small town like that, I was news! Perhaps not many young Englishman turned up there.

The town was essentially a railway head from whence cattle, cotton and leather goods were shipped to Galveston then up the Mississippi

River. Slavery had underpinned its economy; it was Confederate country and very conservative. I was taken to a local ranch where Hereford cattle were bred, and oats grown under special conditions and harvested in a week! The cattle were automatically fed by a mechanical feeder, while the so called "bacon bin" induced pig growth: all this in 1969! I was invited to a kind of rotary club called the Kwana Club, where the speaker that day was an FBI officer. He was of the clear view that communists were inciting the student disturbances across the country, which were almost certainly being led on by the Soviet, Chinese and North Vietnamese governments. He had everyone's rapt attention. What was striking to me was that a police officer should have such pronounced political views and felt free to air them without restriction. What he said was quite clearly what his audience wanted to hear. Texan agriculture and policing were a lot different from the UK.

Go West Young Man

The call sign "This is Houston, this is Houston" became famous in 1969, if it was not so before. Apart from being the oil capital of Texas, Houston was home to the National Aeronautics and Space Administration (NASA), which, since 1961, was handling the Apollo space programme. In only a matter of months a moon landing would be attempted, and excitement was mounting. To be a visitor at the centre then, in late May of 1969, was to be at the nerve-centre of one of the greatest attempts in human exploration, this time to the moon. In just six weeks the launch of Apollo 11 would put the whole of America on tenterhooks.

On a more down to earth level I was on tenterhooks (almost) about my first blind date. To be honest I can't remember very much about it, except that my American hosts were much more excited about the prospect than me! The venue was a restaurant near the Space Centre with a girl whose name I have not recorded (shame on me), but apart from the meeting itself I can't recall much. I don't think the date reached lift off, probably not even countdown! This whole dating process was fairly unknown to me in England; at least in this rather more deliberate American form. In England it seemed more a question of being thrown together with someone by social events, rather than being *put together* in an organised "date".

From Houston I went to San Antonio—the Alamo of Davy Crockett fame, where he reached his *denouement*. From San Antonio, with its Spanish connections, I went to the Mexican border town of El Paso, which seemed then to specialise in quickie divorces. From there the Spanish theme continued through Albuquerque, Santa Fe, and Taos—an artists' colony with notable Indian and Spanish influence, and visited by D. H. Lawrence—and then to a town called Gallup, New Mexico, on the edge of a Navajo Indian Reservation.

I arrived on Sunday night in June to stay with the extended family of the Stones, another SERVAS host. There were a number of unusual things about them. I gleaned that they were a Baha'i family with strong missionary tendencies living on the edge of a very large Navajo Reservation, and that some friends of theirs had gone missing in the Reservation that day. Two Danish girls, Kathe and Dorte, were also staying with the Stones, and like me had recently arrived, and had gone out with a friend of the Stones, an artist called Gordon, but had not returned. It was getting dark and it seemed they were lost.

The Reservation was huge, covering some twenty-seven million acres, about half the size of England. It included parts of Utah, Arizona and New Mexico: wonderful desert country with great outcrops of rock, lush green oases of trees and shrubs, and a plentiful supply of cacti of all shapes and sizes. It was home to some three hundred thousand Navajos— fine looking people, but suffering from poor immunity to diseases introduced by white settlers, awful unemployment, and alcoholism, and still coming to terms with the loss of their way of life.

Our first job was to find the party lost in the Reservation. The police had been informed, as had the Sheriff and the local radio station. At twelve thirty a.m. I set forth with Jim Stone and his daughter Barbara to try and track them down. We were, I suppose, the Sheriff's posse. We returned at two a.m. without them. They were found the next day, after spending a chilly night at 7000 feet, their vehicle stuck in deep sand.

On Monday we recovered from the adventure of tracking down Gordon, Owen Stone (the son of the house) and the Danish girls. We rested, and had a celebration in the evening with plenty of jokes about the lengths people go to in order to have a romantic night out. As it transpired, we were not too far from the truth. But first, the next day we were taken into the Reservation to see one of its great sights: the De Cheely Canyon and Spider Rock. It is a vast canyon, or series of canyons, with a soaring sandstone spire rising from its floor to some seven hundred feet. For the Navajo, Spider Rock has special religious significance, which soon got us talking, and offered the cue for learning more about the Baha'is.

Baha'ism was well suited to life next to an Indian Reservation. The religion originated from Persia or Iran in the nineteenth century and teaches that all religions lead to God and that all faiths are of equal worth, such that the Indians are as valid in their faith as any other. Its main followers were in Iran, India and South America. It sounded appealing, but had the obvious difficulty of reconciling conflicting narratives. We listened attentively, but what happened next was a complete surprise.

That evening the three of us, the two Danish girls and myself, were due to leave for Flagstaff, the Grand Canyon, and then go on to Las Vegas. We went to catch the Greyhound Bus, but at the bus station Owen and Kathe asked us to wait while they talked outside. They came back and Kathe said she wanted to stay as she and Owen were in love! The effects of one night lost in the desert! Our baggage was taken off the coach, and we went back to the house to take it all in. Dorte and I decided to leave the following day without Kathe, who was adamant about staying. Then, when we were about to leave on the morning bus to Flagstaff, Barbara took me by the hand and looking directly into my eyes, she said that "we could get together" and I could stay indefinitely! It didn't take too long to decide... but it was one of those moments where everything hangs in the balance. I said I was leaving for Flagstaff with Dorte!

I think both of us were shell shocked at the turn of events. She at the loss of her travelling companion (at least for a while, although Kathe caught up with her later), I at the sudden proposal! We reached Flagstaff and peered into the Canyon after watching the explanatory film at the Visitor Centre, not quite able to take it all in. The Grand Canyon was certainly worthy of more attention, but geological features, however momentous, weren't uppermost in our minds. We took the night bus to Las Vegas arriving at five in the morning! We (or I) then had an altercation with the manager of a rather seedy establishment, who seized my bag for having a shower in Dorte's room without paying for a separate room, as I was not intending to stay. Surprisingly, now I think about it, I called the police, got my bag back and we left and stayed with another SERVAS host family for a night. Neither of us liked Las Vegas, but Dorte stayed on longer while I took the bus to Los Angeles.

I corresponded by letter with Dorte for a little while when she got back to Denmark (there being no email for another thirty years!). She told me Owen and Kathe were still together and Kathe had become a Baha'i. Owen had travelled through Copenhagen on his way back from a pilgrimage in Haifa, but Kathe's mother had refused to meet him. Dorte had written this heartfelt line in her last letter to me in January 1970: "I wish every people would take each person for what it was and not on account of colour and religion." Sadly, I have long since lost touch, for it would be fun to talk about those days again.

The West Coast

After the ups and downs of crossing Arizona, New Mexico and Nevada I arrived in the promised land of California: that extraordinary state that has probably more deeply affected the life of the world than most countries, and that continues to do so with the deeply powerful effects of Silicon Valley. Its universities shine, its vineyards refresh, its show-biz in equal measure entertains and irritates, its cities enthral, its collected art amazes, its technology leads the world, and its varied population fascinates. And all this on a coastline second to none, on topography that has everything from deserts to redwoods, and over a geological fault that could end it all in minutes.

The coach pulled into the Los Angeles Bus Station: Greyhound had once again done its business. I stayed in the city a couple of days with Mr and Mrs Sherry (a good name!). He worked at the University of Southern California as an economics lecturer; his wife worked with disadvantaged children. They were a charming and kind couple. Los Angeles was founded by the Spanish in the eighteenth century, occupies a wonderful position between mountains to the north and the Pacific, and is the second largest city in the States, with a population numbering around four million.

Although I inevitably went to Disneyland and Marine Land, and was amazed at the energy, size, fun and variety of these theme-parks, the most memorable moment in Los Angeles was pure happenstance. Our host had heard that the President was flying into the local military airport on his way back from Midway Island. Nixon had been in discussion there with the President of South Vietnam about the withdrawal of American troops, currently then at levels of half a million men. In fact, it would be another five years before the end of the conflict. Our hosts suggested we went to the air force base to see the President. So, together with a few hundred others, I was there to greet him. They came over to where we were standing close by the tarmac and came down the line, shaking hands. The President and the First Lady walked past, and I shook her hand! Five years later Nixon resigned, facing certain impeachment for Watergate, while Pat Nixon and their two daughters stood graciously and courageously by him. It was I am sure the closest I will ever get to a U.S. President, and currently at the time of writing in 2020, I don't want to be any closer!

After two days in Los Angeles, which was too big to explore much more, I took an overnight bus to San Francisco and stayed in the faithful YMCA, at $30 a week! I got in touch with a contact of Alan Emery's in Berkeley who ran a small home contract cleaning company with ServiceMaster and I was offered two weeks' employment at $50 a week plus board and lodging in their house. The work was from seven a.m. to four p.m. and consisted of cleaning carpets, bathrooms, walls and furniture and kitchens. The worst house to clean was that of three students from Berkeley University! The well-off haggled when it came to payment, the worse-off paid up and were grateful: an important life lesson. Early finishing times and a weekend at the outset living in the YMCA, gave me time to get "the vibe" in San Francisco: and vibe it certainly was.

We all knew the song by Scott McKenzie, "If you are going to San Francisco, be sure be sure to wear some flowers in your hair" for you are going to meet "some gentle people there", people with "a new explanation". Flower power, headbands, drugs of every kind, thousands of young people, free love, bra burning, rock music, protest against war— "make love, not war"—and for some reason old Volkswagen cars, which were the vehicle of choice and painted, of course, with flowers, were everywhere!

The first "Summer of Love" had been in 1967 when a hundred thousand hippies converged on the city, and in '69 we were still very much in the afterglow. San Francisco itself was and is an immensely attractive setting: the bay, the Golden Gate Bridge, the steep streets going down to the wharfs, the trams, Chinatown, Fisherman's Wharf and the nearby quays. The "scene" was based around the Haight Asbury district where the hippy colony congregated. I wandered the streets, taking in the atmosphere, no doubt filled with smoke from spliffs. Another side to the "Summer of Love" was that there had been twenty-one unsolved homicides in the area.

There was no denying the opportunities for culture of all kinds in the city. I went to a concert at Fillmore West headlining *The Who* from England (still touring in 2020) and performing, among many others, their new song *I Can see for Miles*, along with Woody Hermon's jazz band, with Woody on clarinet and saxophone. And then, contrastingly, I saw Stoppard's *Rosencrantz and Guildenstern are Dead*—still playing recently in London with Benedict Cumberbatch. Then, to add to the range of experiences, after my two weeks' work, I treated myself to two nights in the El Cortez Hotel and watched via satellite TV the investiture of Prince Charles as Prince of Wales in Caernarfon Castle. Talk about culture clash!

My journey through the USA was coming to an end. It was now July and I had to be back in the UK in August. I travelled to northern California, seeing the mighty redwoods on the edge of the Pacific Ocean, some 300 feet tall. I lay on my back looking up their soaring trunks, and then it was on to Portland, Oregon. From there I went to Vancouver Island, Banff and Lake Louise in the alpine majesty of the Rockies, before heading south to Salt Lake City, the home of the Mormons. The Temple seemed to be closed to visitors but there was an expansive visitor centre explaining the story and beliefs of the Mormons: their trek under Brigham Young to Salt Lake, and the origins of the Book of Mormon with its strange conflation of the Old Testament and primitive American history. Combined with knowledge of their practise of polygamy made this another bizarre experience of the opposing cultures of the States in its vast space, which can both accommodate and lose so much.

My final trek home was via Denver, Colorado, and Rapid City in South Dakota, where I saw in the Black Hills the carved heads of the American Presidents. It was whilst in Denver that I saw in a hotel the great event of the moon landing on 20 July, and heard, in real time, Neil Armstrong's rather low-key words, "one small step for man, a giant leap for mankind", as he explained that for the first time in history a human being was leaving footprints in fine lunar dust. There is no doubt that the event which the words recorded set America ablaze with pride and confidence during a period of doubt and self-questioning, due to the course of the Vietnam War in '69. Then, as if to puncture or impair that joy, an incident involving Senator Ted Kennedy in which he drove a car into a creek after a party, bringing about the death of his passenger, May Jo Kopechne, brought politics down to earth with a bump. It ended any likelihood of this third Kennedy brother running successfully for President: both his brothers having been assassinated.

Meanwhile I needed to contact Flight Lieutenant Scroggs of the RAF Movements Unit in New York to apply for a return seat on a RAF flight to Brize Norton, supported by Lieutenant Colonel D.G. Turner in Washington. After a wait in Chicago the seat came up—one more hop on a Greyhound to New York and I was on a flight home on 9 August. Two months later I was a "fresher" at Oxford. In some ways I felt like the Ancient Mariner in Coleridge's poem, greeting new people and places but having to work through all the experiences of the last eight months. I needed somewhere to place all these experiences that had crowded in on me, a means of calibrating them and a new centre to my existence.

Chapter III
Journeys of the Soul

In October 1969 I went up to Christ Church Oxford to read Modern History, which in traditional Oxford terms meant history after the Roman Empire or the classical world. I found myself sharing a sitting room (we each had a bedroom leading off it) with a delightful man, James Gould, who was studying Jurisprudence (Law) and who had a host of friends from Winchester College and the Isle of Wight, where he was a keen sailor, as well as an all-round sportsman and wine taster. Later he would sail across the Pacific from Tahiti to Bali in his cousin's boat, Mayfly. He had recently been to Sikkim, where his father, Sir Basil Gould (much older, and who had died when James was seven), had been the British Political Officer from 1935–1945 and present at the installation of the present Dalai Lama in Tibet. Although there was no indication then, James was to have a tragically short life. He had a heart defect about which he breathed not a word, but two years after leaving Oxford he died in full flight as a barrister. He was the epitome of courage and good humour. When I wrote to his mother after his death, she was kind enough to say he had enjoyed sharing a sitting room with me. I certainly did with him, and could never forget him; his great shock of red hair, his large frame and laugh, and his generous bonhomie.

After my travels around the United States and using sailing as a metaphor, I felt I needed a keel or "centre board" in my own life: something that would both ground and direct me. As I had seen in the States and indeed in a post-war Europe struggling to find its feet after 1945. There were plenty of currents and cross currents at work: one was the pursuit of freedom, whether from communism as in East Germany, or by Afro-Americans tragically denied civil liberty as in the States; another was the search for transcendent meaning—expressed in music, in mind-altering drugs, or in protest against conventional mores, war and capitalism, as seen in the hippie movement in Boston and San Francisco.

While there was also the possibility of settling into all that Oxford had to offer without facing any deeper questions about our purpose on earth, I sensed a spiritual stirring, a quest for meaning and purpose, of wanting to live beyond the immediate, and this had been provoked by questions thrown up by travels, by my brother having found "new life" in Christianity as a student in Cambridge, and by what can only be described as my own inner search for meaning and purpose which I think sooner or later we all face, and must resolve.

Indeed, my housemaster at school had summed up that disposition perspicaciously, by writing as follows in a kind of final report for my father when I left school in December 1968: "I have said that he's very friendly: that's not his only strong point. He has a most equable temperament, yet he's one who thinks quite deeply about today's problems, and he is by no means completely conventional in his conclusions; yet they are delivered with such charm and perhaps, such detachment, that he's never a 'rebel'." It was a perceptive comment. Well, I was determined in a quiet way to dig beneath the surface, and not remain too detached for ever.

In October 1969 I listened to an Anglican Clergyman, Canon David Watson, with a gift of explaining the significance of Christ's life, and in particular his death by crucifixion. He took a passage from Isaiah and explained it. Strangely, as it seemed to me then, the Old Testament was talking about an event some eight hundred years in the future. I quote in full:

Who has believed our message,
And to whom has the arm of the Lord been revealed?
He grew up before him a like a tender shoot.
And like a root out of dry ground.
He had no beauty or majesty to attract us to him
Nothing in his appearance that we should desire him.
He was despised and rejected by men,
A man of sorrows, and familiar with suffering
Like one whom men hide their faces. He was despised, and we esteemed him not.
Surely, he took up our infirmities

And carried our sorrows,
Yet we considered him afflicted.
But he was pierced for our transgressions,
He was crushed for our iniquities;
The punishment that brought us peace was upon him
And by his wounds we are healed.
We all like sheep have gone astray
Each of us has turned to his own way;
And the Lord had laid on him the inequity of us all (Isaiah 53: 1–6
NIV version).

Of course, Isaiah was talking about Christ, the Man of Sorrows, who had come to redeem humankind. I later learnt from a saying of Martin Luther, that to understand Christianity truly, "you must begin with the wounds of Christ". In other words, Jesus came into the world to do something for us that we could not do for ourselves, that no amount of human intelligence, brilliance and skill could achieve, because we are flawed. In other words, my transgressions, iniquities or shortcomings contributed to his sorrows and sufferings, but his dying secured my acceptance and forgiveness.

Much later I discovered a succinct piece of early Christian writing from the third century AD in the *Epistle to Diognetus,* which echoes the words of Isaiah,

But when the time arrived, that God had planned to reveal at last his goodness and his power, he did not hate us, destroy us, or hold a grudge against us. But he was patient, he bore with us, and out of pity for us he took our sins upon himself, he gave up his own Son as a ransom for us, the holy one for the lawless, the innocent one for the wicked, the righteous one for the unrighteous, the imperishable one for the perishable, the immortal one for the mortal. For what else could hide our sins but the righteousness of that one. Oh, the sweet exchange! Oh, the inexpressible creation! Oh, the unexpected gift![8]

Amazingly, these words were first found amongst the packing cases in a

[8] *The Apostolic Fathers*, Vol. II, tr. Bart D. Ehrman (Loeb Classical Library, Boston, MA: Harvard University Press, 2005), p. 151.

fish shop in Constantinople in the sixteenth century, where they had somehow been preserved.

As there was a choice to be made, I could either walk away from what I heard in this address based on Isaiah's prophecy or, in a sincere prayer, I could seek to the follow the one who had given all. I did the latter in a moment of grace and determined with divine aid to start following. I was used to praying in a peremptory kind of manner. As children, our parents would expect us to pray before climbing into bed in a "God-bless-Mummy-and-Daddy-and-the-whole-wide-world" kind of way. We did go to church and years of school chapel did not entirely inoculate me against the real thing. I do remember as a ten-year-old, after hearing the story of Solomon, asking God to give me also the gift of wisdom. I don't believe these prayers were ignored. But here was something different, more deliberate, more conscious, more meaningful: a prayer beginning a new relationship and way of life. Some might say conversion, or maybe for me it was "an inking in of what was previously written in pencil". I did that inking in and it had profound consequences.

What certainly helped me in those early years of "following" was joining with others on the same journey, but also reading: yes, the Bible, which became remarkably alive, like a personal letter written to me. I have increasingly enjoyed and treasured this extraordinary book, but I also appreciated contemporary Christian writers. One then was Malcolm Muggeridge (1903–1990), a journalist, writer, soldier and spy, whose scintillating autobiography *Chronicles of Wasted Time I & II* enthralled, entertained and challenged me: showing how one soul voyaged erratically towards the same light. His was the type of life that appealed to me, working for MI6 in the war in Mozambique, North Africa and in Paris after the liberation.

While in Lourenço Marques (now Maputo), Mozambique, in 1942 he had become deeply depressed and resolved to take his life. With no drugs to hand he decided to swim out to sea, like the poet Shelley off the coast of Leghorn or Livorno, and drown himself. He began to swim, and after a while he turned around to look at the coast, where he caught sight of a light on the quay beaming out to him. Almost involuntarily he began swimming back to the shore. Climbing out of the sea in the early morning he struggled through thick mud towards the light. It was the light of Peter's Café in Costa del Sol, and the light shone through bars of the café in the shape of the cross. Muggeridge takes up the story:

In a tiny dark dungeon of the ego, chained and manacled, I had glimpsed a glimmer of light coming in through the barred window high above me. It was the light of Peter's Café and Costa del Sol calling me back to earth, my mortal home: it was the grey light of morning heralding another day as I floundered and struggled through the black mud; it was the light of the world. The bars of the window, as I looked more closely, took on the form of a Cross.[9]

It was his epiphany. People whom Muggeridge held up in his writings included Mother Teresa with her deep commitment to the poor and dying in whom he noticed, when visiting her in Calcutta, "a special kind of sagacity and sense of the absurd that comes of understanding the world without being in it".[10] He also admired Simone Weil, the French mystic and political activist, Leo Tolstoy and Augustine of Hippo. They all had much to teach. Augustine of Hippo was another because he kept the daily routines of his monastic life, eyes fixed on the "City of God", even as Rome fell in 410 and the Vandals besieged, and "vandalised" Carthage.

As for Tolstoy, if I were ever asked, which I won't be, on *Desert Island Discs* (England's most popular radio programme) what book I would take to the desert island along with the Bible and the complete works of Shakespeare, it would have to be the complete works of Tolstoy. Tolstoy died in a railway station waiting room, running away from his wife's demand, that he change his will so as to benefit his family, rather than Russia's literary circle. His Christian faith had changed him, but, like the rest of us, he too was a work in progress. Years before he wrote:

Five years ago, I adopted the teaching of Christ, and my life suddenly changed; I ceased to wish that which I formerly wished, and I began to wish that which I formerly did not wish. What formerly appeared good

---

[9] Malcolm Muggeridge, *The Infernal Grove: Chronicles of Wasted Time* (London: Fontana, 1973), p. 204.
[10] Muggeridge, *The Infernal Grove*, p. 272.

now appeared evil; and what formerly appeared evil now appeared good. With me happened just what happened to a man who went out for some business and on the way decided that it was unnecessary, and therefore returned. All that which was at the right side, then was at the left side, and that which had seemed on the left was then on the right; the desire to be as far as possible from home gave way to the desire to be as near as possible to home. The direction of my life—my desires—became different; and good and evil changed places. All this was the result of my understanding the teaching of Christ otherwise than before.[11]

In Oxford you could not avoid C. S. Lewis and J. R. Tolkien. I was to devour C.S. Lewis, who just forty years before had knelt in another Oxford room in Magdalen College, not very far away, and famously described that moment in these terms at the end of his book, *Surprised by Joy*:

In the Trinity Term of 1929, I gave in and admitted that God was God, and knelt and prayed: perhaps, that night, the most dejected and reluctant convert in all England. I did not see what is now the most shining and obvious thing; the Divine humility which will accept a convert even on such terms. The Prodigal Son at least walked home on his own two feet. But who can duly adore that Love which will open the high gates to a prodigal who is brought in kicking, struggling, resentful, and darting his eyes in every direction for a chance of escape? The hardness of God is kinder than the softness of men, and His compulsion is our liberation.[12]

For Lewis, as he says, this conversion initially was just to theism, the belief in the existence of God alone. But when he understood the Incarnation, God taking on flesh in Christ, some months or a year later, he rejoiced. He was like a person who having been lost in a forest saw a signpost showing the way out, and his theistic faith turned to fully Christian. He said this happened while seated on the top of a bus taking him to Whipsnade Zoo. He went there a theist; he came back a Christian.

---

[11] Taken from *The Life of Tolstoy*, chapter 10.
[12] C. S. Lewis, *Surprised by Joy* (London: Fontana Books, 1960), pp. 182–3.

He believed that the person at the centre of the Gospel was the Incarnate Son of God pointing the way out of the forest.[13]

While I had taken a new step in my life, in 1969 I certainly didn't know where it would take me, although it had not removed my desire to travel. What I did know was that, as far I was able, I wanted to follow the teaching of Christ, in a relationship with him. And over time this new found discovery gave a new side and meaning to travel

Over the next few years, I took three journeys of significance, as well as a walking holiday in the Lake District with a fellow student Geoff Fazan, where we got lost in a blizzard and came down the wrong side of Hellvelyn! Tragically he was to die young in a motor accident in South Africa in the 1980s and I found myself taking a memorial service for him in a city church in London.

The three longer journeys during these Oxford years and just after were to southern Europe and Yugoslavia, another to Turkey and Iran, and the third to East Africa. Each was important in its own way.

A European Tour

The "Long Vac", as it was called, i.e., the summer months (June to October) allowed for the possibility of travel. Some, like the travel writer and historian, William Dalrymple, managed to go to Xanadu and back in the long vacation.[14] To earn some money, I did some strawberry picking in the fields around Didcot, where there were then a number of fruit farms, and then, for a few weeks in July and August, travelled around Europe with a close friend, Charles Higgins, whose home was nearby,

Charles and I planned to travel through France, where he had family friends, to Corsica, Sardinia, and Rome; across Italy to the port of Bari, and then through Yugoslavia, which was ruled by Tito under a kind of liberal form of Communism. The return journey was to be through Venice, Austria and Southern Germany. Along the way there were a number of contacts to stay with—friends of Charles' family. Initially we hoped to drive, but the car broke down before we left and so it was train, bus and ferry. We would camp, although we had no tent, and would in

---

[13] Lewis, *Surprised by Joy*, p. 189.
[14] William Dalrymple, *In Xanadu* (London: Penguin, 1989).

fact sleep rough by the roadside when not staying with friends, and keep what money we had for food and travel. We were not even identifiable as backpackers, since neither of us had a backpack. We had suitcases, as if travelling to a weekend house-party in the country! We planned our route through France to Valence on the Rhone, Aix-en-Provence and Nice, Corsica, Sardinia and Rome. This was the first leg.

Our first stay was at Château St Maurice, Baix, near Valence, which belonged to a family called the Pousses. On arrival at the Château, we were greeted with an unusual notice in the driveway that read: *Achtung, Ici on Travaille*. Charles had warned me that to keep the Château ticking over, and it was getting very dilapidated, the family were expected to do fatigues each day, and we too were set to work. The use of the word *Achtung*, in post war France, which had recently been so divided, struck me as risky!

Charles had brought some presents for the family: a bottle of whisky and a box of cornflakes. The cornflakes were a novelty (and I think the gift was a bit tongue-in-cheek anyhow). Anyhow they were served as pre-prandial crisps with drinks on the terrace. Chilled sauvignon blanc embellished with the odd cornflake seemed satisfactory to the owners! Charles and I winked at each other, and helped ourselves to more. Despite being American in origin, they were judged *delicieux!*

We left after two days, cadging a lift to Aix-en-Provence with a cousin in their Citroen. From there we took a train to Nice and then a ferry to Corsica, named after *Napoleon*, the most famous son of Corsica. We travelled fourth class, and slept on the deck during the eight-hour night journey, and nothing could have been more exciting than crossing a small part of the Mediterranean for the first time!

In Corsica we arrived at Ajaccio, where we went around Napoleon Bonaparte's house and we were struck by how spacious it was. He was not a typical *sans culotte*, having been born on the island into a family of minor Italian nobility, and entering the French Army as an artillery officer when the Revolution erupted in 1789. We spent a night on the ground in Ajaccio, where the police shone torches in our faces around two a.m. and then moved on. From Ajaccio we went to Propriano, a seaside resort where in typical English fashion we swam, sunbathed and got sunburnt. We then travelled on by bus to Bonifacio, refusing an invitation from a fellow passenger, an older man, to stay in his house in the hills. From that moment he stuck to us like a limpet, even accompanying us to our night quarters on some waste ground near the port. We lent him a groundsheet and my jacket as a pillow! During the night he got closer and closer, so we made sure passports, money and valuables were tucked well inside our sleeping bags. Next morning, we were all set to leave for Sardinia, only to be told the ferry had run aground and would be delayed! There seemed to be no communication between Corsica and Sardinia, which meant a further night out in the open. As friends of this well-known local character, we were, however, given free drinks at several of the bars.

By then we were down to our final 20 francs cash (10 francs to a £), although we did have travellers' cheques. We arrived in Porta Teresa Sardinia on a Sunday, so the banks were all closed and there was no chance of changing a travellers' cheque. My grandfather Whitworth, then aged ninety-two, had given me £10 for the trip, and so we exchanged it on the street and had enough money for the ferry to the Port of Rome. We took a bus in from Civitavecchia to Roma to stay with Marina Neubert and her beautiful daughter Gaya, friends of the Higgins family through the military in France. They showed us around the city, but we were not there long enough there for any romance to blossom, for we moved on to Naples, explored the Island of Capri and then crossed to Bari on the East coast of Italy. There we caught another ferry to Dubrovnik, and Yugoslavia.

In 1970 Yugoslavia was made up of six separate republics, all of which in time would have their own future, although not without war, massacres and bloodshed. At the heart of that divide would be the historic rift between Croatia and Serbia, between Muslim and Orthodox Christian and the state of Kosovo. In 1970, and under the leadership of Tito (1892–1980), Yugoslavia was a stable and relatively open socialist country, with greater freedoms than the rest of the Soviet Bloc from which it had broken in 1948. A Croat by birth, Tito, who was closely supported by Churchill, had become a war hero fighting against the Nazis and organising a guerrilla campaign with the Partisans against Germany. He was made Prime Minister in 1943 and then President for life until his death in 1980, when forebodingly, ethnic and religious differences began to raise their heads. But in 1970, thirty years before I would be there again, it was a peaceful country.

Arriving in Dubrovnik was breath-taking. It is, as Byron said, "a jewel on the Adriatic". The spectacular city walls drop down into the sea, the streets are paved with marble, now worn. Originally Roman, the city was taken by Slavs, and then in the thirteenth century by the Venetians, before being incorporated into the Republic of Ragusa and then the Ottoman Empire. Caught in the cross-hairs of the civil war in 1990, it suffered extensive damage which was later repaired. The city glistens on the shimmering sea once again: beautiful and expensive! From Dubrovnik we headed inland by bus to Mostar and then Sarajevo. Mostar is in Bosnia Herzegovina and is famed for its most elegant bridge, the *Stari Most* or the Old Bridge, built by the Ottomans in the sixteenth century. It lifts high and graciously over the blue-green water of the Neretva River below. Mostar too would be torn apart by the civil war, neighbour turning on neighbour, and the bridge destroyed, although now rebuilt.

From Mostar we went to Sarajevo, famed in the lexicon of European history for the incident that sparked the First World War. Sarajevo had passed from Ottoman control to the Austrian Hungarians, and it was there that a young Serbian Nationalist called Princip fired at the Archduke Ferdinand of Austria and his wife, killing him on 28 June 1914. Austria Hungary gave an ultimatum to Serbia with which they could not comply and Russia supported its Orthodox-Christian ally. Germany came onto the side of the Austria Hungarians and invaded the Low Countries at the same time, which in turn brought France and England into the War. World War I with all its appalling consequences had begun.

Charles was determined to see the spot where the assassination had happened only fifty-six years before. He wrote to his parents as follows, "On Monday 3 August, we went to Sarajevo. It had always been one of my dreams to see where Franz Ferdinand was shot" (perhaps a curious dream!). Of course, Princip is still a national hero here, despite the tragedy that the assassination precipitated. From Sarajevo we took a slow bus to Jajce, famous for its waterfall. We spent a wonderful two days swimming in lakes and walking in the mountains. "To see the real

Yugoslavia, the tourist must go to Bosnia, Hercegovina and Macedonia," Charles wrote to his parents. The countryside was lovely: steeply wooded gorges breaking into rich pasture and meadows, old fashioned farming methods with horse and cart, and bright strong streams of water cascading down hillsides.

It seemed idyllic, although later Sarajevo was to suffer an appalling siege in the civil war from 1992 to 1996. It is a small city that has known intense suffering. Eleven thousand people, including fifteen hundred children, lost their lives when they were pounded by the Serbian army. There was terrible cold in the winters and awful hunger. In 1970 one could not have predicted this. It was a lesson that I was to learn again when in Syria some years later; once again things are not necessarily what they seem. A bucolic idyll can be tipped into tragedy more quickly than one might imagine.

From Jajce we went by train to Banja Luka, Trieste and then Venice, the shimmering queen of the Adriatic, where we went our separate ways. Charles went on to stay with German friends in Cologne, retuning to England mid-August and I travelled back directly to England at the end of the first week of August. The trip had taken about three weeks, and was full of happy memories, interesting events and amusing incidents to treasure. I never expected it would become a source of nostalgia too.

Two years later I was to meet my sister Teresa (Tsa) in Venice for my second-longest trip at the end of my time in Oxford. We would meet up where Charles and I had parted. This time the idea was to go by boat to Greece, then Istanbul, along the Black Sea and into Iran. My sister would fly back from Istanbul and I would travel on alone.

The start was coloured by great sadness. That year, on 23 May 1972 Charles, my travelling companion of two years before, mysteriously died of a brain haemorrhage, or something like it. He was twenty. The shock for his family was incalculable, and for his friends devastating and sobering. It was compounded by the recent loss of my first cousin James in the full flow of talented youthfulness Charles's funeral was on 17 June, just after my finals. I still have the service sheet. It has in it the famous prayer beginning, "O Lord support us all the day long of this troublous life…" I was beginning to learn that despite many advantages we are never far from the unexpected, and from the deep struggles of life. It also made think more deeply about my future.

In May that year I had been offered employment as a management trainee in a timber importing business called William Mallinson, Denny Mott and Dixon, based in 130 Hackney Road London. Since I had mentioned in other interviews with a merchant bank (Hambros) and an insurance broker called Willis Faber that I might put myself forward for ordination, they weren't too eager to employ me! I think I had also been sounded out, in a roundabout way, by the Oxford Appointments Board as to whether I would be interested in being a spy! Although interested (since Berlin days I had read every Le Carré novel to date avidly), I declined! But I definitely sensed the light touch of a fly on the water to see if I would rise to take the bait! Perhaps I said less about ordination to Mallinsons — a timber importer, as they offered me employment. It was not to be a lifetime commitment to timber, however!

The Chief Executive of Mallinsons was a war hero with an acute mind, Sir Tommy Macpherson. He was rightly held in great awe by the staff there. He had gained three MCs in the War (one of only twenty-five men to have achieved such a signal accolade). He was awarded as well Croix de Guerre, the Legion Honneur and a Papal Knighthood for saving the life of an Archbishop near Trieste. He worked behind the lines with the French Resistance after D-Day, holding up German Panzer Divisions in Operation Quinine. Dressed in a kilt and parachuted into France, he was adept at blowing up railway lines, booby-trapping tanks and taking out or destroying bridges. On the few occasions I reported to him, I knew I was in the presence of a man of exceptional ability who exuded great energy and would not suffer fools gladly. After the war he took a first in PPE from Trinity Oxford and very nearly competed in the Olympics in London in 1948, having already beaten Roger Bannister over a mile. Illness prevented an appearance at the Olympics, however. Having offered me employment on 30 May 1972, and asking me when I would be available, the company graciously accepted a starting date of the end of October.

This gave me a few months to kick my heels and travel. So, I met my sister in Venice for a trip, which meant two months of pure adventure, and perhaps that is why Tommy Macpherson approved!

Chapter IV
Crossing Continents

My sister came to Venice from Florence where she had been attending a finishing school, a now unheard-of form of educational-icing which seemed mostly to involve keeping English girls away from Italian men (who they were probably happy to meet in small doses) and teaching them the finer points of Renaissance and Quattrocento art (also in small doses!). There were certainly shades of E. M Forster's *Room with View* about it. Now free from the shackles of her redoubtable minder in Florence, and without stopping to explore the beauties of Venice (on this occasion), we took a passenger boat from Venice to Athens.

The voyage took about three days down the Adriatic, and past places which Charles and I had visited two years before, which was nostalgic. Ship life was quite jolly, although I remember an awful smell of oil and grease in the fourth-class hold that was literally nauseating. It was better to sleep on deck. There was a crowd of young Israelis returning home, since the boat went on from Istanbul to Haifa. There was dancing to a band and Bingo played in five languages! I don't think we won much. When we arrived in Piraeus, the port of Athens, we were ready to leave the restrictions of boat life and head into the great city itself.

We stayed in a hotel in Omonia Square (perhaps a good way of cleansing the smell of the boat!) in the heart of the city, with only a short walk up the hill to the Parthenon. There are few greater sights in the world than that of the Parthenon, which means "virgin's chamber", built in honour of the goddess Athena, and sitting atop the Acropolis. Begun in 444 BC, in the Golden Age of Pericles, the Parthenon has survived despite being caught up in war between the Ottomans and Venetians when explosives were stored there by the Ottomans, and which, in 1687, were exploded in the bombardment of the city. Although damage was done, it was Lord Elgin, the British soldier and diplomat, who took the marbles—the sculptures for the frieze around the Temple that had been overseen by the Greek architect and sculptor Phidias—and sold them to the British government. Residing now in the British Museum they are a running sore between Britain and Greece. (This a highly contentious subject, and the marbles would probably be returned with howls from the British Museum and the British public alike. Yet it would be like the Greeks taking part of Stonehenge on the basis that we could not fully look after the stones and with the permission of an occupying power, as The Ottomans gave Elgin permission). Even without the marbles, the Parthenon combines unequalled power with elegance. The geometric principles of its design create an optical illusion in which seemingly perfect symmetry is achieved by irregular sizes, measurements and heights, conforming to what has been described as the "golden ratio". In other words, geometry, mathematics and architecture have conspired to please the eye to perfection.

Recently a family heirloom has come into my possession: a book of lithographs about an owlet called Athena that was found by Florence Nightingale when touring the Parthenon with her family in 1850. When Athena, then a fully-grown owl, expired while Florence Nightingale was embarking for the Crimea in 1854, her sister Parthenope wrote an account of the owl's life for Florence. Several copies were made with beautiful illustrations, and one was given to my great-great grandmother, Frances Hanford-Flood, a close friend of the Nightingale family.[15] Florence not only had an owlet for a pet but a cicada called Plato and two tortoises named after missionaries working in Athens called Mr and Mrs Hill. The owlet proved very fierce and had to be hypnotised before she would go into a cage. The owlet also ate Plato, no doubt making her even more wise!

On our second full day in Athens, we decided to go on an excursion to Delphi. Just a few hours northwest of Athens, on the slopes of Mount Parnassus, and with a captivating view over the gorges below to a wide plain, Delphi is certainly a spot to reflect on life and the future. Renowned in classical times from the ninth century BC for its ambiguous oracular messages through a Pythian priestess, at the very least it reminds humans of their need for guidance. The silence, produced by the heat of

---

[15] Cecil Woodham Smith, *Florence Nightingale* (London: Constable & Co, 1952), p. 63.

midday, settles like a blanket across the pine clad slopes, giving a pregnant stillness, although such moments are probably rare now, with the ceaseless arrival of tourists.

Much later I read an account of my grandfather Whitworth's visit to Delphi in 1905, then teaching Classics at Eton as Master in College. How different it was then (Greece I mean)! It was a very arduous journey compared to 1972, still less today. They joined a small chartered steam ship from Piraeus, which bumped along the very narrow sides of the Corinth Canal into the Gulf of Corinth. A Professor Gardner from the British School of Archaeology, along with an assistant called Mr Wace, and a party of others including parasol carrying ladies and various Oxbridge undergraduates made up the group of nearly fifty. They disembarked at Itea, hired mules for their baggage and rations and walked the 2000 feet up to Delphi.[16] Lectures from Professor Gardner followed. No photography was permitted by the French, who had exclusive rights of excavation on the site.[17] *Plus, ca change…*

From Delphi, my grandfather and three friends walked north to Thermopylae, where the Greeks had held off the Persians in 480 BC. They then caught a boat near Molos across the Bay of Marathon and through the Straits of Chalcis to the Peloponnese. It was at Marathon that the Greeks defeated the Persians and the runner, Pheidippides, ran the twenty-six miles to tell the awaiting Athenian Senate the news. My grandfather's tour, although demanding, was not so gruelling. They lived on cocoa, eggs and bread, and had hammocks to sleep in. There were virtually no hotels or cafes. They sometimes stayed in Greek homes where they ate the simplest fare. By contrast, in a single day we saw Delphi and returned to Athens, and there was no difficulty taking photographs—the French in their custodial capacity had gone had gone!

Returning from Delphi to the throb of traffic in Omonia Square for a final night was to leave behind an enchanted place for the heat and noise of the city. The next day we left Athens for the eastern Peloponnese, hiring not a steamer and mules, but a car. We decided to spend money on transport and nothing on hotels. We slept on the ground without a tent and in the next few days went to Old Corinth, Epidaurus, Nafplion and

---

[16] *Diary of a Tour in Greece in 1904* (Private Papers), pp. 20–27.
[17] *Diary of a Tour in Greece in 1904*, p. 27.

Mycenae, all places I shall describe in a much later visit to the Peloponnese. Three days of travel around these sights and we were back on a ship bound for Istanbul or, as it was called for most of its life, Constantinople.

It took two days to arrive in Istanbul, across the Aegean and past the Islands of the Cyclades. Of course, the journey from Athens to Istanbul is redolent with Homeric legend: it must have been by this route that the Greek warriors led by Agamemnon and Achilles sailed in their small ships to Troy to recapture Helen, who had been taken by Paris. It was a well-travelled route to one of the great cities of the world; sailing across this sea was truly exciting.

There can be no doubt that great cities are made by their location by water. The location of Istanbul is quite simply breath-taking. It is the hinge between Europe and Asia and was the capital of the Eastern Roman Empire and the Ottomans for near on one thousand and seven hundred years. It guards and sits on one of the great waterways of the world. It is approached from the West through the narrow straits of the Dardanelles, or to give them their classical name, the Hellespont—Helle being the mythical daughter of Athamas, who was rescued by a golden fleeced ram. It was in these Straits, off the Gallipoli Peninsula, that British and ANZAC forces faced such a catastrophic defeat by the Turks in 1915, costing the job of Winston Churchill, whose idea it was, although he was probably let down by his commanders. Sailing through those straits there was much to ponder before the waters opened up into the Sea of Marmara and eventually the Bosporus and the Black Sea. Ships from Turkey, Ukraine, Russia, Bulgaria and Romania and Georgia sailed constantly through from the Black Sea, making this one of the busiest waterways in the world. The blue waters glistened in the sun, and the thought of so many killed from the other side of the world was hard to grasp.

My sister and I had only two days in Istanbul before she flew back to England and I travelled on to Iran. We certainly did not do justice to Istanbul and its many sights on this occasion, although I would begin to do so later on a second visit. Content to simply gaze at the continual movement, sights and sounds on the waterways surrounding the city on all sides, we sipped Turkish coffee and enjoyed bahcevan *kebabi* (skewered meat and vegetables) and "Noah's pudding"—a mixture of walnuts, raisins and honey, which must have kept him going in the Ark—rather than dash round every mosque, church and palace. We did manage the Topkapi Palace, and, like all visitors, were stunned by its spectacular position on the tip of the peninsula that had first boasted the ancient city of Byzantium.

We had also been picked up by two young Turks, Hamdi and Ali, who were intent on showing us the city and more importantly earn a tip which, when it came, they inevitably considered poor payment for their "far-reaching knowledge". They took us to a Turkish nightclub which mainly featured interminable and plaintive Turkish love songs, which ears acclimatised to the Beatles and the Stones found hard to fully appreciate.

My sister took the plane home, and I spent the day before my ship sailed into the Black Sea exploring some of the smaller communities along the Sea of Marmara. I remember practising my rudimentary Turkish, playing *tawula* or Turkish backgammon in some of the many tea shops along the coast. Everyone was friendly, amused to have an Englishman challenge them at backgammon and probably coming off worse.

The next day I caught a ship that went east along the southern coast of the Black Sea. As far as I remember it was a two-day voyage to Trabzon, via Sinop and Samsun. To be travelling across the Black Sea seemed exotic enough, but to begin by going up the Bosporus, with its assorted communities nestling along the banks of this waterway gave a sense of progressive revelation. From the port of Istanbul, we passed the Galata Bridge over the Golden Horn, the finger of water reaching north around the Peninsula of the old city, and then the Dolmabahce Palace or Sarayi, the principal residence of the Sultan from the nineteenth century onwards and the final resting place of the father of modern Turkey, Kemal Atatürk.

The Bosporus is about thirty kilometres in length and at its narrowest is seven hundred metres wide, dividing Europe on the west bank from Asia on the east. I was not aware at the time, but there are two currents at work in the Bosporus: an overcurrent from the Black Sea to the Sea of Mamara, and beneath it an undercurrent (Corrente Sottanno) driven by the heavier saline solution of the Mediterranean going in the other direction. The undercurrent was discovered by Italian oceanographer, Luigi Ferdinando Marsigli, in 1680.[18] Entering the Black Sea, one becomes aware of the many cultures that it supports; interconnected by the all-important waterway.

To the north-east are the Eastern European countries of Bulgaria and Romania, where the mighty Danube empties its precious water into the sea through its wild-life rich delta at the rate of 203 cubic kilometres of water each year.[19] To the north are Moldova, Ukraine and Russia, and the disputed region of the Crimea; to the east is Georgia and the tiny state of Abkhazia, while the south coast falls entirely within Turkey. Other rivers, such as the Don, Dnieper, Dniester and Kuban, empty into the sea also. Yet the sea conceals a secret: it is the world's biggest reservoir of hydrogen sulphate, a toxic substance. Below a depth of two hundred metres there is no life, but above that depth the Black Sea used to team with fish stocks, salmon, Beluga sturgeon carrying rich caviar and anchovy by the ton, all swimming anti-clockwise round the sea. The Black Sea nurtures these nations and its fish, while the Bosporus is the passage to a wider world, a birth channel for the progeny of these nations.

Moving along the south coast, we put in at Sinop and Samsun. Once an important trading port on the route to Cappadocia, Sinop is now a quiet provincial town. Founded as colony by the Greeks and taken over by the Romans, it was an important ship-building town. It was from here that heretic Marcion (c 85–160 AD) came. He himself was a wealthy ship builder and was eager to be as influential in church life as he had been in the ship building world. He came with money to the Roman church, bringing also teaching that said there were two gods: the one of the Old Testament and the one of the New. Only the Gospel of Luke and Paul's Epistles could be trusted, he maintained. It took a very long piece of writing by the North African theologian and polemicist Tertullian to keep the church to the view that there was a single divine mind behind the Old and New Testaments. But now, in 1972, churches in Sinop had long since been replaced with mosques, as the Seljuk and then Ottoman Turks took over the city from the thirteenth century.

---

[18] Neal Ascherson, *Black Sea* (London: Vintage Books 2007), p. 4.
[19] Ascherson, *Black Sea*, p. 5.

From Sinop, I sailed via Samsun to Trebizond or Trabzon, a famous Silk Road city, also made known to English readers by Rose Macaulay's strange and wistful autobiographical novel called the *Towers of Trebizond,* published in 1956 shortly before her death. Macaulay's book highlights the impossible tension between her yearning for a mystical Christianity and her sexual longing for a married ex-priest and writer, Gerald O'Donovan. Perhaps the tensions in the city of Trabzon as it migrated from its Christian past to its Muslim present, reflected the chasms in her own heart. Like so many other provincial cities, Trabzon fell to the Ottoman Turks in 1461. Until then it was the capital of the Rom people and the Comnenian Empire, following the sack of Constantinople in the Fourth Crusade of 1204. For centuries, Greek Christians practised their faith here, provided they paid their taxes and did not ride a horse. The hinterland saw a Christian civilisation built in Greek coastal communities and in fertile valleys, with monasteries such as the Sumela Monastery, which clings to a craggy cliff face some thirty-nine miles from Trabzon. The Greek presence and their worship all came to an end in 1923, however.

Encouraged by Lloyd George, after World War I the Greeks had taken up arms to claim more of Turkey, both along the Ionian coast where great cities like Izmir lie and along the coastal littoral of the Black Sea. It was to be a fateful step. All round the Black Sea, from fifth century BC onwards, Greeks had settled and successfully traded with peoples further inland, bringing grain, oil, and leather to the west. In the north, around the Sea of Azoz and the city of Kerch, a polyglot Greek kingdom emerged, the Bosporan Kingdom, which lasted until the coming of the Huns in the fifth century.[20] Further east, in present day Georgia and Abkhazia, Greeks flourished in the territory they called Colchis.[21] In different forms, Greeks would trade and live in these coastal communities, cross-breeding with Scythians, Huns and Sarmatians until Stalin began his mass deportations of Greeks further east to the Khans (Kazakhstan and Uzbekistan) in the 1930s.[22] From there, many with Greek passports would eventually return to Greece. Greek communities around Trabzon were smashed by the resurgent power of Turkish forces

---

[20] Ascherson, *Black Sea*, p. 211.
[21] Ascherson, *Black Sea*, pp. 237–8.
[22] Ascherson, *Black Sea*, p. 174.

under Kemal Ataturk in 1922. Following the Treaty of Lausanne, Greek and Turkish populations in Thrace and in Greek Macedonia were swapped, and the Pontic Greeks along the southern Black Sea were no more. Churches became mosques, monasteries such as Sumela were deserted and decayed, Greek culture was removed, and two and a half thousand years of Greek Pontic history came to an end. In 1923, the last Metropolitan of Trebizond led 164,000 Greeks "home" to Greece, a country alien to them culturally, linguistically, politically, physically and climactically.[23]

It was here that I left the ship and went by bus to the important Eastern Anatolian Turkish town of Erzurum. By now the terrain was mountainous, going through the eastern Pontic Mountains and then the Taurus, which rise to ten thousand feet. It was crossing these mountains that Xenophon's troops, called the Ten Thousand (c.400 BC), desperate for water and refreshment and returning from a failed campaign in Persia, upon seeing the Black Sea cried "*thalassa, thalassa*" (the sea, the sea).

As a border town, Erzurum frequently fell to invading forces over the centuries: the Arabs, the Seljuk Turks, the Mongols and Persian Sassanids. Eastern Anatolia and Erzurum had been a centre for Armenian and Assyrian Christians in the seventh century. A synod was held there to attempt a rapprochement between the Armenian and Orthodox churches, but with no success. It has long since been Muslim. In 1552 it was absorbed into the Ottoman Empire and by the late nineteenth century brutal efforts were made to clear the Kurdish and Armenian populations from the area. By 1972 it was a provincial centre of Eastern Turkey with a quarter million people.

From Erzurum, I travelled to the Iranian Border which lay right under the greatest and highest mountain of the region, with its distinctive snow-capped double peak, Mount Ararat. Beloved by the Armenian people as their holy mountain, it was now part of Turkey. I would see it nearly fifty years later but this time from Armenia. It was reputed to be the place Noah landed in his Ark when the flood waters subsided. I was told at the time it was a highly secure area, with Turkey and Russia confronting each across the mountains. Some two hundred kilometres on I was at the Iranian border right under Mount Ararat at Dogubayazit. An adventure in Iran was about to begin.

---

[23] Ascherson, *Black Sea*, p. 173.

Iran

The reason for going to Iran at all was that I had met a young Iranian called Hassan, who was attending language school in Oxford. We had become friendly and he had invited me to visit him there. It was too good an opportunity to miss, so now, having travelled for more than a day, I arrived on the bus in the dark at Tehran coach station with only his address in hand. With no mobile phone (not yet invented), and no Farsi (the Iranian language) I decided to take a taxi to his address in the suburbs of the city. I arrived outside the house around ten p.m., got out into an unlit street and promptly fell into a gutter at the side of the road, full of water or worse. I paid the taxi driver, only to discover later I had paid him ten times too much, not distinguishing the colour of the notes in the dark and being unfamiliar with the currency. Dishevelled, looking a bit worse for wear, I presented myself at Hassan's house. Of course, I was given a warm welcome and had a story to tell: the oversea and overland journey from Venice!

It was the first and only time I have been the guest of a Muslim family, and a thoroughly welcoming one. I stayed with them for about a week in all and enjoyed their home in the suburbs of northern Tehran, which functioned as a base for a three-week tour of the country. Hassan could not have been more hospitable, displaying all those laws of hospitality for which the Middle East is justly known, and which is true throughout Iran. From the outset I hardly ever saw Hassan's mother and sisters, however. Apart from an initial greeting, they were secluded in a room at the front of the house; a kind of kitchen and living room area. Occasionally the door was left ajar and I would catch sight of them in their house clothes, although they wore black and headscarves whenever they went out.

Hassan and I ate meals alone in a small dining room where his mother had left out the food. We never ate together as family. Hassan's father was a merchant in the Grand Bazaar, whose corridors of shops extend over ten kilometres. He seemed mostly to be out, presumably fraternising in the all-male society of the Bazaar's shop-holders. The family did not strike me in any way as discontented, and I have often

73

wondered how they fared in the approaching revolution of 1979, for as I travelled around speaking to Iranian and expatriate British, of whom there were many at that time, there was evident unease.

Tehran was a busy modern city in 1972. After Cairo, it is the largest city by population in the Middle East; one of the many capitals that Iran has had over the centuries of its long history. The population today is around fifteen million (a fifth of Iran's total population of seventy million). Among the sights to be seen was the Golestan Palace, built by the former Qajar dynasty, which ruled Iran from 1789 to 1925, and famed for its Hall of Mirrors filled with glass chandeliers, mirrors and sumptuous furnishing. In 1972 the growing and privileged middle classes, encouraged by the Shah's regime, were consciously turning Tehran into the Paris of the Middle East. Indeed, its geographical location made it a city of great opportunities for the better off; the Elburz Mountains immediately to the North were high and already enjoyed by skiers. Beyond the mountains was the Caspian Sea, the largest inland lake in the world, fed by the Volga River stretching north to the Caucuses and Russia, and in the east was Turkmenistan, Uzbekistan and the vast area of Kazakhstan. Iran, or Persia as it was called until the twentieth century, is the hinge between East and West, a country in search of recognition and inclusion among the nations of the world, but which has successfully made itself a pariah to the West. Much of that is due to recent history.

No one could travel around Iran in 1972 without being aware that Mohammad Reza Shah was the *Shahanshah* (King of Kings) of Iran. His chiselled features stared down from posters and pictures in every shop, public space and government building in the country. His family had ruled Iran since his father Reza Khan took power in 1925, when he ended the Qajars' dynasty and built on the Constitutional Law Reforms that had established the Majlis (the Iranian Parliament) in 1907. The Reforms had led to some disillusionment and into this vacuum Reza Khan moved with alacrity and confidence. Reza Khan was "an intelligent, hardworking, forthright and ruthless soldier with an astonishingly powerful memory and a high degree of self-confidence".[24] He was inspired by an Aryan and

---

[24] Homas Katouzian, *The Persians: Ancient, Medieval and Modern Iran* (New Haven, CT: Yale University Press, 2010), p. 200.

pan-Persian ideology that had gripped modern Iranians since the end of the First World War. He served in the Russian Army and came to power with the support of the Russians and the British—joint colonial powers with an interest in exercising influence in Iran and in gaining oil concessions in the country.[25]

By the 1930s Reza Shah had become increasingly despotic; not only that, he was set on accumulating a vast personal fortune. This in turn induced a state of resignation and helplessness among his civil service,[26] but he was still backed, for the time being at least, by the Soviet Russians and the British. That was to change when the Shah gave the Germans increasing influence in running the Iranian railways and in industrial development. The thought that oil concessions might go the same way precipitated both the Russians and British to invade in 1941, and demand the Shah's abdication. He was succeeded by his son, Mohammad Reza Shah, so long as he proved more compliant to Russian and British interests. Mohammad Reza Shah would rule constitutionally from 1941 to 1953, and then as dictator from 1953 until 1979 and the Iranian Revolution led by Khomeini.[27] In 1943, at the wartime Tehran Conference, Stalin, Roosevelt and Churchill committed themselves to Iranian independence.

Following the war Iran faced a host of problems. Neighbouring Azerbaijan wanted greater independence from Iranian influence; Russia sought oil concessions in the north of the country; politically, the country was restless. In these unstable conditions, a new leader emerged through the National Popular Movement: Mohammad Mosaddeq, a lawyer, administrator, intellectual and author, and the likely leader of a more secular Iran. Yet his policy of nationalising the oil industry and removing concessions to BP (British Petroleum or The Anglo-Persian Oil Company) and taking over oil installations provoked a response from the British and American governments, led by the old war-time colleagues of Churchill and Eisenhower.

A CIA and MI6 plot was hatched to remove Mossadeq from power

---

[25] See the Anglo-Russian Convention of August 1907, ibid., p. 185.
[26] Katouzian, *The Persians*, p. 225.
[27] Katouzian, *The Persians*, p. 231.

in August 1953.[28] Mossadeq was tried and sentenced to house arrest, where he remained and died, and with him any further hope of developing a constitutional government in Iran. Nor did Mossadeq have the support of the religious community or *ulema,* who feared his creeping secularism and his links to communists through the Tudeh Party. The short-term gain to Western interests in terms of oil was a heavy price to pay in view of subsequent Middle Eastern politics, and in particular the West's relationship with Iran.

The Americans and British together did in Iran what the French and British failed to do in Suez just a few years later; that is to intervene politically and militarily in another state to further their own interests at the cost of democracy. While the Americans acted with the British in Iran, the United States rightly withdrew all support from Britain and France's actions over Suez, although this was hardly consistent.

The consequence of provoking a coup against Mossadeq was a new temporary Prime Minister, General Zahedi, a placeman of the West. Within two years he was gone, and the Shah took increasing control. By 1963 the Shah entered a phase of absolute power,[29] and by the time I arrived in Iran his control was complete, underpinned by the hated SAVAK secret police. Oil revenues and international aid, especially from the United States, kick-started the economy in the 1960s, but western values were increasingly in conflict with older Islamic ones. Discontent spread as only a section of the population gained from the fruits of the Shah's rule. Elections were still called. The Majlis or Parliament sat, but this was merely a front to the Shah's power. The revolution of 1979, the flight of the Shah, and the accession of Ayatollah Khomeini replaced an autocracy with a theocracy, only now with popular support, and Islam as its *raison d'etre.*

Since 1979, power has rested with the Supreme Leader, as it previously did with the Shah. Only now the Revolutionary Guard and its associates, such as the Quds Force, underpin the Ayatollah's rule, just as SAVAK previously underpinned that of the Shah. Likewise, elections are still called and the Majlis sits, but both can be suppressed or overruled by the Supreme Ayatollah's ruling council. Thus, in Iran, as in Russia,

---

[28] Katouzian, *The Persians,* pp. 245–249.
[29] Katouzian, *The Persians,* p. 253.

there may be a discontinuity of personnel from the days of the Shah or the Tsars, but there is continuity in method of government. Furthermore, in the case of Iran, the country now looks to Russia and not the West. It also seeks to police the Middle East in its own interests, even recently seeing ISIS off from Iraq, where Iran presently seeks greater control. Many of these things lay far in the future, and it would be seven years before the Iranian Revolution occurred, but when it did, what I saw in my next port of call would be profoundly affected.

Isfahan, Persepolis and Kurdistan

Isfahan lies some two hundred and fifty miles south of Tehran, and is the third city of Iran. I travelled down with Hassan in his car and enjoyed the semi-desert landscape, which nevertheless has sufficient rainfall to yield crops in a good year. We went by the holy city of Qom, visited by around twenty million pilgrims every year, and the centre of Shi'a scholarship. We called at a farm near Ardestan on the edge of the Zagros Mountains, which was owned by a relative of Hassan, and had lunch on a shady veranda outside the farmhouse. There were some camels nearby, used on the farm, and I had my first camel ride—no doubt thoughts of Wilfred Thesiger filling my mind, although a short camel ride was a far cry from crossing the Empty Quarter. We then proceeded to Isfahan.

Isfahan is the architectural "jewel in the crown" of Iran, and was the capital of Persia during the years of the Safavid dynasty, which lasted from 1501 to 1722. Its greatest ruler was Shah Abbas (1588–1629), who was to Persia what Elizabeth I was to England. At its height, the Safavid dynasty stretched from the Caucasus, through eastern Turkey, Syria, and the Gulf to Uzbekistan and Afghanistan; in effect from the Black Sea to the Indus or from the Ottoman Turks to the Moghuls of India. Shah Abbas defeated the Ottoman Turks, taking chunks of territory from their eastern borders. He then proclaimed those victories with confidence in the new capital city at Isfahan. Exquisite buildings followed: the Masjed-e Shah Mosque, with its two soaring gateways or *iwans,* which open onto the majestic Naghsh-i Jahan Square with its huge dimensions, and the Masjed-e Sheykh Lotfollah mosque. Opposite them was the great Imperial palace of Ali Qapu. The shimmering water in the square, the blue tiles, the intense patterning and the Arabic script from the Koran made for a powerful expression of Persian power and Islamic devotion. There was no shortage of confidence shown by the Safavid Dynasty, which bore the insignia of a lion holding a sword in its paw and carrying the sun on its back.[30]

The Safavids claimed descent from the Imam Ali, the son-in-law of Mohammad, making them Shia Muslims. The Persian Muslim regarded himself as far older than the more recently established House of Saud of Saudi Arabia. And with the passing of the Caliph, the Ottoman Sultan Mehmed VI, into exile into 1922, Iran saw itself as a senior brother of Islam.

For all this splendour, I came to Isfahan to seek out the Christian presence in this most holy Islamic city. And indeed, there had been a Christian presence in Persia from earliest times. Nestorian and Assyrian Christians had settled in present-day Iraq or Mesopotamia, which had been part of earlier Persian dynasties like the Sasanians. One Sasanian ruler, Yazdgerd I (399–421), shocked the Zoroastrian Persian community by being well-disposed towards the Christians. Assyrian and Nestorian congregations had spread through the region from present-day Iraq into Iran. Indeed, there had always been a close relationship between Iran and Iraq, until new boundaries were created after the Treaty of Versailles and the politics of oil took over.

The creation of Iraq out of the Ottoman Empire at the end of the First World War was to make a state out of an area that had once been part of the Persian Empire—before it was part of the Ottoman Empire—and in which some of the great Shi'ite Holy shrines resided, such as Karbala and Najaf, which received millions of Shi'ite pilgrims each year. With the large Shi'ite population in Iraq ruled at least for a time by a coalition of Sunni Muslims, and indeed some Christians, there was implicit tension between the two countries. This erupted in a costly and fruitless war between Saddam Hussein and Iran between 1980–1988, with half a million lost. Ironically, the Americans supported Saddam Hussein, whom they would later topple in 2003. Iran, at the time, and after the revolution of 1979, was considered the greater enemy.

During the later years of Qajar Shah Naser Al-Din (who ruled from

---

[30] Katouzian, *The Persians*, p. 112.

1848 to 1896), missionaries had once more been allowed into Persia, and in particular to Isfahan. Relations with Britain were good after a spat over Afghanistan, and Queen Victoria had welcomed the Shah with a Grand Review of the Fleet and had made him a Knight of the Order of the Garter. There had been an English missionary presence in Persia from 1869, a branch of the Church Missionary Society, founded in 1799 by William Wilberforce and Henry Venn, among others.

In 1870 Robert Bruce arrived in the Armenian suburb of Julfa in Isfahan, where he began work.[31] On his arrival he found that Persia was facing a famine. Money was raised in England to buy food and relieve starvation. Soon, an orphanage, school and medical mission were established, first among the Armenian population and then among the Persians. The New Testament had been translated into Persian in 1812 by Henry Martyn, a brilliant linguist and chaplain with the East India Company. He sought to present a copy to the Shah whilst travelling through Persia, by way of Shiraz, Isfahan and Tabriz, but he fell ill, and although aiming to reach Constantinople and return to England, he in fact got no further than eastern Turkey, and died there near the Black Sea at Tokat. He was buried by two Armenian clergy who were accompanying him to Constantinople.

In 1972 the CMS Mission was still flourishing in Isfahan. I stayed with one of the student teachers at the school. There was still an orphanage and a school for the blind, and I met several of the staff, including the Anglican bishop of the community, Hassan Dehqani-Tafti. He and his wife Margaret narrowly escaped death after the revolution of 1979 when a gunman broke into their bedroom and emptied five shots at them. Miraculously, they survived; four shots going into a pillow, the other passing through Margaret's hand as she shielded her husband. Their son had no such escape and was shot and killed in Tehran in 1980 by Iranian government agents. Exiled to England they have both now died and are buried in Winchester Cathedral. Their daughter, rather wonderfully, has recently been appointed Bishop of Chelmsford.

The church in Iran, albeit underground, is growing more quickly now than at any stage since the Revolution. Likewise, very many Iranian Christians have come to England and found asylum here.

---

[31]Robin E. Waterfield, *Christians in Persia* (London: Allen and Unwin, 1973), p. 148.

After a wonderful week in Isfahan, in which I visited the great Bazaar, buying some fluted silver vases for my parents which I now have, and viewing the wonderful hand-crafted silk Persian carpets, so intricate in their design and pattern, I moved on to Shiraz, where I stayed with a medical missionary called Dr Ronald Pont and his family. It was just a two-night stop as I delved further back into Persian history by making a day trip to Persepolis.

Persepolis is a little to the north-east of Shiraz, and was the capital of the Achaemenid Empire founded by Cyrus the Great, an empire that stretched from the Indus to the Balkans. It is a reminder, if one needed such, of just how old Persian civilisation is. Achaemenes, the founder of the dynasty, lived in the mountains south-west of Isfahan in about 700 BC. A descendent of his, Cambyses I, took the fateful step of marrying the daughter of his much more powerful neighbour, Astygages, the King of Media. It was their son, Cyrus, the Great who conquered his father-in-law's kingdom, combining the Medes with the Persians and overthrowing nearby Babylon.[32]

Cyrus was an extraordinary character. He preferred mercy to cruelty in victory, and he certainly was a great and victorious military leader. He conquered the Median Empire and the Babylonian Empire, which under Nebuchadnezzar had taken the Jews captive to Babylon; and the Lydian Empire in present day Turkey, with its capital at Sardis, the citadel of Croesus (he of "as rich as Croesus" fame). Cyrus's empire stretched from the Mediterranean to the Indus, the largest yet seen west of China. The Persian capital was at Ecbatana (now Hamadan) in the Iranian Zagros Mountains: cool in summer, well defended by snow and ice in winter. With the traditional Persian capital at Ecbatana, Cyrus created another at Pasargadae. In the hills, he built palaces and a large audience chamber for receiving, in some splendour, tribal chiefs, governors and embassies from his vast empire. In time Cyrus was buried here: in grandeur and simplicity. His tomb still stands, two and a half thousand years on. "From a stone base measuring about forty feet square, six tiers of massive stone steps rise to form the foundation of the tomb chamber itself, entered through a low narrow doorway measuring eleven and a half feet by

<hr>

[32] Sir Roger Stevens, *The Land of the Great Sophy* (London: Methuen, 1965), pp. 10–12.

seven".[33] Inside was a gold sarcophagus carefully orientated to the rising sun.[34] In years to come, sacrifices were made in front of the tomb by the Magian priesthood, and it was descendants of this priesthood, the Magi, who came to offer gifts to the Christ Child in Bethlehem (Matthew 2: 1–12).

Cyrus reigned for near on thirty years from 559 until 530 BC and early in his reign, Hebrew exiles petitioned the great king for permission to return to Jerusalem. The prophet Isaiah had foretold that Cyrus would be like a Messiah, bringing back the Jews to their kingdom.

This is what the Lord says to his anointed (Messiah), declared Isaiah: "To Cyrus, whose right hand I take hold of to subdue nations before him and to strip kings of their armour.... For the sake of Jacob my servant, of Israel my chosen, I summon you by name and bestow on you a title of honour though you do not acknowledge me. I am the Lord, and there is no other: apart from me there is no God" (Isaiah 45 :1, 4).

And so, in the first year of his accession as King of Persia, Cyrus proclaimed that any Hebrew could return to Jerusalem and rebuild the Temple of the Lord there (Ezra 1: 1–11). The Jews began to return from exile, entrusted with the gold articles previously taken from the Temple at Jerusalem by Nebuchadnezzar, whose Empire Cyrus had taken over. For a further thirty years Cyrus ruled his vast empire, and was eventually killed whilst campaigning in distant Uzbekistan, aged about seventy.

If Cyrus was the founder of a great Empire and dynasty, his successors were not so adept at combining power with wisdom. His son, Cambyses II, died campaigning in Syria, after subjugating Egypt, having contracted gangrene from a wound.[35] His younger brother, Bardiya, succeeded him, only to be murdered by an ambitious cousin, Darius the Great. By now the new ceremonial capital was moved from Pasargadae to Persepolis about thirty miles to the south-west. So, on my day out from Shiraz, I too moved from the site of the lonely tomb of Cyrus to the later centre of Persian power and ceremony at Persepolis.

Darius found the earlier capital too remote or perhaps not grand enough, so he built a new ceremonial and royal capital. It was to be the

---

[33] Stevens, *The Land of the Great Sophy*, pp. 229–230.
[34] Tom Holland, *Persian Fire* (London: Abacus 2005), p. 22.
[35] Holland, *Persian Fire,* p. 23.

spring and autumn court of the Persian kings, the summer capital being at Ecbatana (now Hamadan, in the mountains to the north). Approached from Shiraz through rolling hills, Persepolis looks out to the south west over an expanding plain. There a vast platform was raised on great stones, the resulting terrace running 325 x 487 yards back into the hillside. On the platform, reached by flights of steps broad enough for a horse to ride up, embassies were received. The great stone doorways facing east and west are decorated with a winged human figure and a wingless creature with a human head and a bull's body. The Apadana or the palace of audience of Darius, flanked by porches on all sides, measures 195 square feet with six rows of columns sixty feet high.[36] A winter palace to the south, also square, was used by Darius and his successor, Xerxes. If the buildings do not have the elegance and seeming lightness of the Parthenon in Athens, there is no mistaking the sense of power that these buildings project—so much so that the Shah used them in 1971 for a spectacle advertising the history and greatness of Persia, personified by himself.

By their very nature, dynasties wax and wane. Just as in his ironic poem *Ozymandias*, Shelley recalled the ruined statue of that king in the desert which proclaims, "Look on my works, ye mighty and despair", but of which "nothing beside remains", so Persepolis heralds a bygone empire. Indeed, it was the Geeks in the person of Alexander the Great who ended Persian power. Darius, and then Xerxes, had made the conquest of Greece their supreme objective. Darius (522–486) made the Aegean, Thrace and Macedonia objects of conquest and in 492 BC Macedonia had been humiliated and subjugated.

Although the Athenian infantry (*hoplites*) led by Miltiades had defeated the Persians at Marathon, that was not the end of the story. Darius, son of Xerxes and Atossa, daughter of Cyrus the Great, brought a yet greater army of 60,000 against Greece. Crossing over the Hellespont via a man-made bridge, Xerxes entered Europe, took Thrace and Macedonia before threatening Athens and Sparta. It was here that Xerxes' forces were held up by the Spartan king, Leonidas, and his warriors, in an heroic stand in the narrow gorge of Thermopylae. In the

---

[36] Stevens, *The Land of the Great Sophy,* pp. 219–221.

end, sweeping them aside Athens was taken, sacked and destroyed in 480 BC, as told by the Greek historian Herodotus. It would take Pericles and the golden age to see the rebuilding of Athens between 460 and 430 BC, and Alexander the Great would later wreak his revenge.

The subjugation of Macedonia and the destruction of Athens by the Persians lay deep in the Greek psyche, where a desire for revenge smouldered. This desire would find its fulfilment in Alexander the Great, who, having defeated the Persians at Guagemala in 331 BC in present day Iraq, east of Mosul near Arbil, found the way along the Tigris open to him. He took Babylon before heading east to Susa, and thence to Persepolis in the heart of the Persian or Achaemenid Empire. Alexander stayed at Persepolis five months, a place he considered "the most hateful city in the world", being the lair of the Greek's greatest enemy.[37] Having ransacked the Treasury to pay and reward his soldiers, he enjoyed all that Persepolis had to offer.

During his stay in Persepolis, either intentionally or by accident, a fire destroyed this ceremonial city. "Only when Persepolis came to be excavated was the scale of the blaze at last appreciated".[38] The floor of the Hall of Xerxes, with its hundred column colonnade was covered with ash to a depth of three feet.[39] According to Ptolemy's account, it was a calculated act of revenge. Athens was sacked, and now it was the turn of Persepolis. For others, the fire was seen as a prank started by an Athenian woman called Thais, who jested with Alexander that it was for women to bring vengeance on Persia.[40] Whatever the cause, the Achaemenid dynasty was laid low. Persia would rise again under the Sassanians from 224 AD to plague Rome and at times to humble her, until the Seljuk Turks and Islam took hold from the seventh century, before the Mongols came in 1220, and then Tamburlaine the Great.

It was time for me to leave Persepolis, and spend a further night in Shiraz before retracing Alexander's steps to Susa, Hamadan and Sanandaj,

---

[37] Robin Lane Fox, *Alexander the Great* (London: Penguin, 1973), p. 256.
[38] Lane Fox, *Alexander the Great,* p. 261.
[39] Lane Fox, *Alexander the Great,* p. 261.
[40] Lane Fox, *Alexander the Great,* pp. 260–4.

although not by horse, but by bus! I broke the journey from Shiraz to Sanandaj at Shush or Susa, which is one of the oldest continually inhabited sites in Iran. Indeed, there is evidence from pottery of a community there in 4000 BC.[41] It was then the centre of the Elamite civilisation. Much later, in 521 BC, Darius made it the principal city of his empire. A citadel, palace and *apadna* or throne room were built there, using crafts, skills, building materials and precious stones from all over the Persian Empire. It was here under Darius's son, Xerxes, or during Ahasuerus's reign, that the biblical story of Esther and Mordecai was quite probably enacted. Esther, a member of the King's harem was chosen as queen, and used by her uncle Mordecai to save the Jews from a conspiracy of genocide against them.

To make one's way from Susa to Hamadan is to cross a landscape of rolling hills in which life has barely changed in two thousand years or more. Flocks are pastured by Iranian shepherdesses in traditional dress, whose ancestors go back to the ancient Elamite kingdom. Extraordinarily, the tomb of Esther and Mordecai is still to be found up in the Zagros mountains in the city of Hamadan, once the ancient city of Ecbatana, and another of the ancient capitals of Persia.

The small brick-built chapel that contains their tombs is simply but reverently kept in this most Islamic of countries. Indeed, the chapel is reverenced as a holy place by Muslims in the area too. The two tombs, which are distinctly Jewish in form, remind me of the tombs of the Patriarchs in Hebron. Esther's tomb is covered with a white shroud or veil, while Mordecai's with a red one. On the floor are Persian carpets and on the walls are texts in Hebrew. Every year during the Festival of *Purim,* pilgrimage is made here by Jews still living in the country: a Purim feast is held in March or February (depending when 14th Day of Adar falls in the lunar calendar), gifts are exchanged, the poor remembered, and the scroll of Esther read in memory of the deliverance of the Jews. Full of this amazing site in Hamadan (Ecbatana), I caught the bus to the nearby town of Sanandaj, and once again was an object of interest as the only European on the bus.

The bus climbed high into the Zagros Mountains, which rise to eight

---

[41] Stevens, *The Land of the Great Sophy*, p. 243.

thousand feet, and into the heart of Kurdistan. I shall never forget getting off the bus and seeing the Kurds walking along the street. The women were wearing the brightest of dresses, not black like the Muslim women in the cites, but bright reds, greens, and yellows, gilded and festooned with jewellery on wonderful headdresses. Since the Revolution of 1979, the Iranian government has tried to suppress this national dress and the use of the Kurdish language in public, but I don't imagine that they will succeed.

I had come to Sanandaj to meet an extraordinary man, Dr Gardiner, who was working among the Kurdish population. During the Second World War he had been sent with his battalion to guard the oil installations in Persia and prevent them from falling into enemy hands. In the course of his duties, he had met the Kurds, and felt a call to come back and help them after the war. Consequently, he had trained to be a doctor, returned to Kurdistan, raised funds to build a hospital for the region, and became their resident doctor—medical facilities being more or less absent. I found a man inspired by his Christian faith to give himself unstintingly for the Kurds, a people who had a history little short of tragic. It was an inspiring example. Clearly, he was much loved and appreciated by the Kurds I met at the hospital.

The Kurds are one of the largest ethnic groups in the Near East with no state of their own. There are about twenty-seven million Kurds living in the Middle East, half of whom live in Turkey. The rest are split between Iraq and Iran, with fewer numbers in northern Syria.[42] In Iran they make up about ten per cent of the Iranian population, numbering over six million. They are not an entirely homogenous ethnic group, with several languages, and are often split and hampered in their aims by tribal rivalries. They originally shared a nomadic existence in the region of the Zagros mountains and the high plateaus to the west. The nearest they came to having their own state was immediately after the First World War when the borders of Iraq were being fixed in the carve up of the Ottoman Empire. The vilayet of Mosul, a centre for the Kurds, which included Arbil and Kirkuk, was incorporated into Iraq, and no longer part of a projected Kurdistan.[43] In the face of the reality of Turkish power under

---

[42] David McDowall, A *Modern History of the Kurds* (London: I. B. Tauris, 2004), p. 3.
[43] McDowall, A *Modern History of the Kurds*, p. 117.

Ataturk, the Allies turned their backs on the possibility of realizing Kurdistan, even if they had wished it.

The Kurds' life in Iran, as in the other two neighbouring countries, has been a continual struggle, verging sometimes on ethnic cleansing. Different movements have sought to harness Kurdish nationalism in Iran, such as the Komala party, a communist movement that looked towards Soviet Russia for support. But it was not, in the end, effective,[44] nor was the attempt to secede and join the Soviet Union made by Kurds at Mahabad, near Azerbaijan, in 1946.[45] Under the Shah, Tehran was quick to shut down this attempted breakaway republic. This attempt at independence was followed by the formation of the KDPI or the Democratic Party of Iranian Kurdistan. Proscribed as a terrorist organisation, it has led the fight for independence since 1978, including insurgencies in the '80s and '90s. The peasantry, often close to penury, were hardly in position to rebel however, and Kurdish landlords who owned ninety per cent of the land were often unable to agree.[46]

After the 1979 Revolution, the policy of Tehran towards the Kurds was effectively the same as the Shah's, i.e., to prevent the fragmentation of Iran. For instance, a new Constitution following the Revolution made no mention of the Kurds.[47] The double-headed regime in Iran—the Supreme Leader or Ayatollah in Qom and the President and Majlis in Tehran—made Kurdish progress still harder.[48] Both parties were agreed that Kurds were separatists and to be resisted. Enforcement of policies by a Shi'ite government on Sunni Kurdish communities normally ended in fighting, with support from Kurds across the border in Iraq. The Kurds regarded the Ayatollah's intrusion as "dictatorship in the name of Islam".[49] By 1982 there was an all-out offensive against the Kurds, now jointly led by the KDPI and Komala. In the end it led to a stalemate neither side could win. In 1997, with the election of President Khatami, hope of a pluralist Iran with a more autonomous Kurdistan revived. It is

---

[44] McDowall, A *Modern History of the Kurds* 236.
[45] McDowall, A *Modern History of the Kurds*, p. 231.
[46] McDowall, A *Modern History of the Kurds*, p. 256.
[47] McDowall, A *Modern History of the Kurds*, p. 263.
[48] McDowall, A *Modern History of the Kurds*, p. 264.
[49] Shaykh Izz al Din, *Statement in Middle East Report no 113* (March/April 1983) pp. 9–10, McDowall, A *Modern History of the Kurds*, p. 271.

this process that is more likely to succeed, but it is very long in coming.

Kurdish minority communities in Turkey and Iraq, if anything, fared even worse than in Iran. As the crow flies, it is only about one hundred and fifty kilometres from Sanadaj to Halabja, where the greatest atrocity against the Kurds, amounting to genocide, was perpetrated by Saddam Hussein and his commanders in 1988. The appalling suffering of the Kurds in that region is hard to take in. During the later stages of the Iraq-Iran War, Saddam Hussein's chief of defence, Ali-Hassan al Majid ("Chemical Ali") led an all-out assault, then allied himself with the Iranians in the Al-Anfal Campaign, in which thousands of Kurdish villages were razed. The genocide culminated in the infamous chemical attack against Halabja, leaving five thousand dead, including many children, not to mention animals. It is thought that the whole campaign amounted to a death toll of 150–200,000, many in the death camps to which they were taken.[50] Despite this onslaught, Kurds in Iraq have steadily sought self-rule within the Iraqi state. When the fog of war clears after the most recent struggle with ISIL, in which Kurds have been instrumental in defeating ISIL in Syria and Northern Iraq, a semi-autonomous Kurdish region has emerged in Iraq, centred on Arbil.

The Kurds in Turkey also had a history of repression, as well as of violent resistance. Although Ataturk initially used Kurds to oppress the Armenians and the Greeks, at some point after 1923 he turned against them. Kurds were prevented from holding office,[51] denied the use of their language in the public sphere, and starved of education. Indeed, all non-Turkish expression was expunged.[52] Turkish Tribunals had the right to hand down sentences of capital punishment without referring cases to Ankara.[53] Kurdistan was starved of resources, especially in the vilayet of Van. Many were driven from their homes, recalling the mass deportations of Armenians in 1915. Indeed, Christians and Kurds suffered the same fate.[54] By 1930 there was warfare between the two sides, with a battle near Ararat. Brutal repression followed, with large-scale killing of Kurds

---

[50] McDowall, A *Modern History of the Kurds*, pp. 357ff.
[51] McDowall, A *Modern History of the Kurds*, p. 191.
[52] McDowall, A *Modern History of the Kurds*, p. 192.
[53] McDowall, A *Modern History of the Kurds*, p. 196.
[54] McDowall, A *Modern History of the Kurds*, p. 202.

and a law of indemnity, no. 1850, exonerating Turks from killing Kurds.[55] A policy of extinguishing Kurdish identity by reducing Kurdish presence to less than five per cent in any area was then followed by Ankara.

Despite this onslaught of repression, there was a national revival of Kurds in Turkey. Many rural Kurds moved to nearby towns like Diyarbakir, which presently has a population of half a million (up from 30,00 in 1930).[56] Nor is it surprising that a resistance movement willing to use violence was born. This was the PKK, led by Abd Allah Ocalan in 1975. Its creed was communist, its methods violent and often cruel, and it struck remorselessly. It was not universally supported by Kurds, who on religious grounds were unable to reconcile the Marxist tendencies of the PKK with Sunni Islam. The PKK garnered support after Turkish reprisals, however. Often the movement had bases outside Turkey, as in Syria and Northern Iraq, and struck inside the border. The state responded in kind with mass deportations of Kurds, particularly those under the age of fifteen. Some three million were displaced in the 1990s.[57] The PKK has become the voice of Turkey's Kurds, even if it could not bring the state to the negotiating table, which used instead the military and reprisals in response.[58] By 1998 Ocalan was on the run, captured, spared the death penalty and imprisoned on an island near Istanbul.

My short time of only two or three days in Kurdistan in Iran was enough to leave an indelible impression of this people's courage, vivacity, intelligence and determination. They have been there for thousands of years and their presence seems secure, even if their life is still hard. I travelled back to Tehran, leaving Dr Gardiner to continue his care of the Kurds in the hospital he had built. I did not hear how he fared after the Iranian revolution. I had a brief stopover with Hassan in Tehran, but now my focus was getting home and starting work. With heartfelt thanks to Hassan for enabling the trip, I said farewell. I have not seen him since nor heard from him. This time I boarded a train bound for Istanbul, which

---

[55] McDowall, A *Modern History of the Kurds*, p. 206.
[56] McDowall, A *Modern History of the Kurds*, p. 403.
[57] McDowall, A *Modern History of the Kurds*, p. 450.
[58] McDowall, A *Modern History of the Kurds*, p. 440.

would take three days and then a further three on to London. Spending nearly a week in all on trains, it was the longest train journey I have made to date, covering three and half thousand miles.

After Tabriz, the journey took me straight through eastern Anatolia and through the Kurdish territories, and what had been Armenian lands within the Ottoman Empire until 1915. When we arrived at Lake Van, a centre of Armenian and Kurdish life, the carriages were disconnected from the engine, then rolled onto a ferry with a track on board, to be reconnected to an engine on the other side. My carriage companion was an Iranian Zoroastrian businessman who seemed to have an endless supply of pistachio nuts with which he generously fed me. We seemed to be making our own Ararat in the compartment with our discarded shells.

I was sad to leave Iran, for Iranians are hospitable, intelligent, open and direct people. They have a rich heritage of poetry and literature. Somehow, we need to get beyond the megaphone diplomacy, the *fatwas* and the western invective, and engage with each other's cultures. In the past Iranians were a source of silk and then oil. Now their government is a threat and it imprisons, detains and worse without just cause, and yet they are a people of abiding customs, great heritage, deep hospitality and a rich and diverse land. Our dialogue must not be scripted by politicians alone, by the Ayatollahs or Presidents, but by the people—merchants, poets and artists. That would be far more fruitful.

The train eventually pulled into London. After a clean-up and debrief at home, I was soon at my desk in Hackney Road, learning the ins and outs of the timber trade. Although enjoyable, it wouldn't last long.

Chapter V
A Fork in the Road

I duly settled into my job with Mallinson's and learnt the art of selling wood (both softwood and veneered panelling), to the building trade, to banks for their smart counters and panelled offices, and to the yacht building industry that wanted marine plywood. Mallinson's were middle-men, so we phoned the manufacturer or importer and added on a margin. Banks had a higher margin added to their orders, of course!

Because I was a "management trainee", I was occasionally sent to operations that Mallinson's owned, like a furniture business in High Wycombe or to a manufacturer in the Forest of Dean. I would write a report highlighting the strengths and weaknesses of the operation (what did I know?) and submit it to the company. Sometimes the Chairman, Macpherson, would ask me to come up and answer a few questions, which put me on my mettle. Yet despite the firm's interest, I did not see myself as a long-term employee, and at any rate, other things were fermenting beneath the surface.

I did apply for another job which looked as though it would give me greater opportunities. This was with Wallace Brothers of Crosby Square, who ran a Far Eastern business with timber rights in Borneo. They offered me a job in January 1973, which brought me to the crunch of either accepting it, or applying to the Church of England selection board and seeking ordination. As my parents already had one son abroad in Zambia, the thought of another in Borneo was not too appealing, and they encouraged me to attend the selection board conference. By then, I did not need too much encouragement.

The selection conference was in April 1973. Henry Chadwick, the Dean of Christ Church, wrote in his words, "a cheerful commendation", and I had already visited a theological college, Cranmer Hall, Durham and been offered a place by the delightful principal, John Cockerton. The selection conference was held in Yorkshire.

I had been briefed a little about these conferences. One had to lead a discussion on a thorny issue, theological or pastoral or both, in front of the selectors, followed by four or so interviews with each of them. I was young, only just twenty-two, the youngest one could be, so it was not "a done deal". Nor was I up with all the ways of the Church of England—I thought *Compline,* which was on the timetable for both evenings, was a drink before bedtime, a bit like Complan. In fact, it was a rather lovely evening service, with origins in monasticism! I did not reveal my ignorance, so there was no loss of face! I do remember reading a short story by Saki called "The Lumber-room" to some of the assembled company to provide a relaxing moment. I met a monk from the CGA (the Community of the Glorious Ascension, not the Country Gentleman's Association), called Andrew, and the Chairman of the conference had the splendidly Anglican name of Twistleton-Wickham-Fiennes. He was the Dean of Lincoln.

They accepted me, and I started my three-year training at Cranmer Hall, Durham, that wonderful northern city with its majestic and powerful cathedral, recalling saints Bede and Cuthbert, that sits on a bluff above the River Wear. There could be few more inspiring places to study. There would be friends in the college and university, and I enjoyed the theology, particularly Reformation Studies under T.H.L. Parker, which I pursued for an MA after the Diploma. There were also opportunities for ministry in the mining villages in the area, such as Newbottle, which in 1973 was still very active in mining, and a very real education for an effete southerner.

I was ordained in York Minster by Archbishop Stuart Blanch in 1976 after an ordination retreat at Bishopthorpe. The night before ordination we were treated by the archbishop to venison sent down by the Queen from Balmoral that he kindly shared with us. Apparently, this was an annual gift from Her Majesty to the Archbishop. It seemed as if the medieval world of monarch and her archbishops still existed.

My first curacy of three years was in York at St. Michael-le-Belfry, working in the midst of a wonderful church community under the inspiring leadership of David Watson, whom I already knew. Holidays were now much scarcer, with three weeks in the summer and a few days after Christmas and Easter. I nevertheless managed a prolonged trip between leaving Mallinson's and starting in Durham in September, when I went with my sister to visit my brother Charles, who was working as an economist for the Zambian government.

This trip was my first, but by no means last visit to East Africa. Its beauty I found mesmerising, its people warmly welcoming. We flew to Nairobi and I will never forget seeing giraffe wandering across the road just out of the city. In 1973 Nairobi was a small city. We rather daringly spent all our money on an orange Ford Transit Van for sale at the side of the road, which we called "Elly". Elly was kitted out with bunks and a calor gas stove and became our hotel and transport for the next six weeks. Trips to game parks, the Serengeti and Ngorongoro Crater, and up the Kenyan coast to Lamu followed, as well as a drive through Tanzania to Zambia and a visit to Malawi with my brother. We flew back to England, and my brother sold the van for more than we had paid. (Elly had mostly behaved well, apart from one problem with her gear box near Kilimanjaro and a tyre that flew down the road in front of us because it had not been properly replaced after a puncture!) I would return often to East Africa in the future, although in a different way. Once seen, it never leaves your blood.

There were to be no long trips in the coming years, but that is not to say there were no significant short ones. Rather than going off on long treks to faraway places, I arranged over the next four years several holidays with friends in Italy (mostly), and also in France and Ireland. Three times I rented houses in Italy in Tuscany; the first near Monte San Savino at Castello de Gargonza, a castellated thirteenth century hilltop village, which is owned still by the Guicciardini family of Florentine fame for over three hundred years. I invited many guests among them Charles Marnham who was to be my best man and founder with his wife Tricia of the Alpha Course, Bridget Gibbs, my sister Teresa, Nick Bell and Peter Daws.

With the rural population moving away, the Guicciardinis let the properties out for holidays. That year of 1974 was the first full year that these holiday lets began. They were an immense success and they still rent out houses today in this beautiful, romantic place, not far from Monte San Savino and Arezzo. I can heartily recommend them. In the early morning we would encounter hunters with trained truffle-hunting dogs, or a keeper checking the wild boar in the 800-hectare estates. The light was beautiful, the cypresses elegant and the narrow streets charming and flower-filled. The converted olive press hosted concerts in the evenings, and still does, and the chapel is used for mass on Sundays. Count Roberto with his kind manager, Piero Mancini, even had us for dinner back in the '70s. We must have been model tenants!

Another time, in 1977, I rented a house called Spedaletto, also found in an advert at the front of the *Times*, from Georgiana Corsini through her English agent. A group of eight of us went, and the cost was £90 a week *in total*: so, each of us paid £10 for a week's accommodation in a splendid old Tuscan house. In the front hall was a fully stuffed horse, no doubt a much-loved family steed kept now in perpetuity, if not in motion. Not surprisingly, love blossomed among the cypresses and Quattrocento art of Siena and Florence, and Olivia and I started "going out". We were married in 1979, at the end of my first curacy. Ever since then I have always loved the opening sequence of *Much About Nothing,* produced and performed by Kenneth Branagh and Emma Thompson. It captures so well the exuberance of a Tuscan summer and a house party, even if Benedict and Beatrice had much more difficulty tying the knot!

After our wedding, Olivia and I travelled to Israel for an extended course in Jerusalem, to which I will return. I started work at Holy Trinity, Brompton, in 1979, the church where my parents had been married in 1946. We were there for five years of eventful ministry with John Collins, our inspiring vicar. And then, at the end of 1984, after the birth of our first two children, Rachel and Louisa, we moved to Christ Church, Gipsy Hill, near Crystal Palace. Louisa was only two weeks old. I was now a fully-fledged vicar at the age of thirty-three, and we were new parents. The church had burnt down in a fire the year before, and we needed to rebuild it, and the congregation needed leading into a new future. It was just the right kind of challenge for that stage of life.

We remained there for eleven very happy years, enjoying the diversity of South London. With a further two children to follow, Sophia and David. Holidays were mostly in Cornwall or Scotland, or both, with a long drive between the two. I also managed to sneak in a few trips, all of which connected to church work. On two occasions I went with a team to Nigeria, sponsored by SOMA (about which more later). On another occasion I went with a group to Poland, soon after the Iron Curtain came down in 1989. Staying in Katowice, we also experienced both the charm of Kraków and the bleak, chill and abiding horror of Birkenau-Auschwitz nearby which we were taken to one morning. The bleak huts, deposits of hair and shoes in glass cases, as well as the gas chambers themselves, drive home the industrial scale of the genocide committed there in an unfathomable memorial. It left an abiding mark on all visitors.

You will be wondering how Olivia managed with four children, a parish, and me *occasionally* away! The answer is brilliantly, but we implemented a star system that helped. If a certain number of stars were reached, a present would be forthcoming on my return for the children. A black star could knock you back a long way. There were a number of scoring categories: getting ready for school, doing homework, being co-operative, going to bed and tidying up. Of course, a present always materialised!

Amritsar

The best present for the girls undoubtedly came from India, from whence I brought back three colourful dresses with matching head gear. I had gone in the early 1990s to a Christian teaching hospital in Ludhiana, called Browns—named after a pioneering Christian medical missionary—with a surgeon from Kings College Hospital London, John Rennie, who was there to teach key hole surgery. I spoke at a number of meetings and one day took myself off by train to Amritsar, while John instructed the hospital surgeons.

The train passed through the landscape of the northern Punjab. I looked onto the early autumn fields where men were ploughing the land with water buffalo. The Punjab, which is divided between India and Pakistan, is often called the bread-basket of India; and with its large, well-irrigated fields and rich soil, it is easy to see why. The fields stretch away into the distance and its several rivers flow down from Kashmir and the Himalayas, and eventually find their way into the mighty Indus, one of the great rivers of the subcontinent. It is considered one of the most fertile places on earth and is populated by the Punjabi, who divide mostly into Muslim Punjabi in Pakistan and Hindu and Sikh Punjabis in

India. (In 1947 the area was witness to awful ethnic and religious violence when Muslim and Hindu communities separated.) On this day outing from Ludhiana, I was bound for Amritsar, the holy city of the Sikhs, right in the corner of India, just a few miles from the Pakistan border.

Having arrived, I made my way to the Sikh Temple—the most holy site of all the Sikhs. I felt very conspicuous as the only European there. The Temple at Amritsar is breath-taking. At its centre is a golden domed sanctuary in which the Sikh holy scriptures called *gurdwara* (meaning "doorway to God") are found, the writings of Sikh founder, Guru Nanak. Around this central golden shrine is water, bridged by a walkway to the temple. All of this is enclosed in an icing-sugar quadrangle of brilliant white buildings: made up of watch towers, a clock tower, and a sacred tree. Apart from taking off my shoes on entering the temple area, there was ease of access, even in 1993 and for such an obvious tourist as myself. And indeed, I learnt later there was a free meal for all visitors which formed part of the pilgrimage; literally hundreds tucked in. But the serenity cloaked tragedies from the past, however.

In 1984 the temple had been the site of a secessionist move by fundamentalist Sikhs. It had become a place of weapon training for militant Sikhism, and those wishing to promote an autonomous state for Sikhs in northern India. In 1984 the Indian government sent in troops to disarm the militants and take control of the temple area. Margaret Thatcher, I believe had sent in SAS advisers to help end the occupation. Many died in the crossfire and the temple was severely damaged. Elsewhere Sikh troops mutinied in the army, and in October of the same year, Indira Gandhi was assassinated by her Sikh bodyguard. Although religiously-motivated violence runs deep in India and Pakistan, years earlier the British too had been responsible for a massacre.

From the temple I walked into the neighbouring area of Jallianwala Bagh. It was here the infamous Amritsar massacre occurred, when Brigadier General Dyer ordered his soldiers to fire and continue to fire on a peaceful crowd demonstrating against the *Rowlatt Act* of 1919, which granted extension of emergency powers. Hundreds died, and many more were wounded. Vividly portrayed in the film *Gandhi* in 1982 (directed by Sir Richard Attenborough with Ben Kingsley as Gandhi), the incident triggered massive non-violent protests against the British Raj and gave new momentum to the movement for independence, soon to be led by Gandhi, who had recently arrived back in India from South Africa. When I visited, there was little in the way of memorials and no visitor centre. The plain ordinariness of the place and the enclosed nature of the setting—there was nowhere for the demonstrators to hide or run to—brought home the deep tragedy of what had taken place, and the unanswerable injustice. In February 2013, David Cameron visited the site and apologised "for this deeply shameful event" in British history.[59] Then in 2019, the Archbishop, Justin Welby, prostrated himself in penance. I stood and remembered in silence, the only Englishman there on that day.

By 1994, our ten years at Gipsy Hill were coming to a close. The church had been rebuilt and the congregation was growing. We had purchased land in a council estate in the parish where a church community centre was being constructed, and for which funds had been raised. Much youth work had begun and would continue in new and inspiring ways in the future. We applied for and were appointed by Bishop Jim Thompson of Bath and Wells to an exciting post in Bath at Bath Weston All Saints with North Stoke and Langridge. We moved over the summer of 1995, and would remain there till August 2016. Everyone said Bath "was a graveyard of ambition" and I thought that we might be there ten years, but ten easily turned into twenty. The activity and support of the congregations at All Saints Weston and the two villages, North Stoke and Langridge, the beauty of Bath and the surrounding countryside, and the opportunities provided, all kept us there. The time really did fly by.

---

[59] David Cameron, *On the Record* (London: William Collins, 2019), p. 493.

Grandparents, Bartle and Daphne Edwards, with three children in 1926, my mother
in the middle

My Grandmother Alice née Hervey, skiing in Adellbolden,
Switzerland 1906, aged 19. No lifts, and one pole for cross country
skiing.

Woollas Hall, my grandmother's house at Eckington, Worcs. It had
been in the family since the 16th Century, sold in 1949. Now
apartments.

"Anyone for Tennis?" Family group at Flood Hall in 1912. My grandmother Alice seated on the ground, and grandfather Aymer seated on the bench with white slacks.

My mother, a FANY in uniform in 1944, with her mother and two brothers Henry and John (standing) at Hardingham Hall. Her eldest brother Bill was killed in Tunisia in March 1943.

My father in 1945, now a Major, served in the 1st Infantry Division HQ in Caserta. The Neapolitan royal palace was taken over by the Allies.

My mother (second from left) with Ian Hunter, Ursula Whitworth – my aunt – and Madron Seligman (right) at a day's racing at Aiello, Italy in 1945.

My parents were married in 1946 at Holy Trinity Brompton. To fulfil residency rules, they left a suitcase in a nearby hotel. I later worked there as a curate (1979-1984).

My brother Charles and I "fishing" in Winterberg Germany 1956

The author at school: scruffy and undistinguished, but his
Housemaster concluded, "He has been cheerfully charming and
could, I fancy, get away with murder!

My father accompanying President Kennedy at the Brandenburg Gate,
26 June 1963, before his *"Ich bin ein Berliner"* speech. Willy Brandt,
later German Chancellor, in the background.

The house at 6 am Rupenhorn, Berlin built by Eric Mendelsohn

58 Beale St: my lodgings in Boston Jan–March 1969, when cleaning
hospital floors to earn dollars

Greenville South Carolina, Civil Rights Meeting addressed by
Ralph Abernathy

Working in a Home Cleaning business in Oakland California

Charles Higgins, an early travelling companion who tragically died young.
He took Cornflakes to the Pousses at Château St Maurice, Baix who served
them with an *aperitif* before dinner.

Charles' friend Gaya Neubert in Rome. She turned a few heads!

The Bridge at Mostar in 1970 years before it was destroyed in 1993
and later rebuilt.

Iran 1972, seven years before the Revolution, a different call from the minaret!

Riding a camel in Iran!

My brother and sister beside "Elly" the orange Ford Transit Van we
bought off the roadside and travelled in round Kenya, Tanzania, Zambia
and Malawi in 1973. We sold it for more than we paid!

My grandfather AWW – Aymer Whitworth, Master in College, Eton
1908–1917 and then a Housemaster till 1932. He supported my first trip
and had travelled extensively in Greece in 1906 on foot.

Chapter VI
The Road to Damascus

In 2001, having been ordained twenty-five years, I put in for a sabbatical of three months. It would be my only sabbatical in forty years of ministry, in fact, and I was ready for it. There had only been a couple of weeks between parishes and I felt it was time to create some space for reflection and re-creation. The diocese was offering some sponsorship, and so I had to put forward suggestions as to how I would use the time. In the end it came down to three ideas: a road trip with a friend from Bath to Jordan, a joint family holiday with my sister and her family in East Africa, and writing my first full-length book. I am glad that I was able to manage all three, although writing the book took a little longer. And what I started during those three months I have been able to continue over the years: the travel, the writing and reflection.

In the intervening months, the world changed. On 9/11, I was in Bath Abbey attending the institution of a new Rector. The service was conducted by Bishop Jim Thompson, Bishop of Bath and Wells, and news had been coming in through the day of the terrorist attack in New York. We were especially concerned because our daughter, Rachel, who was visiting her uncle in Manhattan, was near the affected area. But all the lines were busy and it was some time before we spoke to them. When I arrived at the service in Bath Abbey, I heard that the daughter of one of our clergy, was on a business trip to New York and had a meeting in the Twin Towers that morning. David, her father, was not at the service but waiting by the phone for news. Naturally, the service was overshadowed by the events in New York, and we prayed for all those caught up in this unimaginable tragedy. Bishop Jim told us he would be broadcasting the *Thought for the Day* on Radio 4 the following day. In the event he gave a moving reflection on Psalm 46: "God is our refuge and strength, an ever-present help in trouble. Therefore, we will not fear, though the earth be moved". "The earth has moved", he said "but we will not give in to fear". Later we heard that David and Anne Prothero's daughter had died in the attack. It was an unspeakable loss.

At the time we did not know how travel in the Middle East might be affected, but it became clear that reprisals would take place in Afghanistan immediately, as part of "the war on terror", and possibly in Iraq, although this did not become clear until late in 2002. It thus seemed quite secure to drive to Jordan, through the Balkans, Turkey and Syria. The plan was that I would set off in May with my friend and tennis partner Michael Fowler, and Olivia, who was teaching in our local school, would fly out at half term and we would spend almost a week together in Jordan. I would give the car, a Peugeot 205, to a missionary working in Amman and we would fly back. I jauntily asked Michael, if he would like to come on a three-week road trip to Jordan (as you do!). He had worked in the Far East and had recently sold a ceramics business, and he very gamely said "yes". More detailed planning followed, but the ball was now in play.

For me there are few more intoxicating activities than planning a route through countries I have always wanted to visit, and building up a web of contacts to meet along the way. The early weeks of 2002 were spent, amongst other things- including my parish ministry, preparing the route and gathering contacts. In fact, the route to be taken was more or less that which an overland pilgrim, or a crusader for that matter, would have taken to Jerusalem in the twelfth century. After all, Amman is only just across the river Jordan from Jerusalem. Not above seeking a little publicity, we got an article in the local paper, the *Bath Chronicle*. The headline was something like "City Vicar drives from Bath to Jordan", which had a suitably watery or even baptismal splash to it! The local Peugeot garage serviced the car, and the mayor posed with us outside the church because we would be meeting her opposite number in Bath's twinned city of Kaposvar, Hungary. So, with suitable civic and mechanical support we set off on our adventure on 10 May 2002. We had identified contacts in Budapest, Kaposvar, Novi Sad, Belgrade, Damascus, and Amman. We hoped to be in Amman by June 2, after covering a distance of approximately 4,500 miles.

We left on May 10, dropping two of our children off at school as we went, before making for the Channel Tunnel. The aim for the first day was to get to Monschau, not far from Cologne. Located near the Belgian border, Monschau is a pretty town with its own castle, set on the River Rur that bubbles its way past the town houses which in places overhang it. The following morning, we set off in beautiful spring sunshine through the meadows of the Eifel region towards the A3 and south to Bonn. This important west-east autobahn took us past Würzburg, Nürnburg and Revensburg to Passau on the Austrian border for our second night.

Passau lies on the junction of the Danube and the Inn. The Inn, which comes down from the Swiss and Austrian Alps (Innsbruck) is fast flowing with a slightly green Alpine tinge, whereas the Danube, one of the greatest rivers in Europe, is more sluggish and statelier, and makes its way from the Black Forest to the Black Sea, along seventeen hundred miles. In Europe, it is second only in length to the Volga. There was time in the morning to go to the open-air market, held under the Baroque cathedral with its vast pipe organ, where, in early May we could buy fresh strawberries and see quantities of asparagus (*spargel*), a regional delicacy. Before setting off we stood at the confluence of the Inn and the Danube looking downstream and realised we would see the Danube again at our next stopping point in Budapest. A river, rather than a motorway, would be a more pleasurable way of getting to Budapest. The Danube gives life to many cities: Vienna in Austria, Bratislava in Slovakia, before making its grand sweeping entrance into Budapest.

It is that *entrance* that makes Budapest so grand and elegant. To the west is Buda, the ancient Magyar citadel of Varnegyed with the Castle district, including St Matthias's Church, and across the river is Pest, the administrative and commercial heart of the city, which saw the high-water mark of the Ottoman Empire's invasion of Hungary in the sixteenth century. On the riverbank is the great Parliament building or Orszagház. The Danube is crossed by the famous Chain Bridge that leads eventually into Andrassy Avenue, which in turn passes St Stephen's Basilica, and ends in Heroes' Square. In Heroes' Square, because of the imposing sculptures of Hungarian warriors there, you are reminded that the Hungarians were a warlike people, who, having conquered the Carpathian Basin in the ninth century, were proud of their martial heritage. They have nevertheless have suffered reversals along the way, principally from the Ottoman Turks, but also from fighting with

Germany in World War I.

We paused in Budapest after the first thousand miles to stay with friends from Gipsy Hill days: John and Jill Mitchell and their delightful two daughters. John worked for the British Council, and in 2002 the focus was all on preparing Hungary to join the EU. There was great excitement about it. For countries that had only recently left the Warsaw Pact, the EU and NATO represented hope, prosperity, and protection from the Russian bear nearby. But old ways die hard in Hungary, and nationalism borne from a populist movement in the face of the refugee crisis of 2015 would again take hold in the country. But all that was still in the future.

For two days we enjoyed much of what Budapest had to offer. We wandered around the Castle District. This time parts of it were closed off because Laura Bush was there, visiting while her husband, President George Bush, attended a NATO Conference. (I am good at meeting, or nearly meeting, President's wives!) We went to a lovely concert in St Matthias's church in the castle district, had coffee and cake in the Gerbeaud Café, enjoying its old-world atmosphere, bathed in the Gellért Spa, with its steam rooms and hot pools all housed in a *fin de siècle* imperial style, saw men playing chess in the hot baths of Széchenyi, and lingered on the Chain bridge that crosses the Danube. There was more to see, but we left Budapest on a Sunday afternoon, having gone to an international church in the morning where the Pentecostal pastor memorably said on Pentecost Sunday, "When God goes tooting, we go scooting!" So, we scooted off to Lake Balaton.

We left the Danube to travel slightly west to the lake, which is the largest piece of water in Hungary. We would re-join and cross the Danube at Mohács. At seventy-seven kilometres long, Balaton is the largest lake in Europe, and with no coastline in Hungary it is a place of leisure and recreation for Hungarians. We stayed near Szántód, a holiday resort with old-world charm and balconied wooden houses in shady streets. Walking out into the lake, which is rarely above waist height, must give welcome relief during the hot continental summers. We had a quiet day relaxing there, and then continued our drive on Tuesday to Kaposvar, where we were to meet the mayor.

The city of Bath is twinned with Kaposvar, and the Mayor of Bath had written to announce our arrival and arrange a meeting with the mayor. We in fact met the Deputy Mayor (a Diplomatic downgrade?) at a restaurant in town to exchange civic greetings and presents, and since his English was far better than our Hungarian we spoke in English! It was an exciting time for Hungary, with optimism generated by the nation's forthcoming entry into the EU. I asked about the changes since the end of the Soviet occupation, and the mayor made it clear that although there were new freedoms, the changes made in the Soviet era had not yet all gone away. Many communist officials still held power, only now in different political guises. Land had not reverted to its original, pre-communist owners. It seemed that agricultural property was still owned by local councils or communes, and farmed by co-operatives. We enjoyed our lunch, exchanged presents—he gave us quantities of succulent strawberries—and then we continued our journey. We were expected in Novi Sad, Serbia, that evening.

The drive through southern Hungary to Pécs was delightfully bucolic. Villages nestled around their parish churches giving way to meadows with grazing cattle; women in black scarves minded a few cows; men rode old tractors. The weather was warm, and the first cut of hay had been taken. This was the best part of travelling by car: slowly, absorbing the sights, sounds and smells, expecting something different around every bend. In Pécs we stopped for a few minutes, but hardly did justice to this lovely town.

Founded by the Magyars in the ninth century, Pécs was established as an ecclesiastical, educational and cultural centre. Later in the sixteenth century the Ottoman Turks took control of the town. A large cathedral, built in the eleventh century and largely rebuilt in the nineteenth, dominates the town square. The atmosphere is one of quiet culture. One of the foremost modern artists in Hungary, Tivadar Csontváry Kosztka, lived here and his pictures *The Solitary Cedar* and *The Rendezvous of Lovers,* as well as others, have become famous. Soon we were on our way again, bound for the nearest crossing of the Danube at Mohács.

Mohács is famous for two things: a crossing of the Danube by ferry and the defeat of the Hungarians by the Ottoman Turks in 1526. Led by Suleiman the Magnificent, the Ottoman forces, superior in men and canon, overcame the Hungarians led by Louis II, who died following the battle. The defeat led to the division of Hungary between the Hapsburgs and the Ottomans, and the decline of Hungarian independence. Bohemia and Croatia were taken over by the Hapsburgs, while the Ottomans took over sovereignty of Transylvania. We were to discover that the Battle of Kosovo was to Serbs what the Battle of Mohács was to Hungary—a defeat that lies heavy in the national consciousness.

Mohács today is where you cross the Danube by ferry. Here the Danube is wide, perhaps almost a kilometre and a ferry crosses it in daytime. We were crossing in the early evening light, the water swift and majestic. We would cross the Danube again in Novi-sad and Belgrade before it turned east for its most dramatic run through the gorges of the Iron Gates into Romania. We were now crossing the border into Serbia, but not without some delay.

There are borders and borders. The Serbian border was not to be our most difficult border crossing. That was reserved for the border between Turkey and Syria, even in 2002, but the Serbian border came a reasonably close second. Even then there were no enforced borders between the Schengen countries of the European Union, and it was striking that when driving from England to Romania, as I did in 2020, that the only place I showed my passport was at the Hungarian-Romanian border.

Going from Hungary to Serbia in 2002 was to move from one culture to another: from Catholic and Protestant Hungary to Orthodox Serbia; from peace to a country that had recently been caught up in a brutalising war; from a country that was part of NATO to one that had recently been bombed by NATO; from a country almost in the EU to one that still had some way to go before being allowed to enter. In a way all this was reflected in the surly attitudes of the Serbian border guards. They were suspicious of the supplies we were taking to a charity in Novi Sad: papers, printers and other stationery. It took about an hour to get through: a visa must be paid for, the car documents carefully checked, car insurance bought and then, eventually, we were waved through. Consequently, we were a little late for the welcoming party in Novi Sad.

Michael, my travelling companion, was a Samaritan—that is, he was a trained telephone counsellor offering support to people who rang the Samaritan help-line, sometimes as their final act of desperation when contemplating taking their own lives. Set up in the city of London by Chad Varah, an Anglican clergyman, Samaritans had wide influence around the world. Michael had been in touch with an associate organisation in Serbia, which was giving support to that war-torn country.

Serbia's history is complicated, and full of twists and turns, highs and lows. And looking at the Serbs you cannot help think of *some* Serbs, if not all, as the hurt young adults of southern Europe, determined to do to others what they believed had been done to them. When thinking about the Serbs, we must remember two things: they are Slav in race and Orthodox in faith. Because of this they are close to Russia, which is also Slavic and Orthodox. And as Slavs, they accrued over time an emotional complexity, a sense of injured pride and idealistic national ambitions that seem to be part of the DNA. All this would lead Serbia to restless adventurism and disastrous choices, a combination that seems to colour all their history.

The Serbian Slavs moved down from Western Siberia to the Balkans in the sixth and seventh centuries, becoming Christian by the ninth. Their greatest years followed the ninth century, when they gained territory along the Adriatic and inland, calling themselves an Empire and ruled by the Nemanjíc Dynasty (1166–1371). Then disaster befell when they were defeated by the Ottoman Turks at the Battle of Kosovo on 15 June 1389, about three miles from Pristina. Although over six centuries past, it is a humiliation which some Serbs feel must be reversed, and consequently a return to a Greater Serbia has been a driver in extreme Serbian policy over the years. On the anniversary of this battle, in 1876, the Serbs attacked the declining Ottoman Empire, depending on the Russians for help;[60] an assassin felled the Archduke of Austria in Sarajevo precipitating the First World War; a new constitution was launched by King Alexander in 1921; and most ominously and recently, in 1989 Slobodan Miloŝević called for a Greater Serbia. The date of 15 June runs like a crimson thread through the history of the nation. And it seems the desire for a Greater Serbia is still to this day very active, not least in Bosnia.

---

[60] Misha Glenny, *The Balkans: Nationalism, War and The Great Powers* (London: Granta Books, 2000), p. 132.

After the break-up of Yugoslavia in the late 1980s, Serbia's nationalists saw an opportunity to enlarge their territory into Kosovo, Bosnia-Herzegovina and their old enemy, Croatia, thus realising the long-held romantic and nationalist dream of a Greater Serbia. At the same time, with the break-up of Yugoslavia, the constituent ethnic populations of several Balkan states made of differing religious traditions of Muslims, Catholic and Orthodox Christians began to pull apart. It was then that Radovan Karadẑić, a Bosnian Serb, and Slobodan Miloŝević joined together to seek this Greater Serbia.

In the bitter fighting of the Yugoslav Wars that followed, a hundred thousand were killed, many were massacred, and rape was used as a weapon of war. NATO intervened in 1992, creating a United Nations Protection Force and eventually succeeded in formulating a peace plan in Dayton, Ohio, in 1995.[61] Karadẑić and Ratko Mladic, his associate in Bosnia, were charged with war crimes in the Hague, including the massacre at Srebrenica, and both are currently serving prison terms there for war crimes. Likewise, Miloŝević was imprisoned at the Hague, but died of a heart attack in his cell. His funeral was attended by tens of thousands of Serbs in Belgrade.

Although the war between Serbia and Croatia and Bosnia had ended in 1995, a further conflict developed between Serbia and Kosovo, lasting until 2001. This resulted in a NATO bombing campaign against Serbia. When we arrived a year later there were still evident signs of it: damaged infrastructure and, more importantly, confusion in the hearts and minds of the population. This, then was some of the background to our arrival in Novi Sad.

As we drove into Novi Sad, we became aware of the physical damage, not least the bombed and broken bridge over the Danube in the centre of the town. We were late for our rendezvous, in part because of the hold up on the Serbian border, but our hosts, members of a Serbian Counselling service in association with Samaritans, were patiently waiting in a car park where we had agreed to meet. We had brought some resources from the UK for their work and were able to offload them. We spent just a day there, staying in the apartment of Slaviko, one of the counselling team of nineteen. It was clear that the war had affected the

---

[61] Richard Dannatt, *Leading from the Front* (London: Corgi Books, 2010), p. 172.

community deeply; there was a sense of abandonment, the block of flats in which Slaviko lived was like a fortress, with steel outer doors covering the normal wooden ones of the apartments, and people's faces were pinched and grim. The city had endured seventy-nine nights of bombing, several had been killed. Miloŝević's Serbian ambition, Slaviko said, took "ten years out of my life".

Despite all this, Slaviko asked his fellow counsellors round for a party the night we stayed. A group of nineteen lively and well-motivated young people crowded into his small apartment. Meeting them, we knew there was hope for the future. They were generally of the opinion that they would be in the EU by 2010, but ten years on, neither a Greater Serbia, nor joining the EU has happened. We turned in late and, since there was just one bedroom, Slaviko slept in the sitting room and Michael and I shared the only bed! It had to happen sometime, but we survived! The following morning, we were given a tour of the city by Cuka, a trainee Doctor whose favourite phrase was, "I fancy", and had a closer view of the bombed "Liberty" bridge over the Danube. We had a lovely lunch at the well-chosen Churchill restaurant, and then we set off for Belgrade.

If in Novi Sad there had been a feeling of lost time as the city was punished for the ambitions of its wayward Serbian government, in Belgrade there was a more pronounced sense of smouldering resentment and surly aggression. There were plenty of young men on the streets wearing black, and with attitude! Our hotel, the Metropole, gave us a distinctly frosty reception. There were prostitutes at the bars. There was little charm and fewer smiles. As with Novi Sad, the city had been bombed by NATO, following the Serbian government's attempt in 1998 to annex parts of Kosovo and drive out Albanians.

On the other hand, many people had seen the fruitlessness of Miloŝević's government, and had stormed the Parliament building in October 2000, forcing a change of leadership and handing Miloŝević over to the Human Rights Court at the Hague. It was a nation deeply conflicted. There was acknowledgement of the brutal attempt to form a greater Serbia, with the attendant massacres, rapes and ethnic cleansing. But there was also growing recognition that progress had to come another way, through closer alignment to the European Union and through burying the hatreds of the past. In 2001, Serbia was inching its way into the future, but with evidence of war all around in the city. It would be a future a long time coming.

Before we left on the trip I had talked to a Serb living in Bath, called Michael Milicevic. He had married an English woman working at the Belgrade British Embassy in the 1950s, and had made a successful career in the food industry in England. He was a member of our church, and personally supervised the production of two hundred beef-burgers "of the highest quality" for our annual summer church bash! His home was in England, but his heart was still in Serbia. His heart had been broken by the tragic murder of his daughter whilst living in England. In time to come, I would sadly take both his wife's and his own funeral. He gave us an introduction to an architect working in Belgrade, called Professor Branco Pešić, who we met on our only full day in the city. He was *the* architect of the huge new Orthodox Cathedral in the city, and he took us around the building and we had lunch together.

The building of the Serbian Orthodox Cathedral in Belgrade was already a long-term project. It began in 1935 and was still not complete in 2001. Modelled on Hagia Sophia in Istanbul, which we would later see, with a central dome weighing four hundred tons, it was designed to take seven thousand people. To cement the Russian-Serbian connection, the Russian Federation promised to pay for the golden mosaics on the walls, with President Putin making a personal promise to underwrite the costs. The golden cross on top of the dome is reputed to be the tallest in the world. It was a privilege to be shown around by the architect Branko and to have lunch with him and his wife. He was friendly and philosophical about the future; whatever happened the cathedral would be built. Memories of bombed buildings in the city, together with this soaring statement of Orthodoxy, served only to underline the complexities of this most Slavic of Balkan countries, where tragedy and fantasies often mingle. The following day we drove out of Belgrade, seeing signs of further bomb destruction as we left. We were bound for Bulgaria.

We would stay only one night in Bulgaria on our way to Istanbul through Thrace. The distance to our destination of Koprivshtitsa in the Sredna Gora Mountains was about three hundred miles. The route took us due south from Belgrade through Niŝ, the birthplace of Constantine and once a lively Roman colony. Over the centuries Empires would trample its streets: the Ottomans subdued Niŝ, building a grisly tower of skulls of people who had opposed them that is still visible today; the Austrian-Hungarians and the Germans in WW II would build a concentration camp here, killing thousands. And it was here that the ultimatum from Austria Hungary was received in 1918 after the assassination of the Archduke Ferdinand, which sparked the First World War. About seventy miles south of Niŝ, we reached the Bulgarian border.

The Bulgarians are another Slavic people-group drawn from the North Caucuses who settled in Northern Thrace. Their religion is Orthodox and their script is Cyrillic, as in Russia. Like Russia, they were evangelised by the redoubtable Saints Cyril and Methodius in the ninth century, and these missionaries gave the Bulgarians the Cyrillic script. For us, being unfamiliar with Russian, it meant stopping the car at signposts and laboriously transliterating the names to make sure we were on the right road to Koprivshtitsa, which, as you might imagine, took a moment or two! Thankfully there was little traffic. One driver, seeing an English registered Peugeot so far from home, stopped to ask if we knew where we were going? A good question! We told him our destination and he confirmed the turning, while at the same time extolling the friendliness of Bulgarians. One thing you can generally be sure of when travelling abroad is that not far away will be a Brit who has made that country his home; they are a ubiquitous race!

After giving Sofia a wide birth, we hastened on to Koprivshtitsa, arriving at our guest house in the evening. The village was delightfully authentic; the houses were wooden in the Plovdiv style, with rich overhanging, red-tiled roofs and stucco painted in red, blue and ochre. Off the main tarmac road, the roads quickly become cobbled lanes where horses and donkey carts could be seen. There was an air, literally and metaphorically, of a mountain culture—a cross between Switzerland and Scotland. We would not have been surprised to hear bagpipes played around the corner. We settled in and enjoyed a Bulgarian meal: *bob chorba*—a thick soup with meat and beans to follow and a robust Bulgarian red wine. We slept soundly.

The reason for coming to Koprivshtitsa was that in 1876 the

Bulgarians attempted to overthrow their Ottoman overlords here. But the insurgency was betrayed to local Ottoman garrisons before it ever took root, and brutal reprisals followed, known as the Bulgarian Atrocities. Shocked at these Turkish reprisals, Gladstone came out of retirement in 1876 to castigate the Turks' brutal repression of their Christian subjects, and the following year the Russians under Tsar Aleksander II took the chance to attack and defeat the Ottomans in the Russo-Turkish War of 1877, ostensibly supporting the Orthodox believers of Bulgaria, but in reality, extending their Empire.

Russia will be Russia: what was true then is still true now. The Treaty of Berlin, agreed by the Great Powers in 1878, gave independence to Romania, Serbia and part of Bulgaria, walking a fine line between recognising these nation states but not weakening the Ottoman Empire to the point where its demise only benefited Russia. This was the epitome of the Eastern Question and the issue thrown up by the decline of the Ottomans, known by then as "the Sick Man of Europe".

In Koprivshtitsa there were memorials to the dead Bulgarian rebels whose uprising had sparked a resetting of Eastern Europe that would last until 1914. We looked at the impressive stone memorials in the centre of the village in the morning and then made our way on a journey that would take us that day to Istanbul, or Constantinople as it was called for seventeen centuries. The journey to Istanbul was just over three hundred miles. We started by going through the rose country of Sredna Gora. In May these roses, *rosa damascena* and *rosa alba*, grow on tall bushes in the undulating hills as far as the eye can see. The petals are harvested by nimble rose pickers, then put in panniers on donkeys and taken to nearby towns for processing. A gentle perfume wafts across the hills. Rose attar or essential oil is produced here; thousands of kilos of rose petals are required for a single litre of attar for the cosmetic and catering industries. To stand amidst roses as far as the eye could see lifted our hearts as well as our nostrils.

Journeying on we came Stara Zagora, where we stopped to watch some Bulgarian country dancing—young men and women in red and white tunics with tight sashes around their waists, dancing to Bulgarian folk music in front of a rather incongruous Soviet-style town hall. It was an unexpected and captivating moment. From there we went to Plovdiv, the second city of Bulgaria, by now coming down out of the hills of Sredna Gora, and the mountains to the north, and onto the plain of Thrace. We had little time to visit the Roman theatre, or the churches filled with frescoes and icons in the Bulgarian Orthodox tradition, and found ourselves instead in the flower market, where the Bulgarian love of bright colourful flowers, especially gladioli, was evident.

From Plovdiv we headed for the border with Turkey, and the Turkish border-city of Edirne. Once called Adrianople, in Roman times in 378, it was the site of one of the most catastrophic defeats of the Roman Legions by the Goths when the Emperor Valens was killed in battle. The Goths did not turn their victory into conquest, however, for they did not know how to besiege a city like Constantinople, which was only a hundred and fifty miles away. Theodosius, a proven Spanish general, was quickly made Emperor and turned the tables on the Goths, settling them in the Roman Empire, and becoming the last Emperor of both the Eastern and Western Roman Empire. (Theodosius also re-established the Nicene Creed and was the father of the remarkable Galla Placidia, whose mausoleum is in Ravenna.)

From Edirne we journeyed in the evening light to Istanbul, arriving at the outskirts of the city as the sun was going down. I had booked a hotel close to the Topkapi Palace, appropriately called the Nomad Hotel. All I knew was that it was not far from the Sea of Marmara and the Golden Horn, so I kept driving downhill, heading for the water's edge, through this huge city of some eleven million people. When we could go no further, I stopped the car and asked for Hotel Nomad only to find we were right outside it—a minor motoring miracle! The receptionist was friendly, and kept saying "lovely-jubbly" and was a keen watcher of Del Boy (David Jason) of "Only Fools and Horses." We went out for a celebration meal of kebabs, aubergines and tomato salad, with two days ahead to explore this astonishing and captivating city.

Constantinople and Turkey

Entire books, like Bettany Hughes', are written about Constantinople or Istanbul. In fact, the city has had three names marking its varied and ancient history. Originally the Greeks called it Byzantion. It is a well-positioned city on a peninsula jutting out into the sea of Marmara, west of the Bosporus, and as such is the final part of Europe before Asia. Alexander the Great seized it—or liberated it, as he saw it—from Persian Achaemenid control in 334 BC. By 150 BC the city had fallen under Roman control and the great Roman Road called the Egnatian Way joining east and west was built, linking Byzantion and Rome.

Following the defeat by Constantine of the Eastern Emperor Licinius in 324, the city was re-founded as the Christian city of *Constantinople*. Churches were built, the original Hagia Sophia, which was later burnt twice in riots during the reigns of Arkadius and Justinian, was completed, as were the Church of the Apostles and Hagia Eirene. New imperial palaces and a street plan were laid out. After Theodosius I (379–395) and the end of the Roman Western Empire, Constantinople became the capital of the Byzantine Empire. Theodosius's son, Arkadius, and his grandson Theodosius II become the first rulers of this new Empire, with Theodosius II extending the city walls.

The Byzantine Empire would continue until the sack of Constantinople by the Ottoman Turk ruler Mehmed II in 1453. During this time the Empire contended with the arrival of Islam (Muhammad died in 632), the Iconoclastic movements of the ninth and tenth centuries, the split in the Church between Rome and the Orthodox in 1054, the disruptive incursions of the Crusades, incessant Byzantine palace intrigues, the rise and fall of dynasties, such as the Komnenos and Palaiologos, and the defeat of the Byzantine army at Manzikert in Anatolia by the Seljuk Turks. Gradually Constantinople became more and more isolated in a sea of Ottoman power, which by now held the Anatolian plain and Arabs in the Levant. By then not even Greek Fire, a way of setting the water alight around Constantinople, processions of the Virgin Mary in defence of the city, or the great iron chain placed across the Golden Horn could keep the invaders out, and in 1453 the city fell to the Ottoman Turks with reverberations throughout Europe.

If Byzantium had lasted a thousand years, the Ottoman Empire—the greatest land-based Empire in the west—lasted from 1453 until the last Sultan and Caliph Abdulmecid II left Constantinople on a train for Paris in 1924, where he died in 1944 on the day of Paris's liberation from the Nazis. Ataturk, the creator of modern Turkey, then took over. In brief, the

Ottoman Empire followed three stages. Its zenith was the sixteenth and seventeenth centuries. Its movement from war to consolidation occurred in the eighteenth century. Its decline followed in the mid-nineteenth century under pressure from an expanding Russia and growing nationalism in its many parts.

In 1523, the Venetian Bailo wrote, "I know of no state which is happier than this one; it is furnished with all God's gifts. It controls war and peace with all, it is rich in gold, in people, in ships and in obedience: no state can be compared to it."[62] Sultans were truly the *Lords of the Horizon*, commanding all that they could see and were the Caliphs of Islam (that is religious and political successors to Mohammad) and the guardians of the Holy sites of Mecca and Medina. Suleyman the Magnificent was truly the greatest of the Sultans (1520–1566). He conquered all opponents until checked by the Hapsburgs under Charles V at Vienna in 1529. He ruled over the Middle East, Jerusalem, North Africa and Eastern Europe, buffered by the Persians to the East and the Hapsburgs to the west.

In this, my second visit to Istanbul, we concentrated on just a few sites, while drinking in the atmosphere, smells, food and views of this great city. Hagia Sophia (Ayasofya) is the greatest legacy of Roman Constantinople. This vast church (until recently designated a museum by the Turkish state but now once again designated a mosque) was the third to bear the name Hagia Sophia. The first Hagia Sophia was begun by Constantine and completed in 360, but was destroyed by fire in 404 AD during riots precipitated by the dispute between John Chrysostom, Bishop of Constantinople, and the emperor's wife, Eudoxia. A new Hagia Sophia was built, only to be destroyed in more riots in the reign of Justinian on 15 January 532. It was then that Justinian, encouraged by his remarkable wife, Theodora, commissioned two architects, Anthemius of Tralles and Isidorus of Miletus, to rebuild Hagia Sophia. Both architects were mathematical geniuses. The result is the building we now have: fifteen hundred years old and as immovable and impressive as when first built, although restored after earthquakes and damage along the way.

---

[62] Philip Mansel, *Constantinople: City of the World's Desire 1453–1924* (London: John Murray, 2006), p. 114.

The vast internal space is created by the huge dome some thirty metres across, and supported by an arcade of forty arched windows. When filled with serving priests, bishops and the full panoply of the emperor it must have created a-never-to-be-forgotten impression. When ambassadors in the 10th century from Kyiv came to see the Orthodox faith for themselves and to advise the King on whether or not to become a Christian or a Muslim, they reported being overwhelmed by the experience. The vaulted space, the ascending plethora of domes and half-domes, the marble columns, the arches and galleries, are all given significance and meaning by the remains of wonderful golden mosaics. Among them we see the *Deësis*, a mosaic from the thirteenth century, depicting the Virgin Mary and St John the Baptist, imploring the seated Pantocrator Christ on Judgement Day. In another mosaic, Justinian and Constantine are seen offering the church of Hagia Sophia and the city itself to a seated Christ. Although now (since 2020 it has been re-designated a mosque by Turkey's nationalist leader and government), but these priceless works of art and faith nevertheless give the abiding feeling of Christian worship.

In contrast to this, in scale if not in faith, is the church of St Saviour in Chora (Kariye Camii—also sadly re-designated a mosque in 2020). As the name Chora suggests, it means St Saviour in the countryside or fields (*chora* means field). Located close to the Theodosian Walls, it is on the perimeter of the ancient city. The church dates from the eleventh century, but its fame lies in the profusion of mosaics and frescoes commissioned by Theodore Metochites, the Prime Minister of Androinicus II Palaelogus. Later exiled in a "cabinet reshuffle", he was allowed to return as a monk to his beloved St Saviour's. He died on 13 March 1332, wishing that this church would secure him a "glorious memory till the end of the world". He need not have worried, it surely has! The frescoes and mosaics, of the same period as Giotto's work in Florence and Padua, are unique and without peer. There are cycles of frescoes depicting the genealogy of Christ, the life of Mary, the infancy of Christ, portraits of the saints and far more. I chose one fresco of the Resurrected Christ raising Adam and Eve from their grave as the front cover of the book I was writing, *Becoming Fully Human*.

If these two churches, now classified as mosques, epitomise

Byzantine Constantinople, two further buildings epitomise Ottoman Constantinople: the Süleymaniye Mosque and the Topkapi Palace. The Süleymaniye Mosque crowns the Third Hill of Istanbul (there are six) overlooking the Golden Horn. It was founded by Suleiman the Magnificent (1520–1566), the longest reigning monarch of the Ottoman Empire, who defeated the Hungarians at Mohács, and took his army to the walls of Vienna and the cities of North Africa. He was not only a soldier, but a poet, a patron of the arts, and ardent lover of his favourite, Hürrem Sultan or Roxelana, a Ruthenian concubine and member of his harem. The mosque was built by the great Islamic architect, Mimar Sinan, whose brilliance expressed the ambitions of Suleiman. Its four minarets rise to a huge dome rivalling that of Hagia Sophia, surrounded by a company of half domes. Inside, vast columns support the central dome and provide a large uncluttered space for prayer, which is complemented by an airy arcaded courtyard outside. Suleiman and Roxelana are buried in separate mausoleums near the courtyard, surely the parents and patrons of this remarkable building.

If Süleymaniye was the greatest of the mosques of Constantinople, the power base was the Topkapi Palace or Sarayi. Begun in 1459, Topkapi was to be the base of Ottoman power, the Court of the Sultan Caliph until in 1856 the court finally moved to the Dolmabahçe Palace on the Bosporus. Sited on the tip of the peninsula overlooking the sea of Marmara, the Golden Horn and the Bosporus, Topkapi's position is unrivalled. Here the Janissaries guarded the Sultan. In the throne room, the Sultan held court and received embassies from throughout Europe and the East. Of greatest interest to the visitor are the quarters of the harem and the Council Chamber where the Grand Vizier administered the Empire, overheard by the Sultan through a grille set in the wall.

The harem, which comprised both the Sultan's family and his concubines, was a breeding machine in line with Islam's teaching on polygamy. If, in theory at least, church courts upheld Christian teaching on monogamous marriage, this was frequently supplanted by the presence of mistresses, as in the court of Henry VIII and many of the Hanoverians. (There were some notable exceptions as in the case of Edward I and Eleanor of Castille and Charles I and Henrietta Maria.) For the Sultans, the harem was a place for pleasure and breeding. The numbers of women in the harem grew from 167 in 1552 to 967 in 1652. Even in 1870 the number was 809.[63] The Empire was scoured for girls to join the harem. Concubines raised numerous children and sometimes yielded a favourite who became a consort of the sultan, as in the case of Roxelana. But the price of such surety of succession was fratricide, and the murder of all would-be usurpers or rivals to the throne on the succession of an heir. A silken cord was used to strangle all claimants once a new sultan had succeeded, sometimes as many as fifteen were strangled in a single day of royal slaughter. Such was the breeding machine of the Ottoman Empire. As someone remarked on another occasion, I believe at a picture of the rape of the Sabines, "how different from the home life of our dear Queen (Victoria)"!

Having taken in some of the unique sights of this extraordinary city over two days and inevitably bought a small Turkish carpet which was very efficiently sent home, it was time to move on. I was to return a few years later. But for the time being, on a fine morning in late May, we crossed the bridge from Europe into Asia, past the ancient sites of the Roman Imperial cities of Nicomedia and Chalcedon and arrived in the late morning at Iznik.

Iznik lies on a lake. It is surrounded by huge vineyards and is the origin of the most famous tiles in Turkey, which were used extensively in the decoration of the Sülemaniye Mosque five centuries before. But for me, as for the Christian church down the ages, its special interest was the site of the Imperial summer Palace of Constantine the Great at Nicaea. And in 325, over three hundred bishops were summoned to hammer out the Nicene Creed, and in particular the nature of the Trinity, during the crisis of the Arian controversy. Not much remains of that great palace where this First Ecumenical Council of the Church was held, but nonetheless it is still evocative of the most important church council in history. What was at stake at the council was maintaining that Jesus was *of the same substance as the Father*, i.e., fully God and sharing with the divine Spirit in the unity of the Trinity. Arius and his followers contended that Jesus was not fully God, but only *like the Father*. Eusebius, the church historian of the fourth century, describes the event when in 325 AD Constantine took to his simple throne in the midst of the bishops:

---

[63] Mansel, *Constantinople*, p. 94.

Now when the appointed day arrived on which the council met for the final solution of the questions in dispute, each member was present for this in the central building of the palace, which appeared to exceed the rest in magnitude. As soon, then, as the whole assembly had seated themselves with becoming orderliness, a general silence prevailed, in expectation of the emperor's arrival. And now, all rising at a signal which indicated the emperor's entrance, at last he proceeded through the midst of the assembly, like some heavenly messenger of God, clothed in raiment which glittered as it were with the rays of light, reflecting the glowing radiance of a purple robe, and adorned with the brilliant splendour of gold and precious stones.[64]

The Creed which, as with most summits, had been drawn up before the Council met, was endorsed by almost all the bishops. We now know it as the Nicene Creed which proclaims the Trinity and the divinity of Father, Son, and Holy Spirit: every Sunday it is said by countless congregations across the world. We lingered for a few minutes among the ancient stones before climbing into the car and driving on to Konya.

The road to Konya took us past some interesting sites. It was a long drive of some three hundred and ninety miles climbing higher onto the Anatolian plain, and leaving to the west Kutahaya, through which Alexander the Great had marched from Pella in Macedonioa in 333 BC on his way to Gordium, where he cut the Gordium (Gordion) knot.[65] Along the road we noticed a field of poppies; on closer inspection I realised that this was my first sighting of the opium poppy whose unripe seed-pod oozes a milky substance, which, when harvested and dried, produces opium. The pale pink flowers waved in the wind; their crop the source of one of the most powerful, contentious, enriching and mind-altering substances in the world—both a gift and a snare. Although for a time the American government sought to suppress the crop in Turkey through payments, it soon returned. The seed heads and flowers waved innocently and insecurely beside the road. By then tired, and affected only by a "road trip", we drove into Konya after dark to a modern Turkish

---

[64] Eusebius, *Vita Constantini* (Limovia, ebook, 2013), p. 116.
[65] Robin Lane Fox, *Alexander the Great* (London: Penguin, 1973), pp. 149–150.

hotel in the centre of town.

Konya (or Iconium in the Roman and Byzantine era) was visited by the Apostle Paul on his first missionary journey (see Acts 14) and is the home of the whirling dervishes based at the Meviana Monastery. It was a former capital of the Seljuk Turkish Empire at the heart of the Anatolian steppes. The dervishes are part of the Sufi sect, a mystical branch of Islam. Although banned by Kemal Ataturk as part of his campaign to create a secular state in 1925,[66] the dancing dervishes proved too popular with local culture and tourists to suppress. The dancers' continuous turning or whirling on the spot along with mesmeric Turkish songs induce a mystical state or extreme dizziness. And the flowing skirts and trance-like demeanour of the dancers is a spectacle. Instead, we had our own rather more prosaic whirling moment in the hotel.

The hotel had been just recently completed and was proud of its modern look, but when it came to the bathrooms, none of the basins had plugs, a minor oversight. Michael had a solution. For just such an eventuality, he had brought a tennis ball sliced in two halves. All you had to do was to press one half over the plug-hole, and suction would hold it in place and water stay in the basin; at least that was the theory! The procedure was enacted, but the force of compressing the half tennis ball brought the whole somewhat unhinged basin whirling to the floor and shattering on the ground! There was no mystical outcome, only a long-suffering hotel manager lamenting the English and their tennis balls!

The following day we enjoyed one of the most scenic drives of the whole road trip: from Konya to Kizkalesi on Turkey's southern Mediterranean coast. From the Anatolian plateau at about three thousand feet, where Konya is situated, the road goes gently upwards to Karaman at the foot of the Toros (Taurus) mountains. Named after the bull, they are a majestic range rising to twelve thousand feet and stretching from Afyon in the west, to the Euphrates and Tigris in the east, feeding those two great rivers and the civilisations that have sprung up around them. We stayed a night at Kizkalesi, along the coast a little beyond Silfike. Kizakalesi has an almost fairy-tale castle in the bay, some three hundred metres from the shore, built by the Armenian Kings of Cilicia in the thirteenth century. It was a charming overnight stop.

---

[66] Mansel, *Constantinople,* p. 416.

The following morning began a day which was to be like no other: from Turkey in the morning to Aleppo in northern Syria in the evening, by way of the Cilician Gates near Tarsus. The names on the road signs that flashed by on this newly-completed EU funded road of minimal traffic were redolent with classical and biblical significance: Cilicia, Tarsus, Antioch and Aleppo. We went through the Cilician Gates, a narrow pass between the Toros mountains. Soldiers from Alexander the Great to the Crusaders had marched this way for millennia. Indeed, along the road were crusader castles indicating that we were soon to enter Palestine or *Outremer*, literally the Crusader Kingdom "beyond the sea". It was through these gates, so familiar because of his home city of Tarsus, that the Apostle Paul went on his first missionary journey to neighbouring Lystra, Derbe, Pisidian Antioch and Iconium—the Galatian churches (Acts 13 and 14). We were now going around the armpit of the Mediterranean, from which Cyprus seems to have been plucked like a jig saw piece waiting to be replaced, and entering the biblical lands of Syria, Lebanon, Palestine and Jordan, with their ancient hinterlands of Assyria, Babylon, Persia and Egypt.

It was a heady and exciting moment, but before we crossed the Syrian border, we left behind the first of these evocative places, Antioch or Antakya, which is now in Turkey. Antakya is now a large coastal city. In ancient times it was known as Antioch, and was founded in 300 BC soon after Alexander the Great invaded the Orontes valley after the Battle of Issus against the Persians in 333 BC. After Alexander's death it became the capital of the Seleucid Empire and then of the Roman province of Syria. It was here, as governor of Syria in 4 BC, that Quirinius commanded that a census be taken in the province including Palestine, requiring every family to go to their home town to be registered (Luke 2:1). In consequence, Joseph and Mary went to Bethlehem. It was here that Peter and Paul ministered to a church exploding with life and missionary vigour in c. 50 AD, and where followers of Jesus were first called Christians (Acts 11;19ff). And it was from here that the Legions of Rome under Vespasian and Titus, both of whom would become Emperors, supressed the Jewish revolt of AD 66 with Roman ruthlessness, destroying the Temple of Jerusalem, just as

Jesus had predicted in AD 70 (Mark 13:1ff) and as described by Josephus in *The Jewish War*. It was here too that Roman Emperors like Theodosius based themselves in a palace on an island in the Orontes, and where the golden-mouthed Chrysostom first preached to an attentive Christian community—the Antiochene school—which was to become well-known for its particular theological perspective. Few, if any, signs of this or indeed of the siege of the city by the Crusaders in 1097 and 1098 remain, but their memories linger on in the place. Then, from Antioch we turned east and were soon at the Syrian border.

Syria and Jordan

Even then the Syrian border was total confusion, and everything could have gone very badly wrong. As I remember, there was a large dusty car park of lorries with several inconspicuous huts, and non-uniformed officials hurrying between vehicles and what looked like temporary checkpoints. The minute I handed over our passports to a "Charlie Chaplain" type figure, helpful, but not in uniform, I regretted it. What was there to say he *really was an official*? What if someone else now asked for our passports, claiming to be the real thing, and we had already handed them over to a fraud? It would have been impossible to identify him in the meleé. There were a few anxious minutes before our friend re-appeared; minutes in which I had visions of our trip coming to an abrupt end. We already had the necessary visas, so we paid for further insurance cover for the car, and, amidst more confusion, were waved through. From the border it is only fifty miles to Aleppo, and about the same distance to Idlib. Rakka, where ISIS or Daesh had its evil headquarters, is about one hundred and fifty miles east, on the upper waters of the Euphrates.

We drove into Aleppo in the evening sunlight, along with others driving home after a day's work. Coming across Hotel Baron, which I had read about, we cancelled a previous booking elsewhere and booked in there for the night. The receptionist was Armenian. She told us her parents had fled Turkey in 1915 during the massacres of her people and they had made their home in Aleppo. She showed us room 238, where T.E. Lawrence of Arabia had stayed while researching Crusader castles in the area before the First World War. She also showed us his unpaid bar bill, framed and proudly displayed behind the bar. I don't know, but I imagine the hotel is rubble now. Having put our luggage in the room we went out to explore the town.

Aleppo was one of the great cities of the Levant, and the second city of Syria once having over three million inhabitants. We made for the *souk* or great bazaar. In 1600 there were fifty-three khans and fifty-six *souks* in Aleppo measuring some eight miles of narrow, vaulted passageways that were locked at night, but in day time presented a bewildering range of merchandise: jewels, carpets, gold, spices, leather, rope, scarves, clothes, hardware—whatever you could want.[67] It was a department store in a thousand shops down myriad alleys. Not as large as the *souk* in Cairo or Istanbul, but nonetheless it gave a vivid sense of trade and interaction, of permanence and survival: how wrong could one be.

Walking the streets of Aleppo, we could not but be aware of the diversity of the city. I noticed a small synagogue, closed but perfectly peaceful, near the Souk al-Attarine, only to learn later surprisingly that one of the greatest and oldest manuscripts of the Jewish Torah, the *Aleppo Codex,* was kept in the Great Synagogue.[68] In Aleppo there were many mosques, including the Great Mosque, which was just a few years younger than the great Umayyad Mosque in Damascus. But there were also many churches belonging to Maronite Christians, Greek Catholics, the Syrian Orthodox Church, and the Forty Armenian Martyrs' Cathedral. Just as the Elizabethan merchant John Eldred observed when he arrived in Aleppo from Baghdad with four thousand camels in 1581, there were Jews, Tartars, Persians, Armenians, Egyptians, Indians and many sorts of Christians in the city.[69] There had been a plural community there, even then, and still in 2002—but what now? Muslims, Christians and Jews jostled side by side, preserving and enabling their own communities. Indeed, in his book about working as a surgeon in Aleppo in the final days before its fall to the Assad regime in 2017, and having been ravaged by indiscriminate barrel bombs, David Nott recalls being prayed for by a priest called Michel in the chapel of the Mar Elias care home for the elderly in the city. As Father Michel prayed for David, he

---

[67] Philip Mansel, *Aleppo* (London: I. B. Tauris, 2016), p. 12.

[68] Mansel, *Aleppo,* p. 29.

[69] Mansel, *Aleppo* p. 12.

recalls that "an electric shiver ran through me filling me with love".[70] Six months later, Michel was himself killed during a barrel-bomb attack while shopping for food for his flock of elderly residents.[71] But that was all in the dark, unseen future, whose tragedy none of us could then foresee.

That night we had a rendezvous with a Syrian doctor, Fateh, and his English wife, Gill, in a restaurant beside the Citadel Square, Gill was the sister of members of our church at home, Nigel and Caroline Dyer. They showed us the marbled Hammam complex where they regularly bathed. Nothing could have been more lovely than relaxing in a warm evening, gazing at the magnificent Citadel, hearing about life there, and, somewhat inevitably, discussing the future of the country following 9/11. Little did we know what that future would hold. When the war started in March 2011 the family stayed as long as they could in the city, but in the end, they emigrated to Australia.

We slept well that night in the Baron Hotel, with so much to recall of a day that began in Kizakalesi and ended in Aleppo. I don't think I have ever had a day of such contrasts: the Mediterranean, the Cilician Gates, Tarsus, Antioch, the Syrian border and then Aleppo. The next twenty-four hours were calmer, as well as being poignant.

In the morning we looked around the formidable citadel at the centre of Aleppo. Built on a natural mound in the middle of the old city, it was first used as a fortification during the time of the Seleucids. In the twelfth century it became a stronghold for Muslim dynasties, particularly during the time of the Crusades. It was built by the Mamluk sultans, who ruled from Cairo until overtaken by the Ottomans from 1453.[72] But, in 2016, it was badly damaged in the Syrian civil war: the moat filled with rubble, the walls broken and the great rampart leading up to the gates damaged. When we were there the high walls were still intact and provided a great vista of the city from their commanding battlements. Now most of Aleppo's population has been either killed, or scattered as refugees in Lebanon, Jordan, Turkey and Germany; not least the engaging, beautiful

---

[70] David Nott, *War Doctor: Surgery on the Front-Line* (London: Picador, 2019), p. 285.
[71] Nott, *War Doctor*, p. 285.
[72] Mansel, *Aleppo,* p. 3.

and lively children of Aleppo who now fill those camps. What future will they have, and will their city ever be rebuilt and habitable again?

From Aleppo we made our way to Qala'at Samaan, a little village to the west of the city, which is the shrine of one of the great desert fathers, Simeon Stylites (389–459). In the early fourth century an extraordinary ascetic movement began in the Egyptian, Syrian and Palestinian deserts, as well as in the city of Caesarea in Cappadocia. Figures such as Pachomius of Thebes on the Nile, St Anthony in the Egyptian desert, Basil of Caesarea and Jerome were some of the leading lights.[73] Although most were either hermits dwelling in caves, cells or sketes, others formed early communities of monks. Some of these ascetics—committed to prayer, meditation and offering counsel in response to the request "Give me a word, father or mother"—adopted extraordinary training (*askesis*). Some stayed awake for days on end, others ate a diet beyond frugality, and others, like Simeon, lived on the top of pillars. Simeon's pillar, though much reduced, was at Qala'at Samaan. It had been as high as sixty feet, but was now the size of "a giant snowball".[74] It was housed in the pleasant ruin of an Orthodox church built in the days of the Byzantine Emperor Zeno.[75] From palaces and hovels, emperors and paupers came to Simeon. And for thirty years he gave advice, offered prayers, and became the most influential Christian leader in fifth century Syria and beyond.

The shrine is on a windswept ridge with stunning views over the Syrian countryside. With the blue sky above, the arches of this ancient church, now a ruin surrounding the remaining part of the pillar, make a fitting monument to Simeon's extraordinary story. The wide views over the Syrian plain below are breath-taking. One can gaze on corn fields already harvested in early June, fig trees and almond groves aplenty, and be forgiven for thinking that Syria is a promised land. And, following a night in Hama *en route* we made our way to the greatest castle in the world, Krak de Chevaliers.

The distance from Aleppo to Krak de Chevalier is about ninety

---

[73] Patrick Whitworth, *Constantinople to Chalcedon* (Durham: Sacristy Press, 2017), pp. 267ff.

[74] Bettany Hughes, *Istanbul* (London: Weidenfeld and Nicholson 2017), p. 168.

[75] Christoph Baumer, *The Church of the East* (London: I. B Tauris, 2016), p. 55.

miles, a little west of Homs. It is one of a string of Crusader castles stretching from north of Antioch to Gaza. Of all these castles, T.E. Lawrence quite simply said that Krak des Chevaliers was "perhaps the best preserved and most wholly admirable castle in the world".[76] Together with another castle, a little to the north, Krak guards the gap between two mountain ranges stretching from Antioch in the north to the Jordan valley in the south. Wonderfully positioned with an all-round view, it was quite simply impregnable to warfare in its day. It has a double curtain wall, with a further inner wall protected by a steep glacis and four round towers. It was built in the twelfth century by the Knights Hospitallers, one of two late medieval crusading orders, the other being the Knights Templars, and it could garrison up to two thousand troops.

After the defeat of the Crusader Kingdom forces in Palestine at the Horns of Hattin in 1187, the continuation of the kingdom and its principalities was precarious. Much of the territory, and Jerusalem itself, was occupied by Saladin and then by the Mamluks, to whom the castle eventually fell in 1271. By then it was a crusader island in a sea of Muslim-controlled territory. To look out from the castle's walls is to imagine the past and the conflicts that this narrow stretch of land has witnessed down the ages. At the same time, it is to contrast the extraordinary beauty of the surroundings with the violence created by the need to possess it.

The previous night we had stayed at Hama, which lies in the Orontes River valley, which runs northwards from the mountains of Lebanon, near Baalbek, towards Antioch, where it enters the Mediterranean nearby. Hama had a peaceful atmosphere with parks along the banks of the Orontes and its famous large water wheels, or *norias,* which in ancient times scooped water from the river and deposited it in aqueducts. Both of us remarked how peaceful the town was, how content the people looked walking arm-in-arm in the evening light, but once again the peacefulness disguised deep seated animosities and fears. In 1982, an uprising in Hama led by the Muslim Brotherhood was brutally suppressed by Hafez al-Assad (the father of the present ruler, Bashar al-Assad), and according to British journalist, Robert Fisk, around 20,000

---

[76] Kelly DeVries, *Medieval Military Technology* (Calgary, AB: Broadview Press, 1992), p. 231.

people were massacred. It was a prelude to, and omen of, what was to follow from 2011. Bashar-al Assad's photograph stared down from most shops and hotels. This seemingly mild-mannered English-trained doctor hardly looked like the merciless war leader he became while maintaining his Alawite tribe's hold on power. In this respect, he would replicate his father's willingness to hold on to power at all costs, with Russian and Iranian support. While the West and Sunni Muslims states remained unsure who to support among the myriad revolutionary groups, some more extreme than others. But all this still lay in the future. In that moment, having visited this great castle, we headed through what would be scenes of bitter fighting in 2013, and then out east towards Palmyra.

The road to Palmyra was due east from Homs and a little short of a hundred miles through the desert—a further hundred plus miles and you would be at the Euphrates, and a little further, at the border of Syria with Iraq. Palmyra was a kingdom built on the trade and taxes from the Silk Route that passed through the oasis. It was an oasis surrounded by hundreds of miles of desert on all sides. From the first century AD, Palmyra was a client state of Rome, but became increasingly independent, until Queen Zenobia established her own empire, rebelled against Rome, only to be confronted by the Emperor Aurelian, and his legions who destroyed much of the city and exiled her to Rome for the rest of her life. It then became the outer limit of the Roman Empire in the east—a buffer zone against the Persians. Intellectual and courageous, Zenobia was not unlike Queen Elizabeth I or the Egyptian Queen, Hatshepsut, a ruler strong on defiance and rich in culture.

There can be few things more beautiful in the world than the setting sun going down behind the ruins of Palmyra Palace, which rises as an architectural apparition in the desert. The graceful columns of the colonnade stretching a kilometre on an east-west axis are as elegant as they are unexpected in such surroundings. Around the central area are tombs, funerary towers, a Temple to Bel, Bel-Shammin as well the remains of a Byzantine church. But Palmyra is greater than the sum of its parts. Its dramatic situation, the surrounding desert, and the light of dawn by which we saw it at five a.m., and later, the light of sunset on the stonework, give the whole an ethereal quality, both entrancing and memorable.

In recent years Palmyra has suffered again, at the hands of ISIL. They occupied the site in 2015 and destroyed or damaged some of the temples and the Tower of Elahbel. But worse still, some two hundred local people were executed in the precincts, including the eighty-three-year-old archaeologist and forty-year custodian of Palmyra: Khaled al-Assad. He was executed on 18 August 2015 and once again Syrian beauty was marred by brutality, and history by hatred. If there was any place I would like to have lingered for another twenty-four hours, it would have been here. But, after a sunset and a dawn and spending some time looking over the site, we were on our way to Damascus. Finally, I could say we were on our road to Damascus.

On the way we came to one of those wonderful signposts that read Damascus 130 Kilometres and Baghdad 200. We passed a train of fifty camels, and camps for the Syrian army. The driver of the camels, with good humour, even offered us a lift! Nearer Damascus we passed through a village of Orthodox Christians. A new large church was being built. There was a butcher selling pork in this mostly Muslim country and an ice cream vendor offering ice cream at twenty scoops for a dollar! Entering the traffic of Damascus was like entering an ant hill after being in isolation: taxis, vans and pedestrians everywhere. It took time to track down St Elias Monastery in Al Touba where we were staying. From there we went to find Eldon and Jane, Mennonite missionaries living in the Old City. We were entertained in their cool and colourful courtyard, replete with a hubble-bubble and heard about life in this teeming city. They talked about low crime rates, no alcohol and social behaviour that would be a model to the West. We nodded sagely!

Damascus is one of the oldest continuously inhabited cities in the world, with evidence of inhabitants from the third millennium BC. Now it is a sprawling city of over two million. It has played host to regimes of every kind, from the Assyrians, the Persians, the Greeks, the Nabateans (of whom we will hear more at Petra), the Romans, the Byzantines, the Umayyad Caliphate in the seventh century, the Abassids and then the Seljuk, and finally, the Ottoman Turks until 1918.

From 1919 it became mandated to the French following the Treaty of Versailles and Sèvres until the Ba'ath Party and the Assad family gradually gained control in the 1960s. Over the centuries almost every power in the region wanted to claim it for themselves. It was the jewel in the Arab crown, but it was to slip from the grasp of Faisal (1885–1933), the Hashemite prince and third son of the Sharif of Mecca who along with T.E. Lawrence led the Arab revolt against the Ottomans in the Great War. Faisal had hoped passionately to rule from Damascus as a reward and recognition for his leadership of the Arab revolt with Lawrence. But the city was not offered to him because an earlier clandestine agreement between Sykes and Picot gave Damascus to the French in exchange for the British retaining a mandate over Palestine, Jordan, and Iraq. It was a case or *realpolitic* undercutting Arab expectations, and for Lawrence it was a source of abiding shame and betrayal.

For all the politics, Damascus was a city of great religious significance. Next to the great Omayyad Mosque was the Mausoleum of Saladin, who had vanquished the Crusaders at the Horns of Hattin and taken Jerusalem. But for Christians, Damascus is known as the city of St Paul. It was on the road to Damascus that Paul, the Pharisee and persecutor of the church, was blinded by a vision of Christ, and where, whilst staying in the street called Straight, his sight was restored by a local disciple called Ananias. And it is here that Paul began his Apostolic ministry, only to be persecuted himself, so that he had to make his escape by being let down from the city wall in a basket (Acts 9: 1–25). We visited the house on Straight Street where Paul received his sight and was baptised.

There are, or at least there were in 2002, a myriad of churches in the old city: the Syrian Orthodox Patriarchate—a Monophysite church (stressing the divinity of Christ) closely linked with the Copts—the Armenian Catholic and Armenian Orthodox Church, the Franciscan Catholic church and the Evangelical church. As we were there on a Sunday, we worshipped with the Syrian Orthodox at St George's Cathedral at Bab Touma, conscious that we were worshiping in one of the oldest Christian communities in the world, using the Syriac language derived from Aramaic, the language of Christ. They are a faithful and resolute people, but the sufferings and difficulties endured by the churches in Syria during the civil war have been many, brought about both by outright persecution and their own internal pressures.

Jordan

The following day we headed for Jordan and to the last country of our journey. The distance from Damascus to Amman, the capital of Jordan, is about two hundred and fifty miles—a day's journey in a car. It takes you past Deraa, and I couldn't help but think again of T. E. Lawrence, whose *Seven Pillars of Wisdom* I was reading, and who wrote these words as he rode frantically towards Damascus (the opposite direction of travel), "I gave liberty to my camel—the grand, rebellious Basha—and she stretched herself against the field, racing my wearied followers for mile upon mile with piston-strides like an engine, then I entered Deraa quite alone in the full dawn".[77]

In a day Lawrence would be in Damascus with the Arab leader Faisal, fêted by the population, but only too painfully aware that France and not Faisal would rule in Damascus. Our "camel", a red Peugeot, had done well and had certainly "stretched herself" and was now covered with desert sand, so we stopped at a garage and at least four Jordanians (as we had crossed a much more peaceful border by then) gave the car a thorough clean inside and outside, ready to be given away a few days later to Malcom, a Church Mission Society missionary working in Jordan.

The plan had always been for Olivia to fly out so we could have five days in Jordan together, and Michael was to visit a wonderful school for the deaf and dumb at Salt, west of Amman. It was by no means the last time Michael and I would travel together, however.

In many ways Jordan is the success story of the Arab Middle East, arguably more so than any other country. A neighbour to Israel, Syria, Iraq and Saudi Arabia, it walks a diplomatic tight rope. Jordan became independent of the British Mandate in 1946, and was ruled by Faisal's older brother, Abdullah, another Hashemite Prince. Abdullah was assassinated by a Jihadist Palestinian when visiting Jerusalem in 1951, probably for his moderate stance towards Israel. His grandson Hussein succeeded in 1952, following his father Talal's abdication due to mental illness. Jordan has played host to two million Palestinian refugees from

[77] T. E. Lawrence, *The Seven Pillars of Wisdom* (London: Penguin, 2000), p. 656.

the 1948 Arab Israeli War, the Six-day War of 1967 and the Gulf War of 1990. A further 1.4 million refugees have come from Syria more recently, as well as others from Iraq (including thousands of Assyrian Christians) and Lebanon. The country appears quietly to get on with the job, and has managed to resist or contain radicalised Arab movements such as ISIL. The present ruler, Abdullah II, Hussein's son, has survived the unrest provoked by the Arab Spring, and is moving towards Parliamentary government.

It is an impressive record, and Jordan is a lacuna of peace in a region of hatreds. The visitor to Jordan will be drawn to a number of unique and extraordinary sites: particularly Petra, the deserts of Wadi Rum and Aqaba, the famous mosaic map of the region in Medeba, the Roman colony of Jerash, and Mount Nebal, where Moses died looking across the Jordan into the Promised Land. We saw all these in the next five days, beginning with Petra.

The view of the Treasury in Petra is one of the iconic sights of the Middle East. Its beautiful classical facade emerges to greet you, chiselled out of almost pink sandstone rock. The day we went to Petra there were few tourists. The 9/11 events of the previous year had reduced tourist numbers, and the fear of an impending strike by the United States, which came in the following year on Iraq, only deflated numbers further. The site was not quite deserted, but certainly quiet. Others' loss was our gain. The entrance to the city past the Treasury is through a narrow defile which gradually reveals the extent of the city built by the Nabateans and imparts a sense of drama and awe. As at Palmyra, the flow of money from taxes on trade coming from the East to the Mediterranean had enabled the building of the city and sustained this civilisation. From around 150 BC, the Nabateans cut extraordinary classical designs into the red sandstone rock, creating a city in the desert and a necropolis too, where this sophisticated Bedouin tribe could bury their dead. But the other essential flow, along with money, was water. Indeed, maybe their greatest triumph was their use of water. During the winter, the Nabateans captured the rainfall in cisterns and reservoirs and then brought it around the city through conduits and channels to homes and buildings, no doubt charging families for the provision.

Once again, as with so many of these ancient sites, it is a place to linger and watch the sun pick out the reds, yellows and browns, and to see the shadows fall across the rose-tinted rock-faces. The mood of the place changes with the light, and makes you marvel at the ambition and ingenuity of it all: engineering and aesthetics harmonise wonderfully with the desert context. Eventually, by the first century AD, what had been a client state of the Romans became part of their hegemony, and in the end the buildings were abandoned to Bedouin shepherds, who used them for nothing more than temporary security from the desert, blackening them with their cooking and warming fires.

Petra lies in the Arabah, south of the Dead Sea. A little further south, and to the east of Aquaba, is Wadi Rum, made famous among the English by the writings of Lawrence of Arabia during the Arab Revolt of 1916. It was a long valley with high red mountains, and crags and cliffs on either side. With evident awe and love, Lawrence describes it best:

Today we ride for hours while the perspectives grew greater and more magnificent in ordered design, till a gap in the cliff-face opened on our right to a new wonder. The gap, perhaps three hundred yards across, was a crevice in such a wall; and led to an amphitheatre, oval in shape, shallow in front, and long-lobed right and left. The walls were precipices, like all the walls of the Rumm; but appeared greater, for the pit lay in the heart of a ruling hill, and its smallness made the besetting heights seem overpowering.[78]

The highest peak within this valley of sandy floors and jagged red rock is Jabal Ram at nearly six thousand feet. In Wadi Rum we were hosted by local Bedouin, equipped, even then, with a mobile phone! They left us alone to hear the silence and contemplate the scenery. We then spent the afternoon at Aquaba, Jordan's precious opening onto the Red Sea and the Mediterranean, through the Suez Canal (through the Gulf of Aquaba). It is a busy port, and a lifeline to the wider world.

Earlier in the week we had visited the ancient site of Jerash north of Amman. I still have the entrance ticket to this Roman colony in my battered copy of the *Seven Pillars of Wisdom,* but we also drove along

---

[78] Lawrence, *Seven Pillars*, p. 360.

the Kings Highway. This ancient route that follows the rim of the Rift Valley on the east side of the Jordan runs past Mount Nebo from where Moses saw the Promised Land (see Deuteronomy 34) before he died. He was prevented from entering the land as he had quarrelled with the Israelites—not a hard thing to do given their obduracy! But from there the Mount of Olives, Bethlehem and Hebron could be seen just tens of miles away on the other side of the Jordan Valley. We are told that aged one hundred and twenty, "his eyes were not weak nor his strength gone," but his time had come. Not even half his age, it was a reminder to me that there are many things we may glimpse, but equally may not be able to enter.

Having handed over the car to Malcolm and Jane and completed the customs paperwork at a small government unit in a back street of Amman so the car could stay in Jordan, we were clear to return to the UK by plane. The previous four weeks had been a trip of a lifetime. Some may prefer to sail or row the Atlantic or lie on a beach; but for me there are few things more enriching experiences than unfurling the past, watching the changing scenery, enjoying many conversations, tasting different foods, and storing away a host of impressions for the future provided by this kind of journey. A good trip certainly leaves you wanting more, and, I am pleased to say, that surely happened.

Chapter VII
Glimpsing the Apocalypse

About six years later I came to an agreement with Olivia (I hope she can remember!) and the Parish of All Saints Weston, that most years I would take a week off for "research" and a pilgrimage with two fellow pilgrims. Fortunately, most of these pilgrimages (if I can invest my travels with that time-honoured name) just happened to be around the Mediterranean and linked in with writing which I was doing! And the month we travelled in was mostly May—to catch the Spring and be there before the tourist season was fully underway. By 2008 these intentions had acquired some substance, as I had published three books, including one that came out of my sabbatical (2002) called *Becoming Fully Human*, which seemed to strike a chord. It would be followed by two other *Becoming* books to make a trilogy. So, with future publications in mind, there was a case to be made for research even if in pleasant climes.

I have learnt that any writing about a place, event or country, or indeed about theology and biblical studies generally, is enhanced greatly by visiting the place where those things happened. There is something about standing in the place, hearing again the story *in situ*, experiencing the climate, seeing the contours of the land, the ancient stones, the way of life, the faces, the birds, the crops, the smells and the light. All this seems to provoke the writing juices and provide insights about the connections between people, place and time. And to have others with whom to reflect and discuss, to laugh and to remember, and to watch your back, is, I think, one of the greatest experiences that life has to offer. Of course, this is most true of the Holy Land (to which we will come), but it is also true of these other trips or pilgrimages around the Mediterranean.

So come May 2008, Paul Bright, a friend from Weston and a recently retired Police Inspector (very useful), and Michael, who had come all the way to Jordan with me some years before, agreed to make a journey following in the footsteps of St Paul and St John, but principally St John. I was hoping to write about John and his writings when I got back. We planned the route, normally over a delightful meal in Paul and Catherine's home, where maps were spread out, the internet consulted and a plan formulated. We intended to fly to Izmir, go to the ancient sites of Ephesus, Samos and Patmos, and then, if possible, visit the sites of the seven churches of Asia Minor. The plan had the flexibility to include, more or less, a nice mix of adventure and structure, a week in length.

Ephesus

We flew to Izmir, on the Aegean coast in Turkey. Izmir, or Smyrna as it was known for most of its life, a principal city of the Levant in the Ottoman Empire, is one of the sites of the Seven Churches of the Apocalypse, to which we shall return.

We hired a car from the airport and drove to Kusadasi, where we stayed at the Liman Hotel run by a certain "Mr Happy": "My real name is Mr Haman, but I am known around the world as Mr Happy!" Happy he certainly was, and there was clearly no end to his reach! He had a lovely roof garden where we had breakfast and supper overlooking the harbour, watching medium-sized cruise ships tying up and disgorging tourists to visit nearby Ephesus. When we heard the muezzin's call to prayer, we knew we were in Turkey. Kusadasi is a small port town, with local shops, such as fishmongers and grocers. It even had a shop that sold "genuine fakes"—leather goods in the style of Dior or Mulberry. And on the street were cobblers to shine and repair shoes. From Kusadasi it was only a short drive north to the ancient site of Ephesus where we went the following day.

Ephesus was one of the great cities of the Ancient World. It was, as with almost all the cites on the Aegean coast of present-day Turkey, originally an Ionian Greek community. The Ionians were one of the main Greek tribes of the ancient world and the city was founded as long ago as 1000 BC. Ephesus was eventually taken over by the expanding Roman Republic from 129 BC, and continued to expand and flourish as a growing Mediterranean port at the end of the trade routes from the East. The buildings that remain more than confirm the wealth, importance, and civic pride of this city.

The most prominent remaining building is the great theatre at the end of Harbour or Market Street. The harbour was then literally at the end of the street, before the sea receded in later times. Construction of the theatre began in the reign of Claudius (41–54 AD), and was completed in the reign of Trajan (98–117). It could seat twenty-five thousand people, not so much for gladiatorial combat as in most contemporaneous amphitheatres, but to enjoy plays and spectacles. It was here that the Apostle Paul was hauled by the incensed silversmiths of Ephesus who were losing trade as people turned away from worshipping Diana or Artemis to Christ (Acts 19). Paul, as on other occasions, barely escaped with his life.

Just to the north-west of the city was one of the seven ancient wonders of the world, the Temple of Artemis (Greek) or Diana (Roman), the goddess of hunting and fertility. The temple was re-founded in the Age of Croesus, the proverbially rich King of Lydia in 550 BC. Destroyed once again, this time by fire, it was rebuilt by the Ephesians in 320 BC. Nothing remains, however, of this spectacular building, except a single lonely column. The city's multi-breasted goddess has long disappeared.

The city of Ephesus is an impressive archaeological ruin, and for the most part, a great Roman city. The road from the harbour leads to the huge theatre and then, turning right or south, Marble Street takes you to the open space of the Agora where citizens assembled for political and civic purposes. On the corner is the Library of Celsus, which was built in 110 AD. Raised on a platform, its façade is an impressive classical construction with niches for statues of Wisdom (*Sophia*) Excellence (*Arete*), Knowledge (*Episteme*) and Intelligence (*Ennoia*). Inside would have been a spacious and well-lit reading room with shelves filled with many scrolls for study. From the library, the Street of Curetes goes uphill to the Upper Agora and the Temple of Domitian. Along and behind the street are further temples, funerary monuments and tombs, rich merchant houses, baths and a brothel. Somewhere in among it all was the Hall of Tyrannus, where for two years between c55–58 AD, we are told that St Paul conversed with all who came about the truth of the Gospel, to the point where Jews and Greeks throughout the province of Asia heard the good news, and thus an important church was formed in Ephesus, also the recipient of one Paul's most remarkable epistles.

One of the most influential residents in Ephesus in the second half of the first century AD was the Apostle John. It is thought that he travelled to Ephesus from Jerusalem in c. AD 67, before the fall of Jerusalem to the Romans in AD 70. The Orthodox church believes John lived on Mount Ayasaluk near Ephesus. It is believed that he wrote his fourth Gospel there, having become aware of the three Synoptic Gospels of Matthew, Mark and Luke, and that he did so after a time of prayerful reflection and exile on nearby Patmos. One early church Father, Clement of Alexandria called it a "spiritual gospel".

Not far from the ancient city of Ephesus are the remains of a large Byzantine Basilica which was built in the sixth century over the tomb of St John. Although little of the church remains, there is a small spot, in among the ruins, which simply says "The Tomb of St John". If true, John's mortal, earthly journey ended here: on a hillside close to the ancient city of Ephesus. He had come from Galilee, followed Jesus as the Beloved Disciple for three years and, after spending many years in Judea and Jerusalem, emigrated to Ephesus. It was such a moment of reflection that gave for me greater resonance and depth to John's life. From there we headed towards the site of Mary's house, buying some succulent peaches and greengages from a roadside seller on the way.

Just a few miles from the Basilica of St John, is the site where, tradition has it, Mary, the mother of Jesus, spent her last years as an elderly woman. This tradition began only one hundred and fifty years ago when a Dutch woman had a vision of the house's whereabouts, and it has been revered ever since as Mary's final home. At least two Popes have visited it as such. The origin of the tradition is taken from the crucifixion narrative in John's Gospel, where Jesus addresses both his beloved disciple John, and Mary his mother, saying, "Dear woman, here is your son" and to John, "Here is your mother". John adds, perhaps writing from Ephesus, "From that time on, this disciple took her into his home" (John 19:26.27). In which case, the argument goes, since John went to Ephesus, Mary went with him, although she would have been of a very advanced age by then.

What was moving about this site was the prayer wall upon which so many visitors had attached prayers for family and friends and indeed the world, all stimulated by the faith of Mary, who as a teenager had rejoiced at the news that she would bear the Christ child.

The visit to Ephesus was more richly layered than I had anticipated: a remarkable archaeological site of a city that had thrived for fifteen hundred years until invading Goths and an earthquake destroyed it; a classical city, which in part embraced Christianity and gave up the worship of the fertility goddess Artemis or Diana; the final resting place of that constructed holy family, St John and Mary. There was plenty to tell Mr Happy back at base, if he hadn't heard it many times before, it might give him an even bigger smile.

Samos and Patmos

The next leg of our journey was by boat to Samos and Patmos. Both islands lie in the Aegean Sea near the Turkish coast. Once part of the Ottoman Empire, they now form part of Greece. When booking the ferry from Kusadisi to Samos, I asked the booking clerk if she had been there, seeing it was only a few kilometres from Kusadasi. "Never," she replied, as if the question were strange. "It is Greece, and we are not welcome there." I was only slowly taking on board the history of the bloody separation that took place between Greece and Turkey in 1922 (not unlike India and Pakistan in 1947), to which we shall return, and the animosity that lingers. As the boat left the Turkish harbour of Kusadasi, the Greek flag was raised.

It was only a short hop from Kusadasi to Samos Town by boat. For that very reason there are now as many as ten thousand refugees there from the east—Syria, Afghanistan, Iran and Pakistan mainly— on Samos or other neighbouring islands. They arrive in inflatables operated by traffickers, and come thereby to one the closest parts of Europe. In 2002 it was as quiet as anything. We had left our car in Kusadasi under the careful watch of Mr Happy and were now proceeding on foot. Samos is a small island, about twenty-seven kilometres long and thirteen wide. It is verdant: producing grapes, honey, figs, olive oil, citrus fruits, figs, almonds and a rich Muscat wine. In spring, the hillside on the northern side is lush with vegetation, flowers and wonderful views of the sea. We had decided to spend two nights on the island, so made first of all for Manolates, a small village to the west and high in the hills, which rose to a thousand metres at their highest, and afforded wonderful views. We took a taxi from Samos town (or Vathy) to Manolates. The houses literally clung to the steep hillside and were surrounded by the gorgeous flowers of bougainvillea, mimosa, and pelargonium. We stayed at "Studios Angela", which could not have been more welcoming. Angela lived up to her own warm-hearted and generous brochure description:

"The village Manolates with a few picturesque houses and taverns which offer local and cheap savours and the sweet intoxicating wine, is lost in the nebula of the mountain Kerki. The road amidst the deep shaded plane-trees, crystal waters and tuneful birds is fantastic. The scenery is embellished by apple-trees, pear-trees and vineyards of grapes. We have taken care of your tranquil, clean, comfortable and friendly stay in our small guest house, with rooms which are fully-equipped with house application (kitchen, refrigerator, bathroom, television). You will have fun with the occasionally barbecue in our bright green garden, you will look far away at the dark blue Aegean and the opposite Asiaminor coastline from your balcony and you will be pleased with the warm humane family relationship with us. The first time is enough to come back to us again and again we are sure of that".

Angela lived up to her billing. On arrival we were given generous glasses of raki, which might well have been "intoxicating", had not Paul, unused to drinking "on duty", thoughtfully "watered' a pot plant, causing its leaves to wilt with pleasure! The views were spectacular, and foregoing the "occasionally barbecue" we tried the "savours" of the local taverna, which seemed as though it were right out of an opera set. I half expected a pop-up opera from Verdi, given the Italians had briefly occupied the island in the war, and opera might well have been the legacy of an opera-singing Captain Corelli figure then. Suitably charmed, we had a restful night knowing all "applications" were ready at hand for a good breakfast.

The next day we did have a walk in the "nebula" of Mount Kerki. In fact, nothing could have been more lovely. Greece, and especially a Greek island in the spring, is an odyssey beyond compare. The walk on the slopes of the mountain was truly lovely; none of us had seen such huge butterflies—white and yellow Swallow Tails and Red Admirals. Even better, we came across another mountain village, Stavrinides, where we enjoyed Greek salad, moussaka and a wonderful thick coffee, before walking back to Manolates.

The next morning, we took a taxi from Manolates to Pythagorio, the main town on the southeast side of the island, from where you take the ferry to Patmos. It is a quiet town on the coast with a pleasant harbour. It takes its name from the Greek geometrician and philosopher Pythagoras (c. 570-c. 495 BC), who pre-dated Plato and Aristotle by well over a hundred years. Pythagoras combined mystical teaching about the transmigration of souls with important geometric principles, the most well-known being his theory about triangles. Here he discovered that if the longest side of a triangle (the hypotenuse) is c and the other two sides next to the right angle are a and b, then the square of the longest side is the same as the sum of the squares of the other two sides. Not only that, but Pythagoras devised a drinking vessel designed to prevent excess. If you tried to drain it quickly, nothing came out, but if you tilted it gently, a steady trickle came forth. In such a way was the excessive drinking of sweet Samos muscat wines checked! Following a meal of more moussaka and muscat wine, we took the boat to Patmos, to see the Cave of the Apocalypse.

The journey from Samos to Patmos of about fifty kilometres takes roughly five hours, although a hydrofoil, which we took on the way back, cuts the journey by half. We had booked accommodation in Patmos with Maria Pascalidis in her simple, no-nonsense pension on the edge of the main town and port, Skala. The reason for going to Patmos was that it was another step in our understanding of St John.

In the opening chapter of the Book of Revelation, we are told by the writer, "I, John, your brother and companion in the suffering and kingdom and patient endurance that are ours in Jesus, was on the island of Patmos because of the word of God and the testimony of Jesus, on the Lord's Day. I was in the Spirit, and I heard behind me a loud voice like a trumpet" (Revelation 1:9–10a). And so, begins one of the most extraordinary books of the Bible; on the one hand the happy hunting ground for religious cranks, and on the other, a glimpse of the near and far future, given to console a church facing increasing persecution at the end of the first century. Its depiction of heaven, its prophecies of judgement on earth—and on Rome in particular—and its vision of a new heaven and a new earth are all part of the final act of the biblical story, and John, through a vision on this island, was to supply it. Patmos is an extraordinary place for that reason, and a beautiful one.

What we know is that John was exiled to this small island, not so far from Ephesus where he had been living, as a punishment for his faith and for not worshipping the emperor, who in 95 AD was Domitian. Domitian was an Emperor of great vanity, irritability and duplicity (but what is new?). In *The Twelve Caesars,* Suetonius tells us: "Domitian was not merely cruel, but devious and cunning. He summoned a bookkeeper to his bedroom, invited him to share his couch, made him feel perfectly secure and happy, condescended to offer him portions of his dinner—yet had already given orders for his crucifixion on the following day!"[79] During Domitian's fourteen-year reign, persecution of Christians was ramped up, and John was exiled and given hard labour, presumably for unwillingness to worship the emperor. (Exile to an island was a common Roman punishment, and by no means the worst, unless you were like Julia, the daughter of Emperor Augustus, exiled to Pandoterina in 2 BC for promiscuity, and deprived of male company, wine and conversation, which for her was a living hell.)

Although some, like the church historian Eusebius, doubted that it was actually the Apostle and Evangelist John who suffered on Patmos and wrote the account of his vision that we know as Revelation, there is no such doubt in the mind of the Orthodox Church. Halfway up the hill from Skala to the Cave of the Apocalypse at the top, we passed the Monastery of John the Theologian. It was founded by the Byzantine Emperor, Emperor Alexis Komninos in 1088 and is heavily defensive in aspect. We were excited to meet a monk from the community there called Pachomius who told us he had previously been a monk on Mount Athos for twenty-three years where he prayed the Jesus Prayer continuously: "Jesus Christ Son of God, have mercy on me a sinner!" He told us that through repetition the Jesus prayer helped him to internalise the presence

---

[79] Suetonius, *The Twelve Caesars* tr. Robert Graves (London: Penguin 2007), p. 303.

of God, and furthermore he believed that God comes to us three times in our lives, in ways that are beyond the normal. Discovering who we were, and hearing of my interest in St John, he promised to show us around the monastery library the following day. But when it came to it, he failed to turn up. The monks are generally very hesitant about showing their treasures to strangers, and this one, it seems, was no exception. This is because in the past travellers have made off with precious manuscripts from monasteries, with the English and the Germans having a particular reputation for filching things from monasteries and elsewhere.

At the top of the hill, we went into the Cave of the Apocalypse; both the monastery and the cave are world heritage sites. It was small and dark and lit by many candles. It was a simple cave with little adornment. Few people were there, and it was entirely possible to imagine John on the Lord's Day, being given this astonishing vision, which he or an amanuensis then faithfully wrote down, neither adding or subtracting anything. If John wondered what his vision meant, and, like Daniel, reeled from its extraordinary visionary symbols, the consolation prize would have been the view outside his cave. There could be no more beautiful view of the surrounding sea than the one afforded from just outside John's cave. Azure blue water stretched away, and the distant Turkish coast could be seen. Hard days of labour must have been soothed by this view, and looking at it, one could be forgiven for thinking that "a new heaven and a new earth" (Revelation 21:1) had already come.

We had a late lunch at a small taverna near the monastery with more wonderful views, and then went back down for an evening stroll around Skala. Patmos seemed more peaceful than mainland Turkey. Walking a little way out of the town we found a place to swim in the warm Mediterranean waters—what could be more delightful—and then supper in the square. This time the moussaka was not so good, a reheat of a batch made a few days before, I suspected. But we talked about our plans for the next three days; we decided to head off from Kusadasi the following afternoon and do the tour of the sites of the Seven Churches of Asia Minor addressed in the book of Revelation. We would go first to Miletus (not one of them) and then to Laodicea, Philadelphia, Sardis, Thyatira and Pergamum. As we had already seen Ephesus, we would pass Izmir or Smyrna on the way back to the airport. It could just be done in the time, and with Paul as a police-trained advanced driver, we had every confidence we would.

The Tour of the Seven Churches

Following an abortive attempt to see the monastery library the next day, we took the fast boat back to Samos, the taxi to Samos town or Vathy, and then the boat back to Kusadasi. We were true island hoppers that day and, having collected our car, drove south to Miletus.

In its day Miletus was the principal Ionian Greek city on the Aegean coast, although as at Ephesus, the sea has now receded by a few miles. The city had an active shrine dedicated to the goddess Demeter who saved the people from eating only meat by blessing their harvests of corn and other crops from the earth.[80] The remains of the city are almost entirely Roman, and towering over all else is the immense theatre completed around 100 AD in the days of the Emperor Trajan. Like the theatre at Ephesus, it could seat an audience of twenty-five thousand, and its acoustics were said to be excellent. Around c. 58 AD the Apostle Paul came here on his way back to Jerusalem, having completed his third missionary journey. He called the Elders of the Ephesian church to meet him on the beach of Miletus, where he gave them a final stirring address (Acts 20:13ff). He committed them to the grace of God knowing that in Jerusalem he would be arrested. The account concludes movingly with these words, "When he had said this, he knelt down with all of them and prayed. They all wept and embraced him and kissed him. What grieved them most was his statement that they would never see his face again. Then they accompanied him to the ship" (Acts 20:36–38). We lingered in the theatre awhile, having read the account in Acts, and then, as the day was moving on, made tracks for Laodicea. We arrived in the evening light a short while before the site closed.

Sometimes you imagine a place from the little you have read about it, but Laodicea was nothing like my imaginings. I thought of it as a small, crowded city with a church that had become "lukewarm" in its devotion and for which it was powerfully rebuked. In fact, what we found were the remains of a city on a plateau on the side of an escarpment with huge sweeping views of mountains in the distance. Made famous by its

---

[80] Robin Lane Fox, *Pagans and Christians* (London: Penguin, 2006), p. 103.

black wool, Laodicea had become rich on its export of fabric and wool from the flocks that pastured in the vicinity. And there was a curious link to the Pre-Raphaelite artist Holman Hunt, also. Not that he ever went to Laodicea, but he did depict a saying of Christ to the Laodiceans in his pictures entitled, *The Light of the World,* each of which hang in Keble College and St Paul's Cathedral. In the picture Hunt represents Christ's words spoken to the Laodiceans, "Here I am, I stand at the door and knock. If anyone hears my voice and opens the door, I will come in and eat with them and they with me" (Revelation 3:20). It was a powerful invitation to invite Christ into the centre of a church that had become lukewarm. It was a challenge as much to me all those years later.

We stayed the night near Laodicea and first thing the following day we went to visit the hot springs at Pamukkale (Hierapolis). The rebuke to the Laodicean church of not being "lukewarm" makes more sense when you discover that, down the road, there are some important hot springs. Here is something to emulate spiritually. Indeed, the hot-water springs cascade out of the hillside at 38° C, depositing a calcareous white sediment that quickly dries and solidifies. Papias was the Bishop of Hierapolis in the late first century. He was certainly passionate in his faith, although inaccurate in his accounts of "The Sayings of the Lord" (of which only fragments remain). Yet he was part of the circle of that area, and according to Irenaeus—the great second century Greek Bishop of Lyons—Papias was known to the Apostle John and Polycarp of Smyrna.[81]

From Pamukkale we went to the next Roman site of Philadelphia, now in the modern Turkish town of Alaşehir. The remains of the ancient city of Philadelphia were very scant and hard to find. Eventually we found them. They comprised the remains of two sides of a triumphal arch in a pleasant garden with a mosque in the background, a few sarcophagi long since robbed or vacated, the bases of columns, pieces of fluted pillars lying on their sides all interspersed with flowering oleander, but with a general atmosphere of peace, as befitted a Roman city dedicated to brotherly love. Of all the churches addressed in the Book of Revelation they received unalloyed praise: "See, I have placed before you an open

---

[81] Irenaeus, *Adv, Haer. 5.33.*

154

door that no man can shut" (Revelation 3:8). For many generations that must have been true. After our visit to the site, we came down to earth with a not-to-be-repeated snack at a greasy-spoon café!

From ancient Philadelphia we moved north to Sardis and Thyatira. Sardis is a little to the west of Philadelphia, near the present village of Sart. The remains are much more extensive than Philadelphia, and with signs of great wealth. It was an important manufacturing centre in the Kingdom of Lydia, of which Croesus was the legendary King in c. 550 BC, according to Herodotus. The town made woollen products and worked precious metals, mostly silver and gold. Among temples to Aphrodite and Artemis are the substantial remains of an extremely fine synagogue with floor mosaics displaying the wealth of the Jewish community. The most prestigious building left standing is the gymnasium, with a classical façade composed of Ionic columns supporting a gallery of Doric columns, which in turn support a gracious pediment—enough to inspire anyone going to the gym for a workout! By contrast Thyatira, located by the town of Akhisar, had few classical remains left. Reproved in Revelation for tolerating Jezebel in their midst, it seems they had been compromised by a female prophet given to promiscuity, for which judgement was to come (Revelation 2:18–25).

The last site of our busy five-site day was Pergamum, or present-day Bergama, not far from the Aegean coast. Pergamum was another Greek colony, then absorbed into the Empire of Mithridates VI before being conquered by Rome in 88 BC. The town was greatly patronised by the Emperors Trajan and Hadrian and was given the status of a Metropolis, or leading city of the Province of Asia, above Ephesus and Smyrna. Some of that expansion may still be seen today in the Acropolis above the modern town. The most impressive ruins are the slender columns of the Temple of Trajan, the theatre set into the steep hill below the Acropolis and the scant remains of the Temple of Athena commanding a view over the plains below. But for me, there was a special connection. Pergamum's greatest classical structure, the Pergamum Altar, can be seen in Berlin in the Pergamum Museum. There this vast sacrificial altar, built by the Greeks in the second century BC, with its wonderful friezes, is the central feature of that extraordinary museum.

I remember visiting the museum as a boy in the early 1960s, and now, nearly fifty years later I was standing on the site from which it had been taken. It was a moment of connecting the past with the present. We then travelled a short distance to the coast and to a delightful resort just north of Izmir called Foca.

Izmir is the Turkish name of the city that once was called Smyrna. Smyrna was not only the site of another Greek and Roman colony, but was to become one of the great cities of the Levant in the eighteenth and nineteenth centuries. Now it is one of the largest cities in Turkey, with a population of more than three million and has a new Turkish name, Izmir. Little remains of the important classical city, but its history resonates down the centuries.

In the second century AD, Smyrna had a remarkable Christian leader in Bishop Polycarp (69–155 AD). Irenaeus tells us that Polycarp, like Papias, knew and heard the Apostle John speaking in Ephesus as a boy. From early on, the Christian community in Smyrna was singled out for persecution. In Revelation the church was told, "I tell you the devil will put some of you in prison to test you, and you will suffer persecution for ten days. Be faithful to the point of death and I will give you the crown of life" (Revelation 2:10). This warning could not have been more prophetic for Polycarp, who, in a wave of persecution in the second century AD, was called upon by the governor to worship the Emperor. He refused and was threatened with martyrdom. Brought into the stadium, the scene unfolded thus:

The Proconsul asked if he was Polycarp. When he said he was, the Proconsul began trying to persuade him to make a denial [that he was a Christian), saying "Have respect for your age" along with other related things they customarily say: "Swear by the Fortune of Caesar, repent and say "away with these atheists" [i.e., Christians—because they did not believe in the pagan gods). But Polycarp looked with a stern face at the entire crowd of lawless Gentiles in the stadium: and gesturing to them with his hand, he sighed, looked up to heaven and said, "Away with the [true) atheists". The Proconsul became more insistent and said "Take the oath and I will release you. Revile Christ." But Polycarp responded, "For eighty-six years I have served him and he has done me no wrong. How can I blaspheme my king who saved me?"[82]Shortly thereafter, Polycarp was burnt at the stake.

Burning was tragically to be part of the city of Smyrna's history too. In the early nineteenth century, the city would become a trading centre in the Levant. Although Ottoman, Smyrna would play host to as many as six hundred Greek ships a year and the numbers would only increase.[83] Greeks, Turks, Jews, and Armenians made up the population of 130,000 by the 1830s.[84] Soon British and French immigrants would be added to the mix, receiving concessions or "capitulations" as they were called, for trade from the Ottoman Empire. The port expanded with a new jetty called the Cordon that extended fifty yards out into the sea.[85] The fashionable *beau-monde* would promenade in the evening, and cafés and newspapers abounded. Figs, raisins, cotton, liquorice, opium and carpets were traded. Thousands of ships visited every year.[86] Schools and churches were opened. Family dynasties were established, such as the Whittals (English traders), the Girauds (French) the Effeindis (Armenians) and the Batlazzi (Greeks). Horseracing, football, theatre and publishing all came to town. And a cosmopolitan Turkish Governor, Kamil Pasha (1895–1907), held sway: speaking Turkish, French, Greek and English. Out in the bay a British or French warship was frequently anchored and could be summoned by their respective Consul to keep the peace or make a point to the Ottoman rulers. But it was all to end tragically in flames

The end of Smyrna resulted from the policies and actions of two national leaders, Eleftherios Venizelos and Kemal Mustafa (Ataturk). The former precipitated it; the latter enacted it. Venizelos was the nationalist leader of Greece who emerged out of the complex and very divisive politics of Greece around the First World War. Initially supported by Lloyd George, Venizelos began a major invasion of Turkey in 1919 to secure old Ionian Greek communities. This strategy continued

---

[82] *The Apostolic Fathers,* vol. I, Loeb Classical Library, vol. 24 (Boston, MA: Harvard University Press, 2003), p. 381.
[83] Philip Mansel, *Levant: Splendour and Catastrophe on the Mediterranean* (London: John Murray, 2010), p. 45.
[84] Mansel, *Levant,* p. 55.
[85] Mansel, *Levant,* p. 156.
[86] Mansel, *Levant,* p. 160.

in 1921 under King Constantine of Greece, the great grandfather of Prince Philip. But after initial success, and getting almost as far as Ankara, the Greek forces were checked and turned back by Kemal Mustafa.[87] By August 1922 the Greek front had collapsed, and some Greek troops committed atrocities as they retreated, sparking mounting resentment.[88] The Greek community in Smyrna was soon threatened, and the final tragedy began.

On 9 September 1922, Kemal entered Smyrna with his troops. Although at first restrained, the Turkish citizens abetted by Turkish soldiers then exacted revenge on the Greek and Armenian communities. The nationalist Greek Archbishop Chrysostomos was arrested, humiliated and tortured; his beard was cut off, and his eyes were gouged out before he was torn apart.[89] British and French nationals began to leave by way of the ships in the harbour. Then the fires began: first the Armenian quarter, where fifteen thousand perished, and then the main city down to the quays and waterfront. The fires blazed from September 13 for nearly ten days. Many thousands died, hundreds were raped, and thousands were sent to labour camps in Anatolia. The Cordon was piled with bodies desperate to escape the flames. It was said that the flames reached so high that they could been seen the other side of the Aegean on Mount Athos. The place where promenades had nightly taken place was now a charnel house. It was the end of Smyrna as it had been known for centuries: a cosmopolitan trading centre of the Levant full of vitality, culture and colour, now for the most part a heap of ash.

As we skirted modern day, Izmir, once known as Smyrna, searching, rather frantically, for the airport in the darkness of the early morning and needing a little divine help to find it, we could barely piece together all the experiences and epiphanies of the week. So much had been seen: the classical city of Ephesus, the natural beauty of Samos, the Cave of the Apocalypse on Patmos, and the sites of the seven churches of Asia Minor. There was plenty to tell the people at home and in due course a book would appear on St John.[90] And I would be soon be back in Greece, this time on Mount Athos.

---

[87] Mansel, *Levant*, pp. 209ff.
[88] Mansel, *Levant*, p. 212.
[89] Mansel, *Levant*, p. 214.
[90] Patrick Whitworth, *Word from the Throne* (Shanghai, Donghong Co. Shanghai, 2011).

Chapter VIII
To the Holy Mountain

After the success of the trip to Ephesus and beyond I was ready for another journey, this time to Athos. Some years earlier, like so many others, I had read and loved William Dalrymple's *From the Holy Mountain*. In it, Dalrymple gives an account of a journey that starts from one of the monasteries on Mount Athos. From there, and using John Moschos' anthology, *The Spiritual Meadow*, as his guide, he explores the very ancient, but equally vulnerable church of the Middle East. Moschos was a wandering monk of the late sixth and seventh centuries from Mar Theodosius near Bethlehem. While there would be no time to follow Moschos's journeyings, so well described by Dalrymple anyway, something more limited, but still revealing, could be undertaken in a week.

The plan was to fly to Thessaloniki, spend a day there and then drive to Philippi, the place Christianity first touched down in Europe. We would then go to Mount Athos for three nights before heading to Mount Olympus and the burial site of the Macedonian kings. It had the makings of another multi-layered journey: part Pauline, part monastic and part Macedonian: reaching from 350 BC to AD 950. My companions were Michael, now on his third trip with me, and Tom Peryer, the recently retired Director of Education from London Diocese, and an advocate of Academy Schools for which he had recently been awarded an OBE. Again, we met to discuss the journey and decided to set out in early May, but on Day I there was a small snag.

Tom had inadvertently picked up his wife's passport and on arrival at the security check in Bristol Airport, the official gave him an old-fashioned look and in best officialese said, "Sir I don't think this is your passport, I imagine it's your wife's". Blanching, Tom realised his predicament. There was not enough time to go back to Bath from Bristol and retrieve his own passport and still make the flight, so we had to leave without him! On the plane Michael and I made mental bets as to whether he would come at all. I believed he would, and sure enough, the next morning we received a text to say that he would be arriving in Thessaloniki at seven thirty a.m., having caught an overnight flight to Athens and an onward connection to Thessaloniki. He had barely missed anything, just an evening in Thessaloniki—the wonders of modern travel. We picked him up in our hire care and spent the day in Thessaloniki.

Thessaloniki or Salonica

Michael and I had arrived in Thessaloniki in the early evening after picking up the hire car, and found our accommodation near the centre of town. From there it was only a short walk to the water's edge, for the city is situated on the Thermaic Gulf in the North Aegean. The location could not have been more splendid. It was a warm day; the city was alive at the evening hour; the atmosphere was animated and people were filling the waterfront cafes and restaurants. But, as is so often the case with great cities in this part of the world, be it Smyrna, Alexandria, Beirut, or Istanbul, the brilliance of the location masks the troubled reality of its history. It is easy to be serenaded by the easy charm of a city and forget the route it has taken to get to where it now is, and what it has lost along the way.

Like Constantinople, Thessaloniki (or Salonica) has a Greek, Roman, Slav, Byzantine, Venetian, Ottoman and Greek past, and the change-overs from one to another have often been steeped in violence. As well as that, the three Abrahamic faiths, we so often see wrestling each other in the Middle East, are intertwined in these periodic struggles as well. Jews, Muslims and Christians all have their own histories, and agonies in Thessaloniki.

The origins of the city are Greek and then Roman. Thessaloniki was in fact the name of the daughter of Philip of Macedon, the half-sister of Alexander the Great. Her husband, General Cassender, founded the city in her honour in c. 316 BC, giving it her name. By 168 BC, Thessalonica was part of the Roman province of Macedonia. It would remain in the Roman Empire, first as part of the Roman Republic, and then as a part of the Eastern Empire after Diocletian had divided it, during which time Emperor Galerius ruled in Thessaloniki. In Theodosius's time (379–395), it became the second city of the Eastern Empire. It lay on the Egnatian Way linking Rome to Constantinople, was an important garrison for troops, and the administrative centre of the empire. In many ways these transitions of power are not just the story of this city, but also the story of the region as a whole.

Thessalonica was also a Christian centre. St Paul founded a church here in c. AD 55 on his second missionary journey taking the gospel to Europe. He wrote two compelling epistles to the Thessalonian Christians, modelling virtues in Christian ministry and allaying anxieties about the *Parousia* (the Second Coming of Christ) and the destiny of Christians beyond death. Later, during times of persecution, Demetrius, a Christian whom Galerius executed, became the patron saint of the city. And much later, in the ninth century, the indefatigable missionaries Cyril and Methodius travelled from Thessalonica, becoming missionaries to Slavic peoples to the north, and giving them the Cyrillic script and Orthodox faith.

From the ninth to the fourteenth centuries, during the decline of Byzantine power in the region, Thessalonica fell prey to a succession of Byzantine, Bulgar and other local rulers, and after being taken by the Venetians in 1423, fell to the Ottoman Sultan Murad II in 1430. The city was then incorporated into the Ottoman Empire for over four hundred years. One of the most important events for the future was the arrival of thousands of Sephardic Jews, fleeing both the Inquisition in Spain during the reconquest of Andalusia and the edict banishing Jews enacted by Ferdinand and Isabella in 1491. Large numbers of Jews came to Salonika, as indeed many went from Salonica to Constantinople.[91]

The city from that time became part Muslim, part Greek Orthodox Christian and part Jewish, and with the relatively light touch of the Ottoman Empire towards minorities in this period they co-existed effectively, creating a prosperous and diverse city, typical of the Levant. But with the nationalist movements that followed the Napoleonic wars, all that was about to change. Although much of Greece was liberated

---

[91] Mark Mazower, *Salonica: City of Ghosts* (New York: Harper Perennial, 2004), pp. 46ff.

from Ottoman rule in 1821, Thessaloniki and Macedonia remained under Ottoman control. Suppression of any attempts at independence in Macedonia were brutal, so it was only a matter of time before further rebellion against a weakening Ottoman Empire would bring liberation from the Turkish yoke. Thessaloniki was at the centre of these events.

At the turn of the twentieth century, the movement for constitutional reform in the tottering Ottoman Empire was pioneered by the Young Turks in Thessaloniki. The Sultan was forced to accept the government of the Three Pashas during the period of the First World War. Furthermore, the eventual leader of Turkey, Mustafa Kemal (Ataturk) came from Thessaloniki. If on the one hand the city fostered revolutionary Turkish action, it was also the apple of the eye of the Greek government. And in 1912, during the second Balkan War, the Ottoman governor of Thessaloniki surrendered to a Greek insurgency.

In the First World War, Salonica became the centre for Allied operations in the area against the Germans, Austrian-Hungarians, and Bulgarians. Then, in 1917 there was a devastating fire in the city, and, following the First World War, the separation of Greeks and Turks. This division of Turks mirrored what happened in Smyrna, except here it was the Turks who were ejected and thousands were forced to flee. (For an insight into this event see the vivid novel, *Birds without Wings,* by Louis de Bernières.) Equally, hundreds of thousands of Greeks from the Turkish mainland and Pontic communities now settled in Thessaloniki. The ethnic change of the city was given a further tragic twist during World War II, when the very large Jewish population, dating back to their first arrival from Spain in 1480, was wiped out by Nazi pogroms in the area. A city typical of the Levant, with a racially mixed population, a culturally rich heritage, and wide mercantile interests, became a still beautiful, but more signally Greek city of more monochrome culture.

In our half-day there we saw some of the great sights: the Arch of Galerius and the Rotunda, the Church of St Sophia, the remains of the Roman Agora and the Church of Agios Dimitrios. But we had another important task to perform and that was to obtain the passes needed to admit us to Mount Athos, which we did not yet have, and without which we would not be allowed onto the Holy Mountain.

Tom and I had been on the quest for these passes for a number of weeks before our departure, but had made only partial progress. In the first instance, I had discovered that priests in holy orders (outside the Orthodox Church), had to apply for permission to His All-Holiness the Ecumenical Patriarch of Constantinople for an *evlogia* or written permission to visit Mount Athos. I had in fact obtained this through the good offices of the Bishop of London, Richard Chartres a good friend of the Orthodox Church, but now the three of us needed a further document granting us permission to enter Mount Athos, and according to my *Pilgrim's Guide to Mount Athos* only ten passes were issued each day for those not belonging to the Orthodox Church.

Tom had applied to the Bureau for Pilgrims for reservations, but had been told there were none left. We still had none on our arrival at Thessaloniki; nevertheless, we made for the Executive of the Holy Mount Athos's Pilgrim's Bureau on Egnatia Street. Before we went there, we visited a church called Hagia Sophia (Holy Wisdom), for some needed wisdom and help! Hagia Sophia dates back to the fifth century, and although rebuilt several times, its oldest parts could be older than Justinian's Hagia Sophia in Constantinople. Its great dome has a remarkable mosaic of the Ascended Christ.

While in the church we met a middle-aged man called Giorgio, who turned out to be a highly skilled carpenter making furniture for churches and only recently back from Athos himself. Michael got talking to him about our visit and said that we had come to Thessaloniki to go to Mt Athos, but did not yet have our passes. Giorgio said he was a good friend of an official, Christos, who worked at the Pilgrim's Bureau, and would accompany us there! He explained our predicament to Christos, whom Tom had contacted from England, and who now said he would give us two documents or passes, but that I must apply for the third pass in the office at our point of departure at Ouranopolis—i.e., letting it all go down to the wire. We looked at each other, we needed three! I sensed this was a test of our patience, so saying many *eucharistos* (thank yous), we left. Over a coffee with Giorgio, we were assured that all would be well at Ouranopolis. While at the Bureau, we were also given further instructions for getting to Mount Athos. We had to take the two reservation permits we had obtained and present them at the Bureau at

Ouranopolis (in Greek: literally the Heavenly City). There we would exchange them for a *diamonitirion* which entitles the bearer to hospitality from a list of monasteries on Athos. But before we did that, we had a previously arranged assignment: to go to Philippi and see the place where Christianity arrived in Europe around 55 AD.

Philippi

We left Thessaloniki in the late morning to drive to Kavala, (once called Neapolis), the nearest town to classical Philippi, and where Paul had landed from Samothrace (Acts 16:11) on his way to Europe from Troas. It was about one hundred and twenty miles along the fast, coastal road, and we stopped on the way for a picnic lunch of bread, olives, feta and fruit, arriving in Kavala in the evening. Kavala was a pretty seaside town, and the old town had steep, narrow cobbled streets. The next day we made for Philippi, which was about ten miles north.

Philippi was the chief town of the Roman Province of Macedonia. It was here that Paul came to preach the gospel for the first time in Europe. It was a significant Roman colony, and nearby Octavian (later the Emperor Augustus) and Mark Antony had defeated Julius Caesar's assassins, Brutus and Cassius, in 42 BC. In Philippi, Paul went first to a riverside place of prayer, where, among others, Lydia the purple seller believed. Paul was then imprisoned for delivering a fortune teller of an evil spirit, because this damaged her owner's income. He experienced an earthquake whilst in gaol, but evangelised the Philippian gaoler and his family. By the time he left, a church had been formed out of this diverse community: a businesswoman, a gaoler and his family, a slave who was once a fortune teller and no doubt a few others. Such were the origins of the European church! Who says it was not diverse? We saw the theatre or agora, with its remaining pillars, colonnade, and mountains in the background; the prison cell (or what was left of it!) where Paul and his companions were gaoled; and various Byzantine churches. We read the account of Paul's time there, then left for Athos, taking the inland route through the town of Drama, which certainly lived up to its name in terms of scenery.

We were on our way to Athos and its entry point of Ouranopolis.

When we struck the sea and followed the beautiful coastal road to the peninsula of Athos, we passed Stagira, the birthplace of Aristotle, who had been the tutor of Alexander the Great. Indeed, our own journey could be summed up as a search for wisdom: the wisdom of the Greeks epitomised by Aristotle and Plato—with Aristotle searching around him and Plato within him—and the wisdom of Paul, who preached that the foolishness of God is wiser that the wisdom of men (1 Corinthians 1:18). Now we were keen to explore the wisdom of the Holy Mountain on prayer. Such thoughts were enough to prepare us for the Holy Mountain.

Mount Athos

We were to spend three days on Mount Athos. The maximum time open to most pilgrims from outside the Orthodox church is four nights, but three fitted our timetable well and seemed an appropriate number. Before a very pleasant night at Ouranopolis, we had to get our *diamonitirion*. I still did not have a letter from the Pilgrim's Bureau at Thessaloniki granting permission, but on phoning, we were told the reservation was forthcoming, and so each of us received our *diamonitirion*. All was well. That night there was a procession through the town; our hotelier, who was also the mayor and as rotund as you might expect for one holding such an important office, led the procession along with the local priest. It was a very charming Greek community moment!

The origins of Athos as a Holy Mountain go back a thousand years. By the tenth century, the monastic tradition in the Orthodox Church was at least seven hundred years old. Egypt, Syria, Palestine and Cappadocia all had strong monastic traditions, and in the West, Benedict of Nursia had begun the Benedictine Rule from around 510 AD, heavily influenced by the eastern tradition through Cassian (360–435) who had settled in Marseilles. Legend has it that Athos was bequeathed to the Virgin Mary. It is *her garden*, her personal domain, and as such she is the only woman to be venerated there, hence the all-male population that even extends to domestic animals.

In Coptic and some Orthodox theology, especially in the *monophysite* doctrine of Cyril of Alexandria, which stressed the divine nature of Jesus, Mary is *theotokos*, meaning the Bearer or Mother of God.

Consequently, there are many icons devoted to Mary in the monasteries on Athos. Although there is evidence of individual hermits living in isolation on the peninsula from the ninth century, it was a monk called Athanasios who founded the first monastery on Mount Athos in 961. It was called the Great Lavra and began what is called Athonite spirituality with its devotion to Christ, Mary and prayer. The peninsula was given special protection by the Byzantine Emperors and from the tenth century was settled by monastic communities.

The peninsula of Mouth Athos is a kind of monastic republic with its own administration, although geographically still part of Greece. It is fifty-six kilometres in length, and stretches from the place of Xerxes's Canal in the north, close to where it joins the mainland, to the tip, which is occupied by the Great Larva Monastery and its estate. Down the middle of the peninsula is a range of hills and mountains, climbing to Mount Athos, which near the top rises to nearly seven thousand feet. The terrain consists of wild mountainous hillside, inaccessible coastal inlets, steep gorges, dense vegetation of low shrubs, wooded peaks, small streams and rivulets, chestnut trees, pine trees and rocky scree. Around the well-fortified monasteries are areas of farmland, olive groves, beehives (the queen is permitted since she is wild!) vegetable plots and some farm animals (male only). All this is framed by a deep blue sea and frequently a cloudless sky. In summer, the temperatures are hot; in winter, freezing cold. So, it is here that some twenty principal monasteries, and other *sketes* and hermitages are scattered across the peninsula for prayer, community life, instruction, hospitality, and spiritual engagement on behalf of the world. It is here that monks in harsh, but beautiful surroundings have chosen for over a millennium to assemble to pray, either on their own or in community. Every pilgrim's experience will be both similar and distinct: the variety created by the different communities, the time of the year, the personal spiritual journey of each pilgrim, the conversations between pilgrims and monks, the worship and individual prayer. It is an experience both purging and renewing, and to start with, a little strange.

Like everyone else, one arrives at Mount Athos by boat, travelling from Ouranopolis to Daphne on the west coast. It is a two-hour trip along the coast with opportunities to see several monasteries from the boat. The most arresting is the now Russian monastery of Panteleimonos, with its green rooves and Russian onion domes on its *katholicon* (chapel), which was taken by the Russian Orthodox church from the Greeks in 1839. Being Russian, it has by far the largest capacity: space for fifteen hundred monks. President Putin has apparently visited it on more than one occasion! Now about fifty monks permanently reside there, just a fraction of the three hundred and sixty-two monks in the Great Lavra monastery.[92] Yet life in the Russian monastery was not always eirenic. In 1913, a group of Russian monks rebelled against their Prior at Serai, another Russian community, over the issue of the correct way to address God. All that is now left of Serai is a shell and rows of skulls in the charnel house![93] The Tsarist government at St Petersburg sent three gunboats to quell the rebellion. Some bystanders were wounded and eight hundred and thirty-three monks arrested. The Patriarch in Russia was outraged when he heard of it. When we alighted at Daphne, and caught a rickety bus to Karyes, the central town of Mount Athos, it was thankfully all very quiet and peaceful, with no gunboats to be seen!

To be honest, Karyes had a rather Klondike feel to it, that is, a bit like a male-only mining town. The absence of the female touch was everywhere felt, especially when it came to shop windows. Try as they might, the monks who ran the shops evidently found window-dressing a bridge too far; there was nothing appealing about the way the wares were presented. But then we weren't there for retail therapy; in fact, we were there for quite a different kind of cure! But it was the only "town" on the Peninsula and the only shops. There is a sort of central track or spine along the peninsula and we took a bus north towards Vatopedi, our first monastery, walking the last part of the journey.

Vatopedi is one of the largest monasteries of Mount Athos, and is situated on the north-east coast of the peninsula. The legend is that the young son of Theodosius I, Arcadius, was shipwrecked off the coast, but the boy was saved when caught in a bramble bush, which in Greek is *vatopedi (vato* — bramble bush, *paedion* — child). In reality, the monastery was founded in the tenth century after Great Lavra (Monastery) at the time King Edgar was crowned King of England in

[92] Graham Speake, *Mount Athos* (New Haven, CT: Yale Publishing, 2007), p. 174.
[93] Speake, *Mount Athos,* p. 159.

Bath. It is a mixture of a Byzantine fortress, a spiritual campus and a hive of industry and prayer. It has its own harbour, kitchen garden, vineyard, olive grove and farm. Like a castle, with a great courtyard, a Byzantine bell tower and large gatehouse, it is as impressive in structure as it is in prayerfulness. At the gatehouse we showed our *diamonitirion* to the man on the gate and were allowed in and shown to the guest house.

On arrival we were given a drink of *ouso* and some *loukami* to eat, and shown our quarters up in the attic of a newly-refurbished guest block. A huge amount of work had been undertaken to develop and maintain the extensive buildings. It reminded me of the continuous work of maintenance and development that goes on at an Oxford or Cambridge College or a cathedral. With a bit of time before Vespers, we walked down to the beach where a newly constructed wooden shelter provided shade from the hot sun before it set on the other side of Athos. The house martins flew in and out of their nests in the roof, the sea was blue, placid today and inviting. It was truly idyllic and peaceful.

We returned to the monastery for Vespers, where the monks were hastening to the *katholicos* or church where prayer and worship is the centre of the community's life. Attired in their black full-length robes, black pillar box hats and fine beards they seemed to glide swiftly and noiselessly around the buildings. Prayer was announced, not by a bell, but the smashing of one piece of wood against another called a *simantron*. It became a familiar, yet strangely insistent sound.

A monk's life is divided into a threefold rhythm of prayer, rest, and work. The prayer or worship is mostly in the morning (early) and evening. Vespers is the last service of the day beginning at six p.m. and preceding the evening meal. The *katholicos* (1312) was dark after the bright sun, with numerous golden candelabra hanging from the ceiling and some large freestanding lights. Many icons are venerated by the faithful on the *Iconostasis*—the screen behind which only the celebrating priest presides. Remarkable bands of frescoes depicting Christ's life, that of the Virgin, and an array of saints and wooden seats surround the ceilings of the main church. In Vatopedi there are seats in the centre of the church too. The service is sung by a monk, but we caught only some of the Greek, such as *kyrie eleison* (Lord have mercy) among long stretches of liturgy. At the end of the service the holy relics are brought out: fragments of the true cross, the skull and preserved ear of John Chrysostom, a finger of John the Baptist encased in silver, the preserved withered arm of a monk who had damaged an icon (a warning!), part of the reed on which Jesus was offered a sponge of water at his crucifixion and the girdle of the Virgin Mary. The orthodox pilgrims come forward and receive prayer and a blessing in the presence of these relics, and are given a prayer card for any friend or relative who has been prayed for.

After Vespers we went to the Refectory, the second most important building in the monastery. It was very old, twelfth century, with seats around small stone tables and metal plates. We ate vegetable soup, some fish, feta cheese and a little watered-down red wine. The meal was eaten in silence, while listening to a reading from the Church Fathers (which we couldn't understand). At the end, the Abbot rang a bell, and the monks left first with the pilgrims forming a guard of honour. The impression was one of discipline and order.

After the meal we mingled with other guests and some monks, meeting them and hearing something of their stories. There was a French monk who once had run a restaurant in London, and in his spiritual journey from restauranteur to monk was greatly assisted by Michael Harper, whom I knew as the founder of SOMA (to which we will come) and who had become an Orthodox Priest, having previously been an Anglican. By contrast, Tom met a fellow Greek pilgrim who was a submarine engineer and desperate to find a wife. At least he had come up for air, but of course it could only be a prayerful search at Athos! We learnt that HRH Charles Prince of Wales had his own room in the monastery and the novelist Geoffrey Archer had been there, perhaps for inspiration! We went to our quarters by ten p.m., for we had an early start at four a.m.

The main prayer in the *katholicos* is from four a.m., which then leads into the Eucharist or Liturgy. In many ways the prayer from four a.m. is a preparation for the liturgy of St John Chrysostom at six thirty a.m. We arrived in darkness and gradually, with the lighting of candles and the arrival of dawn, the church lightened. Different monks took it in turns to lead the service; monks came and went. The liturgy is the centre of the Orthodox faith, together with the teaching of the Fathers, and it is by digging into the significance of both that renewal has come to the wider community. This occurred through the Kollyvades movement, embraced by St Nicodemus of the Holy Mountain, and which published the fourth century work of the *Philokalia* in 1782. "Indeed, the *Philokalia* has acted as a spiritual 'time bomb', for the true 'age of *Philokalia*' has not been the late eighteenth century but the late twentieth century".[94] And in the dark days of Ottoman Rule and Nazi occupation "it was the Holy Liturgy which kept Orthodoxy alive",[95] together with the writings of Symeon the New Theologian and Gregory Palamas, of whom there is a near contemporary portrait in Vatopedi. Indeed, one might argue that what they did for Orthodoxy, Ignatius Loyola did for Roman Catholicism and John Wesley for Anglicanism. In those early hours we were witnessing the lifeblood of Orthodoxy on display in the sacrament and the words of the ancient liturgy that surround it.

After a breakfast in the refectory of brown bread, cucumber, tomatoes, salty olives, peanuts, and halva, we collected our gear from our quarters and made for the harbour to catch the boat that would take us towards Iviron. There is a harbour at Iviron, one of the oldest, senior monasteries on Mount Athos. It was founded for the Iberians or Georgians, who also had become followers of St Athanasios, in the Caucuses in 980.[96]

As we did not have a reservation there and wanted to make more progress south, we kept walking. Passing a *skete* with two or three monks and a helper, we stopped for lunch. We ate our provisions and were given a glass of ouzo after several glasses of water, as we were hot from the journey. We walked on to Karakalou. If Vatopedi represented the grander, larger monasteries on Mount Athos, Karakalou was much smaller, with about fifty monks. It nestled in the hills, smiling, and welcoming with its geraniums, roses, and other plants in pots around the walls. Not used to the large numbers of pilgrims of Vatopedi, we were kept more at arm's length, and as non-Orthodox were restricted to the narthex in the *katholicon,* reprimanded for indecorous behaviour when we crossed our legs, and had to eat separately from the monks. A young Finnish monk who spoke English kept an eye on us, and earlier I was told by another

[94] Timothy Ware, *The Orthodox Church* (London: Penguin, 1997), p. 100.
[95] Ware, *The Orthodox Church,* p. 101.
[96] Speake, *Mount Athos,* p. 55.

that Anglicans were heretics for altering the Nicene Creed! So perhaps the smiling *outside* the monastery was not fully reflected by the messages *inside*. Nonetheless, we enjoyed our stay. After Vespers we ate bean stew and an orange, and cheerfully went to bed.

The following day we gave the early prayer service at four a.m. a miss, but arrived for the liturgy at seven a.m. Breakfast of pasta and feta cheese was eaten in silence. Afterwards we made our plans for the day and decided to go to Simonopetra, the most dramatically situated of all the monasteries overhanging a cliff in the southern part of the peninsula. As it was near the tip of the peninsula, the trip involved going back to Karyes, and then taking the rickety bus to the small port of Daphne and from there a boat. You get used to Athos's travel system of boats, buses, and boots. Simonopetra had its own landing stage, and as we arrived in the early afternoon, we could see its walls rising sheer above the cliff, about a thousand feet above us.

Simonopetra was first founded in the fourteenth century by a Serbian prince and rebuilt in 1567. It had been the brainchild of "the most worshipful Lord Oxiotis Agas", an official at the court of Wallachia or present-day northern Romania, and had also received patronage from Stefan the Great of Moldavia by the Black Sea.[97] Princes of Wallachia continued to give their patronage to the monastery, especially after a devastating fire in the sixteenth century. As with other monasteries, support would come to Athos from kingdoms far away: Iviron from Georgia, Chilander from Serbia, Panteleimonos from Russia and Stavrinikita by the Phanariot prince of Wallachia, Sherban Cantacuzino. In other words, Orthodox churches from Byzantium, Greece, Georgia, Romania, Serbia, and Russia founded monasteries on Athos, and these monasteries waxed and waned with the fortunes of those nations and national churches: sometimes dynamic, sometimes hitting *stasis*.

As we stepped out of the boat onto the landing stage at Simonopetra and looked up, the cliff face and walls of the monastery towered above us. Once upon a time the way in was to be pulled up in a basket and in through a window of the monastery. Thankfully we could walk, even though in the midday heat! When we eventually arrived at the entrance after a steep climb, we were told that they were full, there was no room

---

[97] Speake, *Mount Athos*, pp. 127–9.

at the monastery (not having been able to make a reservation before), so there was nothing for it but to walk back down again, and continue along the coastal path for a few kilometres to Grigoriou. On arrival at this monastery, likewise perched on a cliff above the sea, we waited anxiously for an hour to see if we would be admitted, otherwise it might have to be a cave on the cliff face—a true hermit's existence—but in the end we were welcomed. We were allocated Room 2 in the guest wing, with breath-taking views across the sea, looking west, and a balcony as well. Tom had smuggled in a bottle of wine in his knapsack, so we were all set for a final evening on Athos.

Gregoriou was also founded by a Serbian prince in the late fifteenth century, but much more recently in 1974 it had undergone a period of spiritual renewal. This meant a renewed commitment to community or coenobitic life, a clear organisation of duties, an openness to pilgrims, an Abbot who ruled the community well and contributed theologically to the wider church, and an aspiration to increased inner spiritual growth among the Fathers. In other words, the more demanding and purposeful the Antonite "rule" was, the more likely the community would gain the new recruits on which its future rested.

Gregoriou was middling in size, but seemingly purposeful, relaxed, and integrated as a community. It had a lovely courtyard with a well at the centre covered by a shelter decked out with frescoes of the great well-stories of the Bible—I could feel a sermon series coming on! Hearing the clack of the *simantron* we went to Vespers, followed by a supper of tomatoes, courgettes, and potatoes, with some stewed peaches for pudding, and this time without a reading. Afterwards, we sat on our balcony mulling over the day and watching the sun setting over the sea and the Sithonia peninsula, some forty kilometres way.

The next day was Sunday and we got up for the four-a.m. service and liturgy. The combined services proved to be five hours in duration and took us to an important Sunday breakfast, which formed part of the overall worship. Tom ventured further into the *katholicon* from the narthex, but was firmly escorted back to sit with uncrossed legs in the narthex! We ate cheese pie, an apple and had some red wine for breakfast. There was a reading throughout the meal. The refectory, with its views over the sea, its marble pillars and arcades with frescoes made for a beautiful and airy setting. But when it came to sharing consecrated bread as part of breakfast, as non-orthodox we were not allowed to participate. As breakfast continued beyond nine thirty a.m., we thought we had missed the water taxi at the quayside, but we need not have worried. The taxi was late and when it arrived it was full and so we waited a further two and a half hours for the next ferry! Athos has its own time, rhythms, conventions, and timetable, which gradually takes over your own. The wait on the quayside and the four-hour journey by boat to Ouranopolis afforded plenty of time to reflect on our three days there, and to read.

When the writer John Julius Norwich came to Athos in the 1970s, he wrote that with declining vocations at the monasteries "the unanswerable fact is that Mount Athos has become an anachronism", but you can't be too sure.[98] In the first half of the twentieth century there was a steep decline in vocations in the twenty monasteries, from 7,432 in 1903 to 1,171 in 1971—the loss of six thousand monks, but since then there has been a steady rise to 1610 in 2000 and almost a fifth of those are in Grand Lavra.[99]

Two things are fundamental to the health and growth of the monastic life. The first is the validity of this search for tranquillity, inner peace and a deeper knowing of God in Christ. In the fourteenth century this path was challenged in the so-called Hesychast controversy, which questioned the validity of a life dedicated to a search for *hesychia* or tranquillity, both in the individual, but also on behalf of the church in the world. The controversy produced some profound responses, notably from Gregory Palamas, the Archbishop of Thessaloniki (1347–59), which bolstered the ancient Orthodox theology that God may be *known*, but remains *unknown* beyond our *knowing*. Exploration of that *Cloud of Unknowing* may be made through prayer and in turn can resource the understanding, mission, and life of the church. Some of the great teachers of the church, such as Gregory of Nyssa, Evagrius of Pontus, Clement of Alexandria and especially Pseudo-St Dionysius, a fifth century Syrian monk, and Maximus the Confessor, taught the efficacy of this path of prayer. Such a life of prayer, focussed in the Jesus prayer— "Lord Jesus Christ Son of God, have mercy on me a sinner"—is not only valid, but it is the core of

---

[98] Speake, *Mount Athos*, p. 169.
[99] Speake, *Mount Athos*, p. 174.

Athonite spirituality. As long as this remained at the centre, uncorrupted, Athos would flourish. Movements of renewal in monasticism, stimulated by the example and teaching of particular individuals such as Fr Theoklitos, author of *Between Heaven and Earth*, Fr. Vasileios of Iviron, and Fr. George of Grigoriou, have had good effect. Such men have attracted new vocations to the monasteries, especially the much-desired younger vocations.[100]

Furthermore, many of the monasteries have in recent years taken a step from the *idiorrhythmic* to the *cenobitic* system of monastic life, that is, a movement from the individual *(idiorrhythmic)* way of the monastic life to a common *(cenobitic)* way of life based on poverty, chastity and obedience to the Abbot. As noted earlier, the countervailing truth appears to be that the more that is demanded, the healthier the response; whereas the less that is demanded in terms of corporate commitment, the more fragile the response. Of course, there were *sketes*, or hermitages where individual monks lived, pursuing their own individual vocations as solitaries, and we could see these dotted along the coastline, but in a monastery, *common purpose* seemed the *sine qua non* of vitality.

Monasteries that pursued a combination of genuine worship expressed in the liturgy, communal prayers, a pathway of personal growth and holiness, together with a role of teaching and spiritual direction and openness to pilgrims, were most likely to flourish in a world craving tranquillity and beauty. There was no need to be gloomy about the future. As always, the quality of future vocations would have within them the seeds of the Holy Mountain's renewal.

As we waited for our ferry to take us back to Ouranopolis, I leafed through a book I had brought by Henry Chadwick, the Dean of my old Oxford College, entitled *East and West: The Making of a Rift in the Church*. The rift referred to is between the Orthodox churches of the East and the Latin Church of the West, including both Roman Catholic and Protestant churches. It came about through the rivalry of Old Rome and New Rome (Constantinople), because of the way the West changed the creed to include the statement that the Spirit proceeds from the Father *and* the Son (and not simply the Father, as stated at Nicaea) without agreement; through the sack of Constantinople in the 4th Crusade in

---

[100] Ware, The *Orthodox Church*, pp. 130–131.

1204; through the breakdown of relations between Cardinal Humbert of Rome and the Patriarch Michael Cerularius in 1054; and as a result of the final break at the Council of Florence, 1439. We had experienced what that break meant on the ground—at times we were excluded—but was it too much to hope and pray that Athos would also be a place of healing, and that the past would not define the future?

We left Athos both thoughtful and entranced. There is nowhere else quite like it. Back at Ouranopolis we picked up the car and drove to the other side of Thessaloniki for the night. The weather had broken and a sudden storm enveloped us. The following morning, we drove part of the way up Mount Olympus, Greece's highest mountain at nearly ten thousand feet, and walked among its profusion of wildflowers. We wandered through the ruins of the Greek city of Dion and then drove to Berea (Veria), somewhere the Apostle Paul visited after being thrown out of Thessaloniki (Acts 17:10ff). It now boasts seventy churches and is called "little Jerusalem". Finally, we went to Vergina, the burial site of the Macedonian kings. It was here that Philip II, the father of Alexander the Great, was assassinated at the wedding of his daughter Cleopatra. Only recently discovered, the tombs have yielded remarkable gold jewellery including exquisite gold-leaf diadems with filigree as fine as a spider's web.

These tombs brought our visit to a close: Thessaloniki or Salonica, Philippi, Mount Athos, and Mount Olympus. The self-imposed exile of the monks on Athos brought to my mind the theme of "exile": an important theme in the Hebrew scriptures and a ready metaphor for describing the church on the margins of society in the west. Once again travel was the companion of reflection. Back in our beds in Bath that night, it was a reflection that would shape future writing.[101]

---

[101] Patrick Whitworth, *Prepare for Exile* (London: SPCK, 2009).

Chapter IX
Into Africa

Many of my generation will have watched the film *Out of Africa,* based on the compelling story of Karen Blixen, whose Christian name, Karen, was subsequently given to a suburb of Nairobi near the Ngong Hills. The opening line "I had a farm in Africa..." spoken in English, but with a Danish lilt, has become a classic one liner—even if lagging a little behind as a film one-liner, "I don't give a damn", uttered by Clark Gable in *Gone with the Wind.* The acting of Meryl Streep early on in her career, the sweeping cinematography of East Africa, and the romance of Karen Blixen and Finch Hatton set to Mozart in the African bush all made for a decidedly European take on Kenyan life, but one that nevertheless left a lasting impression.

I had first gone to East Africa in 1973 and would go again with my family in 2002, but in between I joined SOMA (Sharing of Ministry Abroad), an organization which, at the invitation of African bishops, sends teams to bring encouragement and renewal to dioceses in Africa. I led my first team in 1992 and have led twelve since, three to Nigeria, the rest to Malawi, Tanzania, Kenya, Uganda and South Sudan, and to some of these countries more than once. In this chapter I want to recall two of these visits with a purpose: one to Nigeria and the other to South Sudan—both countries with huge challenges, courageous people and erratic governments.

Nigeria

In 1991 the Bishop of Aba, Augustine Iwuagwu, and his wife Grace stayed with us for two weeks at Gipsy Hill. Looking back, I am not quite sure how Olivia managed it, as we had four small children including one-year old David. The following year I was invited to lead a team to Aba in Eastern Nigeria and then again in 1995 to the Diocese of Bauchi.

Nigeria was the creation of the British. It owes its early exploration and commercial exploitation to what might be called "gunboat trading", exercised by Edward Hewett on behalf of the National African Company operating in the Niger and Oil (Palm) Rivers of the region in the 1880s.[102] Led by Sir George Goldie, in 1881 the company had been given reluctant permission by the Gladstone government to trade in the Niger region. It traded Manchester cotton fabrics, old rifles and other goods for palm oil.[103] As was frequently the case in Africa, entrepreneurial and forceful colonialists badgered an oftentimes-reluctant Liberal government under Gladstone to give British protection to commercial, and expansionist projects, not conceived or driven forward by Whitehall, but by colonial adventurers on the ground. Never was this more the case than in 1890, when Leander Jamieson, encouraged by Cecil Rhodes, and guided by the hunter Frederick Selous, pushed north from the Transvaal in South Africa to occupy present-day Zimbabwe.[104] On that occasion a Conservative government led by Lord Salisbury was more amenable—and hence the name of Salisbury in Zimbabwe (now Harare). By 1897, the Salisbury government had appointed Lord Lugard to consolidate the various trading British Protectorates in West Africa and Nigeria to stymy French and German interests in the region. The Northern and Southern Protectorates of Nigeria were joined together and Lugard became the first Governor of Nigeria in 1914. By 1960 Nigeria was independent, but forming this varied country, with its large Muslim and Christian populations, into a single entity was never going to be easy and by 1967 Nigeria was riven by a tragic civil war.

There are four large people groups in Nigeria, along with many smaller ones. The main groups are the *Igbo* in the east around Port Harcourt, numbering over thirty million and almost entirely Christian; the *Yoruba,* a people group of both Christians and Muslims of over forty million in eastern Nigeria around Lagos and Ibadan, and also in neighbouring countries like Benin and the Ivory Coast; the *Hausa,* a group of seventy-five million people spread through north-western Nigeria and sub-Saharan Africa, with a Sunni Caliphate based at Sokoto

---

[102] Thomas Pakenham, *The Scramble for Africa* (London: Abacus, 2010), pp. 191ff.

[103] Pakenham, *The Scramble for Africa,* p. 192.

[104] Pakenham, *The Scramble for Africa,* p. 374.

in the north west; and the *Fulani,* a Muslim people of about fifteen million pastoralists spread through the Sahel region, including Northern Nigeria. These diverse groups of people were put together by the British as Nigeria.

Christian missions, particularly the Church Missionary Society, had been active in the region from the end of the slave trade in 1807. One Igbo, Olaudah Equiano, had himself been active as an abolitionist in England, and, encouraged by the movement for abolition, had published *An Interesting Narrative of the Life of Olaudah Equiano* in 1789 (which went through nine editions), in which he writes from personal experience about the horrors of the slave trade and how as a boy he was shipped from West Africa with two hundred and forty-four others to Barbados. He served there as a Lieutenant in the British Navy, but was eventually freed by an American Quaker and found his way to England. There, having become a Christian, he joined the abolitionist cause. He was supported by the redoubtable Countess of Huntington and married an Englishwoman, Susannah Cullen, with whom he had two daughters. What an extraordinary story! But he wasn't the only Nigeran to make a lasting impact. The other great figure of the Nigerian Mission was Samuel Ajayi Crowther (c1820–1891), whose story was also connected to the slave trade.

Ajayi was the descendent of a Yoruba king, Abiodun. He was captured by Fulani slave raiders and sold to the Portuguese in 1821. Intercepted by a British naval vessel, the Portuguese trader was boarded and Ajayi, together with other members of his family, were set free at Free Town, Sierra Leone. He was cared for by members of the CMS in Sierra Leone. His abilities, especially in languages, were soon recognised, and he was taken to England where he was baptised, taking the name Samuel Crowther after the vicar of Newgate! He later returned to Nigeria, began the translation of the Bible into Yoruba, which was completed in the 1880s, went on several British expeditions up the Niger in the 1850s, and then, towards the end of his life, began an Igbo Primer and Bible translation. He founded the Niger Mission in 1857 and the Bonny Mission in 1865.[105] Samuel was consecrated as the first African

---

[105] Augustine Iwauagwu, *The History of the Anglican Church in Ngwaland* (Awa, Nigeria: Educational Publishers, 2000), p. 1.

Bishop of the Anglican Communion in 1864, was granted a DD by Oxford University, and read the Lord's Prayer in Yoruba in the presence of Queen Victoria, who remarked on the melodiousness of the language! His son Dandeson served as an Archdeacon in the delta region of Port Harcourt, where he acquired land for a church and school building through the British Commissioner for Lands in the 1920s.[106] Dandeson knew the remarkable Scottish missionary in nearby Calabar, Mary Slessor (1848–1915), who famously stopped the infanticide of twins among the Igbo people.

If this is some of the background to missions in Nigeria, which now boasts the most populous Anglican church in the entire Anglican Communion, as well as the largest national population in Africa, it did not come without struggle and awful pain. In 1967 Nigeria fell into civil war, which was to lead to a single word—Biafra—with desperate images of starving children, resonating in Britain through the first collaboration of hunger relief and rock culture. This was to come to an abiding crescendo much later with Band Aid in 1984 with *Do they know it's Christmas?* prompted by the famine in Ethiopia, performed by Bob Geldof, and written by Midge Ure, whom, as it happens, we would later meet at a school prizegiving in Bath.

In 1967, however, Britain was gripped by the images of a terrible civil war in Nigeria and of children bloated by starvation with matchstick limbs. The plain facts were that the substantially Christian East and the Igbo people wanted to secede from the newly-independent state of Nigeria, taking with them the oil (petroleum) production around Port Harcourt (itself the cause of human rights' abuses in the region of the Niger Delta). The Federal Nigerian government, supported by the British government, blockaded the area with devastating results: the starvation of families and children that affected between five hundred thousand adults and two million children, civilian deaths, and a further one hundred thousand military casualties. The war dragged on for three years (1967–1970). When I went with a team to Port Harcourt and the Diocese of Aba in 1992, it was only twenty years since the ending of that shattering civil war and it was still remembered well.

The Diocese of Aba had been formed twenty years before in 1972,

---

[106] Iwauagwu, *The History of the Anglican Church in Ngwaland*, p. 5.

and Bishop Augustine had taken over the reins in 1987.[107] Augustine, like Crowther, was a linguist and had completed the huge task of translating the Bible into Igbo. What I remember of the visit in 1992 are the packed churches; the very warm welcome; the exchange of kola nuts, which is an Igbo sign of greeting; the speeches made at the drop of a hat; pounded yam and cassava galore; and taking a team, some of whom had barely been out of South London before, into a completely different culture. Thus, on arrival at security at Port Harcourt, the security officers in uniform held your passport, expecting a bribe before returning it! After all, we were perceived as rich Westerners, while they were in poorly-paid posts with large families and relatively few opportunities for adding to their income. We did not encourage the habit, but it was a shock to see just how brash it was. It was a different mindset, a different culture and a different world. And in many ways, it was a preparation for another visit to a very different area three years later.

In 1995 I was invited to go with another team, this time to Northern Nigeria, to the Diocese of Bauchi. If the great rivers of Nigeria—the Niger and the Benue—form a Y stretching up towards Lake Chad in the east and to Mali with its famous proverbial capital of Timbuktu in the north west, then Bauchi lies somewhere close to the centre of the Y, in a semi-arid sub-Saharan landscape. Our host was Bishop Emmanuel Chukwuma, a man not slow in coming forward, and who had taken on this new diocese four years before. Jos Diocese was to the south on the plateau and Kano to the north, which was where we had arrived on our flight from England. As I looked out of the aircraft windows, I was impressed more than ever with the Sahara Desert, and its immense and inhospitable expanses. And I found myself surprised that here and there life is supportable in these deserts of southern Algeria and Niger which were passing below.

Six of us arrived at Kano airport: Alan Goddard, Evelyn Ighamre, Emma Kimberley, Peter Rouch and John Lamb. Apart from myself and Evelyn, none had been to Nigeria before. It was an adventure. A blast of hot air in the high 30s Celsius hit us when we stepped off the plane and walked across the tarmac to the single passenger building. We were met by the bishop, who whisked us off to Bauchi, about a hundred and fifty

[107] Iwauagwu, *The History of the Anglican Church in Ngwaland*, p.13.

miles south. Bauchi is almost the size of Wales, but without the green hills and sheep! It was a Hausa area, although some Igbo people had moved north into the towns and formed the basis of the church there. Our programme over the next week was varied and interesting. On Sunday I spoke in the Cathedral, and together we took meetings of young people, youth leaders and clergy. Some church services were as long as three hours. Collections might include the offering of a goat led bleating up the aisle and then tethered outside. One day we took a day conference on leadership for around forty clergy and lay leaders. And at the weekend, members of the team travelled about seventy miles on the very slow and rutted roads to the extremities of the diocese—places like Gombe in the east, Azare in the far north and Boi in the south west. Top speed on parts of these roads might be only 5mph, so travel took a long time. These Christian communities were in the Styx and hardly ever saw anyone from Bauchi, let alone from South London! Their churches could not have been simpler: breeze blocks and a corrugated steel roof on a good day, otherwise just a tree. The pastor's house was often very cramped. They were frequently not paid at all and existed on gifts from the congregation and produce from their very meagre patch. A pastor would be fortunate to have more than three books. We had novelty value, but I hope we brought some encouragement also.

Alongside these opportunities for mutual encouragement, with our talks translated into either Igbo or Hausa, there was important work to be done as advocates for the church in Bauchi to the Muslim leaders there. In 1991 religious' riots in the area were caused by rumours that Christian butchers were trying to sell pork to Muslims, which sounded almost like the cause of the Indian Mutiny. That such things could cause riots, death, and the burning of property in the late twentieth century came as a revelation to me. Yet it had a particular resonance, because in the religious riots that followed, the Cathedral had been burnt down, and was still just a burnt-out shell. To mitigate persecution, the bishop had arranged a number of key visits to leaders in the city to create the impression that the churches in Bauchi had wider contacts in the UK, something that might help their standing. These visits were to the military governor of Bauchi State, to the local Emir or Muslim Ruler and to the State Radio Station for an interview.

We were ushered into the State Governor's main meeting room, with plenty of very well-dressed flunkeys in flowing robes and Nigerian fezzes acting as ushers—there is never a shortage of people in Nigeria, which at nearly two hundred million now has the largest population of any country in Africa. There was an atmosphere of quiet deference and power in the room which we don't often find in England! I was ushered to sit next to the State Governor, whose official title was His Excellency Naval Commander Rashid Raji, and who was dressed in full naval uniform and gold braid. He was a long way from any ship in Bauchi! After we were all sat down around a table as big as I have ever seen, with nearly thirty people around it, including our team (who were intrigued as to what would happen next), the speeches began. Bishop Emmanuel introduced us and then it was my turn. I thanked them for their welcome, explained the purpose of our visit was to maintain links between the churches of the Anglican Communion, and then, chancing my arm a little, added that Her Majesty's government was looking forward to the restoration of democracy and the replacement of the military government! I knew this to be the case as it had been expressed in the House of Commons the week before we left. I then presented the Governor with a copy of *Basic Christianity* by John Stott, pointing out that John was a Chaplain to Her Majesty the Queen, and therefore, by implication, this was a very good book (which it is). His Excellency responded by saying that reading was one of his interests and he would read it for a better understanding of the Christian faith. After some refreshments and some further conversation between our team and the officials, we left. The bishop judged the visit to have been a success. I thought it was the nearest I would come to representing, without them knowing, HMG and felt I had missed a career in the Foreign Office! We then moved on to meet the Emir.

The Emir is the traditional African ruler and a Muslim. Throughout Africa there are two layers of government or influence: the national and the traditional. In Uganda there are traditional kings still, and in West Uganda near the Ruwenzori mountains, there is a King of the Rotoro people whose palace is near Fort Portal which I have visited. These traditional rulers still have real influence in their regions, but the executive power belongs to the national government. The Emir was a traditional ruler who lived in a large clay or mud coated house, wore traditional clothes of robes and a turban, and was presumably the leading Muslim figure in the community and a leader of the Hausa in the region. The meeting had none of the frisson of the Military Governor's reception and the agenda was much more one of "it is good to be there, we appreciate the welcome and our hope is that Christian and Muslim communities can live peaceably together". It seemed to go well, although the Emir was fairly inscrutable.

In West Africa and the Sahel in recent years, as in the Middle East, some Muslims have of course become radicalised. Neighbouring states like Mali, Burkino Faso and Algeria are dangerously infiltrated by extreme Muslim groups. In Nigeria since 2002, Boko Haram (meaning: Forbidden Education), have become a malevolent influence in the region, both for the government and for the Christian population. Located in the north-east corner of Nigeria in Borno Province, the group has ready access to Chad, Niger, Cameroon, and not so far away, Sudan. Members can slip away too easily into a neighbouring state to evade capture or detection. The kidnapping of two hundred and seventy-six girls from their boarding school in Chibok in 2014 was the nadir of Boko Haram's activity: at once cowardly, and at the same time terrifying and tragic for the girls. The group seeks to destabilise the area through suicide bombings, kidnappings and terror.

Our last port of call in the city was the state broadcasting radio station. The radio stations were then mouthpieces for the government, and the previous interviewee had been a Major General from the capital Abuja, no doubt speaking for the military government. Our message was much the same as before: we were thankful for our welcome, and hoped for peace in the city, and restoration of democratic government. The bishop seemed pleased with our words, so much so that he made me a commissary for him in the UK, and a canon of Bauchi Cathedral. I am not sure what a commissary does, and I must have been the only canon of a burnt-down shell of an Anglican Cathedral with nowhere for anyone to sit, let alone a canon!

When we boarded the plane home after so many varied experiences, we at times had to pinch ourselves that it had all been real, so different was it from life in South London. Although I went once again in 2000 to

Nigeria's Owerri Diocese at the invitation of Cyril Okorocha, I have not been back since. But in 2013 I went to the newest country then in the world: South Sudan.

South Sudan

In the nineteenth century it seems that almost every European country "had to" scramble for a part of Africa. The French took over countries in the North— Morocco, Algeria, Tunisia, Chad—and almost all of West Africa, apart from Nigeria, Ghana and Sierra Leone, which were held by the British. The British occupied Egypt, controlling the Suez Canal and the sea route to India, and were still expanding south, taking East and Southern Africa in the 1890s. The two Empires (French and British) met in an Imperial stand-off in 1898 at a small town on the White Nile, now in South Sudan, called Fashoda (now Kodok), north of Malakal. The French were expanding to the East and the British further south into the Sudan to join up their East African colonies of Uganda and Kenya with Egypt, in order to create a continuous red line from Cairo to the Cape, a route that had become an explorer's dream (see Ewart Grogan's book *From Cape to Cairo*, which tells of a journey that took this twenty-five-year-old adventurer two and a half years).

Meanwhile the King of the Belgians had established a rapacious regime in the Congo, portrayed in Conrad's novel *Heart of Darkness*, and after 1918 took over Rwanda and Burundi. The Germans held Tanzania and Namibia till World War I; the Portuguese held Mozambique and Angola; and finally, the Italians had Libya. It is worth remembering this when China is criticised for involvement in Africa now. It has been done before, nor was it benevolent.

Sudan has figured strongly in British colonial history. The names of General Gordon, the Mahdi, the fall of Khartoum, the Battle of Omdurman, Winston Churchill and Kitchener all feature in the story. General Gordon was reluctantly sent by Gladstone's government to suppress the Muslim revolt led by the messianic figure of the Mahdi in Sudan, and to reverse the earlier destruction of an Egyptian army under British command in 1883. Although Gordon reached Khartoum, he was soon surrounded by the Mahdi's forces, which were called the *ansar*. A relief force was sent by General Wolseley in Egypt, but arrived too late. Khartoum had been taken, a slaughter ensued, and wearing his Governor's gold-braided uniform, Gordon died a hero, fighting on the steps of his palace. For the public at home Gordon was a Christlike figure resisting Islam, and Gladstone was perceived as Judas. Such was the humiliation that the event nearly brought down Gladstone's government. Queen Victoria showed her displeasure and a further army was sent from Egypt under General Sir Herbert Kitchener—of *Your Country Needs You fame*—to punish the Mahdi. At the Battle of Omdurman, Kitchener inflicted punishment; there were 30,000 Sudanese casualties while the British suffered only around four hundred. Winston Churchill took part as a lieutenant in the 21st Lancers, and was critical of Kitchener's merciless attitude to prisoners and the desecration of the Mahdi's tomb. Sudan was by then a household word in Britain.

The future of the Sudan was fraught with problems. It was initially governed by the British as a joint protectorate with Egypt. In 1956, after three years of self-government, Sudan was given independence. In such a vast and diverse country, the differences between north and south soon dictated the future. The Islamic north sought to govern the Christian south. The tribes of the south resented interreference from the north, and eventually the bitterness escalated into civil war. In fact, almost continuous civil war resulted with Anyanya I (1955–1972) and then Anyanya II (1983–2005). Anyanya means poison. For much of the second period of civil war the north was led by President Omar al Bashir (1989–2019) and the Sudan People's Liberation Army was led by the charismatic figure of Dr John Garang from the Dinka tribe. Dr Garang wanted the south to be a loosely-federated nation within Sudan, in which all of the elements of South Sudan might be merged. But there were uneasy alliances in the SPLA, especially between Garang, and then later Salva Kiir Mayardit, and Riek Machar from the Nuer tribe, who had a different vision of a fully independent South Sudan. Sometimes this tipped over into bloody ethnic violence between the tribes, and indeed led to separate military organisations. From 1989 –2019 Omar al-Bashir led a military dictatorship in the north, using the Janjaweed to brutally supress the Darfur region through rape and massacre, whilst at the same time intimidating the south. The civil war between north and south eventually concluded with peace talks and a referendum for Independence was agreed which was overwhelmingly carried in January 2011, with South Sudan formed in July 2012.

Over the years there had been a lot of Christian missionary activity in the south, and there was a small, vulnerable, but active Anglican church in the North. Roman Catholic missions first came to the country in 1842, led by Daniel Comboni, the Vicar Apostolic of Central Africa, who founded the Verona Brothers and Sisters to work there. Other Protestant missions, the Sudan Interior Mission (1893), and the Sudan United Mission (1904) had been at work in Sudan for a century. Christian Missionary Society Missionaries eventually reached Sudan, and in 1905 Llewellyn Gwynne was appointed Archdeacon of Sudan, under the overall jurisdiction of the Archbishop of Jerusalem. Thereafter 139 CMS missionaries worked in Sudan between 1905–1964.[108] In other words, there is a rich legacy of Christian work, with many dioceses and schools established, albeit living precariously during protracted periods of civil war and continuous shortages.

In March 2012, in the weeks just before Easter, a small team of three of us went to Maridi in South Sudan. Maridi is a town to the west of Juba, not far from the Congolese border. It had been the focus of previous visits in much more difficult circumstances. Don Brewin a previous Director of SOMA had been there in February 1999 when the civil war between North and South was ongoing. On that occasion, while teaching a seminar in the diocesan compound, six bombs were dropped by an Antonov aircraft circling low over the town! The visitors escaped and were able return to teach their seminar entitled *"Discerning the Spirit of God in the Midst of Chaos"*, a very appropriate seminar for the times!

Our small team consisted of Janet Darg-Forsyth who had been to Sudan several times before and was a mother of four, Nigel Rawlinson, an A&E Consultant at the Bristol Royal Infirmary, who was also ordained and working with me as an associate minister at All Saints, Bath Weston, and myself. We flew to Kampala and had two nights at the Mission Aviation Guest House there meeting, among others, Harriet Ntegeka, a gifted worship leader and singer. This was a necessary stop, because at that stage there were no direct flights from London to Juba, the new

---

[108] Don Brewin, *It Will Emerge* (Self-published 2002), pp. 649 ff.

capital of South Sudan, plus we needed twenty-four hours in Kampala to obtain a visa to enter South Sudan. This we did, and used the time both to prepare our teaching for the forthcoming conference in Maridi and visit the Mulago Hospital in Kampala and the cathedral with its famous Namirembe ("Full of Peace") Guest House nearby.

We noted the memorial in the cathedral to James Hannington from Hurstpierpoint in Sussex, who, after one visit to East Africa, had in 1884 been consecrated Bishop of Eastern Equatorial Africa by Archbishop Benson. He arrived at Mombasa and proceeded to go inland. By then King Mwanga II of Buganda had become suspicious about incursions by Europeans into his kingdom and Hannington and his group were arrested. They were all speared to death. Hannington's final words were "Go tell Mwanga, I have purchased the road to Uganda with my blood". Myanga was received into the Anglican Church while in exile in the Seychelles in 1900, taking the name Daniel. Since then, the Ugandan Church has become well known for its courage in the face of persecution. Thus, in the years of Idi Amin, Archbishop Janani Luwum became a modern-day martyr in 1977. His statue occupies one of the niches on the west front of Westminster Cathedral, which is reserved for twentieth century martyrs. Having been issued with our visas, we left the following morning to fly to Maridi with the Missionary Aviation Fellowship. It was a dramatic journey.

The flight from Kampala to Maridi took us over some of the most spectacular scenery of the Great Lakes' region of East Africa. We took off from Kampala airport, from whence the Missionary Aviation Fellowship flies. The MAF, supports thousands of development, aid and missionary organisations throughout the world and transports much needed medical care. It is said that there is a MAF flight taking off or landing somewhere in the world every four minutes, and is this the busiest airline in the world. Our Swedish pilot began the flight with a prayer and off we went. Leaving Lake Victoria to the South we headed north-west to Lake Albert and the great river system of the Nile, passing close to Murchison Falls where the White Nile moves through a narrow canyon issuing spectacular spray. (I was later to visit these Falls following a Mission in Hoima, Uganda, in 2015.) Flying north-west, we crossed into South Sudan with the Congo to the west and landed on the simple grass landing strip at Maridi Airport. The arrivals and departure lounge was a hut with a corrugated steel roof, there were no formalities just goats grazing in the grass.

In late March the temperature is hot in the high 30s Celsius. The landscape was still green, dotted at regular intervals with huge mango trees whose fruit was eagerly awaited in just a few weeks' time. Tracks led off from the rutted roads to villages of tukels made of brick or mud walls and thatched roofs. There are places where wells have been dug providing clean water, and where women and children congregate in the evening with their colourful plastic buckets. We stayed in the diocesan compound in our own individual tukels with a central bathroom that had shoulder-high walls and a bucket of water. Water was delivered by a bowser each day and we ate together in a common room in the centre of the compound. There were some long-term missionaries there, like Lynn Treneary, and several UN workers with their white 4x4s and UN markings parked around. It was a reminder that the country, just a year on from independence, was coming out of a protracted civil war.

Maridi is in a fertile area with several different people groups in the state and at least eight different languages spoken. Juba Arabic is the *lingua franca*. Most people exist through what they can grow, and a small percentage of people are employed or have a salary. The leadership of the diocese was both talented and committed. The Bishop, Justin Badi Arama, was travelling on behalf of the Archbishop of South Sudan for much of the time we were there, but since then has become the Archbishop of South Sudan in 2018 with a huge task. In 2012 he was ably supported by others in his team in Maridi, including Archdeacon Tito, Captain Gerusoma and others. They hosted us for ten days.

What could we bring to a war-torn country from comfortable Bath must be a question that is going through your mind? After all, in twenty years of civil war nearly two million had lost their lives. Yet all in our visits, and in the many others made to the Congo and to South Sudan by SOMA, the fact that we *have come at all* is in itself seen as a message of solidarity, of prayer, of fellowship and of encouragement. The links formed by our forebears are still cherished, and their sacrifice in coming with the message of Christ—and often losing their lives through disease in the process—are not forgotten, or passed over lightly. We were there for two Sundays, and on the first I preached in the large brick-built cathedral with Bishop Justin present. I spoke from Second Isaiah 40 and those words so well known to us from Handel's Messiah, "Comfort ye, Comfort ye my people". First spoken to the Jewish people coming out of exile in Babylon, they are words that offer reassurance, hope and comfort. During the week, from Monday to Friday, the three of us led a conference for thirty: mostly clergy and youth leaders. Our themes were restoration, forgiveness, leadership, and the role of women in the church and nation. All these themes were vital for rebuilding the country. One night a young man came called Emmanuel came to our community room in the compound. His brother had been part of the SPLA army, had become an alcoholic, and was often aggressive. His father had died, his mother had AIDS and would not take treatment. We talked and prayed. Another had a very sick child; there being so little medical care, he had taken the child to the witchdoctor and felt guilty at having done so. We prayed for peace and blessing for him and his family. In a moving moment we wrote all our burdens on paper and placed them at the foot of a home-made wooden cross and sang together. We were strengthened. We were encouraged and there was renewed hope for the future.

At other times during the week, we went to the local Haddow School, named after an Englishman who gone there as a missionary and died from malaria. There were seven hundred children in the school in bright magenta uniforms. We spoke, and presented them with some footballs. They sang and danced in the dusty open-air playground in the way that only African children can. We went to a local clinic or dispensary where Nigel could practise his medical skills, and we were shown round this two-room surgery. Grateful for drugs provided by Diocese of Salisbury, its resources were nonetheless meagre. In the coronavirus pandemic there are presently only four ventilators in a country of eleven million people. On the final Saturday we went to the neighbouring Diocese of Ibba a little to the west, where we met Bishop Wilson who had come to the conference. He spoke about his diocese and then he showed us the house where the Lord's Resistance Army had abducted the diocesan youth worker. The Army is a rebel movement in Northern Uganda, South Sudan and the Congo. Now largely on the wane, the LRA kidnapped children, turning them into child soldiers for their cause of anarchy and violent disruption, and causing them deep psychological damage.

The tragedy is that since our visit the country has descended further, this time into internal civil war, largely on ethnic grounds between the Dinka and Nuer peoples and their leaders—both pastoralist tribes with age-old feuds. This lasted until February 2020, when a new transitional government was formed. The war consumed a further four hundred thousand lives. Archbishop Justin Badi estimates that nearly eighty per cent of the population has been displaced either internally, or to refugee camps in Northern Uganda. Once again, the country experiences the long uphill struggle to rebuild. In Maridi there was some fighting, but many of the same faithful people in the churches are rebuilding their fragile communities and give some cohesion to such a fractured society. In 2019, Omar al-Bashir was deposed in Khartoum to face justice for atrocities in Darfur amongst other things. Could it be a new beginning? There have been many false dawns.

Before we returned by MAF flight to Kampala, we had a day out near Maridi, going to the amusingly-named nearby town of Bingo which lay on the edge of the Lantoto National Park on the Congolese border. It was a large area of forest stretching as far as the eye could see. There were no paths and if you ventured too far into the forest from the road then almost certainly you would get lost, and never come out again! We flew back to Kampala thoughtful and humbled by the difficulties and courage of the people we had met. And then it was on to Nairobi where our flight to Heathrow was delayed by twelve hours. It was another night in Nairobi airport before arriving back to the different world of Britain, with much to think about.

Other SOMA visits would follow, to Western Uganda, called Bunyoro Kitara, to Nairobi and Nakuru (twice), to Kenya, Malawi and Tanzania. Paul Bright and Jo Skinner were often on the team, as were Francis Awando and Georgia Omwa from Nairobi and Tom and Wiola Hola Peryer from Bath—all up for an adventure, as well as others besides.

While in Uganda I was mindful that in 1900 there had been a scheme to make the country a home for the Jews. In 1900 the British Colonial

Secretary Joseph Chamberlain offered Theodore Herzl, a founder of the Zionist movement, land in Uganda as a homeland for the Jews such was the imperial mindset of Chamberlain. The offer was not accepted, but of all the struggles in the world, perhaps there is none greater than that of Israel to fulfil its destiny, and to this we now turn.

Chapter X
Israel: Then and Now

It was 27 September 1979, our first full day in Israel, not three weeks since our wedding in Kingsclere, Berkshire, followed by a honeymoon on the west coast of Ireland in Connemara. We were standing on Mount Scopus in the bright morning sunshine, and it was going to be a hot day with temperatures expected to reach the high thirties Celsius. We were looking south towards Jerusalem's Lion's Gate and the Dome of the Rock on the Temple Mount (Haram al-Sharif), the gold dome of the Al-Aqsa Mosque catching the sun that was still rising behind us. We were having an orientation day, after arriving the evening before for a ten-week course put on by St George's, Jerusalem. I was in between curacies and we had been given the opportunity to attend this course, which was to prove foundational for the next forty years of work. I was even offered a job at St George's College as part of the teaching staff four years later.

From the vantage point of Mount Scopus next to the Hebrew University, we went past the Augusta Victoria Hospital built by Kaiser Wilhelm II's wife of the same name, to the Mount of Olives facing the Temple Mount. Between the two mounts lies the Kidron Valley, with its surround of tombs below the walls of the Mount. The Jewish belief is that when the Messiah comes, the just will rise from their graves and be led through the Golden Gate, which is presently all bricked up. Going past the road leading "from Jerusalem to Jericho", we went around the City of David, or the Silwan, and over the valley of Gehenna to the Jaffa Gate where we disembarked from our minibus with fellow course members for an afternoon walk around the old city. As we entered, to our right was the Armenian Quarter and beyond it the Jewish Quarter leading to the Western or Wailing Wall of the Temple Mount. To the left of the Jaffa Gate was the Christian Quarter with the Church of the Holy Sepulchre. That site is shared by a bewildering array of churches: Greek Orthodox, Roman Catholic, Armenian Apostolic, Coptic, Syriac and

Ethiopian Orthodox. The Via Dolorosa, the Patriarchates of the Copts, the Latins, the Greek Catholics and other churches besides are nearby. Then, beyond the Christian Quarter and beneath the Temple Mount is the Muslim Quarter.

Arriving in Jerusalem is a bewildering experience: both thrilling and daunting at the same time. How are we to understand this multi-layered, multi-textured city and land over which more blood has been spilt, and more hopes raised and dashed than almost any other? Jerusalem is both a synonym for paradise and a symbol of unresolved conflict. To start with, we need the perspective of the past in order to hope to understand the present. The story of the Jewish nation and Jerusalem is a long and complicated one, but a survey may be helpful.

The History of Palestine from c.2500 BC to 1979

Palestine has been settled for at least six thousand years. Megiddo (Armageddon) in the north near Haifa has been inhabited since the early Bronze age of 3500 BC. By the time of the middle Bronze age, around 2000 BC, Palestine was settled by the Amorites and Canaanites. The Amorites were a Semitic people who had drifted west from Mesopotamia to dwell in Palestine where they worshipped the god Amurru. The term Canaanites was a catch-all name for the Semitic peoples who lived in the region.

At some point around 1880 BC, Abraham, a wandering Aramean from Ur of the Chaldees—identified with present-day Nasiriyah in southern Iraq on the Euphrates a little north of Basra—met with God. A calling by God to depart for a land "I will show you" (Genesis 12:1) marked the beginning of God's covenant with Israel. By degrees Abraham emigrated to Palestine, basing his family at Beersheba in the Negev. Eventually he secured an heir called Isaac, the father of Esau and Jacob. Jacob, although the younger son, succeeded through the connivance of his mother Rebekah. Jacob had twelve sons through four wives, including his favourite Joseph. And it is Joseph who was sold into slavery in Egypt by his brothers who provides the way out from famine for the family, and the way into a tempestuous future.

The Israelites became slaves to the Egyptian Pharaohs from c.1650

BC to 1250 BC. This is a period of time covering some of the greatest Pharaohs in Egypt: the Queen Hatshepsut (1478–1458 BC), Thutmose III (1458–1425 BC), Amenhotep III (1388–1351 BC), Akhenaten (1351-1334 BC) Tutankhamun (1332–1323 BC) and Ramses II (1279–1213 BC). Some of these, notably Tutankhamun, have become very familiar to us. And perhaps it was during the great builder Rameses II's reign that the Israelites- now well over a million people from the original sixty immigrants who had come with Jacob to escape famine four hundred years before- left Egypt in the Exodus led by Moses, the lawgiver.

The period from 1250 BC to 597 BC was for the Israelite nation a period of a few peaks and many troughs, ending in destruction and exile. The struggle continued. For forty years the Israelites wandered in the desert. Formed as a nation by the experience of slavery, by deliverance through Moses, through desert wanderings and through receiving the Law or Torah, they occupied the promised land after defeating the Amorites. Yet they never completely rid the land of the pagan practices. The brew of exploitation of the poor, sexual licence and pagan worship t would continually dog them. High points were the Kingship of David, and the early years of Solomon's reign, but neglect of the Law and the wilfulness of rapacious kings took their toll. Solomon built a magnificent Temple in Jerusalem of which the Western Wall, rebuilt by Herod, remains; but this was no insurance policy against national tragedy. The Kingdom was divided into the Northern Kingdom, Israel, with its capital at Samaria, and the Southern kingdom consisting of the tribes of Judah and Benjamin, with its capital at Jerusalem. Both kingdoms would fall to regional powers: Samaria to the Assyrians in 722 and Jerusalem to the Babylonians in 587 BC. The struggle continued.

Before the destruction of Jerusalem in 586 BC, ten years after its capture by the Babylonians, many thousands of Israelites from the ruling elite went into exile. The period of exile covered about seventy years and was a time of purging and purifying for the Jewish community.

When the Jewish exiles returned first during the reign of their Persian overlord, Cyrus the Great (c 540 BC, and see the Cyrus Cylinder in the British Museum) and then in the reign of Artaxerxes, the nation found its future, if not its autonomy. Jerusalem would still be a pawn in the regional power play: first the Macedonian Greeks, then the Seleucid

Empire, and finally the Romans all governed Jerusalem. Occasionally, there would be unremitting opposition from Jewish nationalists. Thus, in 166 BC Judas Maccabeus led a revolt against the Seleucid King Antiochus Epiphanes IV out of which came the Hasmonean Monarchy. The Hasmoneans were the ancestors of Herod the Great who became a client king of the Romans and received his *imperium* from Octavian, later called Augustus, in 30 BC. Twelve years later Herod began rebuilding the second Temple and just before Herod died in 4 BC, Jesus was born in Bethlehem.

During this period, Messianic expectation of someone who would come and deliver the Jewish people increased. Jewish sects proliferated. The Qumran community in the desert was formed: committed to purity, frequently praying and washing, and copying the Jewish Scriptures with painstaking care and producing what we know as the Dead Sea Scrolls. At the same time, the Pharisees and the Hassidim immersed themselves in the Jewish Law, while the Sadducees pursued a more Hellenised, rational and elite form of Judaism. Then around that time a new unlikely group formed around Jesus the Nazarene, born in mysterious circumstances, a teacher and healer who claimed to fulfil the prophecies of Isaiah and who taught a new righteousness summarised by the Beatitudes and that heralded another Kingdom, but not of this world. He was crucified by the Romans, delivered over to them by the Jewish leaders and the mob. So now in Jerusalem there are not just the remains of the Temple but an empty tomb as well.

In AD 70 the Temple was destroyed. Once again, the Jews rebelled against their Roman masters. Legions were sent from Antioch under Titus and Vespasian, both of whom would become Roman Emperors. And as Jesus predicted (Matthew 24:1–2), Jerusalem was encircled, the Temple burnt to the ground (as recorded by Josephus in his *Jewish War* VI), and the city was destroyed. After a further revolt in 135 AD the Jews were now excluded from their own city except for twice a year. A temple was built to Jupiter on the Temple Mount. Jews increasingly made their future away from Palestine in the Diaspora where they had been spreading for over two hundred years. Indeed, it was in Alexandria that their scriptures were definitively collected and published in Greek by seventy Jewish scholars in the mid second century BC.

The church then grew. Initially seen as a Jewish sect, it increasingly diverged. But it was led at first by Jews: Paul a converted Pharisee, Peter, James and John, fishermen from Galilee. Their writings formed the scriptures of Christianity. They envisaged a new community of Jew and Gentile, inheriting not land but the promises of God (Ephesians 3:6 and 2:11–22). Yet they were persecuted remorselessly. Less accommodating even than the Jews to Roman paganism and Emperor worship, they became the new scapegoats of the Roman Empire,[109] until one Emperor, Constantine, had a vision of Christ before a battle at Milvian Bridge in Rome in 309. Soon after, through the Edict of Milan in 313 AD, Christian worship was tolerated. Indeed, Constantine built churches in Rome, Palestine, Jerusalem, and in his new city of Constantinople, raised bishops to the purple, remitted their taxes and made them judges.

With Christianity now accepted, even patronised in the Empire, Christians flocked to Palestine. The emperor's mother, Helena, built churches at Bethlehem and at the Holy Sepulchre. Pilgrims from Bordeaux and one Egeria from Italy travelled to the Holy Land. Jerome (c347–420), Paula and Julia Eustochium settled in Bethlehem in a monastic community. Jerome translated the Bible into Latin there (the Vulgate), while loading criticism on his opponents. But with its new-found room to breathe, division came to the church. Firstly, there was the controversy over whether the Son was the same substance (*homoousios*) as the Father, which argument, although settled in theory in the Nicene Creed (325 AD), continued to divide the church for a hundred years. More serious in its consequences was the controversy about how to define the nature of Christ as both God and Man. The Nestorians, following Nestorius the Archbishop of Constantinople, believed that Jesus had two wills: one human, one divine. The Alexandrians and North Africans believed that Christ's human nature was incorporated into his divine nature and called themselves *monophysites*, while Christians in Rome and many in Syria and Constantinople believed the human and divine wills of Christ were perfectly and co-equally intermingled, and this was best expressed in the Chalcedonian definition of 451 AD. The Chalcedonian definition could not heal the divisions, however. The

---

[109] See Tertullian's *Apology*, TANF, vol. III.

Nestorians went East becoming the Church of the East establishing themselves in Assyria and Baghdad and even reaching out to China, planting communities in Singan—memorialised by the Nestorian Stele of 781, now in Xian's Beilin Museum, and recording the arrival of Christianity in China in 635, bringing "luminous religion".[110] The *monophysite* churches included the Syrian, the Coptic, the Ethiopian and the Armenian Apostolic, and were separated from the others. Whereas the Orthodox churches, the Roman churches and the Melkite Syrian churches held to the Chalcedonian definition, the others did not. Yet all of them would now seek a presence and representation in Jerusalem and the Holy Land, making a bewildering assortment of churches which are there to this day.

Amidst all this debate, controversy and confusion, a new voice was raised in the deserts of Arabia, in Medina and Mecca, which would profoundly change Israel and Palestine: the arrival of Islam. The Prophet Mohammad lived from 570–630 AD. Although there was a brief revival of Byzantine power in Jerusalem in the seventh century under Heraklion, the newly-motivated Arab forces submissive to Allah arrived and conquered Jerusalem in 638. It was now a three-way struggle between the Jews, the Christians and the Muslims, with religious aspirations focussed on a single city, Jerusalem, and its surrounding countryside of Palestine. By 692, Caliph Abd al Malik Ibn Marwan had built the Dome of the Rock, the second holiest site of Islam after Mecca, and then beside it his son Walid built the Al Aqsa Mosque for more everyday worship. The Temple Mount had been turned into a holy Islamic shrine.

For the coming centuries Jerusalem would be controlled by different Muslim dynasties, apart for the relatively brief period when Jerusalem and Palestine came under Crusader control. From 660, Jerusalem was controlled by the Umayyad dynasty of Damascus. They deputed Muawiya to be governor of the Holy Places in Jerusalem, which he did with commendable equity.[111] Some Jews retuned and worshipped in a

---

[110] Bettany Hughes, *Istanbul: The Tale of Three Cities* (London: Weidenfeld and Nicholson, 2017), p. 271.
[111] Simon Sebag Montefiore, *Jerusalem* (Weidenfeld & Nicolson), pp. 178–9.

subterranean synagogue called ha-Meara below the Temple Mount.[112] From 750, having ruthlessly deposed the Umayyads, the Abbasid dynasty ruled as Caliphs from Bagdad and took charge of Jerusalem. Their rule reached an apogee under Harun al-Rashid (763–809): a correspondent with Charlemagne and from whose court portions of *One Thousand and One Nights* were derived. It was a golden age of literature, philosophy, mathematics and astronomy in Arab culture. Greek works were translated into Arabic and Syriac, and learning flourished.

Yet the power of the Abbasids was challenged in Palestine by the Crusades, and in Egypt first by the Fatimids and then the Mamelukes basing their rule in Cairo. Also, in Anatolia the Seljuk Turks had already defeated the Byzantines at Manzikert in 1071. The Fatimids gained control of Jerusalem and Hakim Bi Amr, a Fatimid ruler, began a reign of terror against Christians and Jews from 1004.[113] Although the Byzantine Emperor, Constantine X Doukas (1059–1067), managed to secure a Christian Quarter in Jerusalem, with the arrival of the Seljuk Turks in the region a new appeal went to Rome from Constantinople "to come over and help us" and Pope Urban II called the First Crusade in 1095, or "Taking the Cross" as it was called. A rag-tag army of monks, mercenaries and knights made their way south-east and cross-country, dying from disease on the way, eventually taking Antioch in 1096 and then Jerusalem in 1099 amidst copious bloodshed. The crusader kingdoms or Outremer had begun, with their own orders of Knights Hospitallers and Templars becoming the go-to military chivalric orders in Europe, and underpinned by a new theology of "indulgences" for those who took the cross.

The crusader kingdoms would prove short-lived. The Second Crusade (1147–1150) provoked by the Fall of Edessa to the Seljuk Turks boasted King Louis VII of France and Conrad III of Germany as its leaders, but it ended fruitlessly. Indeed, a new Turkic/Kurdish military star-commander emerged soon afterwards called Salah ed Din (Saladin), who defeated the Crusader forces emphatically at the Horns of Hattin in Galilee in 1187 and then took Jerusalem. Jerusalem would not leave Muslim control until General Allenby walked into the Holy City in

---

[112] Montefiore, *Jerusalem*, p. 186.
[113] Montefiore, *Jerusalem*, p. 198.

December 1917: "A Christmas Present for the Nation", said Prime Minister Lloyd George. Attempts to regain Jerusalem by the Crusaders failed. King Richard the Lion Heart retook Acre at great cost to England while the Fourth Crusade (1204) descended into chaos, ending with the sack of Constantinople, and providing another reason for the break between the Roman Catholic and Orthodox churches.

The remaining Abbasid dynasty was ended with the Mongols taking Damascus in 1258, who in turn were overtaken by Timur or Tamburlaine (1336–1405). It was then the turn of the Ottoman Turks to become the dominant regional power, and they were so for nearly five centuries, taking Constantinople as their capital in 1453. Sultan Suliman the Magnificent defeated the Mamluk army in 1516, and rebuilt the wall of Jerusalem, thinking himself, with just a little prompting from his wife Roxelana, the new Solomon of the age.[114]

Following their diaspora, which had begun in the third century BC, the Jews continued their penetration of the cites of the Roman Empire. There were large communities in Alexandria, North Africa, the Eastern Mediterranean, Rome, Persia, Mesopotamia—in fact a list is provided by the record of those present at the Feast of Pentecost as narrated in Acts 2 (Acts 2: 8–12). The Arab occupation and Muslim Caliphates from 638–1917 only spurred on this process. The Christian church, often encouraged by the Church Fathers, *vehemently* blamed the Jews for the death of Christ. Jewish communities then spread into Northern Europe, Eastern Europe, Russia and eventually to the new world. Jews became skilled craftsmen, moneylenders, industrialists, retailers, scientists, artists, politicians and bankers in these communities. Often successful, frequently resented or envied, they were continuously persecuted, attacked, placed in ghettoes as in Venice, expelled as in England in 1270 or Spain in 1492, and finally, and most terribly, subject to the pogroms and the liquidation of the concentration camps and holocaust of Nazi Germany. The chief memorial of this is Yad Vashem in Jerusalem.

In the nineteenth century two movements occurred simultaneously. One was the renewed Christian interest in the sites of the Holy Land, and the other was the Zionist desire for a homeland for the Jews in Palestine.

---

[114] Montefiore, *Jerusalem*, p. 292.

In 1859, Tsar Alexander II's brother, Grand Duke Konstantin, visited Jerusalem and established a steamship company to bring pilgrims from Odessa. And in 1862 the British followed suit when the Prince of Wales, "Bertie", rode into Jerusalem. New churches and missions were constructed by the Great Powers including by the Kaiser and the Americans. Kaiser Wilhelm II entered Jerusalem on a white charger in 1898. Alongside this, by the mid nineteenth century, there was a stirring of Zionism, that is, the desire for a permanent homeland for the Jews. Early visionaries for this were Moses Montefiore, Rabbi Zvi Hirsch Kalischer from Prussia and Yehuda Hai Alchelai from Sarajevo. It was Theodore Herzl who gave organisation and momentum to the movement in the 1890s, however. At the Zionist Congress in Basel in 1897, Herzl boasted, "I founded the Jewish state".[115] Already in the 1860s there were Jewish settlers arriving in Palestine, with a second wave coming in 1882. On 2 November 1917, and following lobbying by Chaim Weizmann, Arthur Belfour, previously Prime Minister from 1902 to 1905, and now Foreign Secretary in Lloyd George's wartime cabinet, wrote to Lord Rothschild these far-reaching words in what became known as the Balfour Declaration:

His Majesty's Government view with favour the establishment in Palestine of a national home for the Jewish people, and will use their best endeavours to facilitate the achievement of this object, it being clearly understood that nothing shall be done which may prejudice the civil and religious rights of existing non-Jewish communities in Palestine, or rights and political status enjoyed in any other country.[116]

Since the British were now in control in Palestine and about to take Jerusalem by defeating the Turks and deposing the Jemal Pasha ruler, this was no idle promise. And the Declaration was confirmed in the Versailles Peace Treaty of 1919. The British Mandate in Palestine was ratified by the League of Nations in 1922, by which time there were eighty-two thousand Jews settled in Palestine, or twelve per cent of the population.

---

[115] Montefiore, *Jerusalem*, p. 375.
[116] (R. J. Q. Adams, *Balfour: The Last Grandee* (London: Thistle Publishing 2013), p. 433.

It was one thing to promise a homeland for the Jews in Palestine, it was quite another to do so whilst "not prejudicing the civil and religious rights of non-Jewish communities". There was tension from the start, and this was compounded exponentially by the inexpressible tragedy of the Holocaust in Europe from 1936 onwards. Six million Jews perished in unimaginable horror. The moral imperative on the Allies—Britain, France and the US—to execute the policy of the homeland only increased. Between the wars the British sought equable treatment of Jew and Arab and appeared successful.[117] Yet Arabs feared the increasing presence of the Jewish community and in 1936 there was a full-scale Arab revolt in Jerusalem. Eventually this was suppressed in 1938 by the British, but at the same time the Irgun, a Jewish para military nationalist force, and the Haganah were established. And it was at this point that a two-state solution was first mooted.

After the Second World War, as British policy would not allow an increase in immigration, the British formed the target for Israeli nationalism, and the Haganah, the Palmach brigades, the Lehi and the Irgun became the means of prosecuting Israel's independence and ejecting the British. The assassination in 1944 of Lord Moyne, the British Minister of State in the Middle East, and the bombing of the British Headquarters in Jerusalem (the King David Hotel) caused Churchill to rethink the policy of Zionism, saying in the House of Commons, "I can assure the House that the Jews in Palestine have rarely lost a better or more well informed friend".[118] Lord Moyne, the most obliging and charming of the Guinness family, and a good friend of Churchill, was mown down as he stepped from his car. Later the bodies of the two assassins who had been tried and hung were repatriated to Israel and in 1975 were given heroes' funerals in the presence of Yitzhak Rabin.[119] As to Jewish leaders, Yitzhak Rabin, Ariel Sharon, Moshe Dayan and Menachem Begin cut their teeth in these para military organisations before the latter became the Israeli Defence Force.

With the founding of the state of Israel in May 1948, war broke out and lasted in different phases from 1947 to 1949. Israel came out on top against a coalition of Arab states led by King Abdullah of Jordan, gaining

---

[117] Montefiore, *Jerusalem*, p. 442.

[118] Martin Gilbert, *Churchill and the Jews* (New York: Simon and Schuster, 2007), p. 225.

[119] Artemis Cooper, *Cairo in the War 1939–45* (London: John Murray, 1989), p. 324.

sixty per cent of the area designated to the Palestinians in UN Resolution 181, as well as the area mandated to Israel. The Arab nations refused to recognise the state of Israel and the United Nations' solution of 1947. At the end of the 1948 war, seven hundred thousand Palestinians were displaced, mostly to Jordan, where they remain as permanent refugees to this day.

In 1956, the Suez Crisis saw the attempt by Britain, France and Israel to depose the Egyptian leader, Nasser, and take the Suez Canal. The attempt failed because of opposition from the United States. Anthony Eden, the British Prime Minister, resigned and the country was humiliated. Nasser remained in power and Egypt gained outright control of the Suez Canal.

This was followed by the Six Day War in June 1967. Provocation by Egypt in closing the Straits of Tiran led to pre-emptive strikes by Israel, which destroyed the Egyptian air force on the ground. Likewise, Syria and Jordan were defeated. Israel gained the Gaza Strip, the Sinai desert, the West Bank and East Jerusalem. In 1973, humiliated Arab nations launched a new offensive on *Yom Kippur*, the Jewish Day of Atonement. However, after initial success in Sinai and the Golan Heights, Arab forces were pushed back. Israeli forces retook the Golan Heights on the Syrian border and in the south advanced as far as Suez, just miles from Cairo, before a ceasefire was brokered by the UN. In subsequent negotiations and the Camp David Settlement led by President Jimmy Carter in 1978, Israel agreed to restore Sinai to Egypt, but kept its gains from previous wars.

It was into this land and complex narrative that we arrived in 1979. Every stone, hillside, town and community told something of this story. They also begged questions to which we were hard put to provide an answer. Blood cried out from the soil and yearnings were felt around every corner. There were three geographical areas we visited in either 1979 or 2011 that begged the deepest questions.

Sinai and the Negev

In 1979 Sinai was still under Israeli control and was about to be handed back to Egypt following the Camp David peace negotiations. As part of our programme, we were to spend a week in the Sinai on a safari led by

Ora Lipschitz, a feisty academic from the Hebrew University who taught religious studies and who ran a business taking tours to the Sinai. Napoleonic in stature and outlook, she had a blaze of white hair in the midst of tousled black mop. She had a Mercedes truck on which our week's provisions were carried. She also had prodigious energy, both mental and physical, and thought everyone else should be able to keep up. We started as she meant to go on, and left Jerusalem at four a.m. on Monday 15 October 1979 and would not return till the following Monday. We took our clothes for the week, were promised feasts every evening on the desert floor, (so would not be living on a combination of manna and quail like the children of Israel) and would sleep *a la belle étoile.* There was little doubt it was going to be an adventure. What is more, Ora had quite a sceptical view on Moses and his Exodus experience—presumably wondering why on earth he took forty years to cover the comparatively short distance from Egypt to Canaan. But then again, Moses didn't have a Mercedes truck!

After *reveille* at four a.m., on day one we drove due south through Hebron and Beersheva to Timna, just a few miles short of Elat on the Gulf of Aquaba, the Israeli port of entry from the Red Sea and the Indian Ocean. The desert landscape here is majestic and dramatic. From the floor of Wadi Arabah that comes out of the Dead Sea, the mountains rise to three thousand feet. The atmosphere is hot and eye narrowingly bright and you realise you are in a harsh, unforgiving environment. In the 1930s, the archaeologist and rabbi Nelson Glueck gave the site the name King Solomon's Mines, believing that copper was mined here for Solomon's building work in Jerusalem. His associate and expedition photographer Professor Ben Rothenberg discredited the link, however, and instead proved that the workings were much more likely intended for an Egyptian temple. Ora, happy to overturn any theory that was too neat and sentimental and unsupported by evidence, gave her support to Rothenberg, whose hypotheses have stood the test of time. We drove on down, ready for a rest, and hit the Gulf of Aquaba (or Elat to Israel) where we snorkelled just off Coral Island, and saw the amazingly colourful tropical fish there.

On day two Ora gave us a lecture about the Sinai as we stood gathered around the truck. The desert is about ten thousand years old and is essentially a landscape of rocks made up of: limestone, red sandstone, white sandstone, and quartz deposited by the sea, volcanic rock as in the case of Mount Sinai itself, and most recently, granite. Rainfall is extremely localised and as it may rain only once a year, plants must be able to exist in these conditions. The most common tree is the acacia which is found in the Rift Valley and can have roots extending twenty-five metres deep. Temperatures can reach forty degrees, so we warned off dehydration. The warning signs of dehydration were yawning, not wanting to drink (ironically), a headache, dozing off, diarrhoea and impatience (some of which symptoms I suffer from at much lower temperatures!). After a further swim we moved south down the coast road until we turned into the desert proper at Wadi Nasib. Driving up over the pass between mountains of about four thousand feet we descended into the Wadi that leads to St Catherine's Monastery.

When we arrived at Wadi Nasib in the afternoon, it was raining— that once-a-year event. We learnt that the Bedouin who inhabit the desert believe that rain is a sign of political change, and since Sinai was about to be transferred back from Israel to Egypt, they were right! What was immediately evident was that the Wadi sprang to life with the rain. Literally within hours flowers were springing up from nowhere, adorning the rocky and sandy soil. We went for an adventurous walk down the steep-sided Wadi into its narrow gullies. We camped nearby overnight and we were off at six thirty a.m., heading for St Catherine's Monastery, hoping to arrive before the main inundation of tourists later in the morning. On the way we passed a Bedouin trap for leopards. The story was that during the British Mandate, ibex were hunted almost to extinction, from the 1920s onwards. In turn, the leopards that had previously hunted the ibex started killing the Bedouin goat herds. The Bedouin then began hunting the leopards to preserve their herds. But leopards now only exist in Oman, and no longer in the Sinai or the Negev.

We arrived at St Catherine's in the early morning, but already other tourists were there. It was easy at that time to visit from Israel, but in more recent years the Sinai has become insecure, with some attacks by Islamic extremists. Arriving at St Catherine's was a dramatic and memorable moment. It lies at the foot of Mount Sinai or Horeb and is fortified by a high encircling wall. It was founded in memory of an early

Christian martyr, Catherine, who was first tied to a wheel and tortured before being executed (hence the term Catherine Wheel which has given its name to a firework!), and then carried by an angel to Sinai. The monastery was rebuilt during the reign of Justinian 527–565, who had built Hagia Sophia in Constantinople. The Monastery is also home to the Chapel of the Burning Bush recording God's revelation to Moses that his name is YAHWEH (Exodus3:13ff). With a nice touch of humour, the monks had identified a nearby bush as the original, and had placed a fire extinguisher there! The monastery quickly became a place of pilgrimage and the very early pilgrim Egeria recorded visiting there in the fourth century in her account *Peregrinatio*, written in the late fourth century.

The greatest treasures of the monastery are its manuscripts, and for one that it no longer has: *Codex Sinaiticus*. *Codex Sinaiticus*—along with *Codex Vaticanus* and *Codex Alexandrinus*—is one of the most comprehensive and earliest manuscripts of the New Testament. On a second visit to the St Catherine's in 1859, Constantin von Tischendorf discovered *Codex Sinaiticus,* and in what became a disputed story, left with the manuscript which he then sold to the Tsar of Russia for 9,000 roubles, passing the money back to the monastery. Later Stalin offered the Codex for sale and the British government, with the aid of a public subscription, bought it in 1933, since when it has been on display in the British Museum.

Codex Sinaiticus is to St Catherine's what the Elgin Marbles are to the Parthenon, except in the case of the Codex there is a paper trail of purchase. Despite the loss of *Siniaticus,* the monastery library boasts one of the largest collections of Greek, Arabic, Coptic, Georgian and Armenian manuscripts in the world (some three thousand).

That night we camped near the monastery, and as usual, Ora spread out her red gingham table cloths on the desert floor and we gathered around as a group as if for the last supper. We were camped close to a Bedouin group who had been invited to join us for the meal and who made us delicious flat bread, beaten out over large hot stones and cooked on the charcoal fire. While eating the bread we heard about their lifestyle. The Bedouin come from Saudi Arabia, just across the Gulf of Aquaba and are nomads of the desert. Theirs is a patriarchal tribal system in which it is family that provides identity, not location. Their movement is determined by the need of their herds of goats and camels. In the summer they pasture their goats close to their wells, but in the winter go up into the mountains. The women have a greatly-respected position in Bedouin society. The harshness of the conditions makes dependence on women all the greater and generally Bedouin in that area (although not in the more settled conditions of the Negev) have one wife as they are so nomadic. The women wear a black burqa even in the desert leaving their mouths covered, to the Bedouin the most sexual part of their bodies, and their noses pierced with a ring (some customs are immemorial: see Genesis 24:47, 65). Yet it is a way of life, which, even in 1979 was under threat.

Full of the day's events we went to sleep early, for the following morning we would begin our ascent of Mount Sinai at three a.m. The mountain is nearly eight thousand feet high but we had a good start at St Catherine's at nearly five thousand feet. It was a little under three thousand feet of steady uphill walking. The aim was to arrive at the summit before sunrise and enjoy the spectacular view of the red peaks of the surrounding range. As the sun rose over the red mountain range to the East, more and more features were picked out by the rising sun. The Book of Exodus tells us that is was here that Moses received the Ten Commandments from the hands of angels, only to find that the impatient Israelites had persuaded Aaron to make a Golden Calf (see Exodus Chapters 20 and 32). When we arrived at the summit, we found a church, a mosque and "conveniences"—not available to Moses—and we had a memorable Communion Service together.

We had a further two days in the Sinai and on one of those it rained heavily—major political change must have been in the air—and we had to rig some polythene over our sleeping bags. The desert did flower but at the same time I found a scorpion sheltering in my shoe! Olivia and others were glad to have a hair wash—we had been six days on the move without bathrooms and at times she wondered what she had signed up to at our wedding just six weeks before! Our drive back to Jerusalem from Elat was delayed by flash floods in the Judean hills. I did not realise that rain could be so torrential in an area so well known for its desert, but we saw that conditions could change in an instant.

Apart from an excursion with a friend to the Dead Sea where we did the obligatory newspaper reading while floating in that syrupy water, we did make one other visit to the Negev, to the site of the Qumran

Community and Masada. On the way to Qumran, we drove along a roller coaster road over the mountains from Arad to Masada, location of the final and awful stand of the Jewish Revolt in AD 73/74. Rather than fall into the hands of the Xth Roman Legion under Lucius Silva, who were inexorably approaching the walls and gates of this Hasmonean fortress, Josephus records that the 960 Sicarii rebels, including many women and children, took their own lives.[120] When we went there again in 2011, I noticed that a group of teenagers were having a Bar Mitzva and many young Israeli soldiers were on an induction course of the Israeli Defence Force, further evidence of the harsh realities that are inculcated into Israelis from an early age. Who would think of having a birthday party in a place notorious for mass resistance and suicide?

From Masada we went to Qumran, the site of the Jewish monastic community, most probably Essenes, who were there from c.130–105 BC. They were in their way a religious resistance movement, first against the Hellenization of Judaism and then against Roman control. The Essenes called for a life of purification and detachment, set around the study of the Jewish scriptures, which they faithfully copied, and for waiting for the Messiah. The copying of the scriptures as an act of worship resulted in the Dead Sea Scrolls: the Jewish scriptures stored in jars in the Qumran Caves. Discovered between 1947 and 1951 by shepherd boys and others in a succession of caves, they are probably the greatest archaeological discovery made in Israel in the post-war period. And in a real way they are a reminder of how much the scriptures, and other writings, lie at the centre of Judaism. Their copying was peerless; their preservation little short of miraculous. Residing as they did in clay pots for two thousand years in the intensely dry atmosphere of the Negev, they are remarkably preserved and were marvellously found. These sites completed our exploration of the Negev and Sinai. The themes that came from it were ones of preparation, formation, resistance and defiance. By contrast we were then to go to Galilee.

Galilee

If you asked most English pilgrims to the Holy Land to identify their favourite places, they would probably say the Garden Tomb in Jerusalem

---

[120] Josephus, *The Jewish War,* Book VII (London: Penguin 1972), pp. 382ff.

and Galilee. The former is how we imagine the empty tomb to be, and the latter has the serenity and peace so prized by the English in their love of the countryside and a serene landscape. The peace of Galilee is preferred to the intensity and confusion of Jerusalem or the severity of the Negev and Sinai. In 1979 we spent eight days in Galilee and a further two in 2011.

Given most of Jesus' ministry took place in Galilee before his passion in Jerusalem, the place names in the area evoke his ministry, his teaching, and miracles. In this way Christ's life is spread out over the hills, lake, shoreline and fields of the region. On the way up to Galilee from Jerusalem, you pass through Nazareth, from which town Jesus took his name, Jesus of Nazareth. It was here that his family lived, his father Joseph working as a carpenter, and his mother Mary going on to have a large family of Jesus's brothers and sisters (Matthew 13:55,56). It was here too that Jesus was rejected by the local people for his indirect claim to be the Messiah who was to fulfil the prophecies of Isaiah (see Luke 4:16–30). They wanted to throw him off a cliff. In Jesus' day Nazareth was nothing special; in fact, one of the disciples, when first told of Jesus' hometown, exclaims, "Can anything good come out of Nazareth?" (John 1: 46). It is still an ordinary town of seventy thousand with a mostly Muslim and Christian population, although situated in Israel.

In 2011, one of our group, Wiola, recounted an extraordinary story. In 1942 her mother aged fourteen had arrived in Nazareth. Her mother, Maria, together with thousands of others had been ethnically cleansed by Stalin from Eastern Poland near Vilnius. Aged twelve Maria had been deported with her family from her home to a labour camp, where for two years the adults did forced labour. In a kind of amnesty with the British Government, Polish General Anders was permitted by the Soviet regime to lead an evacuation of seventy-seven thousand Polish troops and forty-three thousand civilians in a great trek from the Soviet occupied territory to the Middle East. Travelling by various means of transport, they journeyed through Tashkent Central Asia, via the Caspian Sea, Persia and Iraq and, in her mother's, case ending up with many Polish school aged children in Nazareth where she received an education obtaining her *matura* certificate awarded by General Anders, before going to Britain at the end of the war in 1947. Wiola would be educated with General

Anders' daughter in London in the 1950s, before marrying Tom and settling in Bath.

On the steps of the boarding school in Nazareth where her mother had been sheltered and educated, we listened to Wiola reading Psalm 84, which proclaims how God shelters the refugee like a swallow being given a place of shelter in the dwelling places of the Lord Almighty (Psalm 84: 1–4). It was a special and very moving moment.

Around lake Galilee are the places so well known to us from the Gospels. There is Capernaum, which Jesus made his base during those years of ministry and where the home of Simon Peter may be found. The Mount of Beatitudes may have been the site of the Sermon on the Mount; Mount Tabor the place where the Transfiguration occurred. There too are Magdala, from whence Mary Magdalene came; and nearer to Nazareth, Cana of Galilee, where Jesus turned the water into wine. And at the heart of these communities is the lake named either Galilee or Tiberias, after the ruler who was Roman Emperor for the bulk of Jesus' life.

In February 2011 when we went out onto Lake Galilee in a boat, it was hazy and entirely still. Going further out into the lake, cutting the engine off and drifting in silence with our thoughts and reflections was probably the moment we most wanted to capture for ever.

It is not a silence we wanted to break; it was not an experience we wanted to end, especially by re-entering the questions and conflicts of Palestine, but enter we must.

The West Bank and Gaza

The West Bank is the area of Palestine to the west of Jordan from Jenin, a little north of Nablus in the north, and to the south of Hebron, and which includes the north-west corner of the Dead Sea. East Jerusalem formed part of the West Bank—although the United Nations called it a separate entity. Originally part of Jordan in 1948, the West Bank was captured by the Israeli Defence Force in the Six Day War and since then has been administered by the Israeli Ministry of Defence, but through the Palestinian Authority. It is regarded by the United Nations as an Occupied Territory. Israeli control has led to the establishment of Israeli settlements in a particular zone (Area C) of the West Bank, so that Jewish settlers now number about 300,000. In this area there is direct Israeli rule. The Palestinian population numbers approximately 3.5 million in the entirety of the West Bank. Many of the Palestinians work in Israel and so enter Israel on a daily basis. With less new investment in the West Bank, this encourages economic dependency on the Israeli economy.

Since 1979 there has been a deterioration in the relationship between Israelis and Palestinians. Palestinian refugee camps in Southern Lebanon have made for a ready recruiting ground for Palestinian or Arab extremist groups. One result was the firing of rockets into Northern Israel from these positions in June 1982. The response from Israel was *Operation Peace for Galilee*. By August 1982 there were thirty-five thousand Israeli troops outside Beirut. This incursion and the merciless aerial bombardment of Beirut resulted in the deaths of fifteen thousand Lebanese, with forty thousand wounded and four hundred thousand displaced.[121] Meanwhile, the refugee camps of Sabra and Shatila, in part radicalised by extremist Arab groups, suffered massacres of up to three thousand people by Lebanese Christian Phalangist groups operating in concert with the IDF.

Again in 1996, Israeli forces attacked Hezbollah positions in Southern Lebanon after more than six hundred rocket attacks on the town of Kiryat Shmona. Although bombing resulted in many casualties and much structural damage, Lebanon would not renounce Hezbollah, whose programme of social integration in the country was by then well advanced. Despite this, in the 1990s, Yitzhak Rabin made substantial progress towards a settlement through the Oslo Accords, but in 1995, having won the Nobel Peace Prize, he was assassinated. As is often the case in the region, those who seek accord with the enemy tend to be assassinated. It was true of Rabin then; it was true of the Egyptian President Sadat in 1981; and it was true of King Abdullah of Jordan, who was assassinated in Jerusalem in 1951.

After the failure of the Camp David Summit convened by Clinton in 2000, a new initiative was needed. By 2002, in the aftermath of 9/11 and a year before the Iraq war, a new "Road Map for Peace" was outlined by President Bush, in which an autonomous West Bank Palestinian administration was proposed, although the issue of Israeli settlements

---

[121] Philip Mansel, *Levant* (London: John Murray, 2011), pp. 337–8.

prevented its fulfilment. Israel wanted forty-four per cent of the West Bank. The Palestinian leadership would consider land swaps, but not reduction of the West Bank. The Palestinians were ill served by their leader Arafat, but the Israelis proved intransigent about the settlements. By 2000, following the failure of Camp David and the provocative walk by Ariel Sharon onto the Temple Mount, a second *Intifada* began of Palestinian resistance to Israel. This resulted in flashpoints in Gaza, Bethlehem, and Jenin as well as rocket attacks and suicide bombers from Gaza and elsewhere that lasted until 2006.

From 2003, Israel began to build a wall and security fences all around the West Bank, along the border with Egypt from Rafah to Elat, and around Gaza. Israeli settlements were withdrawn from Gaza by Sharon and now it is a Palestinian enclave ruled initially by Hamas, who were elected in 2007, and now jointly with Fatah. Gaza is 41 kms long and up to 12 kms wide with 1.85 million Palestinians inside it, one of the highest population densities on earth. All its borders are closed and it is not free to import or export without Israeli permission. There have been repeated flare-ups between Gaza and Israel since 2007, resulting in substantial loss of life, although almost always disproportionately among the Palestinians. In 2014, among many adults, five hundred and fifty Palestinian children were killed. In the most recent flare-up along the Gaza border in 2018/19, the IDF forces shot over a hundred Palestinians protesting close to the border, but within Gaza. I have never been to Gaza, but was brought close to its tragedy through an event in 2003.

Whilst at Oxford I formed a close friendship with Anthony and Jocey Hurndall. We went on several holidays together and I stayed in their house in Islington during my first job in London. They went on to have four children, the oldest son being Tom, who was also Olivia's godson. He was a photographer and a writer. He had attended Winchester College and was taking a break from studying photo-journalism at Manchester. In 2003 he attended a *Stop the War* demonstration against the Blair government joining the war against Iraq. On the march Tom was given a leaflet about becoming part of a human shield in Baghdad and was determined to go. He stayed in Baghdad until the outbreak of war in March and then moved to Jerusalem and then finally Rafah in Gaza, where, while courageously protecting children from sniper fire near the border, and wearing an orange Hi-Viz jacket, he was shot in the head by an IDF sniper. Tom never regained consciousness. He was operated on in Beersheva and flown back to England where he died on 13 January 2004. I visited him in hospital in London while he was unconscious, and prayed, but Tom was soon to die from his wounds. It was the nearest I got to the tragedy that is Gaza. Jocey told me later that Tom's death was like a bomb going off in their family.

It is the Jewish philosopher Martin Buber who said, "There is a tragedy at the heart of things". There is the inestimable tragedy in the treatment of the Jews in history, especially the Holocaust, and sadly still in the present day. There is tragedy of the treatment of the Palestinians, and their continuing substantial losses. No party is blameless. Hate, revenge, poverty and occupation are an ever-churning cycle. Of course, there are still human joys: love, marriage, birth, family—but too often against a background of sadness and deep loss. When Balfour made his declaration that there should be a homeland for the Jews, he envisaged self-determination for both peoples in Palestine, and said that "nothing should be done to prejudice the civil rights of existing non-Jewish communities in Palestine". To create two states means both sides giving up some cherished goals, and taking people with them. In seventy-two years, it has not been possible, and until such time as it is, the wound only festers and the cycle of violence and antipathy continues to churn. And if we have learnt anything, it is that poverty and injustice induces extremism. We may say that people should not react with violence to injustice and poverty, but when have they not?

When in the West Bank in 2011, we visited the famous sites of the area. We went to Bethlehem and the church of the nativity. To get there from Jerusalem one must go through the Israeli security wall and be checked. For one who grew up in the shadow of another wall in Berlin there was a sense of *déjà vu*. In Berlin it took twenty-seven years before the wall came down. But this wall was higher, and much longer, going around the whole West Bank. In Bethlehem we visited the Shepherd's Fields, recalling the invitation to the lowly shepherds to see the nativity and the angelic chorus of "Glory to God in the Highest and on earth peace, goodwill to all upon whom his favour rests" (Luke 2:14). We visited Bethlehem Bible College that trains Arab Christians to be pastors and leaders in their communities, and that relieve the needs of the poor in the neighbourhood. It was founded by the inspiring visionary, Bishara Awad who had been to Bath several times. We visited Hebron and the tombs of the Patriarchs, which had high security around them. The women in our party wore capuchin-like habits with pointy hoods to accommodate religious sensibilities when visiting the tombs, now set in a mosque! I baptised several in the Jordan River with an Israeli border guard just feet away. And finally, we walked down to Jericho from St George's Monastery in Wadi Kelt, remembering the man who fell among thieves and the despised Samaritan who was the hero of the occasion. Incidentally, Samaria is the present-day West Bank.

And so, at the end of February 2011, we flew back to England, concluding my second visit to Israel/Palestine separated by nearly thirty-two years from the first. Although in 1979, it had been just a few years since the Yom Kippur war, in 2011 relationships seemed more entrenched, more embittered than ever. There are, of course, no easy answers. The conditions for peace seem as elusive as ever. But encouraged by the nations of the world, Israeli and Palestinian should fulfil the original vision of 1917 of self-determination and the peaceful co-existence of both communities, living in dignity and security. We should reserve final words for the greatest of all Jews, who said, "Blessed are the peacemakers for they will be called sons of God" (Matthew 5:9).

Chapter XI
Down to Egypt

It was becoming a discernible pattern that my trips would coincide with some upheaval, political or otherwise in places I went to. The year before this visit to Egypt I had travelled with family members to Moscow and St. Petersburg, only to be marooned in the latter for an additional four days because of volcanic eruptions in Iceland. Frantic return bookings were made, followed by cancellations, as one airline after another took our reservations and then cancelled them due to the persistent ash cloud. Eventually we flew back via Dusseldorf, after making the most of the extra time with further visits to the Hermitage in the Winter Palace, to Pushkin's house, where we saw the sofa upon which the great peot lay dying, but still receiving friends, following a duel, and to Dostoevsky's flat in the suburbs. There we discovered how the great man worked: he wrote all night and his wife typed the manuscript all day! For these extra four days we had decamped from our hotel to stay with an older Russian couple as bed and breakfast customers. They told us how they survived when St Petersburg was besieged for three years by the Germans during the war. They had suffered terrible deprivation, being reduced to dismantling the furniture and burning the wood for warmth, and boiling the ends to extract the glue, which they then ate!

The occasion for this trip to Egypt in 2011 was this: having been the Rural Dean of Bath for seven years from 2003 to 2010 (quite a lot of extra work, but no extra pay!), I asked the diocese if I might take four weeks paid leave in May of 2011. I had already led a group to Palestine in February that year, as described in the previous chapter, but this was additional! They agreed. The plan was to go to Egypt, which had become increasingly unstable in the early months of 2011 following the start of the Arab Spring. It was to be something of a repeat of the trip of 2002, that is, friends and I would drive my now ten-year-old Peugeot 207 to Egypt, donate it to the Bishop of Cairo, with whom I was in touch, and

I'd then fly back with Olivia, who would join me during half-term for a cruise down the Nile as part of my 60th birthday celebrations. At least that was the idea, although it did not work out quite like that.

Michael, who had come with me to Jordan in 2002, and Richard, the senior partner of a London law firm—and was in need of a change of scenery— agreed to come with me. Initially, we had thought of getting to Egypt by crossing the Straits of Gibraltar and then driving across North Africa, but it quickly became evident that this was a non-starter: the border between Morocco and Algeria had been closed for years and Libya was in turmoil, with the Gaddafi regime having only a few months to go. In fact, we wondered whether we should go to Egypt at all in May, and seriously considered going overland to the Crimea instead! In fact, as we now know, in less than three years Crimea would be invaded by Russian forces in February 2014, but we might just have got there. However, the plan was settled: we'd drive from England to Venice and take a car ferry from Venice to Alexandria, then on to Cairo and some other places in Egypt before the Nile cruise with Olivia and a flight home. It had the makings of a special trip. Although the country's future was uncertain, Egypt seemed relatively calm after the Egyptian Revolution of late January 2011 when Mubarak was overthrown. We set off on in early May.

Bath to Venice via Slovenia

As in 2002, we drove to Monschau for our first stop and then on to the German Alps, staying at Mittenwald where the hotel receptionist wore Tyrolean costume and had a pay booth that looked a bit like one of those shelters on a cuckoo clock from which a happy *fraulein* pops out whenever the hour is struck. We ate generous servings of stew in the local *stube* and had a look round a very baroque church before heading off for nearby Slovenia and the scenic town of Bled.

Slovenia is one of the successor states of the former Yugoslavia— now eight in number. It is one of the smaller new Balkan countries, with a population of two million, a capital at Ljubljana and a small piece of Mediterranean coastline between Italy and Croatia. The country has its own language of Slovene, and the people are Slavic, although intermixed with neighbouring Germans, Italians and Hungarians. During the war (1939–45) large numbers of Slovenes were purged by the Germans, Italians and Hungarians, each wanting a slice of their territory. The land was for a time trisected. In addition, the Partisans led by Tito massacred numbers of Italians in Istria. Much of that territory is forested, as we found out, and it was in these forests north of Trieste that the Partisans, supported by British members of the SOE led by Sir Fitzroy Maclean (see his enduring classic account, *Eastern Approaches)*, fought a guerrilla campaign against the German and Italians.[122]

Early on in Slovenia we visited Bled which is indeed a beauty spot: a small spa town set on an emerald green lake with a castle at the far end. The lake has an island with a church, and pilgrims came there in numbers in the medieval period. Later, during the Victorian heyday of spa towns, the town's warm spa waters were developed, and soon Bled became a favoured holiday resort. There is no gainsaying its picture-postcard beauty. From Bled we headed into the heart of Slovenia, stopping in the capital of Ljubljana for a coffee. In fact, there could not be a better place to stop for a coffee. It is a lively, young, picturesque city, buzzing with life. With its medieval castle on the hill, its white (*bela)* buildings rebuilt after an earthquake in 1511 and cafés overlooking the Ljubljana River, what more could we wish for! Plus, there was a festival in town that day, with old soldiers marching, and bands playing. It all made for an unforgettable scene. From Ljubljana we headed south into the meadows and the forests of the countryside towards Ribnica, and to a village called Dane.

As the guide book said, Dane is at the end of the line, with nothing but forest to the south and west until the Croatian border, and beyond that, even more forest until the Adriatic coast at Rijeka. The bed and breakfast where we stayed was hard to find, but worth it, and described "as the best place to stay in the area". We learned that a forester lived nearby and knocking on his door we discovered that his house was literally stuffed, filled in fact with stuffed animals. And confronting us when we first entered, there was a stuffed bear! The forester told us that bears were common in the forest and that the forest was so extensive he would go into it for weeks on end, living in cabins dotted around its heart.

---

[122] John Earle, *The Price of Patriotism* (Brighton: The Book Guild, 2005), pp. 17ff.

The next day we headed south into Croatia and the Istrian Peninsula. At the border post of Bodna Kupi we had to show our passports for the first time since leaving England (Croatia was then not yet a member of the EU), before driving into Croatia, my first time back since visiting Dubrovnik in 1970. Croatia is a beautiful country with a European coastline second to none. We were heading for Rovinj in the Istrian Peninsula. Once part of the Roman Empire, Istria was successively governed by Goths, Avars, and Franks and more latterly by Venice, Austria, Italy and then Yugoslavia. The interior is hilly, rocky and charming: bedecked with coronilla, myrtle, honeysuckle, cistus and vines. It is a place to meander through slowly.

Arriving at the coast we made for Rovinj, a delightful old-world seaside fishing port with a steep promontory overseen by the massive church of St Euphemia. Euphemia was martyred in Chalcedon near Constantinople for being unwilling to burn incense to the Emperor Diocletian, in 303 AD. Her bones are buried here, which made the church a significant site of pilgrimage in the medieval period. Later it was overtaken in trade by nearby Rijeka and Trieste, but it has lost none of its old-world charm.

The following day we had one of those memorable drives along a beautiful European coastline from Rovinj to Venice: from the jewel of Istria to the great pearl of the Adriatic. Along the way we heard news that would change the shape of the trip. Back in Germany, Richard, never long parted from his Blackberry (in the days before the iPhone) had spoken with an Egyptian client: "At the moment we are driving to Egypt via a ferry from Venice" he said. The client responded, helpfully as it happens, by asking if we knew there were import duties levied on foreign cars on arrival in Alexandria, and that the car would be impounded until the tax was paid. "No, we did not know: I had not been told this by the bishop's office. So, I rang the office and waited for a reply. A few days later it came. "Yes, we would have to pay an import duty and it was likely to be in the region of £3,000". Well, there was only one thing to do and that was to give the car away in Venice where we were staying for two nights. After all, it was only worth £1,000 and Olivia and I were anyhow booked to fly back from Cairo!

With these developments turning over in our minds we drove along the Istrian coast to Venice, perhaps not quite giving the scenery the full attention, it deserved! What we did notice was that the nearer we got to Venice the more expensive and luxurious the houses and hotels along the coast appeared. *En route* we stopped at Trieste.

Trieste is a large commercial centre and a hub for trade into southern and eastern Europe. It has both a large container port, but also elegant classical buildings along the waterfront in the city centre. It has extensive banking and finance facilities that support industries, many of which have their headquarters here. Its fine waterfront has many cafés, which is not surprising, as this is the coffee trading centre of southern Europe. Stopping for a coffee was thus obligatory, and, seeing a statue of James Joyce, I learned that he had lived here for ten years, on and off, from 1904–1914, along with his partner and later wife, Norah Barnacle.

Trieste had been a centre of the arts and literature for years, but the war bitterly divided the city between Italians and Slovenes. In 1944 it was occupied by the Germans and then by the Yugoslavs under Tito for "forty days", a time when many Italians and anti-Communists "disappeared". Eventually it came under Joint US-British command under Field Marshall Alexander having been liberated by the 24th Guards Brigade with whom my father served as an Intelligence Officer during the war.

After a brief glimpse of this historic and great city, it was time to move on to its renowned neighbour, in whose cultural shadow Trieste lies. We arrived in the late afternoon, parking the car in one of the car parks on the city's outskirts and then taking the vaporetto (water bus) into the heart of the city. Arriving in Venice is never anything but exciting, but this visit had turned into a mission to find a home for the car. We ate outside that night, at a restaurant near La Fenice Theatre, famous for its opera.

At the hotel I explained our predicament and asked whether the receptionist knew of any charity in Venice who might like a car. He couldn't think of any, but suggested I go to St Mark's and ask for Father Fabrizio in case he could help. So, splitting our forces, and with the goal of finding a "home for the car", Richard and I set off one way, Michael another. Arriving at St Mark's—this wonderful Greek-styled church based on the Church of the Holy Apostles in Constantinople—I asked for

Fr. Fabrizio and was told he was in the sacristy, robing up for a service. I was taken to the east end of the church and entered a room with enough space, I imagined, for a large number of clergy to assemble for a grand occasion, such as the institution of a new Doge. Fr. Fabrizio patiently listened to my explanation about needing to give away a car. He heard me out and kindly said that he did not need a car just at the moment, which is just what I would have said if the same thing had happened to me in England just before a service! And of course, a car *in Venice* was even less likely to be needed.

We continued with sight-seeing, wandering around the streets and dipping into churches and buildings. To go into a church in Venice, as in Florence or Rome, is often to be overwhelmed by the sheer profusion of artistic talent on display, and perhaps no more so than in the Church of the Friars (Santa Maria Gloriosa de Frari). In it we found works by Titian, Donatello, Bellini, Girolamo Camapagna, Sansovino and others, including a monument to Canova. From there we wandered into the *Scuola Grande* of San Rocco—one of the six great guilds of Venice— where we were amazed by the cycle of paintings by Tintoretto in the upstairs assembly hall. The extraordinary wealth and talent of Venice, based on a ruthless maritime empire constructed in the shipbuilding and armaments yards of the Arsenal, was definitely on show. Having made no inroads into our problem over the car, we made our way back to the hotel to see if Michael had been more successful. It could be said we hadn't tried very hard.

In his resourceful way, Michael had found a taker. Seeing lots of locals going in and out of what looked like a government building, he had approached the receptionist and begun the story. She did not understand him, except that it was something about "giving away a car— *mamma mia Inglesi*". Thinking he might be trouble she summoned the policeman who kept watch in the hallway. Michael explained the situation: "A car to give away… today… come to this hotel tonight and you will be given the ownership and registration documents". The police officer's name was Danilo, a Venetian police officer who paid us the honour of believing our story. His family had been to Scotland many times; his mother particularly enjoyed that country. He would come that evening, he said, and meet "Patricio". As Jan Morris wrote in her book about Venice, "there are few kindlier policemen than those who patrol the canals in these little speedboats, or solemnly potter about, buttoned in blue greatcoats in flat-bottomed skiffs".[123] Danilo was certainly one such individual. He came around that evening. We went through the documents and agreed to meet at the vaporetto stop near St Mark's in the morning. We'd then go to the car, and Danilo would take us to the port of Venice and the "car ferry"! Richard, meanwhile with trouble brewing in his firm back home needed to fly back to London to pour oil on troubled waters.

Everyone kept to the bargain. Danilo now had a car and kept in touch with Michael, who later stayed with his family just outside Venice. We had no import duty to pay, but sadly the bishop did not receive a run-around car for his staff. In fact, without Danilo I don't think we would have found the quay for the ferry to Alexandria anyhow. It was run by Visamar and the ferry was sailing for Tartus in Syria and then on to Alexandria—three days' sailing—but there were less than twenty people on board this brand-new ferry! The Arab Spring and the emerging civil war in Syria had taken their toll and there were virtually no takers for the ferry.

Soon after arriving on board, we heard over the ship's loudspeaker that because of the war, we would not be stopping at Tartus in Syria. We would be sailing direct to Alexandria instead. We soon met the other passengers: a couple driving a 4x4 from Cairo to the Cape, and six German motorcyclists who were going touring on their BMWs in Egypt. The car deck was startlingly empty, with room for four hundred cars and twenty lorries. The days stretched out ahead of us, like the coastline of Italy in the Adriatic. For some reason there were no benches on deck. In the daytime I sat on the boards, with my back to the funnel's housing and read *Julius Caesar* and *Antony and Cleopatra* by the bard, and Lawrence Durrell's *Alexandrian Quartet*. We were going to Alexandria, after all, where Anthony and Cleopatra died and Julius Caesar fell for Cleopatra's charms. The three days went by slowly but enjoyably, interspersed with summonses to the ship's dining room with its bright orange plastic chairs and the same ten passengers, and occasional games of scrabble with Michael. It took over a day to lose sight of the Italian coast, and sail past

---

[123] Jan Morris, *Venice* (London: Faber and Faber, 1993), p. 27.

the coasts of Albania, Corfu and the Peloponnese, then a further day to Crete and another half-day to Alexandria. I knew the port of Alexandria was not far away, when, leaning over the side of the ship, I saw a customs boat drew alongside, and boxes of what looked like cigarettes thrown into the hands of the waiting customs officers from our ship! I realised that things would be different in Egypt, and was glad that we did not have the car, there was as no knowing what we would be charged in import duty and there would be no leaving before we paid it.

Alexandria

Alexandria is a city whose name conjures up many impressions. Founded by Alexander the Great *en route* to the oracle at Siwa in the Western Desert, it became the capital city of the Ptolemies from 305 BC until the time of Cleopatra, whose death in 30 BC marked the city's transition to Roman rule.[124] Augustus (Octavian), who had hunted down Cleopatra and Antony, absorbed Egypt into the Roman Empire. By the second century AD it was famed for its library, its lighthouse, and its intellectual and commercial prowess. Here Platonic and Jewish studies flourished, producing the Septuagint (the Greek translation of the Hebrew Bible) and a philosophic school headed by Plotinus, the Neo-Platonist. Here too the Coptic church flourished. The church was first planted by St Mark, the Gospel writer in the first century AD, whose body was stolen by the Venetians to give Venice more spiritual clout and gravitas—hence St Mark's Venice. Alexandria produced a succession of almost pharaonic bishops so commanding were they, like Athanasius and Cyril. They stood for Orthodoxy, and brooked no compromise. Cyril could "rent a mob" of monks to kill a pagan philosopher like Hypatia, or destroy a pagan shrine. Yet despite its profound Christian foundations, Alexandria would fall to the Muslim Caliphate in the seventh century AD. The Coptic church was far more ancient than Islam, although its own Coptic language is now preserved only in its liturgy. Arabic then became the *lingua franca* of Egypt.

In the Middle Ages, the centre of power drifted south from Alexandria to Cairo, which became the capital of the Fatimid Caliphate

---

[124] Robin Lane Fox, *Alexander The Great* (London: Allen Lane 1973), pp. 200ff.

in 969, then of the Ayyubid dynasty of Saladin, then of the Mamluks—a military order of Islamic knights—until it was absorbed into the Ottoman Empire from 1517. Alexandria was not to rise again to prominence until the nineteenth century and the arrival of the singular character of Muhammad Ali in 1830, who came as an Ottoman governor and founded a dynasty and made Alexandria a great Levantine city.

Ali became the pasha or ruler of Egypt and transformed Alexandria from "the saddest and most deserted place in the world" to one that was militarily secure, politically stable and commercially and culturally buoyant.[125] Apart from his expansionist ambitions in Arabia, Syria and Sudan, he managed to attract Greek, French, Jewish and British investment to the country, and to Alexandria in particular. Cotton and banking became the staples of Alexandrian life and from these came a host of other business opportunities and forms of cultural life.

Although Ali never became fully independent of the Ottoman Empire's oversight, he virtually founded a dynasty which was to last until the abdication of Farouk I, a successor, in 1952. A palace, the *Ras El Tin* (Cape of Figs), was built above the western Harbour in Alexandria and here Ali held court with the envoys and consuls of the world. He sat, in some magnificence, overlooking the harbour and his beloved navy, smoking his seven and half foot pipe encrusted with diamonds and with a gilt bowl.[126] By 1848, French culture dominated the city with 300 élite Egyptians educated in Paris, including the Pasha's sons. The city was rebuilt with the *Place des Consuls*, where consulates occupied pride of place, and the English church of St Mark's was built in typical Gothic style nearby. The city was gaining a reputation for luxury and sensuality built on the backs of a majority Egyptian population who would not forever applaud European social superiority.

In 1869, after ten years of construction, the Suez Canal was opened and jointly owned by Britain and France until 1956, becoming the new artery to India and the East. The stability of Egypt became part of British foreign policy and when riots broke out between Jews and Greeks, and

---

[125] Mansel, *Levant,* p. 56 citing Francois-René, Vicomte de Chateaubriand II, *Itinéraire de Paris à Jerusalem et de Paris à Jerusalem* (Paris, 1846), p. 141.
[126] Mansel, *Levant*, pp. 63ff.

Egyptian nationalism became more insistent, Britain intervened.[127] By 1882, British and French gunboats had arrived in the harbour of Alexandria and a naval bombardment of Alexandria by fifteen ships of the line in support of the Khedive followed, and British occupation resulted. The British years, which spanned 1882 to 1952, were about to begin. But colonial wars first took place to establish British hegemony, and then two world wars followed, in which British armies sought to control both the artery to India and the East and the transfer of oil from the Gulf to Europe. Egypt became the hinge of empires for those seventy years, and controlling it meant prosperity in Britain and France. British and French families would be drawn there for war or for commerce, and among them some of my own ancestors.

Under the Khedive or Pasha, from 1882 to 1918 Alexandria became a truly cosmopolitan city of the Levant. The Khedive and then the King—after 1918 with the collapse of the Ottoman Empire—provided the foundation stone of Egyptian society, but were underwritten and guided, more or less, by British Pro-consuls, such as Lord Cromer, Evelyn Baring, Consul General from 1878–1907 and then the British Ambassador, Sir Miles Lampson (1936–1946). These two men pretty much spanned the entire British period, and were literally the power behind the throne.

Alexandria boasted a diverse array of personalities and talent: from the actor Omar Sharif, who starred in *Dr Zhivago*, to the Nazi Rudolf Hess; from Mohammed Fayed, the owner of Harrods, to Gamal Nasser, the first President of Egypt. All were born in Alexandria.[128] There were clubs of all kinds: The Union Club for British Officers, the Alexandria Sporting club, a race course and a further eighty charitable and academic societies overseen by Prince Omar Toussoun, a cousin of the royal family. Commercial life was mostly developed by the Greeks. Trading in Egyptian cotton was of paramount importance for a hungry, world-wide market, supported by a stock exchange and banks. The Benaki family were a leading Greek mercantile family.[129] When it came to literature,

---

[127] Mansel, *Levant*, p. 116.
[128] Mansel, *Levant*, p. 133.
[129] Mansel, *Levant*, p. 137.

Constantine Cavafy (1863–1933), the Greek-Egyptian poet (much admired by E.M. Forster, who worked there for the Red Cross from 1916–1920), headed a cast of poets and authors who were thoroughly at home in the multi-layered society of Alexandria. This international community was supported by many schools: nearly seven thousand children went to French-run schools and a further nine thousand to other foreign schools. The city was truly a melting pot of cultures.

But all this was in the past. When Michael and I arrived by ship, surely the best way to arrive in Alexandria, the city was and had been a fully independent Egyptian city for sixty years and was no longer what it once was.

We had two days there and we checked into a fairly dilapidated hotel on the front overlooking the sea. The next day we went to the new Alexandrian Library, to whose director we had an introduction from Martin Palmer (a great traveller, broadcaster and environmentalist) who then lived in the parish of North Stoke which I looked after. The Director was busy, but an assistant gave us a splendid guided tour. Following in the tradition of the classical ancient library of Alexandria in the Serapeum, which was destroyed in a fire in c. 250 AD, this world heritage project lives up to its famous predecessor. The building itself is remarkable: designed as a huge open room with terraces of books and reading stations beneath a sloping roof with portholes for controlled sunlight, it stretches down to a perimeter lake and eternity pool water feature. It forms part of the University of Alexandria, and is thus well used by the students and a fitting successor to the great library of old, with a permanent display of ancient Arabic manuscripts from the ninth century. (The original classical library is said to have held four hundred thousand manuscripts, all lost!)

In contrast to the peace of the library there was a demonstration going on outside. We discovered it was a group of Coptic Christians demonstrating over the lack of security provided by the government for their worship. Indeed, 2011 proved a particularly bad year in Egypt for persecution of the Copts. The persecution was not the result of Christian missions encroaching in a Muslim country, but sheer resentment at their presence. For the Copts are an ancient Egyptian group as we have noted, worshipping Christ as they have done since c. 60 AD. In Alexandria on 7 January 2011 (their New Year's Eve) a bomb exploded in the Coptic Church of St Mark and Pope Peter, killing twenty and injuring ninety-seven. It was a massacre. This happened only four months before our visit to Egypt, and there had been many other incidents and attacks elsewhere on Coptic Christians and their churches. No wonder the Coptic community was so raw, but also so resolute. Given that the whole country was in ferment since the toppling of the government of Hosni Mubarak on February 11, it was the right time for the Coptic Church to make its voice heard as the future constitution was being decided, and the place of minorities affirmed.

That evening we had a meal in the Montgomery Bar in a local hotel. All around the bar were black and white photographs of General Bernard Montgomery, who had virtually liberated Alexandria from German attack in November 1942. El Alamein, which is in fact the name of a humble railway halt about sixty kilometres to the west of Alexandria, was where the 8th Army engaged German forces under the highly-regarded German commander, Marshal Edwin Rommel. A newly-resourced 8th Army (from the Americans) under the can-do leadership of Montgomery, forced the retreat of German and Italian Forces between 23 October and 11 November 1942. Of the victory of Alamein Churchill famously said, "It was the end of the beginning". Before it nothing had been won and afterwards nothing was lost. My father arrived with the 24 Guards Brigade on SS Samaria as part of Operation Torch, which landed in Algiers on 9 March 1943. They swept the remaining Italians and Germans from North Africa before invading Sicily and Italy together with the 8th Army.[130] Being in Alexandria, just a few miles from El Alamein, was a reminder of just how close German forces came to realising their objective of breaking through Egypt to seize the oil installations of the Gulf. Alexandria and Cairo were in panic and no one writes more vividly of those days than Olivia Manning in her *Levant Trilogy*. While the Battle of Stalingrad was underway in the East on a different scale of attrition, both campaigns marked turning points in the war and in both, vast numbers of prisoners were taken. The Wehrmacht

---

[130] Nigel Nicolson, *The Grenadier Guards in the War 1939–1945 Vol II* (Gale and Polden, Aldershot 1949), p. 312.

was overstretched by fighting on two fronts, North Africa and Russia, and the *coup de grace* was delivered in Normandy in 1944.

When I turned-in that night so many impressions of Alexandria crowded my mind and begged for attention: the classical city of Octavian, Anthony and Cleopatra; the great library now re-born; a city revived by Muhammad Ali Pasha as a polyglot Levantine capital; the nearby Suez Canal and the British years of influence; the cockpit of war of 1942; and now a nation seeking a new future with an ancient minority of Christian Copts seeking re-assurances of security and care in the wake of attacks. It was enough to keep a person awake all night!

The following day we did some fairly desultory sight-seeing of some of the Roman antiquities of the city, including the misnamed Pompey's pillar which is near the ancient Serapeum, the classical shrine which housed the great library. The pillar is misnamed because although the great Roman General Pompey, one of the Triumvirate who ruled the Roman Republic (0–48 BC), was murdered on board a ship in the harbour of Alexandria on the orders of Ptolemy XII, the pillar was in fact set up in honour of Diocletian (284–305 AD), the emperor more than two hundred years later. In the evening we went to a service at St Mark's Anglican church, where it was obvious how uncertain the future was since the Egyptian revolution in February, the throwing out of the old guard, and the attacks on the Coptic Church. We brought greetings from England and I was able to say a few words when they gave space in the service to welcomed any visitors among them. The service and Gothic church, which would have passed muster in any English market town, seemed like an island of Anglican normality, if there is such a thing, in a sea of change.

Cairo

The next day we left for Cairo by train. Had we had the car we would have visited a place called Tel-el-kebir on the way, a place with family connections. It lies about halfway between Alexandria and Cairo, not far from the city of Zagazig, on a canal flowing west from Ismailia and the Suez Canal. Here in 1882, my great-great uncle and great grandfather, who may not have even known each other, were part of General

Wolseley's force of twenty-five thousand regulars against an Egyptian force led by Arabi (Urabi), who had entrenched his force of about eighteen thousand soldiers near the Sweetwater Canal which joined Cairo with Ismalia. The battle started on 13 September 1882 at five thirty a.m. and during it my great grandfather, twenty-seven-year-old William Mordaunt Marsh Edwards from Hardingham, Norfolk of the 74th (Highland) Regiment of Foot, stormed an artillery placement on foot, killing some of the gun crew and becoming wounded himself. For this he was awarded a Victoria Cross. My great-great uncle on my father's side, Captain John Hanford Flood of the 19th Hussars, was General Wolseley's "galloper" (i.e., message-taker). The *Kilkenny Moderator* recorded Colonel Hanford Flood's death with the following dramatic description:

"Captain Flood was ordered to convey a message to the general commanding a division. To do which the young officer had to traverse a wide tract that was literally swept by Arab bullets. Captain Flood settling his monocle in his right eye, grasping the reins, pressing his knees tight to his horse's side set his charger at the gallop. The handsome young officer with the tawny hair, the light of battle illuminating his handsome face, swept across the bullet swept plain with as much concern for danger as if again he were following the county hounds at home in pursuit of a fox across the stonewall country of the Ballyhale."[131]

The obituary writer of the well-named *Kilkenny Moderator* and, perhaps not without a bit (or should I say a lot of poetic licence) of Irish blarney, goes on to say that this was the turning point of the battle! The result of the battle was more than uneven: British fatalities were put at fifty-seven and Egyptian deaths at two thousand. More happily, the VC's granddaughter, and the galloper's great nephew, my parents, were married in 1946. And I can't imagine that Tel-el-Kebir was on their minds for a moment!

I was sorry to miss the battlefield then and the chance to reflect on this little-known imperial campaign; instead, we were on the train to Cairo. (I was later to visit the battlefield in November 2020, in the midst

---

[131] *Kilkenny Moderator*, 19 August 1911, Obituary.

of the Pandemic, when recording some lectures on the Cappadocian Fathers in Heliopolis!)

When we arrived at Cairo's mainline Ramases Station and caught a taxi across to the Anglican cathedral hostel on Zamalek, I was quite relieved not be driving, given the unbelievable traffic and driving habits of Cairo, although I do like a challenge. With its twenty million inhabitants and their vehicles crammed onto every millimetre of the roads, progress was like bread rolls going through an intestine. It was exciting to have our first glimpse of the Nile and arrive at Zamalek: an island on the river, heavily populated with large hotels, embassies and the well-known El Gazira Club. In the days of the British, it also had a race course, a golf club and a country club. The Anglican Cathedral was close to the great river, so the sporting British of Zamalek could say their prayers without going far from their playground!

During two world wars, Cairo had been a centre of British military and social life and the place in which the uneasy relations between the Egyptians and the British were played out. On 28 June 1917, General Allenby— "the Bull" — having been transferred from the Western Front at Arras, arrived in Cairo to take command of the Palestinian Campaign, and inject new life and vigour into its prosecution.[132] His mission was to take Palestine and break the power of the Germans and Turks there. My grandfather, Bartholomew Edwards (son of the VC subaltern), served in the campaign with the Rifle Brigade. By Christmas 1917 the campaign had resulted in the taking of Jerusalem and the defeat of the Turks. It was a campaign that became as celebrated for its more eye-catching officers, such as T.E. Lawrence, Colonel Richard Meinertzhagen and the coming leader, Archibald Wavell, as for the battles won. It effectively opened up the whole of the Middle East to a political settlement in 1918 that was to set the parameters for the region's future, and its many continuing conflicts. In 1917, the main aim was to break the power of the Turks in the region, but more especially to secure oil for the modern industrialised economies of the British and French. And it was on account of that oil that the British under Wavell found themselves back in Cairo in 1940 with another army, this time to defend it from the Germans and Italians whose need for oil was urgent.

---

[132] Brian Gardiner, *Allenby* p115 (London: Cassell & Co, 1965), p. 115.

Between the years 1940 to 1944, Cairo was an extraordinary melting pot of talented individuals and traditional callings, of military power and diplomatic skill, of conflicting British and Egyptian interests, of regular soldiers and of the new military adventurism of the SOE (Special Operations Executive), of exploration and relaxation, of literary interests and of the need simply to let off steam. The city was a magnet that attracted the displaced royal families of Greece and Yugoslavia as the Germans pushed south, eventually taking nearby Crete in May 1941. It also had more than its fair share of authors, artists and poets. Cecil Beaton was an official war photographer at the front.[133] Freya Stark lit up conversation with her travel anecdotes and opinions. Olivia Manning, the author of the *Balkan Trilogy* and the *Levant Trilogy*, and her brilliant husband Reggie Smith, who worked with the British Council, looked for opportunities to shine. The Anglo-Egyptian Union, which boasted such names as Robin Redden, Bernard Spencer and Lawrence Durrell, founded the literary review *Personal Landscapes,* considered "the most influential literary magazine to come out of the war years".[134] Among these *literati* were soldiers like Enoch Powell, who would never remove his tie,[135] David Sterling planning the next adventure into the desert behind enemy lines with Fitzroy Maclean, and a German spy named Eppler who had been guided across the desert to Cairo by the great Hungarian desert explorer, Almasy.[136] The latter had discovered the Cave of Swimmers in 1933 and its prehistoric cave-art that depicts fish swimming in a desert cave, proving that the Gilf Kebir of Libya had once been by the sea or alongside a lake (This is a mesmeric part of the film *The English Patient*). As the writer Charles Johnston put it in his notebooks, "You arrive there [Cairo] from the material and emotional austerity of England, and before you know where you are, two hundred most intimate friends are dining with you by candlelight at small tables in a garden."[137] It was not quite the same as the Duchess of Richmond's Ball on the eve of Quatre Brass and Waterloo, but with two hundred thousand soldiers ready to engage the Germans at Alamein nearby, there

---

[133] Artemis Cooper, *Cairo in the War* (London: John Murray, 2013), p. 187.

[134] Cooper, *Cairo in the War*, p. 156.

[135] Cooper, *Cairo in the War*, p. 151.

[136] Cooper, *Cairo in the War*, pp. 211–212.

[137] Cooper, *Cairo in the War*, p. 230.

was more than a touch of the same.

Nor was it possible to keep Winston Churchill away from Cairo, as it was the main theatre for British troops until the Normandy landings. He first came in August 1942 after the loss of Tobruk, and saw to the replacement of General Auchinleck with General Montgomery (after the premature death of General Goss in an air accident). He came again after the conference in Casablanca in January 1943, once more after the victory of Alamein, and again for the Cairo Conference in November 1943 with Roosevelt and the Chinese leader Chiang Kai-Shek. Lastly, he came for a meeting in the desert with Egyptian King Farouk and the patriarch of the present Saudi dynasty, Ibn Saud, in February 1945, where they showered him with gifts.[138] Winston was told that Ibn Saud would not permit the drinking of alcohol in his presence, but unphased he had some glasses of medicine. Ibn Saud, not to be outdone, gave Winston a trousseau for his harem![139]

On our first full day in Cairo, we decided to walk from Zamalek to Tahrir Square. It was not far and the walk over the Nile, with the city laid out before us on the east bank was scenic, but as ever there was an immense volume of traffic along the main arterial roads close by, and a cloud of fumes. On arriving in the square, which had become familiar from broadcasts of the Egyptian Revolution just three months previously, all was peaceful. On the north side was the Egyptian Museum with its treasures of the Pharaoh's tombs, and particularly of the boy pharaoh, Tutankhamun. Looking like newcomers, we were accosted by a certain Dr Ali who said we should go to his friend's shop that sold perfume and papyrus. We did so, and I bought a papyrus with Egyptian hieroglyphics depicting a judgement of a soul! It depicted scales on which a person's heart was weighed: either the soul was innocent like a feather or guilty like a stone. If innocent, then Horus led the soul into paradise and everlasting life. There was no doctrine of grace, but the image served to show what we found out later, that death and the afterlife was an ever-present reality in ancient Egypt. On a more practical note, Michael thought I had been ripped off, maybe I was but I am pleased to have the picture!

---

[138] Cooper, *Cairo in the War*, p. 328–9.
[139] Cooper, *Cairo in the War*, p. 328.

We walked around the square, imagining the scenes of January and February a few months before, when the world's eyes were all on Cairo. At that point there were high hopes for the future of Egypt. It was still only sixty years since the "independence" of Egypt from the British. On that fateful day of 26 January 1952, the Egyptians made it clear that they wanted to be rid of the British. Although there was a garrison of eighty thousand troops still in the country near Ismailiyah, the Egyptian population, led by a combination of the Muslim Brotherhood and other groups, demonstrated their intolerance of the British presence. In Cairo, the Turf Club, Shepheard's Hotel—the hang out of the British in Cairo—Barclays Bank, Thomas Cook, W.H. Smiths were all burnt down.[140] British troops did not intervene, for the writing was on the wall. King Farouk was sent into exile, despised for his lack of Islamic devotion, his indolence and opulence, and the army, led by Gamal Nasser, took over. In effect the army and its front men have ruled ever since. And the Suez Crisis of 1956 in which the British with French and Israeli assistance, sought to regain control of the Suez Canal ended in British humiliation. The debacle marked the end of Britain's imperial role in the world: one of the main arteries of the British Empire, the Suez Canal, had become a stumbling block, it was nationalised by the Egyptian government. One can argue the end of British imperialism happened in Egypt.

The years between 1956 and 2011 followed a pattern. Wars with Israel ended in Arab defeat, although the first successes of the Yom Kippur war in 1973 were celebrated by the Egyptians. Attempts at a Pan Arab movement floundered on the individual aspirations of Arab states. There were increasing numbers of terrorist attacks on Coptic Christians, tourists and government buildings over the years—the worst on 17 November 1997 when sixty-two people, mostly tourists, were murdered at Luxor. President Sadat, who had succeeded Nasser in 1970, was assassinated for his accommodation with Israel and his allegiance to the United States. Sadat was succeeded by Mubarak (1981) in a referendum in which he was the only candidate. The economy could not keep pace with the population explosion which led to poverty and unemployment, the bane of the Arab world. The army in Egypt kept control, but increasingly used torture and detention without trial to get its way. It is a

---

[140] Cooper, *Cairo in the War*, p. 343.

way of governing the army and its political front men have continued ever since.

In 2011, the spark of the "Arab Spring" (winter?) that began in Tunisia spread to Cairo, and groups of young secular social-media savvy Egyptians occupied Tahrir Square, as did members of the Muslim Brotherhood representing the more grassroots popular Islamic movement among the poor. For weeks there were huge crowds in the square until Mubarak abdicated, later to be tried. Elections in 2012 resulted in a victory for the Muslim Brotherhood's candidate, Mohamed Morsi, but when a purge of judges took place, who were then replaced by the Brotherhood's nominations intent on imposing Sharia Law more comprehensively, the more secular Egyptians walked out of the Ruling Council. The army stepped in, appointing Field Marshal el-Sisi, the current ruler, whose appointment was "validated" by presidential and parliamentary elections. The hopes of February 2011 of neither party— the secular young or the populist Islam Brotherhood—were realised. When we talked to the Bishop of Cairo, Bishop Mouneer Anis, after apologising for not bringing him his car, he spoke of the heated discussions between the parties in a constitutional conference led by the temporary government he had attended that day. His object was to procure security for the Christian minority in the country for the future, but he realised how difficult it would be to get real change.

The rest of that first full day in Cairo we wandered the streets. We went into a mosque that seemed quite busy, where we got the distinct impression we were not wanted. We went on to another mosque more frequently visited by tourists called after its builder, Ibn Tulun. It is the oldest mosque in Cairo, dating to the Abbasid period (750–1258) when Cairo was ruled from Baghdad. It has a large courtyard at its heart with a fountain, pleasantly designed spaces, and a restored minaret, which we climbed. From the minaret there is a fine view of Cairo: a little to the east is the citadel with its palaces, museums and antiquities. To the north is the Abidin Palace, which had been the seat of the Royal family until King Farouk was deposed in 1952. We were getting the hang of Cairo: its incessant traffic, its vast population, the mighty Nile, its many mosques, its history, which although dating from the classical site at Heliopolis, was more fully developed by the Fatimids from 969 AD onwards. The next few days we were determined to explore Coptic Cairo.

Coptic Cairo and Beyond

Over the next three days we would visit the ancient centre of the Coptic faith in Cairo, based at the enclave at Mari Girgis in the southern part of the city; the famous church in the cave dedicated to St Simeon the Tanner in "Garbage city"; and we would stay two nights in the great Coptic Monastery of Saint Macarius the Great outside Cairo.

The word Coptic is simply derived from the Greek word for Egyptian. The church in Alexandria was founded by St Mark, associate of St Peter and author of the second Gospel, who came to Alexandria around 50 AD. Under powerful leaders, the Alexandrian branch became a formidable force in the ancient Orthodox church from the third century AD. Copts now make up ten to fifteen per cent of the population of Egypt. Often persecuted, and under-represented in government, they do not have the security they need. They are led by a Pope, have experienced considerable revival in recent years and a have rich history of scholarship, mission and prayer in Egypt and beyond.

We took the metro to Mari Girgis and stepped into a place that was quiet and restful. At the entrance there is an ancient Roman tower dating back to Emperor Trajan (98 AD), and in the compound there are a number of churches, a synagogue and the Coptic Museum, with many icons from Coptic churches. These icons are more vernacular in type than the more stylised Greek forms: the faces are rounder, the eyes are larger, attire is simpler, and cruelty and violence is generally avoided, with the result that a sense of peace and quiet joy emanates from them. One icon of the Archangel Michael shows the influence of ancient Egypt, with a staff in one hand representing eternity and immortality, and in the other the weighing scales signifying the Last Judgement which are so common in Ancient Egyptian tomb paintings. Looking at these icons it was interesting to see how Coptic Christianity gathered up some of the themes so prevalent in ancient Egypt, which were then given fresh meaning by Christian artists. It was as if the Archangel Michael had replaced Anubis.

From this enclave of ancient Coptic Churches, we went to a vibrant Coptic mission on the outskirts of the city, and to Garbage City at the base of the Muqattam hills. It is here that Coptic Christians known as the *Zabbaleen* are responsible for garbage collection around the city. Garbage is piled high in great mounds in the streets and on the roofs of houses for sorting: some is recycled—even by the resident pigs—while some is burnt. But also here, from the 1990s an extraordinary Coptic church began to be carved out of the mountainside, forming an auditorium capable of holding thousands. Every week on a Thursday evening it is full, and is an oasis of vibrant worship in the unlikeliest place in the city: the church of the rubbish collectors dedicated to St Simeon the Tanner.

The next day we left Zamalek for a two-day stay in a Coptic monastery in Wadi Natrun, some hundred kilometres north-west of Cairo past Sadat City and past the great military compounds that enclose both military and industrial facilities. Egypt has been from the third century a place of desert spirituality and monasticism. It was along the Nile, in the Nitrian Desert and in the Theabid, that much of this movement in the church began, and where the Desert Fathers and Mothers were to be found. One of the greatest ascetics alongside St Anthony was Macarius the Great (c300–391 AD), and the monastery dedicated to him was our destination.

The monastery is a mixture of fortress and refuge. It is surrounded by a high perimeter wall enclosing a large space in which there are gardens, a chapel with a high bell tower, accommodation blocks, the refectory and a very well-stocked library open to all. There is a chapel devoted to the memory of the Forty-Nine Martyrs of Scetis who were killed by the Berbers in 444 AD. The monks, of whom there were about a hundred, attired in long black robes and a black head covering, were friendly and active. The monastery had undergone a revival during the long papacy of Pope Shenouda III (1971–2012) and his predecessor, Pope Cyril VI, before whom it had been reduced to as few as six monks. There is now an impressive link between the monks and the coachloads of Coptic church members who visit the monastery most days to enjoy a day of refreshment and retreat.

The guest master, a monk named Bartholomew, was assigned to explain to us the workings of the monastery and the present position of the Coptic church in Egypt and its core beliefs. After decades of growth in both Egypt and the United States, the Church now felt better supported in its experience of persecution and its refusal to compromise with the government: for the Copts discretion was not the better part of valour. Bartholomew was critical of leadership in the Church of England for suggesting giving way to Muslim proposals to include Sharia law into British law, and of any proposed watering down of Christian teaching on marriage. In the Coptic community, sex before marriage, divorce, and gay marriage are all considered deeply regrettable.

Our meals mostly consisted of boiled eggs, lava beans, pita bread and feta cheese often surrounded by flies, and our cells or cubicles were hot and not free of mosquitoes which I chased all night. All of this was a mild taste of the ascetic life. After two days we went back to the flesh pots of Cairo for a final Sunday in the city. We worshipped at the newly-completed Cathedral, which hosts a large number of Sudanese refuges, had lunch with the Editor of the *Arab News*, met the bishop in the evening, and ate our final meal together in Egypt at La Bodega in Zamalek. The following day Michael went on his Nile Cruise and I headed out to the desert.

The Desert and The Nile

I was determined to visit the desert as well as the Nile; and with Olivia flying out in three days' time, this seemed the perfect opportunity. I asked around for a tour or safari to the desert and in the end, one was recommended. My guides picked me up on the Monday for a three-day excursion into the White Desert. I was the only guest, and two young Egyptians, Rash and Mohammad, were my companions for the next three days. I soon discovered that they were devout Muslims, since for the next three hours we had on the radio a fervent Muslim preacher. Had it been a year or two later, after the emergence of extreme Muslim groups such as ISIS operating in Egypt, I would have been a lot more hesitant about being on my own! My guides occupied the front seats of the 4x4; I was in the back. We headed south-west from Cairo towards Bawiti. Initially we were travelling through the suburbs of Cairo, not far from the Pyramids of Giza, and then we struck south. After at least two hours the preacher was thankfully turned off and I could begin to appreciate the scenery. We stopped at Bawiti for a drink and a quick look at the museum, which seemed more like a bunker, but nevertheless contains ten golden mummies found at the nearby Bahariya Oasis, and dates from the Graeco-Roman period from 300 BC. We drove on with the scenery becoming ever more the desert you might expect. At one point we stopped, and Rash beckoned me to go with him to a knoll a few hundred yards from the road. We climbed to the top of this bump and there all around us were sea shells. Once upon a time all this desert was under water. We drove on to the Farafra Oasis and the beginning of the White Desert.

As I had not seen any pictures of the White Desert, I was not prepared for the extraordinary landscape that confronted us. After visiting the gushing spring at Bir Sitta, we headed east driving off-road across the desert floor and into a forest of chalky rock formations that rise up from the ground to be crafted by the desert winds and tiny particles of sand and ice. The result is a ventifact: rocks sculpted by the wind into weird and bizarre shapes going as far as the eye can see across the four hundred square kilometres of desert. Some formations look like spires, others like camels, or old men sitting up to speak. There are chickens, and houses, and some are like giant balls balanced on poles: a whole orchestra of rock sculptures. Among and between them, were small mounds, sand dunes and rocky bluffs. There was no end of looking, nor of being enchanted and surprised by the landscape that stretched ahead of us.

As the light is gone by six p.m., we stopped early, at four, to set up camp: each in a one-man tent not far from the vehicle. In the evenings the wind gets up, so a breaker was needed to shelter behind and where Rash could set up the stove for the evening meal. The temperature would drop quickly from forty degrees Celsius, and soon the large-eared desert foxes would be circling the vehicle, looking for scraps. Having lost all fear because of the many safari groups that pass through, they would come almost right up to us, and then run off. There were few other visitors on account of the instability in the country. We only saw one other vehicle with some German travellers. And when the sun disappeared, the extraordinary desert night sky gave us a twinkling canopy above, beyond anything I had seen before. I don't think I have been anywhere so remote, so far from the madding crowd. Pulling down the zip on the tent for the night and reading a novel, I savoured the mild adventure of it all.

The next two days we wandered through the desert sometimes in the vehicle, at other times on foot, carrying a large bottle of ice that thawed quickly in the sun, just walking slowly and looking. We moved a little north to the Black Desert (Saha Suda). Here there is a change in the desert floor from sandy beige to black, the sediment of black volcanic rock of great density that is strewn over a wide area makes the scenery look like something out of Star Wars, eery and forbidding. One morning at breakfast a snake moved close to the vehicle looking for food. Rash caught sight of it and a hunt began as it slithered under the vehicle. It was eventually caught and despatched; an incident perhaps in keeping with the Black Desert.

We moved off to the west towards the great sandy expanse of the Gilf Kebir Plateau and closer to the Libyan border. It was here that the Hungarian explorer Lázsló Almásy found the cave art called the Cave of Swimmers that figures in an episode of the film *The English Patient*. Unable to get that far, and to the cave that is probably closed to visitors, we enjoyed the dunes—there are five different types of dunes, of which four are in Egypt—and then returned to the road back to Cairo. That night I met Olivia at Cairo airport with plenty of sand still in my boots and the following day we flew down to Aswăn.

The Nile

If ever a river created a civilisation, it was the Nile. If Alexandria, Cairo, the Coptic Church and the desert had already made a deep impression, it was all completed by the Nile. The river itself, which flows from Ethiopia (the Blue Nile) and from the great lakes' region of East Africa (the White Nile), converges at Khartoum into a single mighty river, is one of the phenomena of the world. Every year, until the building of the hydroelectric dam at Aswăn, there was an inundation of water irrigating the fields close to the river and thus providing crops to sustain Egypt and its population. We were to spend four nights on the Nile. It could have been forty, such was its entrancing effect.

Two things combine to make the Nile so beguiling. It is the cruise itself, travelling at a steady but sure pace along the downstream current, passing scenes of local agriculture which appear to be frozen in time. You see oxen ploughing, men and donkeys, crops ripening or being harvested along the banks. The other is the contrast between the settled life of the fields and the movement of the powerful river as it carries crafts of all kinds, from the elegant and romantic single-sail Felucca, to the little boats taking local people out fishing or moving about. Once again, because of the Arab Spring and the Revolution in February, our cruiser was less than half full, and the sights much less crowded than normal. We went from Aswăn to Luxor, a distance of about two hundred and fifty kilometres, with several stops along the way.

The High Dam, which replaced an earlier British-built dam, was the great symbol of Egyptian independence in 1952. Built with the help of Soviet engineers, the High Dam more effectively controlled the flow of water, regulating the inundation so as to irrigate without washing away crops. At the same time the river drove great turbines to generate electricity for the whole of Egypt and for export. The scale of the project, which involved the diverting of the river, and the removal of temples to Abu Simbel, was vast—involving forty-three million cubic metres of material. The lake created to the south, Lake Nasser, is over five hundred kilometres long and is, we were told, infested by crocodiles. At Aswăn we looked over the Temple of Philae, saw how an obelisk was taken out of the rock to be floated down the Nile, and then had English tea aboard the boat. It did seem at times like an episode out of Agatha Christie's *Death on the Nile*. Thankfully, there were no murders; perhaps because there was no Belgian heiress on board!

The Temple at Philae was certainly one to get your eye in. It was moved onto higher ground on an island when the High Dam was built and was thus approached by a small boat. Recent by Egyptian standards, it was built in the age of the Ptolemies in third century BC, although the cult of Isis at Philae goes back much earlier. Two courtyards are guarded by great *pylons*, which we quickly learnt are not the ungainly and unwelcome metal giants carrying electricity across lovely English countryside, but massive gateways to Egyptian temples. Inside the courtyards we were introduced to the main characters of Egyptian mythology: Isis, the goddess of healing, health and life, the protector of women and children and the wife of Osiris. Osiris is the god of the dead, of resurrection and fertility. Together they were the parents of the hawk-headed Horus, the protector of Egypt, of whom the pharaoh was the living embodiment. Amun (like Aten) the god of the sun, was the self-created one and supreme among all the gods, and came to the fore especially in the New Kingdom (to which we will return), while the jackal-headed Anubis oversaw the dead and mummification. These were the essential elements of Egyptian mythology; simpler, if anything, than the plethora of gods in Greek and Roman mythology with which we tend to be more familiar. The overriding concern in Egyptian life was preparation for death and the afterlife, which, in the case of the Pharaoh, led to the pyramids, to the necropolis in the Valley of the Kings, and to their tombs becoming repositories of untold treasures and mysteries.

It would not be an unreasonable summary of the next part of the cruise down the Nile from Aswăn to Luxor to say it had to do with taxes and death. As Benjamin Franklin famously said, "But in this world nothing can be said to be certain, except death and taxes". The truth of this was certainly well signalled on the Nile. Further downstream we reached the Temple of Kom Ombo. As with all Egyptian temples, they are a shrine to a particular god, in this case to Haroeris (a form of Horus) and Sobek the crocodile god. Built by Ptolemy XII, the temple followed the traditional design of forecourt, outer hall, inner hall, outer and inner antechambers, and a sanctuary where offerings were made to the gods. Outside the Temple, and nearer to the river, we found the Nilometer and here we come to the subject of taxes. The Nilometer measures the rise and the fall of the river. The higher the river rises, the higher the taxes, for the annual inundation is likely to result in greater irrigation of the fields and hence more food and income. The Pharaoh would tax accordingly.

Further downstream we came to an impressive temple dedicated to Horus at Edfu. The same pattern of construction was evident: pylons at the entrance, a large court of offerings with a colonnade, a library where sacred texts were stored on papyrus, an outer and inner hypostyle hall, a room for the preparations of offerings, and the sanctuary of Horus. And on the east wall of the temple, a Nilometer. Again, it was the priest's job to inform the Pharaoh's civil service of the level of inundation, for the priest was both a civil servant and a religious officer.

A hundred kilometres further and we were at Luxor, the capital of Upper Egypt, Royal Thebes. With Karnak and Luxor on the East Bank and the Temples of Al-Deir al-Bahari, Medinat, the Colossi of Menon and the Valley of the Kings on the West, it is quite simply in its entirety a "treasure house of countless wealth".[141] More than anything else, Thebes is the showcase of the New Kingdom 1539–1069 BC (the 18th–20th Dynasties) and the great stage of Egyptian kingship. The 18th Dynasty had a succession of eye-catching Pharaohs. Thutmose III (1479–1425) was the warrior conqueror who made inroads into the Levant, subduing all rivals.[142] His co-regent and aunt, Hatshepsut (1473–1458), was the Elizabeth I of the dynasty, a devotee of Hathor the mother goddess, and wily and skilful in diplomacy. She built the Temple of Deir al-Bahari, "one of the most remarkable buildings in ancient Egypt".[143] Amenhotep III (1390–1353), whose long rule gave him ample opportunity for self-promotion, commissioned the Colossi of Memnon in Western Thebes: statues of himself over sixty feet high guarded his mortuary temple.[144] There followed the heretic Pharaoh Akhenaten: "His seventeen-year reign and the tumultuous decade which followed were perhaps the most exhilarating, uncertain, dynamic and bizarre period in Egyptian history".[145]

Amenhoteb IV married the dazzlingly beautiful Nefertiti, whose sculpted head is now in Berlin, and then changed his name to Akenhaten. He changed his worship from Ammun to Aten, the sun god, and made himself into a personification of Aten, changing the main seat of power and the main place of worship to Akhetaten, much lower down the Nile at Amarna, south of El-Minya. Construction began there on a prodigious scale.[146] Mortality overcame Akenhaten's dream, and in the end his last daughter by Nefertiti married her nine-year-old half-brother,

---

[141] Homer, *The Iliad*, Book IX.
[142] Toby Wilkinson, *The Rise and Fall of Ancient Egypt* (London: Bloomsbury 2010), p. 243.
[143] Wilkinson, *The Rise and Fall of Ancient Egypt*, p. 243.
[144] Wilkinson, *The Rise and Fall of Ancient Egypt*, p. 265.
[145] Wilkinson, *The Rise and Fall of Ancient Egypt*, p. 279.
[146] Wilkinson, *The Rise and Fall of Ancient Egypt*, pp. 283–287

Tutankhaten, who restored the traditional worship, taking the name by which we all know him: Tutankhamun. Together this teenage couple had two still-born daughters, lovingly mummified and placed in the tomb with their father, to be discovered three hundred thousand and twenty-two years later in the most spectacular archaeological find of all time, by Howard Carter, funded by Lord Carnarvon.

Having gazed in awe at the Deir el-Bahari, the Temple of Hatshepsut, with its reliefs that record her birth, the triumphs of her reign and her expedition to the land of Punt with strange animals and exotic plants, we walked up the Valley of the Kings, surely the most famous necropolis in the world. We visited the tombs of Ramasses III, IV, and IX—Pharaohs of the 20th Dynasty. The tombs comprise a succession of rooms in descending levels until the tomb itself is reached. The rooms are decorated with vivid wall paintings and the chambers would have contained all that was considered necessary for the Pharaoh's transition to the afterlife. Their forbear, Ramesses II (1279–1213), was the Henry VIII of the 19th Dynasty. He checked the Hittites at Kadesh on the Orontes in Syria, saving the day by his prowess, and then began extensive building in Egypt, including the Ramesseum in Thebes and the temples and huge statues at Luxor, Memphis and Abu Simbel.[147] Often associated with the name Ozymandias in Shelley's famous sonnet, Ramesses II is also thought to have been the Pharaoh whose "heart was hardened" at the time of the Exodus of the Hebrews and the associated plagues (see Exodus 5–11).

Taking our leave of the Valley of the Kings and Queens and after a wonderful night at Luxor seeing the *son-et-lumière* at Karnak, we headed back to Cairo for a final night near Giza. If ever there is an example of a Pharaoh preparing for death in life, whilst at the same time demonstrating his absolute power, it is Khufu and his great pyramid. Built on a limestone stratum called the Mokattam Formation, the pyramid took two decades to build.[148] The work started at Khufu's accession, with four thousand men working in teams to bring cut stones on sledges from the nearby quarry and put them in place. Over two million stones weighing at least a ton each were required. The mathematics involved was as extraordinary as the organisation. In 2545 BC it was the largest building

[147] Wilkinson, *The Rise and Fall of Ancient Egypt*, pp. 324 ff.
[148] Wilkinson, *The Rise and Fall of Ancient Egypt*, p. 81.

project on the planet. (The great Wall of China would not be completed until the Ming dynasty (1368–1644). In the pyramid the family's burial chamber, with all that they supposedly would need for the afterlife. Leading from the chamber were shafts or channels pointing upwards and outwards to the circumpolar stars which never set: a metaphor of the king's eternal destiny. And nearby was the pyramid of his successor-but-one, Khafra, almost as large as Khufu's, and alongside that the Sphinx: the symbolic figure of a being with the body of a lion and the head of a human, symbolizing a combination of courage and wisdom. It was a good place to leave Egypt: its ancient history, its modern history, the world wars fought around its territory, and its hopes for the future after its most recent revolution. It had been an extraordinary month since leaving England.

Chapter XII
Balloons over Cappadocia

In 2013 I visited Cappadocia in central Turkey together with Tom and Paul. Tom had already journeyed with me to Athos; and Paul to Ephesus, Patmos and the sites of the Seven Churches of Asia Minor, so we were getting used to travelling together.

The plan for the trip was to go to Istanbul and straight on to Kayseri, the provincial capital of Cappadocia. We would then return overland to Istanbul, where our three wives would meet us for a long weekend, before returning on the second May Bank Holiday. For me, the main purpose of the trip was to discover more of the background of three men I was thinking of writing about: the Cappadocian Fathers who lived in the fourth century AD and who had a profound influence on the church (although some may not have heard of them). I was instinctively drawn to them, had started to read about them, and was dipping into their writings, about which more in a moment.

We flew from London Heathrow to Istanbul (everyone's passport was present and correct!), and at Istanbul we transferred to an internal flight to Kayseri, the modern name for the Roman city of Caesarea, the capital of Roman Cappadocia. In two hours, we were in Kayseri from where we caught a taxi to our hotel in Ürgüp, where we stayed three nights in a single room. Thanks to the wonders of modern travel, we were settled into our cave hotel in the heart of Turkey and eating very Turkish food in a cave restaurant in Ürgüp by the evening.

The first thing I must point out is that in this part of the world, most things happen in caves. There are cave houses, cave hotels, cave restaurants and cave churches, all to do with the remarkable geology of Cappadocia.

This geology is almost unique. Some ten million years ago there was strong volcanic activity during a period when continents were forming— the early Miocene era. Lava produced by these volcanoes formed on a plateau a layer of tufa rock, which varied in hardness. The flow of rivers and water in the area then contributed to the erosion of this rock, leaving behind the present conic shapes in the valleys of the region. Bizarre, almost comical, rock formations resulted, from whose bases chimneys of tufa rock known as "fairy chimneys" protrude. These chimneys consist of tufa cones, sometimes looking like the pointy hoods of monks, with a boulder or cap on the top. The cone is of tufa, but the cap is made of harder, more resistant rock, such as lahar or ignimbrite. In Cappadocia there is a collection of shapes: caps, cones, mushroom-like formations, columns and pointed rocks. It is these shapes that make the landscape so amusing and mesmerising. The larger formations can be hollowed out relatively easily, making possible the construction of cave-houses, hotels, restaurants, churches, and in several places, whole underground cities.

Cappadocia was settled by the Cappadocians in about 700 BC. There were, however, much earlier temporary settlements to the north-east of Kayseri around Kültepe. These were trading colonies established by Assyrian merchants from Mesopotamia on the Anatolian plain at the cross-roads of trade routes— north-south and east-west—as far back as 2000–1750 BC. To the south of Kayseri lie the Taurus mountains and, further south, the city of Tarsus on the Mediterranean, passed which we had travelled on my way to Syria in 2002. To the north of Kayseri is Ankara and the route to the Black Sea; to the east is Persia and Mesopotamia; and to the West the route to Ankara and Constantinople.

From the fourth century BC, Cappadocia came under the influence of Greece, following its conquest by Alexander, and by 160 BC had its own Greek king, Ariarathes IV, who had become a client king of the Persians (2210–163 BC). It was the Romans who would soon become the overlords of Cappadocia as Cappadocia became a frontier province abutting Armenia under the Emperor Tiberius. Although Cappadocia had by the third century AD become a well-established Roman province, it was also vulnerable to attack by the Sassanid armies from Persia. By the fourth century AD, with the new toleration of Christianity in the Empire, it had developed a strong Christian presence.

There appears to have been a Christian presence in Cappadocia from as far back as around 55 AD. Jews from that region were present on the day of Pentecost (Acts 2: 9). The Apostle Peter addressed his first letter to those residing in Pontus on the Black Sea and Cappadocia (1 Peter 1:1). Pliny the Younger was the governor of the neighbouring provinces of Bithynia and Pontus, and he reported to Emperor Trajan on the activities of Christians in his jurisdiction.[149] When Origen, the great third century philosopher and exegete, came to Caesarea Marittima in Palestine around 230 AD, he trained one Gregory Thaumaturgus (the wonder worker) and later bishop of Neo-Caesarea, who then became a missionary to Cappadocia.[150]

Gregory came to work in Cappadocia and had a powerful effect on one family who were to become leading Christians in the province, as well as being part of the provincial landowning elite. St Basil of Caesarea's grandmother, Macrina, became a devout believer, then likewise her daughter Emmelia, the mother of Basil, Gregory of Nyssa and of their older sister Macrina, whose life would be written by Gregory Nyssa.[151] This family, together with Basil's university friend, Gregory Nazianzen, were to have a lasting effect on the development of Christianity over the next eighteen hundred years, and their influence is still felt today.

In brief, each of these men, known as the Cappadocian Fathers (not forgetting their devout sister Macrina), contributed a strand to their overall mission and thought. The background to their lives was the great controversy that had erupted in the early fourth century over the divinity of Christ. Arius, a priest from Alexandria, persuasively maintained that "there was a time when Christ was not". In other words, in his pre-incarnational existence, Christ was a created being and not "of the same substance as the Father". Although the Council of Nicaea, convened by the Emperor Constantine, in 325 AD, upheld the divinity of Christ in the Nicene Creed, a number of bishops, plus the new Emperor Constantius, rowed back from that orthodoxy. Each of the Cappadocian Fathers sought to promote the orthodoxy of Nicaea in striking ways. Gregory Nazianzen (c. 330–390) did so in his eloquent set of *Orations* given in Constantinople in 379. Basil (c. 329–379) wrote the long *Contra*

---

[149] Pliny, *The Letters of the Younger Pliny*, ed. Betty Radice (London: Penguin Classics, 1963), pp. 293ff.

[150] Philip Rousseau, *Basil of Caesarea* (Berkeley, CA: University of California, 1998), p. 4.

[151] Rousseau, *Basil of Caesarea,* p. 3.

Eunomium against the Arian position as put forward by a philosopher Eunomius; and, having been made Bishop of Caesarea in 370, Basil encouraged his fellow bishops to hold the orthodox line. Gregory of Nyssa (334 –395) also burnished his Orthodox credentials by writing, like his older brother, his own *Contra Eunomium.*

There was more to the Cappadocians than doctrinal orthodoxy, however—not that orthodoxy was unimportant at that critical juncture in the development of Christianity. On arrival at Kayseri, I asked an English-speaking Turk whether Basil of Caesarea was still remembered in Kayseri. He surprised me when he said he was, for after all it is now an entirely Muslim city. He said they still had a feast day when Basil was remembered in the city. Why was that, I asked. "Because he helped the poor" came the quick reply. Indeed, in 369 Basil set up a monastic community in the city called the *Basileiados*, which developed over a number of years following a famine. It was financed by Basil's own inheritance. A whole range of buildings were established to care for the sick, welcome the traveller, and distribute food and clothing to those in need.[152] Alongside the institution, a group of monks were professed who followed a rule written by Basil, and in which he himself took part, washing the feet of the poor. This monastic community was one of the first of its kind in a city-setting, for in Egypt such communities were more found in more isolated locations in the desert.

Alongside upholding orthodoxy and taking compassionate action was a deep commitment to prayer. This was a fundamental part of each of the Cappadocians' lives. It was sometimes called the *philosophic life*, and centred around withdrawal to a remote place for several days for contemplation and prayer. Although each was dedicated to this practice, Gregory of Nyssa made it a major part of his life. In various works, such as *The Life of Moses*, and his commentary on the *Song of Songs,* he wrote mystically about prayer and its effect. This prayer was spurred on by a concept of the soul ascending to God and leaving behind the restraints of what they called "this garment of skin", and in the process experiencing "sober inebriation", joy and transformation.

Prayer was the means of penetrating the incomprehensible and invisible nature of God. These three things: doctrinal orthodoxy,

---

[152] Rousseau, *Basil of Caesarea,* p. 141.

compassionate action inspired by a desire for social justice, both undergirded by contemplative prayer, are what made the Cappadocian Fathers so inspiring for generations to come.

Churches in Göreme and the Surrounding Area

Until 1071, Cappadocia formed part of the Byzantine Empire, but on that date, just five years after the Normans conquered England at the Battle of Hastings, there was a change of power in Cappadocia and seven hundred years of Christian rule came to an end. This followed the Battle of Manzikert when Alp Arslan, the leader of the Seljuk Turks from Khorasan north of Iran and east of the Caspian Sea, swept through central Anatolia, taking charge in central Armenia and Cappadocia. From then on, the Turks would rule central Turkey (as we now know it). Gradually, the Christian Community would dwindle and the area would become increasingly Muslim, but what the Christians left behind in the cave churches with their art may still be seen and admired today, especially in Göreme.

Göreme is just a little to the north east of Ürgüp, where we were staying in our cave hotel, enjoying breakfast on the roof and a fine view over the town. The landscape around Göreme has many fairy chimneys and the Kiliçlar valley nearby is also filled with these "stone hoodies". In a small area around Göreme are countless churches and monasteries, some with intriguing names like the Snake Church (Yilanli Kilise). Inside is a fresco of St Onuphirios: a beautiful woman who had pleaded with God to protect her from men's advances. Her wish was granted: she grew a beard and her face was disfigured. In the church there is a picture of a figure of a half-man half-woman with a beard and breasts, but a well-positioned shrub growing up "her' legs shields her modestly. The fresco represents a lesson in ascetic living, where beauty is renounced for the sake of virginity, yet leaves behind the thought "be careful what you pray for".

The churches in Göreme have long since been abandoned. Their heyday appears to have been the ninth to the twelfth centuries, when a number were excavated from the tufa rock and decorated. The oldest church is the Tokah or Buckle Church. It has a single nave, and a barrel-vaulted ceiling, but lost its apse when a new church was added to its east wing. The wall paintings are in a simple provincial style, the later frescos more metropolitan. The simpler frescos tell the main stories of the Gospels: the Nativity, the coming of wise men, the massacre of the innocents, the flight into Egypt, the ministry of Jesus, the last supper, the betrayal by Judas, the crucifixion, deposition, burial and resurrection. The background is a homely green and the figures are mostly dressed in red. By contrast the new Buckle Church is decorated with frescos painted in blue of the deepest lapis lazuli, and tell of the cycles of Christ's life as well as events in the life of St Basil.

The jewel among these churches of Göreme is the Dark Church. It is further up the rock face, and accessed by a winding staircase that leads into a rectangular, barrel-vaulted narthex, which in turn opens into a cruciform church at the centre of which is a dome with four columns and three apses. Because there is only a single tiny window in the narthex, it is called the Dark Church. But what it lacks in natural light, being in a cave, it makes up for in spectacular and vividly-coloured wall paintings. It is as if all the sophistication of the capital, Constantinople, has come to the provinces. If St Saviour's in Chora, Istanbul, is the most spectacular of all the churches after Hagia Sophia there because of its frescos and mosaics, the Dark Church in Göreme is no less impressive. Almost every wall is covered with frescos, beautifully executed and still freshly coloured, the style distinctly Byzantine. A cycle of the nativity and passion are especially striking. One fresco of a dynamic, victorious, risen Christ dragging Adam from the grave is an echo of the same theme in St Saviour's, Chora, and demonstrates the consistency of Byzantine art. And on the central dome is a Christus Pantocrator.

Having looked around the churches we sat on the rocks outside and Tom read one of St Basil's many letters. In fact, after Cicero, there are more letters from Basil than any other author in classical literature. The subjects vary from doctrinal exhortations upholding Nicaea, to pastoral letters restoring fallen Christians; and from fundraising appeals addressed to wealthy Romans to missives for the bereaved. He could be harsh, as he was to his brother Gregory of Nyssa for deceiving him by forging a letter seeking to heal a breach with their uncle. On that occasion he said, "I write these words to upbraid you for your fatuity—which I consider at no time befitting a Christian and entirely out of place at the present moment".[153] Or, after pages of condemnation for her actions, he says to a woman who has broken her vow of virginity, "If you give yourself to Him, He will not delay, nor in His kindness will He disdain to carry you on His shoulders, rejoicing that He has found His sheep which was Lost".[154] It was tough love: for all the art of the churches, there lay behind it a demanding Christian community.

Underground, Overground, Wandering Free

Our remaining two days in Cappadocia before catching an overnight coach to Istanbul were spent exploring the amazing scenery of the region: going underground, walking along its canyon valleys and floating serenely above in a balloon.

We began by going underground. The tufa rock had made it possible to excavate space for underground cities, and that is what had happened. For security in times of trouble whole communities could live as troglydites underground. There are at least one hundred and fifty underground and cliff settlements of this kind.[155] A few of these cities were capable of holding up to thirty thousand people for short periods. As with the one we visited, these sites were on several levels. There were long corridors off which apartments were created with wooden doors that fastened from the inside. The corridors were broken in places by large millstones that could seal off the passageways. Apertures in the middle of the millstones could be used for observation, and for shooting arrows. Linseed oil was used to burn in lamps, food was stored in larders, and latrines of the long drop kind were provided with lime.

On the upper levels, horses were stabled with ramps to the surface. Fodder was kept nearby. Kitchens were provided communally, and water was stored nearby. Special ovens called *tandirs* produced daily rations of bread. Barley, wheat, vegetables and oil were kept in large earthenware jars still visible. Wine was kept in cellars and wineries kept production

---

[153] *St. Basil's Letters Vol. I*, ed. Roy Deferrari, Loeb Classical Library, Vol. 190 (Boston MA: Harvard University Press, 1963), p. 359.
[154] *St. Basil's Letters Vol. I*, pp. 283–311.
[155] Murat Ertugurul Gulyaz, *World Heritage in Cappadocia* (Istanbul: Unal ikizoglu, 2009), p. 83.

going from the grape harvest. As in Kaymakli, chapels were carved out to provide places of worship. All in all, human life could continue for weeks on end until danger passed and the population could move back to their above-ground villages. It was an impressive expenditure of energy and ingenuity aimed at maintaining life when invaders came through— generally from the east.

The city we visited, and probably the one most frequently visited, was Derinkuyu, which probably dates from the Hittite times, (1600–1000 BC) although it was used into the Roman area and beyond. It had up to eight levels and covered a surface area of four-square kilometres. Here apartments with their own kitchens were grouped around a central ventilation shaft and passages up to ten kilometres long linked one underground community with another. Yet despite the ingenuity of design, it was a relief to get into the fresh air and the bright natural light.

Another feature of Cappadocia is the canyon-like valleys that flow through the region, carved out by rivers running through the soft Tufa rock. The most scenic of these is the Ilhara Valley, which weaves for fourteen kilometres below the surrounding plateau. It is as if the floor of the valley has dropped down a few hundred feet to form a gorge, which is irrigated by the river that feeds a profusion of flowers, trees, shrubs and wild life. The river in this valley is the "Potamus Kapadukas" or the River of Cappadocia, now known as the Melendiz River, and which found its way through the cracks in the basalt and andesite lava. It now wiggles its way through the canyon. Roses, irises, poppies, the tall nigella Damascene (part of the Persian series), and the bright and fresh blue flowers of Omphalodes Cappadocia and its white-flowered sister Omphalodes Linifolia or Venus's navel can be seen. To be in Cappadocia in spring is very heaven.

Not surprisingly others found the valley to be a place of inspiration and along the river many chapels and monasteries sprang up between 300 and 1200 AD, when the exodus of Christians began. They have long since been deserted. The wall paintings are patchy and missing parts of their subjects, the tombs in the churches are empty spaces (you can try them out for size, and we did!). There are about twenty-five of these chapels in the valley, which must have been a veritable canyon of prayer.

We took an afternoon walk in another valley closer to Göreme. It was likewise a canyon where the river had cut through the high-rise cliffs on each side, providing places to scramble, but more importantly, a continuous dovecote. Pigeons or doves were an important part of the agricultural and cultural life of Cappadocia. Dovecotes, facing east or south, were hollowed out of almost all the cliffs and fairy chimneys of Cappadocia. Dove or pigeon droppings were then gathered for fertiliser and the eggs used to fix or glaze paint. Boys, functioning as the fairy-chimney-sweeps of Cappadocia, were sent up to the collect the eggs from these dovecotes.

For our third dinner in Göreme, we chose a rooftop restaurant in town. Anna Shea, a Canadian human rights lawyer, who we met on one of our tours, joined us. Like us she loved the area, and was and is enthusiastic about Turkish culture, art and landscape. We chose to eat the Cappadocian speciality, a pottery kebab. Cooked in individual earthenware pots the kebab of beef or chicken is cooked slowly with tomato, peppers, aubergine, potato and garlic. When served, the waiter brings a hammer and cracks the pot open in front of you. It is a bit of drama than any visitor can't fail to love. Eaten with flat bread, other spicy sauces and a Turkish red wine, what could be more delicious?

The following day was our last in Cappadocia, and like thousands before us we chose to go on a balloon ride to survey the Cappadocian scenery from above. Meeting early in the morning outside the town we joined scores of other balloons in a drift across the terrain. We could see it all plainly: the rocky canyons with a green thread of trees and shrubs running like a ribbon along the canyon floor, showing the presence of a stream; the fairy chimneys protruding from the floor with their caps on, standing to attention like immovable sentinels; the broad plateau worked hard by women in traditional dress with only hand tools to help them in their back-breaking work; and shepherds pasturing their flocks of sheep. It was a timeless scene as we drifted above with only the noise of the burn in the balloon that we might gain height. After an hour or so we came down, chilled by the early morning air, and were given a glass of Turkish fizz and a certificate of our adventure.

We were moving on to Istanbul by coach. It was a journey of seven hundred and fifty kilometres and would take over eight hours. It was my first overnight coach journey since visiting the United States in 1969.

The coach, scenery and language might have been different, but the experience of an overnight coach journey was much the same: the fitful sleep, the occasional stop and the disembarking into cold night air. The journey would take us through the new capital (Ankara) to the old capital (Istanbul). Indeed Istanbul, literally translated, means "to the city", and is a corruption of the old Greek *"'s tin polin"*.[156] Thus if you are going to the city from somewhere you were going "Istanbul". We were going there to meet our wives who were flying out for a weekend.

Back to Istanbul

The bus followed the route of the old Silk Road from Persia to the Mediterranean, where there would have been many *caravanserais* on the way; indeed, there are still several of these in Cappadocia where a caravan, a group of travellers journeying together, put up overnight with their mules, camels or horses. It is interesting how in English the use of the word has morphed into a mobile home towed by a car, which in effect means taking your own *caravanserai* with you. And what a *caravanserai* is on land, a convoy is at sea, only for shelter a convoy must reach port.

We arrived in Istanbul, this vast city of some sixteen million inhabitants, early in the morning, and having left our luggage at the Orient Express Hotel, began a bleary-eyed morning of sight-seeing, taking buses across the city. Knowing that with Olivia, Katherine and Wiola, we would look at some of the main sights together, we headed for the more recent parts of the city, those dating at least from the nineteenth century.

At Carlowitz near Belgrade, a Peace Treaty was struck between Austria Hungary (the Hapsburgs) and the Ottoman Empire or the Sublime Porte as it came to be known in 1699. Arbitrated by the English and Dutch, it marked a moment of transformation in the life of the Ottoman Empire, which went from being an offensive to a defensive empire. (Something similar happened with the Roman Empire in the second century AD, when Hadrian built a wall on the Scottish border.[157]) It was now an Empire of Viziers, Janissaries and Dragomans, the latter

---

[156] Steven Runciman, *A Travellers Alphabet* (London: Thames and Hudson, 1991), p. 55.
[157] Philip Mansel, *Constantinople* (John Murray 2006), p.145ff.

the multilingual advisers or guides who acted as middlemen between the incoming European powers to Istanbul and the Sultan. As in other cities of the Levant, Phanariot Greeks, Armenians, Jews, the French, the Russians, the Austrians and the British, not only had embassies, but whole communities settled in the city. Some families, like the Mavrocordatos and the Cantacuzenos, could glide between Ottoman, Greek, Wallachian and French interests with social skill and linguistic expertise. The Phanariot Greeks occupied the area of Istanbul called Phanar or the Fener district mid-way up the Golden Horn in the old city. The greatest of the Phanariot Greeks, and displaying their polymath tendencies, was Nicholas Mavrocordato, who would "retire to his library, to study botany, learn Hebrew, read the latest French books or correspond with the Archbishop of Canterbury".[158]

The embassies of the great European powers took up residence at Pera on the hill above Galata. The area is easily identified by the Galata Tower, once called the Tower of Christ and built in 1348 by the Genoese, who had followed the Venetians to Constantinople after 1261.[159] The European embassies clustered around Pera, and as trade concessions were made to the European powers, so there was incessant to-ing and fro-ing between the embassies and the Vizier's office near the Topkapi Palace. It was in a wooden house on Pera that in 1717 Lady Mary Wortley Montagu, the British Ambassador's wife, dressed up in Turkish clothes, paid court to the Sultan, wrote home to Congreve, Pope, Lady Bristol and Lord Cadogan, and gave birth to a daughter before sailing back to England on the *Preston*.[160] She painted a vivid picture of life in Istanbul in the eighteenth century. For the next two centuries, until the demise of the old Constantinople after the First World War, and its most ancient ethnic communities such as the Greeks and the Armenians, the city was a centre of European diplomacy.

For the few hours on the day of arrival we ranged over the area of the city we would not have time for in the next two days. This took us further west into the Old City, and the area known as the Third and Fourth Hills, towards the Fatih Camii Mosque built by Mehmet the Conqueror and designed by the great architect of the city, Atik Sinan. Attached to

---

[158] Mansel, *Constantinople*, p. 157.
[159] Bettany Hughes, *A Tale of Three Cities* (xxxxx), p. 380.
[160] Isobel Grundy, *Lady Mary Wortley Montagu Comet of the Enlightenment* (Oxford: Oxford University Press, 1999), p. 134ff.

the mosque are eight madrassas or Islamic schools. It was on this site that the Church of the Holy Apostles was built, where Emperor Constantine was buried and which was surpassed in scale only by Hagia Sophia. A ruin by the time of the Fall of Constantinople in 1453, the church became a builders' yard for the new mosque, which was constructed from stone from the ruins. The original mosque was destroyed in an earthquake in 1766 and little remains except the courtyard of its replacement. Nearby, on the Fourth Hill, are the remains of St Polyeuktos, a church from the early sixth century built for an imperial princess, Anicia Juliana, a member of the Imperial family and descendent of Theodosius I.

As always, in amongst the arcades, the hotels, and the modern shopping streets of Istanbul, there are at least seventeen hundred years of history in an architectural mosaic of the past. Mid-afternoon we returned to the hotel to wait for the others to arrive, and when they did, we were ready for dinner on the rooftop restaurant with its views across the Sea of Marmara, for the position of the city on the sea lanes of the Bosporus mesmerises and makes for endless fascination.

Over the next two days, we saw the classic sights of Istanbul: Hagia Sophia, the Blue Mosque, Topkapi Palace, the Covered Market and Spice Market, and the great mosque of Suleymaniye. Paul and Catherine went to have a Turkish bath and massage at Cemberlitas Hamami, operating since 1584, where they were massaged to an inch of their lives! But the highlight for all of us was a boat trip down the Bosporus in brilliant sunshine.

Perhaps the best way to catch the atmosphere of Istanbul is from the water and the great sea lanes that pass by the city. There are plenty of boats touting for business below Topkapi Palace. Once aboard and out on the water the geography comes to life. Ahead is Asia, on the other side of the Bosporus, and the road we took to Konya and beyond in 2002. Soon we would go under the first of two bridges that cross from Europe to Asia. Behind us was the Golden Horn: the finger of water stretching north and dividing parts of Istanbul. Over it the Galata bridge, which was built in the nineteenth century that consuls and embassies might make their way from their palaces to the Sublime Porte, and for which in 1519 the polymath Leonardo da Vinci put in a design to the Sultan. Now it was thronged with people lingering and meandering along, what is for the most part, a double-decker bridge a kilometre long, with kiosks and shops on its lower deck.

We made our way in full sunshine up the Bosporus to Ortaköy, passing the white icing cake palace of Dolmabahçe. The palace, with its three hundred and four rooms, was the creation of Sultan Adbulmecid I (1839–1861), who moved there permanently from Topkapi on 7 June 1856,[161] in a statement of imperial power made by the Ottomans soon after the Crimean war. The palace has the largest throne room in the world, and the opening banquet on 22 July 1856 saw the British Ambassador, Stratford Canning, and the French Commander, Maréchel Pelissier, seated either side of the Grand Vizier, below the Sultan. They had something to toast: they had seen off the Russians—even if in a very unsatisfactory campaign we call the Crimean War. More British troops had died from cholera than in the fighting despite Florence Nightingale's nursing. And despite the throwing away of lives in the glorious but hopeless Charge of the Light Brigade it became an inspiration for an upcoming imperialist age. By 2014, after a short absence since 1991, the Russians were back in the Crimea. Rightly or wrongly, it was their backyard, and giving it up to the Ukraine in 1991 was regarded by Putin as a huge mistake. It was their naval window, via the Black Sea, onto the Mediterranean.

We sailed as far as the fortress of Rumeli Hisari, where the Bosporus is just seven hundred metres wide and where the Persian King Darius took a grand army across a pontoon bridge designed by Mandrocles of Samos to invade Greece. The fortress there was built for Sultan Mehmet II who captured Constantinople in 1453. It was designed to hold the Bosporus and prevent any re-supply of the besieged city. Before reaching the Black Sea where I had been in 1972, we turned around. Tom and Wiola stopped off to look round the Dolmabahçe Palace properly, while we wandered round the streets of old Istanbul and then enjoyed a final dinner with some Americans we had met in Göreme, before flying back to London the following day.

---

[161] Mansel, *Constantinople*, p. 272.

Send-off Party from Bath to Damascus: Julie from Peugeot Motors in Westbury who prepared the car, the author, The Mayor of Bath with greetings to the Mayor of Kaposvar Hungary, and Michael Fowler my travelling companion. 2002

Bomb Damage in Belgrade in 2002

A meeting with the Architect, Branko Pešic, and his wife. Architect of
the new Cathedral of St Sava in Belgrade. 2002

The Village of Koprivititsha in Bulgaria where the uprising against
Turkey in 1875 led to the Bulgarian Atrocities, highlighted by William
Gladstone in 1876. 2002

The remains of the Emperor Constantine's palace at Nicaea (Iznik)
where the Nicene Creed was hammered out in 325 AD. 2002

A field of Opium Poppies by the roadside in central Turkey 2002

The modern approach to the ancient city of Antioch: the nearby border
between Turkey and Syria was a nightmare in 2002

The view from the Citadel of Aleppo in 2002. Today this is mostly destroyed

The Citadel, built in 12th Century, now badly damaged

The Church of St Simeon Stylites c390-459AD and the remains of the
rock upon which he lived. Emperors and peasants consulted him

The famous water wheels at Hama transferring water from the Orontes to Aqueducts, much destroyed by the Civil War – everything seemed so quiet then.

Palmyra: the city of Queen Zenobia in the desert – The Colonnade. 2002

The Library at Ephesus 2008

Angela's place on Samos, overlooking the dark blue Aegean

Which one is called Pachomius and has spent 23 years saying the Jesus prayer in Athos?

Tom (left), Patrick and Michael. Permissions, called *Diamonitirion*, in hand ready to visit Mt Athos for three nights, 2009

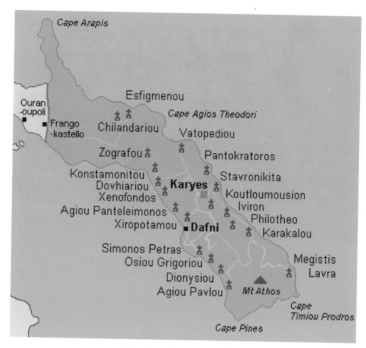

A Peninsula of Monasteries

Team meeting with Mufti of Bauchi and the Bishop, Nigeria 1995

Meeting with Lay Leaders in Bauchi Diocese

Setting off with Nigel Rawlinson to Maridi South Sudan

Arrivals at Maridi: no queues at arrivals or departures! 2012

Jerusalem and the Temple Mount with the Dome of the Rock, 1979

On safari with Ora in the Sinai for a week, thankfully not 40 years!

Olivia, newly married, November 1979

Chapter XIII
No Chickens in Kyiv

Of all the trips that I have been on, this one had the most extraordinary genesis. Occasionally, we would get a call in our church office from someone wanting to use the church for a concert or to make an appeal for support. I remember one year it was a group of male singers from St Petersburg who wanted to come and sing. I gladly agreed and a few of us put them up before the concert. It was a warm summer's day, and the Russians wanted to sunbathe. I looked out of the Rectory window to see all five wearing only their underwear, soaking up the sun! I told Olivia that she had better not go out into the garden: perhaps thoughts of headlines in the *Bath Chronicle* came to mind: "Rector's wife with five Russian men in underwear in Rectory Garden!" At any rate, they sang the better for the sun that evening; and, as always with unaccompanied Russian part-singing of church and folk songs, their performance was extraordinarily accomplished and beautiful.

A year or so later we received another call: "Could a Russian nun (a Belarusian nun, in fact) come and make an appeal in our church?" She came to a Tuesday morning service to tell us her story, as translated by Wiola, our resident interpreter as they both spoke Polish. The nun was in Bath for three weeks and had a stall in the Christmas market raising money for her convent in Minsk. In fact, she and others came back every year for the next few years. We got to know them, and we learnt about their extraordinary work in Minsk.

The convent was started by a member of the Russian Royal family, and a great Aunt of Prince Philip, Duke of Edinburgh (1921–2021). The founder of the Saint Elisabeth Convent in Minsk was the Grand Duchess Elisabeth, who was married to Grand Prince Sergei Romanov, the son of Tsar Alexander II. Sergei became a polarizing figure in Moscow when in 1891 he expelled some twenty thousand Jews; many came to the East End of London. Elisabeth was the daughter of Princess Alice Hessen Darmstadt, the third child of Queen Victoria who died young aged thirty-five and was named after the extraordinary St Elizabeth of Hungary.

Elisabeth was therefore a grandchild of Queen Victoria and her niece was Princess Alice of Battenberg, the mother of Prince Philip. Prince Philip's mother, Alice, was married to Prince Andrew of Greece and Denmark, and had herself worked in an Orthodox nursing order of nuns giving help to Jewish refugees, for which service she was recognised as one of the "Righteous among the Nations" at Yad Vashem in Jerusalem. Both Alice and her Aunt Elizabeth were buried in the Orthodox church on the Mount of Olives.

Princess Elisabeth was part of the tragedy that befell the Romanov family in the Russian Revolution. She married Sergei, the fifth son of Tsar Alexander II, the liberator of the serfs, who himself was assassinated in 1881. They had married in the chapel of the Winter Palace in 1884, when she was twenty and very beautiful. Like her mother, Princess Alice—the daughter of Queen Victoria, she was also devoutly Christian. Her younger sister Alix would marry the last Tsar, Nicholas II, in part through Elisabeth's own encouragement. Elisabeth's husband suffered the same fate as Alexander II. He was assassinated in the Kremlin in 1905 by a socialist revolutionary, Ivan Kalyavev.

Elisabeth went into deep mourning following her husband's assassination, but later visited her husband's assassin in gaol to tell him she had had forgiven him, and would plead for clemency for him if he repented of his crime. Instead, Kalyavev sought death at the hands of the system, so as to become a socialist martyr. In 1909 Elisabeth sold all her jewellery, founded a convent in Moscow called St Mary and St Martha, (the sisters of Lazarus), and became its first Abbess. The aims of the convent reflected the names of its patrons: contemplative prayer (Mary) and practical action (Martha).

Soon after the Russian Revolution, Elisabeth was arrested with other members of the royal family (but not with the Tsar's close family). They were thrown down the shaft of an abandoned iron mine. Grenades were lobbed in after them, but most of the group died of wounds suffered in the sixty-foot fall, and of starvation. Elisabeth's remains, after initially being taken to Beijing, were buried in Jerusalem at the Orthodox Church of St Mary Magdalene in Gethsemane. Her niece, Prince Philip's mother, would eventually join her there. Elisabeth is one of twenty modern martyrs depicted in statues in niches on the west front of Westminster

Abbey.

The sister convent in Minsk was founded in 1999 and called St Elisabeth's. It states its aims as providing "spiritual and social help for the sick and suffering". In line with these aims they run a home for the disabled, another for children with learning difficulties, and provide shelter for those needing care. Alongside is the daily cycle of worship and prayer in the convent. Sitting and listening, being and doing does indeed fulfil the calling of Mary and Martha in the Gospels (Luke 10:38–41, John 11: 1–44). Hearing of their work, I was anxious to see it for myself, and also the city of Minsk, which had been largely rebuilt since its devastation in the World War II.

I have always been fascinated by Russia, its literature and history, and the surrounding countries too. After my A levels, I read *War and Peace* sitting on the flat roof of my schoolhouse. Later, I would avidly read more Tolstoy, also Dostoevsky, Gogol, Turgenev, Pushkin, Chekov, Pasternak and Solzhenitsyn. Just recently I enjoyed a new production of *Uncle Vanya* in Bath's Royal Theatre, which Rupert Everett produced and acted in. It was an amusing, lyrical and melancholic play, as Chekov generally is.

My parents first took me to Leningrad (as it was then) and Moscow in 1975, in days when Russian tourism was supervised by the Soviet Tourist Company *Intourist*. I remember being given a large menu in an Intourist hotel on Gorky Street, Moscow, and ordering something. It seemed that everything I chose was off the menu, eliciting a firm Soviet *niet*. I said, "Perhaps we should do it the other way around, what actually *is* on the menu?" Two things! Choice was an illusion then, and no doubt despised in Leninist Russia as a western capitalist value. At school, like most of my contemporaries, I had my poster of Che Guevera on the wall and asked for literature about the communist party from the Soviet Embassy. They sent a good wodge of Marxist-Leninist gobbledygook and interminable minutes of International Comintern meetings, equally opaque. Yet dig beneath all that and the history of Russia cannot but fail to both fascinate and appal.

Some years before I went on this trip in 2013, I had talked with John Lawrence, who'd been a press attaché attached to the British Embassy in Moscow during the war. He lived in one of the villages I looked after just outside Bath and had written extensively on the Soviet Union. As a Christian, he had drawn attention to the suffering of the church there under communism through Keston College of which he was President (its director was Michael Bourdeaux). The Lawrence family had lived in North Stoke for centuries, still owned land there, and the names of Sir John's ancestors filled the walls of St Martin's North Stoke, the church of the village where he lived. His ancestor, Sir Henry Lawrence, had died in the siege of Lucknow in the Indian Mutiny in 1857. He encouraged me to go to Russia if possible and gave me a copy of his history of Russia. When I visited him in hospital in his final days, he had a copy of the Greek New Testament on his bed. I think he was the only man I knew to be thus equipped. He told me he had been taught classics by my grandfather at Eton, which created a bond between us.

It was more difficult to get into Belorussia than I had anticipated, however. Three of us were to go, the same three who had been to Cappadocia the year before, and we intended to travel by train via Paris, Berlin and Warsaw and spend three nights in Minsk before returning. With this in mind, and when in London for meetings, I called in at the Byelorussian Consulate for visa application forms. There was no answer, but I spoke through an intercom to a "receptionist" and was told to email for the forms. They came eventually. I filled them in and returned them. We were refused and asked to provide a personal invitation from a member of the convent. Sister Ekaterina kindly obliged. We submitted new applications. These too were refused. We were then asked for sponsorship from the Department of Religious Affairs in Minsk. This seemed like a long shot in the time remaining, and despite the help of an agency in London specialising in obtaining visas, nothing was forthcoming. With just a few days left before we were due to depart, we changed our final destination from Minsk to Kyiv: no visa was needed for Ukraine. The route would remain the same: Paris, Berlin, Warsaw and Kyiv. We were to leave on Thursday, 28 November 2013.

London to Kyiv

Eurostar took us to Paris with a toast of kirsch as we left St Pancras. Picking up speed in Northern France, we arrived at the Gare de Nord two- and a-bit hours later. We walked the short distance to Gare de l'Est and had some supper at an art nouveau café before boarding the overnight train to Berlin. It is a ten-hour journey, with nine trains a day covering the thousand kilometres from Paris. As John Lawrence wrote in his book on Russia, east of Cambridge there is nothing higher than the Gog and Magog Hills between East Anglia and Moscow.[162] The journey to Berlin strikes north from Paris, goes through Belgium, and then into Germany past Cologne and Hanover.

I had been back once to Berlin since we left as a family in 1963 at the height of the cold war. I had gone with Olivia and our children in 2003 to see the sights forty years on that had been so familiar in my childhood, but of course the most notorious sight, the Berlin Wall, had long since gone. So much had been built or re-built since 1989. The Reichstag, Germany's parliament building, destroyed by fire by the Nazis in 1933, had been re-built by the architect Norman Foster with its now famous glass dome. There is now a Museum of the Wall where Checkpoint Charlie once was: recalling the original building, the grief that it brought to the city's inhabitants, as well as significant moments like Kennedy's visit and its downfall.

During the two days we spent in Berlin we stayed at an apartment linked to a hotel at Spandauer Bucke near Alexander Platz. From there we could walk down the Unter den Linden through the Brandenburg Gate into the Tiergarten. We found the memorial to all the Jewish victims of the war: a maze of concrete blocks of differing sizes on sloping ground covering a wide area. Visitors were left to their own thoughts amidst this brutal sea of unyielding structures. Not far away we found a monument to Hayden, Beethoven and Mozart, but disfigured by gunshot. More than any other city, Berlin recalls the vicissitudes of war and the effects of division. While Paul and Tom went for an evening tour of the Reichstag, I went to the nearby Christmas Market now in full swing and then together we had a typical German meal of pork, sauerkraut and mounds of potatoes. How different from the delicacies of French cooking: nations can be described by their food.

The following morning, we went to the museum district, where there was nostalgia for me in revisiting the Pergamum Museum which had been in East Berlin when I was there as boy. Now that I had been to

---

[162] John Lawrence, *A History of Russia,* (Bromborough: Meridian Books, 1993), p. 16.

Pergamum in Turkey, from which the altar had been taken, it meant much more. Nearby, in the Neues Museum, is the head of Nefertiti, the wife of the heretic Pharaoh Akhenaten, which came from Amarna on the Nile. In the afternoon we hired bicycles and pedalled down to Lake Havel and the Grunewald Forest to see the "house by the lake" my family had lived in fifty years ago. It was as I remembered, but locked, with no chance of nosily going inside. The industrialist who owned it had sculptures by Barbara Hepworth and Henry Moore, no less, in the garden. No wonder it was well locked and guarded! From there we went to the old Olympic Stadium where the 1936 Games were held, and where my father had worked, and which is now a football and athletics stadium. There has recently been a debate about erasing the Aryan figures on a frieze in the building. We pedalled back to Alexander Platz, turned around, and, in the evening saw a ballet of the life of Tchaikovsky at the Schiller Theatre. The following morning, we were on the train to Warsaw.

Warsaw is a more or less straight line six hundred kilometres east of Berlin across the north German plain. The train left the Ost Bahn station in Berlin at 9.37 a.m. and arrived at three p.m. in Warsaw—plenty of time to finish reading Antony Beevor's grim tale of the fall of Berlin in 1945.[163] It was also Advent Sunday, which reminded me of the Advent hymn, "Thy Kingdom come O God", for its plaintiff cry was so appropriate to the terrain we were crossing, where the largest armies in human history had assembled, confronted and fought each other: "When shall all hatred cease?"

When we arrived in Warsaw, we were met by Wiola, a friend of Paul's who stayed with him and Catherine in Bath. Thinking that we had just a few hours in the city, Wiola took us to look around the centre and its amazing reconstruction after the war. Of the nine hundred and eighty-seven pre-war listed buildings, seven hundred and eighty-two had been reduced to ruins. Bridges, railway lines, streets and the water system of the city were destroyed by the retreating German forces. No city suffered more from the Nazis. Following the 1943 Warsaw Ghetto uprising by the Jews and the subsequent Warsaw uprising by the resistance in August 1944, the city was subjected to systematic destruction by the German army. And while the destruction continued, the Red Army waited nearby

---

[163] Antony Beevor, *Berlin* (Penguin 2007).

until it was complete. It is estimated that eight hundred and fifty thousand Poles perished and the Jewish population was transported to Auschwitz-Birkenau.[164] When Eisenhower visited in 1945, he pronounced that the sight of the derelict and devastated city and the subsequent loss of human life was more tragic than anything he had ever seen.

Yet from 1945 on, Polish people began the herculean task of rebuilding the centre of the city as it had been before. The architects Roman Piotrowski and Józef Sigalin, began the mammoth task of removing the rubble and rebuilding the old centre of the city. With all records destroyed, and as a reference to the original townscape, they used pictures of the old town by Marcello Bacciarelli and Bernardo Bellotto. In this way, they re-created the charm, vivacity and sense of continuity of the Old Market Place and the Castle Square. It is a triumph of human persistence and ingenuity, and demonstrates the deep desire to recreate the architecture of the past to bring comfort, national solidarity, continuity, and hope for the future.

Our whistle-stop tour with Wiola continued: we dropped into a café for a coffee, briefly visited the Artist's Church where a service was underway, passed by the huge Cultural Palace built by the Soviets in the typical "best" tradition of Soviet architecture, with all its monochrome form, but still the highest building in Warsaw, and then headed back to the station. We thanked Wiola profusely for her kindness, settled down to a Polish stew in a station restaurant and then ambled to the platform to find the 21.00hr sleeper to Kyiv, only to find it had left four hours before at 16.50! In the sudden change of destination from Minsk to Kyiv, we had neglected to alter the departure time of the Minsk train in our itinerary! We would have to rebook our tickets for a day later and do a certain amount of regrouping! On the positive side we could look forward to another half day in Warsaw.

We rang Wiola in the morning, admitting our mistake, having spent a night in a shared room in the Polonia Palace Hotel. Wiola took us to the new Jewish Museum, which was barely complete, and which traces the story of the Jews in Warsaw in all its harrowing detail. Then it was a walk in the Royal Gardens with its fine statue of Chopin, before hastening back to the station to make sure we were in good time for the sleeper to

---

[164] Tim Sharman, *Poland* (Zanesville, OH: Columbus Books, 1988), p. 22.

Kiev that left daily at 16.50. We were glad that we had had some lunch at the station as there was no restaurant car or food outlet on the train for the entire sixteen-hour journey to Kyiv. We were confined to our carriage and sleeping compartment and had to hand over our passports to the carriage attendant. We quickly realised we were in a different culture.

I have always had a rather romantic view of sleepers, and the journey to Kyiv certainly did its best to dispel this—although not entirely successfully. I have enjoyed sleepers across Germany in the 1960s to Berlin; from London to Inverness or Fort William (the latter across the Scottish almost-tundra of Rannoch Moor); and from Paris to Milan through the Alps. Of course, the pinnacle of sleeper experiences must be the Trans-Siberian Express or the Trans Canada taking in the Rockies, but those experiences have been "by proxy only" through the likes Joanna Lumley, or with Michael Palin or Michael Portillo. Nevertheless, Warsaw to Kyiv must be, for me, the most memorable, if the least romantic.

Installed in our compartment with three bunk beds (two of them in the upright position so we could sit on the bottom bunk) and having handed over our passports, we settled down for the journey. In all, the trip would take fifteen hours (plus two-hour time change) and would cover about eight hundred kilometres. For reasons that will emerge, the train was not in a hurry. It drew out of Warsaw, and we settled down to reading, scrabble and looking out of the window. From Warsaw we headed south to Lublin, following at first the course of the Vistula River. Once a wealthy town on the trade routes that connected the Baltic to the Black Sea, Lublin escaped wartime destruction and retains its old-world charm. From Lublin the railway strikes due east for the Ukraine. By then rumours were circulating that disturbances had begun in Kyiv. In fact, there were signs of real unrest, which was starting to be reported in Western Europe by the end of November, and, since we had left England, had developed further and the so-called Euromaidan Revolution was underway.

In a neighbouring compartment some journalists from Germany were making their way to Kyiv to report the story, and we got talking to them. Darkness fell well before we reached the Ukrainian border, and at midnight we decided to get into our bunks for sleep. About an hour later, having just nodded off, border guards came on the train to inspect our passports, which we had to first retrieve from the guard of our carriage. The burly Ukrainian border police shone a torch in our faces, removed our passports for examination, and wanted to inspect our luggage for drugs. To this end they were accompanied by an Alsatian. Our passports were returned after about half an hour later. Meanwhile there was a lot of banging beneath the train, and an inspection panel in the WC was opened so as to give a view of the track. We learnt that the bogeys of the train were being repositioned for a wider gauge in the Ukraine and Russia.

This border between Poland and Ukraine marks a real cultural boundary between West and East, and, for all the desire among some Ukrainians for a closer relationship with the EU and the West, there was no doubt we were entering a different world. After nearly two hours at the border, we proceeded through the night towards Kyiv. Standing by the corridor-window early the next day the great flat expanse of the Ukraine stretched ahead until we reached Kiev mid-morning.

Kyiv and the Ukraine

In order to have some understanding of the Ukraine and its history, perhaps the easiest way is to divide its past into three broad periods: its original founding in the eleventh century until 1686 when lands east of the Dnieper came under Russian rule; its submission to Imperial Russia and then the Soviet Union; and thirdly the period since independence in 1990, or the last thirty years.

The founders of Ukraine are the Vikings: those self-same peoples who colonised half of England, destroying much of Anglo-Saxon civilisation on the east coast until reversed by Alfred the Great. Called Varingians by the Greeks of Constantinople, these Slavs came down the rivers and trade routes that connect the Baltic to the Dnieper and the Dnieper to the Black Sea. They mixed with the local Polans to form Rus, and by 830 this combination founded a settlement atop the sandstone bluffs that became Kyiv.[165] Their ruler Volodymyr then had to decide on his religion. Initially he worshipped a pagan god called Perun, to whom he even made human sacrifices. Then, wanting something more contemporary, he enquired of the Muslim Bulgars nearby. He liked the idea of having many wives, but was not so keen on circumcision and abstinence from pork and wine! An embassy then went to Constantinople and on attending worship in Hagia Sophia reported as follows: "We did not know whether we were in heaven or earth; upon earth there is no such sight or beauty, we do not know what to say; we only know that there, God is present among men and their service is the best of all lands. We cannot forget that beauty: every man, if he tastes sweetness will not then partake of bitterness: even so we cannot live here."[166] And so Kyiv was founded as a centre of government for the region and of Orthodox worship, with an emphasis on liturgy, mystery and humility. One of their early saints, St Theodosius of Kyiv (d 1074) insisted on poverty and self-abasement.[167] The golden days of Kyiv followed: those of Vladimir the Great (980–1015), and of Yaroslav the Wise (1019–1054). Then, in 1234 the Mongols arrived and totally destroyed Kyiv. Ukrainian Rus would now undergo a change.

The area which we now know as Ukraine would be divided. Once the power of the Mongols declined, a new hybrid Russian state, part-Slav, part-Mongol, emerged further east in Moscow under Ivan the Great. Later this state would be given a new centre on the Baltic at St Petersburg by Peter the Great. Many great Russian families had Mongol origins: as Napoleon said once, "Scratch a Russian and you will find a Tatar".[168] Kyiv now faced west, and was absorbed for years to come into the Lithuanian-Polish Kingdom that became the dominant force in that part of eastern Europe. In the Union of Lublin (through whose town we passed on the way to Kiev) western Ukraine was shared between Lithuania and Poland. Meanwhile, in the south, in the Crimea, and on the Black Sea, a Tartar kingdom or khanate was well established, and by 1648 a Cossack kingdom, called the Cossack Hetmanate, emerged in

---

[165] Anna Reid, *Borderland: A Journey through the Ukraine* (Quezon, Philippines: Phoenix, 2001), p. 6.
[166] Lawrence, *History of Russia*, p. 33.
[167] Lawrence, *History of Russia*, pp. 36–37.
[168] Orlando Figes, *Natasha's Dance* (London: Penguin Books, 2003), p. 361.

central Ukraine including Kyiv. These different parts of the patch-work quilt that was Ukraine remained until the great Russian expansion under the Empress Catherine (1729–1786) and her first minister, Potemkin.

The second great phase of Ukraine's history is a story of Russian colonisation, whether under the Tsars beginning with Catherine, or by Soviet Russia from 1916 onwards. Both forms of government pursued imperial policy: one was Tsarist, the other was Soviet Communist. The remorseless onset of Russian power on the northern littoral of the Black Sea continued. In 1709 the Cossacks of Ukraine, allied with the Swedes under Charles XII, were crushingly defeated at Poltava by Peter the Great, well east of Kyiv. Typical of Ukraine today, the town of Poltava cannot decide whether to depict the battle as a great victory for Russia or a tragic Ukrainian defeat.[169] By 1764, the Cossack Hetmanate was abolished and the lands west of the Dnieper were partitioned between Austria and Russia. By 1783 Crimea was annexed by Russia, and four years later Catherine the Great left on a royal progress down the Dnieper arranged by her lover and first minister Potemkin to see her "New Russia".[170] Odessa was founded in 1794 as polyglot, free-port city on the Black Sea, planned by the French aristocrat Duc de Richelieu, the first city prefect.[171] It was supplied with corn by the Polish, and populated by Jews. Merchants, artists and émigrés including Pushkin, a political exile from Tsarist St Petersburg gravitated to this new polyglot city.

Pushkin wrote his great poem *Eugene Onegin* in Odessa, having seduced the governor's wife, Countess Vorontsova, and for his pleasures he was sent away by her husband on a roving commission to track locust damage in the Dniester region.[172] The Russian grip on Ukraine intensified, and by 1876 all Ukrainian-language publishing and teaching was banned in face of a growing Ukrainian intelligentsia at Lviv led by Taras Shevchenko. At the same time up to a quarter of million Ukrainians were re-settled in Siberia.

When the First World War began, 3.5 million Ukrainians fought with Russia, France and Britain, while two hundred and fifty thousand fought

---

[169] Reid, *Borderland*, p. 53.
[170] Reid, *Borderland*, p. 57.
[171] Neil Ascherson, *Black Sea* (London: Vintage, 2015), p. 127.
[172] T. J. Binyon, *Pushkin* (London: Harper Collins, 2002), p.133, 176ff.

with Austria and Germany: once again the nation divided with Ukraine as a battlefield, especially around Lviv.[173] Kyiv changed hands with "dizzying frequency between the Germans and the Russians".[174] At the end of the war, at the Treaty of Versailles, Ukraine was split, this time four ways: a newly-formed Poland taking the west, Russia the east, Bukovina next to Moldova was taken by the Romanians, and the Czechoslovaks had the south-west corner of the country. Yet as soon as one war ended, another began, this time following the Russian Revolution of 1917. Ukraine now became a battlefield between the White (Tsarist) and Red Armies. Millions of people were displaced, and a further 1.5 million killed. Although the Soviet government encouraged some intellectual independence for the Ukraine, worse was to come when Stalin fully took control, and the policy of the collectivisation of farming began.

The result of this collectivisation was the Great Famine or *Holodomor* of 1932/3. *Holodomor* means death by starvation. Most recent estimates believe that between four and seven million perished. The accounts, as of all starving populations, were appalling; the greatest irony was that it happened in the bread basket of eastern Europe. The Ukrainian, Victor Kravchenko, who was told to go to Petrovov, seventy-five miles west of Dnipropetrovsk, described it as follows:

Again, we were oppressed by the unnatural silence. Soon we came to an open space which, no doubt, was once the market place. Suddenly Yuri gripped my arm until it hurt; for sprawled on the ground were dead men, women and children, thinly covered with dingy straw. I counted seventeen. As we watched, a wagon drove up and loaded the corpses on the wagon like cordwood.[175]

A further twist to this story was that when Kravchenko published his memoirs *I chose Freedom* —a publishing sensation—having defected in 1944 to France, the French Communist party brought an action in Paris against him in January 1949, claiming the work a travesty of the truth. Only after the most sensational trial, with many twists and turns, did the

---

[173] Reid, *Borderland*, p. 97.
[174] Reid, *Borderland*, p. 101.
[175] Ivan Kravchenko, *I Chose Freedom* (New York 1946), cited by Reid, *Borderlands*, p. 129.

court find in favour of Kravchenko, and communists in France began to realise that the Soviet Union was not the paradise they wanted it to be, but a cauldron of repression and lies.[176]

The Second World War piled on slaughter and genocide towards the Jews, slavery, and further famine on an already troubled nation. Even before the war began, the Soviet Union had deported 1.6 million to the labour camps in Kazakhstan and Siberia.[177] The German Barbarossa invasion began on 21 June 1941. By September, Kiev had surrendered, and Jews in their thousands were driven at gun point into a ravine known as Babiy Yar where thirty-three thousand were gunned down and the ravine filled in, but "the earth did not stop moving for some time after".[178] The same happened at Odessa, which fell to German and Romanian troops in October, as well as other towns in the Crimea. The grisly statistics go on. The Wehrmacht deported over two million Ukrainians to Germany—over half of them women—to work as slave labour in munitions and mining and other heavy industries.[179]

Any hopes that Germany would support Ukrainian nationalism were dashed. Some four million Ukrainians fought with the Russians, but little respect was paid them after the war: deportations continued, especially of Crimean Tartars, and Ukraine, with its great waterways, became an industrial and agricultural heartland of the Soviet Union. Its future was to explode in the nuclear disaster at Chernobyl on 26 April 1986. Fifteen years later Ukraine was given its independence by a moribund Soviet Union, but it was to be a rocky path to true independence.

The story of independence, simply put, is that Ukraine is pulled two ways: towards Russia and the West, and in particular the United States. And around this basic tension there are trade-offs for Ukrainian politicians from one side or the other. After a slow start and an economic contraction in the 1990s, Ukrainian independence became more defined in the Orange Revolution of 2004. In a rigged result, the Russian-supported candidate Victor Yanukovych was initially declared the winner. Massive demonstrations followed in Kyiv, which overturned the

---

[176] Artemis Cooper and Antony Beevor, *Paris after Liberation: 1944–1949* (London: Penguin, 2017), pp. 338ff.

[177] Reid, *Borderlands*, p. 151.

[178] Reid, *Borderlands*, p. 155.

[179] Reid, *Borderlands*, p. 162.

result as affirmed by the Supreme Court. The opposition candidate, Victor Yushenko, was found to have been poisoned by the Russians, but he and Yulia Timoshenko came to power. Timoshenko was a NATO and EU-leaning candidate, courted by both sides. In 2006 Yanukovych (the Russian candidate) was returned to power and Timoshenko imprisoned on charges of corruption. When we arrived in Kyiv in December 2013, the uprising was against Victor Yanukovych with Timoshenko's release demanded. To complete the story, Victor Yanukovych was eventually deposed in the Euromaidan Revolution of 2013/14. Timoshenko was released and a new Western-leaning President Poroshenko was elected. Then, in March 2014, Putin occupied the Crimea after a plebiscite in the region supposedly voted for Russian intervention. Civil war followed in the Eastern Ukraine, the Donbas region around Donetsk and Luhansk north of the Azov Sea. And as I conclude this book in early 2022 a brutal and unprovoked attack on Ukraine is underway. So far, the characteristics of this war are the logistical and tactical failures of Russian forces, the patriotic and spirited resistance of the Ukrainians, the incessant shelling and the encirclement of cities in the South and East like Mariupol and Kharkiv and the displacement of millions of refugees. But Kyiv survives as do the great cities L'viv and Odesa. The brutality and evil of Putin is more than matched by the inspirational leadership of Zalensky.

When we stepped off the Warsaw train into Kyiv central station, we were hardly aware that the nation was in ferment with what would be known as the Euromaidan Revolution (after the central square of Kyiv) brewing. We were immediately aware, however, that although geographically European, Ukraine has a very different culture from our own. We first had to buy our return tickets to Warsaw for Thursday afternoon (after two days in Kyiv). There seemed to be a kind of martial atmosphere. We were repeatedly told off by burly Ukrainian women for asking for tickets at the wrong kiosks. After five attempts we found the right booking office and were issued with a handsome, important-looking return sleeper ticket to Warsaw. Once outside the cavernous station we found a taxi to take us to the Great Lavra Monastery where we were to stay for two nights.

When our journey to the St Elisabeth Convent in Minsk had fallen through, Sister Ekaterina had recommended we stay at the Kyiv

Pecherska Lavra (Great Lavra), and kindly made reservations at their guest house. Far from just a single institution, the monastery was in fact a great complex comprising a cathedral, other churches, a training college for priests and monks, guest house and a whole mountainside of underground chapel caves. I had never seen anything like it. It was all spread within and upon the mountainside high above the Dnieper River, which swirled below. For sheer drama of location, little could compare. The great golden onion domes of orthodoxy shone in the clear, cold December sky, as they had for near on a millennium since first founded in 1051. It was now a focus of Ukrainian cultural and religious identity, and a World Heritage site.

We settled into our rooms in the guest house before walking along the ridge on which the monastery and buildings were set. There we saw many memorials to the resistance of Ukrainians to the German invasion. There were others recalling famine, depicting waif-like girls seeking food. We returned to the monastery at about three p.m. and explored some of its many sights, walking down the hill until we came to the entrance to the underground passages that led to many chapels, much like the catacombs in Rome. The chapels were small, decorated, and often devoted to a holy person or saint whose bodily remains were dressed in a shroud or colourful robes and could be seen in a glass coffin. We walked back up the slope to the top and into a huge open space where stood the Cathedral of the Dormition with its eleventh century bell tower that had been badly damaged in the war. In the courtyard a huge bell hanging on a low sling was solemnly struck by a sole bell-ringer. We learnt that it was a saint's day and the Bishop of Kyiv would be attending the liturgy. The cathedral was fast filling up and soon the liturgy was underway.

It is hard to describe the drama of the Orthodox liturgy: The priests and bishops in their golden copes, the candelabra ablaze with candles, the copious swinging of incense throughout the building, the large standing congregation which at times parts to allow a priest or assistant through, the singing of the congregation which swells like a wave through the worshippers, offset by the solos of priests singing the readings or the liturgy, and the soaring iconostasis through which the bishop passes to celebrate the Eucharist. It is not didactic, it is not simple or plain, it is not restrained, and it does not directly appeal to the mind.

It is emotional, communal, and theatrical, mystical and spiritual. It is an experience, the like of which we do not have in western Christianity, whether in Rome or Canterbury. It appears to have sustained a nation through unbearable losses. Marx dismissively called it the opiate of the people; I would call it more an infusion of the soul.

After an hour and a half, we slipped outside into the freezing air. The service would continue for three hours in all. We went for a meal, having hardly eaten since lunch the previous day. We all ate fish, perhaps from the great Dnieper River or perhaps from the Black Sea further downstream: trout (Tom), sea bass (Paul) and turbot (me). Nothing ever tasted better. We were also getting ready for a big day tomorrow.

The day began at about four a.m., when, knowing it was another feast day, we went back to the cave churches within the mountainside. We followed the *babushkas* on their way down the wide path leading to the entrance to the mountain; it was very dark. These elderly grannies, attired in black, seemed like the backbone of the Orthodox church. Whenever we passed a cross, a shrine, or an icon, they crossed themselves in the orthodox fashion: three fingers to their head, shoulders, chest and the ground. It seemed like an action of humility and reverence, and of prayer for divine protection and blessing triggered by a holy memory. We descended deeper inside the mountain down the labyrinthine passageways that occasionally opened into a space large enough for a chapel, and where a small congregation had assembled and a service was underway. For nearly two hours we wandered, paused, reflected, joined in as best we could, until by six p.m. we were ready to go back for breakfast. But the guest house had little to offer except bread. Perhaps it was also a fast day!

After breakfast we took a taxi down into the city centre and made for St Sophia's Cathedral. Built by Yaroslav the Wise in 1054, the cathedral is as part of original Kyiv. A plethora of green domes and gold crosses surround the main golden dome and cross, which rises above the others. Inside, mosaics adorn the domes, cupolas and walls, with a clear connection to the Byzantine art of the period. There were only two or three other visitors. In fact, there were more attendants preventing photographs being taken than either worshippers or tourists! Although it had been fourteen years since independence—before which the cathedral would have been classed as a museum rather than a place of worship—it was still being restored. Apparently, the reason for this sense of isolation was that several branches of the Orthodox church had laid claim to it when it was transferred back from state to ecclesiastical ownership and the resulting paralysis had halted restoration. We looked around the outbuildings of the Bell Tower, the Bishop's palace and a bakery. It felt like a neglected island near the centre of town. There was no doubt that the Pecherska Lavra Monastery was much more the heart of the Ukrainian Orthodox Church.

From St Sophia we walked to Maidan Square, the centre of the town, where musically-minded revolutionaries were limbering up for another day of protest. At that stage of the protest, about seven days in, was a more light-hearted tweaking of the government's Russian-leaning nose. All that was to change after Christmas, when the government sought greater control, shot some of the protesters and provoked a far more serious response. By late February 2014, one hundred and thirty protesters and eighteen police officers had been killed. On 22 February the President fled to Russia. When we walked round the square it was more like a pop festival than a revolution, with a main stage and bands playing through the day. There were stalls promoting the objects of the protesters, especially the release from prison of Julia Timoshenko. We talked to the protesters, waved a Ukrainian flag and absorbed the atmosphere. If a few hundred people kept the square in the daytime, by evening the number swelled to thousands. By February it was hundreds of thousands.

Moving on from our encounter with the friendly revolutionaries, we passed the City Opera House and bought tickets for Turandot that evening. After a pizza, eaten near a rather schmaltzy Golden Gate, I settled with Paul for a quiet afternoon of reading. It was not easy to find a cosy café. Kiev has an atmosphere of raunchy rawness and rather brutal modern architecture mixed in with an occasional jewel. Tom went in search of art to buy. At six thirty p.m. we returned to the Opera House for the evening performance. By now it was dark and growing cold. Inside the Opera House it was bright, warm and spacious, with huge areas devoted to hanging coats. We took our seats, conscious of the fact that in

1911 in this very opera house, the reforming Russian Prime Minister, Pyotr Stolypin, was assassinated in the presence of Tsar Nicholas II and two of his daughters by an anarchist, Dmitry Bogrov. I imagined him bloodied and slouched over his seat as the Tsar looked on. On that occasion they were watching the *Tale of the Tsar Saltan* by Rimsky-Korsakov. By contrast we heard Puccini's *Turandot* with its well-known solo *Nessum Dorma*. Although there was no star like Pavarotti, it was a workmanlike performance, memorable for the sheer numbers of people in the cast and orchestra. The cost, too, was remarkably low, presumably well subsidised by the state. Afterwards we made our way back to the monastery guest house and next day, after a quiet morning in which Tom bought a handsome icon, we went back to the station to catch the sleeper to Warsaw. This time we *caught* the train, and now knowing there was no dining car, took some provisions on board.

In Warsaw we were met at the station by Wiola and taken to see more of the city. We went to a museum dedicated to the Warsaw Uprising, with a harrowing film of original footage of Jews being taken to concentration camps and the destruction of the city by the German army following the uprising. Then we went to a church where the heart of Chopin was buried and finally to a memorial dedicated to the Polish officer class executed by the Soviet forces in the Katyn Forest and elsewhere. In 1940, after the Ribbentrop-Molotov pact led to the partition of Poland, twenty-two thousand Polish officers and members of the intelligentsia were massacred by Russian forces under the direction of Stalin and his chief of security of Beria. It was a lot to take-in in a morning. We flew home that afternoon. Back in Bath, preparing for Christmas three weeks later, the week in Eastern Europe seemed unreal. It would take time to process, especially as the situation in the Ukraine deteriorated.

Occupying these islands, separated from the continent by a small piece of water and defended historically by a sizeable navy, has placed the UK in a position of great privilege. Nevertheless, the forces of nationalism, national socialism and Marxist Leninism that swept our continent in the twentieth century inevitably caught us up in their very costly consequences. Travelling to these places only re-enforced my belief that we should play our part in shaping the future of Europe. For most of the twentieth century, Europe struggled bitterly with the forces of nationalism, anti-Semitism, communism and national-socialism, which led to untold suffering.

Indeed, going to Berlin, Poland and Ukraine you become exposed to a scale of hardship and suffering we could barely understand. Now, once again, we can no longer be bystanders in a European war.

Chapter XIV
Islands in the Sun

Among the glories of the Mediterranean are its islands, large and small. Many a lazy summer holiday has been spent on them. Over the millennia, cultures have risen and fallen across them. In the Western Mediterranean are the islands of Corsica, Sardinia and Menorca, Majorca and Ibiza. Some of these we have touched on already. Dividing the Western Mediterranean from the East, and thereby subject to conquest and cultures coming from all directions, are Sicily and Malta, lying more or less in the middle of what the Romans called proprietorially *Mare Nostrum* (Our Sea). In the Eastern Mediterranean, or the Aegean, among a host of smaller Greek Islands, the principal islands are Crete and Cyprus. And down the Adriatic Coast are a plethora of islands also. Islands of all kinds abound, each with its own microclimate, culture and story to tell. In the space of a few years we went to Cyprus, Malta, Sicily and more recently, Crete.

Cyprus

In 2013 Michael and I spent a week in Cyprus. There was no revolution, just the normal standoff between the Greeks and the Turks, but the spring of that year saw the height of the financial crisis in Cyprus, following the banking crisis of 2008.

The Cypriot economy had gone into recession in 2009, and by 2012 was in dire straits. The Bank of Cyprus was failing, in part because of the withdrawal of very large Russian deposits from its central bank (made in the first place because of very favourable tax rates in Cyprus), thus leaving the bank's depositors vulnerable. A loan of ten billion Euros was made by the ECB (European Central Bank) on the condition that no further Russian money be withdrawn and that any depositor could only access 100,000 Euros of their own money. The rest of their holdings would be taken by the Cypriot government in exchange for government bonds. There was no run on the bank, because the banks were closed, and cash machines would issue only small amounts.

While in England such a measure would have resulted in an unspeakable crisis—imagine the government taking over all bank deposits above £90,000 and issuing government bonds instead—in Cyprus the move was met by many with a shrug. It also underlined the complexity of financial arrangements in Cyprus, with large amounts of Russian money gaining high interest rates and paying low tax, resulting in insufficient funding for services. Cyprus was a cocktail of dubious financial interests ready to explode, which it did. It is a complex place historically, ethnically, strategically and culturally, and all that makes it fascinating too. Nor is it very different in these respects from Malta and Sicily. Each is more than susceptible to "rackets", and we all know about Sicily and the Mafia. They are certainly "islands in the sun", but they have unhealthy sub-cultures of corruption.

We left for Cyprus on an overnight flight from London Heathrow to Larnaca in May 2013 on the grounds of wanting not days on the beach in the sun, but instead to follow a little in the steps of St Paul and Barnabas who came to the island in c. 49 AD. We would trace their path, to some extent, from Salamis in the east to the former Roman administrative centre of Paphos in the west.

Cyprus has an extraordinarily strategic position close to the Levant or the Middle East. Its eastern tip, the pan-handle, lies only a hundred kilometres from Latakia in Syria. It is for this reason that two British bases outside Limassol and Larnaka were "leased" by treaty from the Greek Cypriot Government when Greece gained its independence from Britain in 1960. It is from here that military missions, involving both the RAF and the SAS, have been frequently undertaken in the last thirty years and more. Currently, British forces are involved in preventing any resurgence of ISIS in northern Syria and Iraq in that complex and dangerous situation.

After our overnight flight to Larnaka we stopped for a coffee on the road to Famagusta near the British Sovereign base at Dhekelia. A beach café was just opening up, and there we found a retired Brit collecting the Daily Mail, and waiting for the café to open to get his morning coffee.

He lived out there more or less permanently, had nothing but praise for the lifestyle, and cheerfully told us his winter fuel allowance received back home kept him warm in Cyprus, with a glass of red! We moved on after our coffee, passing signs to the notorious resort of Agia Napa, where a combination of alcohol, drugs and sex have produced more than one clash between the Cypriot justice system and young British men and women, mostly ending in tears.

We headed north to the Turkish area—an explanation of which we will return to—crossing from the Greek Zone into the Turkish Zone at Pergamos (there are seven crossing points between Greek and Turkish Cyprus, otherwise there is a physical barrier between the two sectors). From there we headed north through fields of artichokes, almost head high, until we hit the main road from Nicosia and turned east.

We arrived at Famagusta with its many layered history going back to the Ancient Greeks, the Crusades, the Venetians, the Ottomans, the time of Shakespeare, the British and the Turks. Although it is a quiet and a relatively unimpressive town, it has had a kaleidoscopic back story: the Mycenaean Greeks settled there from the ninth century BC and the colony is mentioned in Homer's *Iliad*. The Greeks called the city Amochostos, meaning "buried in the sand," which suggests its coastal setting. Nearby, the colony of Salamis flourished from the sixth century BC onwards and did not finally dwindle until the seventh century AD. It was at the time of the Crusades that Famagusta took on new significance, with its fine bay for ships and easy access to the coast of Palestine. It became what Cyprus has been ever since: a staging post for military intervention in the Middle East. In 1191, Richard I, *Coeur de Lion*, came to Cyprus on his way to Palestine to rescue his fiancée, Berengaria of Navarre, whose ship had run aground on Cyprus's rocky shores. Being Richard, he conquered the country while he was at it, taking it from the Byzantine ruler, Isaac Comnenus, and was married to Berengaria in the Governor's chapel in Limassol. She saw very little of Richard thereafter, never set foot in England and had no children, so it does not sound a very happy marriage. Richard seems to have been far closer to his mother, Eleanor of Aquitaine who admired his martial spirit.

Another Norman Crusader, Guy de Lusignan, left his mark on Famagusta, in the form of a Crusader church called St Nicholas. It had a simple interior in the Gothic style with large columns along the nave made with stone from Egypt. Now it is a mosque. Nearby was the church of St Peter and St Paul, the latter, as we shall see, also made his mark in Cyprus. The old walls of the city were built by the Venetians and overlooking the harbour was Othello's tower.

It is said that in 1481 Leonardo da Vinci visited the city and advised the Venetians on its defence. The Othello Tower resulted. It is more a mini-castle than a tower, strongly built, with look outs on its four corners, and much space to store ammunition and food. It was called Othello's tower by the British because of the connection with Shakespeare's Othello, who as a General in the Venetian army came to Cyprus to drive out the Turks, with whom he had less trouble than with his wife Desdemona! The British could not resist attributing the Venetian tower to Othello and introducing the Bard made Cyprus feel more homely. After looking round Famagusta, we headed in the early afternoon to our hotel, the Crystal Rocks, which seemed remarkably deserted, as indeed the eastern, Turkish, side of Cyprus did as a whole.

The division of the island between Greeks and Turks goes back to the flare-up of animosity between the two communities at the end of British rule. British rule had begun in 1878, but after Independence and the removal of British authority, the two communities of Greeks and Turks quickly showed signs of unease and rivalry. By 1963 there was intercommunal violence and the displacement of twenty-four thousand Turks. Gradually the Greeks, led by Archbishop Makarios and the Greek government, sought *enosis* (unity) with Greece.

In 1974 the Turks responded with a full-scale military invasion of thirty thousand troops into the eastern part of the island. Large numbers of Greeks and Turks were displaced into their own ethnic regions of the island: the Greeks in the south and west, the Turks in the north and east. A Green Line was established, dividing the capital Nicosia, and guarded by a United Nations Peace Keeping force. Attempts at further reconciliation have not been successful. Greek Cyprus was admitted to the EU in 2004, and the United Nations annually calls upon the Turkish administration to return to the *status quo ante* 1974, but there seems little likelihood of this, especially under the present Turkish regime of Erdogan.

After a very pleasant evening at Crystal Rocks, we headed off to the ancient city of Salamis in the morning. Salamis was a very significant

Greek, and then Roman, city on a par with Ephesus. It had all the features of a thriving Roman town: a colonnaded gymnasium, baths, a theatre and an amphitheatre still to be excavated. We read the account of the Apostle Paul's arrival with Barnabas in Acts 13:4 from Seleuchia in Pieria, the port of Antioch, and how he preached in a synagogue in Salamis. We then moved on to the nearby church dedicated to Barnabas: The Church of Apostolos Varnavas. It was in a quiet grove of olive and pine trees. It is a simple Byzantine church with a collection of fine icons, for which it is now classed a museum. Not far away was the tomb of Barnabas, who is said to have been martyred on the island. He was the first Bishop of Cyprus.

One icon was of a later bishop of fourth century Salamis, called Epiphanius (c. 320–403), a noted heresy-hunter strongly opposed to the great third century theologian and commentator, Origen, who he considered too Platonist in his belief in the ultimate reconciliation of all things i.e., that there was no judgement or hell. In his book *Panarion* (meaning medicine chest) Epiphanius identified the various heresies in the church.

After looking around the delightful archaeological museum in the quiet cloister by the church we set off for our next stopping place, Keryneia, still in the Turkish Republic of Cyprus.

To get there we headed north to Lefkonoiko and then through the Pentada Ktylos range of coastal mountains that rise to nearly three thousand feet. We had lunch under an olive tree, munching our bread, olives, cheese and an apple before finding a cove on the coast where we could swim. This part of the island is deserted and remote. Although the Turkish Cypriot government maintains that there are one hundred and twenty thousand inhabitants, the population seems much sparser, or is mostly concentrated in Turkish Nicosia. We arrived in Keryneia in late afternoon. It is the main Turkish port on the northern coast with connecting ferries to Silifke on the Turkish mainland, through which we had driven twelve years before on our way to Amman. We stayed in the well-named Nostalgia Hotel two minutes' walk from the harbour, along whose walls we meandered in the evening sun. It was a picturesque town with a castle, pretty harbour, geraniums and bougainvillea, and old-world charm: a place to linger in, certainly. We had inadvertently parked close to St Andrew's Anglican Church, and when we left the following day, I could hear a group of ex-patriots singing the hymn, "Great is thy faithfulness". It was another slice of the multiple mix that is Cyprus: amidst "all the changing scenes of life", which the island had undergone, this British community continued its life and worship.

We left in the morning for the Troödos mountains. On the way out we passed signs to Bellapais, where Lawrence Durrell wrote *Bitter Lemons of Cyprus* in the 1950s, a book about his life on the island at a time when the movement to get rid of the British was growing ever stronger. Durrell was in process of becoming estranged from his second wife, Eve, a Jewish Alexandrian who figures as Justine in his *Alexandrian Quartet*, and whom he had met in that city during the war. Instead of reproducing the idyll that he had known in Corfu in the 1930s so lovingly brought to the screen by ITV, Cyprus had a bitter taste for Durrell and he left precipitately in 1956, after just three years. The island was once again in ferment, and the Cypriots by then loved to hate the British.

Passing Bellapais we made for St Hilarion, a castle on a clifftop overlooking the north Cypriot coast. Named after a monk who had escaped from Palestine and made a cave in the cliff his cell. The site was later developed by Guy de Lusignan in 1191 for its military capability of commanding the north Cypriot coast. A crows-nest castle resulted. It's a steep climb to the top and up to the tower of John of Antioch, but once at the summit the views to the coast are beyond stunning. We descended slowly, rewarding ourselves with a cup of coffee, and went off to Nicosia to find a check point to cross the Green Line into the Greek Cypriot Republic. Nicosia seemed a jumble of small shops and busy streets, with the Turkish language giving way to Greek; mosques giving way to churches, and differing cultures and communities abutting one another. Eventually, we found the crossing point from Turkish Nicosia to Greek Lefkosia, two parts of the same divided city. There we could see the ancient Venetian walls, the Ledra Street crossing, the archbishop's palace, and the Liberty monument commemorating those who fought against British rule in the years of the insurgency. My overall memory is of a city congested with traffic, however, and it was a relief to get out of the town into the countryside and take the road south to the Troödos Mountains.

Troödos Mountains

We stopped in an orange grove, so plentiful in Cyprus, and had our usual picnic lunch of bread, olives and cheese *en route*. Within two hours we were in the mountains heading for Pedoulas in the Marathasa valley beneath Cyprus's Mount Olympus at nearly eight thousand feet.

Pedoulas turned out to be a place of great interest and charm. We stayed at the Christy's Palace Hotel, which had an Alpine atmosphere and was good value at 25 Euros a night. The proprietor took the long view of the country's financial woes, knowing that given the beauty of the island, things would come around in the end. He said philosophically we just have to be patient. The village, which was set on a steep slope, had several attractions of note, particularly the Byzantine Museum, where icons from several of the village chapels were on display. A fine depiction of St Luke holding the Gospel caught my eye. Nearby was the spectacular Chapel of Archangelos, the Archangels. A World Heritage site, it had a spectacular display of icons of the Archangel Michael, floor to ceiling in size, imposing and authoritative. The village had several shops in the high street and a grocer selling cherries by the trunkful. The cherry harvest had just finished and there were cherries everywhere, as well as other fruits and vegetables. I bought a small bottle of cherries to have with ice cream at home! Not enough ice cream eating was done for the cherries hung around the fridge for ages! In the evening we ate slow cooked pork with wine and herbs (*afelia*) at a restaurant called *Platanos* (meaning plane trees) in the village centre. We learnt from the patron that the owner of Easy Jet, Stelios Haji-Ioannu, came from the village where he still had a house, and which he pointed out to us. Stelios was a generous philanthropist in the neighbourhood, and much praised there.

In the morning we visited a monastery of some significance called Kykkos Monastery. On arrival it felt a well-endowed and influential institution. Archbishop Makarios, the first President of Cyprus, and very much in the warrior-priest mould, was evidently trained here. Regarded as the father of the nation and initially the main advocate of the policy of union with Greece, he survived four assassination attempts. He had been exiled by the British to the Seychelles for campaigning for independence. While he wanted the peaceful evolution of an independent Cyprus, he realised latterly that *enosis* was not possible without community violence. More fiery Greek nationalists wanted *enosis* at any cost and were prepared to fight; and this tension was made more acute when the Greek military Junta with its nationalist aims seized power in 1967. Like Kenyatta in Kenya, Makarios was the one the people wanted, however. A very identifiable figure in his black robes and black hat he raised the profile of Cyprus world-wide, as he sought an independent status for Cyprus while maintaining a close relationship with Greece. His hopes were dashed by the Turkish invasion in 1973, although the international community supported the Greek Cypriot desire for a return of territory annexed by Turkey. Having looked around the monastery we went to the top of the hill where Macarios's tomb and a monument can be seen, along with a panoramic view over the region. We then walked along nature trails in the pine forest, admiring the array of wild asphodels, orchids, *paeonia mascula*, Cyprus germander, prickly junipers and *rubus sanctus* (the holy bramble!). It truly is a beautiful area.

The following day we left Pedoulas for Paphos and took a track off the main road running through the forest. What we lost in time, we gained in beauty. Travelling on average at twelve kilometres an hour we went extremely slowly for about ten kilometres along a rocky dirt track before joining a made-up road at Pana Panagia. The fleshpots of Paphos are the heart of the tourist industry in Cyprus, but for all that, the large Capital Coastal Resort we stayed in did have a wonderful position on the coast. There were quite a few Russian families there who generally avoided talking to their children at breakfast by giving each of them had a hand-held device while devoting themselves to their own mobile phones. Michael, who doesn't even own a mobile phone, found this beyond comprehension!

As it was Sunday we decided to go into the old town and see what was happening. We followed signs to the ancient Roman centre, parked and walked in. We could see the ruins of the centre ahead of us, and sounds of singing from a church of the hymn, "I will tell the wondrous story". It was a moving to hear those words drift across the Roman remains, as it was here that Paul met and converted the Roman governor two thousand years ago. When a Jewish sorcerer called Elymas repeatedly tried to prevent Paul from speaking his message to the governor, he was temporarily struck blind. The proconsul, Sergius

Paulus, "an intelligent man", was naturally impressed by this and asked for an explanation. He too heard and believed Paul's message, and became a Christian (Acts 13:4–12).

It was then that Saul changed his name to Paul, underlining his mission to the Gentiles, and taking the name of this élite Christian convert out of respect. It was touching to hear the singing all these hundreds of years later and to meet a Roman Catholic congregation and their priest, Father Jim, borrowing a Greek Orthodox church. We chatted to some members of the congregation including some keen bridge players. We returned to the hotel for a leisurely afternoon. The following day was our last full day, and we left for Larnaka in the morning.

Larnaka is one of the principal towns on the island, one hundred and twenty kilometres along the coast from Paphos. It has all the features of a Cypriot town: a coastal position, a Greek and Persian pedigree, and a history of Ottoman invasion. These days it has a large, mixed and quite poor population. Many Greeks arrived in 1974, fleeing the Turks and starting life again. There were Armenians, Palestinians, Syrians and Lebanese. When we arrived in the afternoon, Larnaka was *en fête*, with a crowd already assembling along the waterfront. Bands were playing on a stage, stalls were being erected, food from something like a food bank was being given out to the needy. We wandered into a town centre church to discover an ornate Orthodox building with an extraordinary ascription.

The church was Agios Lazaros or St Lazarus, a clue in itself. Lazarus of Bethany, the friend of Jesus whom he raised from the dead, and the brother of Martha and Mary (see John 11: 1–44) was "finally" buried here. According to tradition he came to Cyprus and became a bishop, appointed by Barnabas. There is no doubt that Lazarus would have had quite a story to tell! In 890 a tomb was discovered bearing his name and the inscription: "Lazarus, friend of Christ". The tomb lies beneath the apse to this day.

We enjoyed our final evening in Cyprus. We would leave with the sense that whatever financial and community problems the island faced, especially in the more populous Greek part, it was one more part of the chequered history this island has weathered. Whatever happens, the beauty and variety of the island, if well preserved, will always attract. Its location so close to the turbulent Middle East will always make it of great strategic value and its sunshine will always attract visitors.

Malta

One of the reasons for going to Malta in February 2017 for three nights was to explore the island where Olivia's grandfather had been stationed right after the war in 1946. Her grandfather, Admiral Sir Peveril William-Powlett, was a descendent of a distinguished Tudor statesman, the Lord High Treasurer, William Paulet. By playing his cards carefully, or to put it more nautically, by tacking in the prevailing wind, Paulet had managed to survive intact whilst serving in the administrations of Henry VIII, Edward VI, Mary I and Elizabeth I. That has to be quite a feat! He was one of the few to survive in office through those tempestuous times.

Olivia's grandfather, however, who was Captain of HMS Fiji in the war, and later a Vice Admiral, took part in the Battle of Crete (1941). His ship sank and he and most of the ship's company were rescued from the sea by other British vessels in very costly battles with the German air force.

Crete is an island I sailed around on the voyage from Venice to Alexandria and visited only recently properly visited with Olivia in September 2021. In many ways Crete fills in the gap between the Pharaoh's Egypt and the rise of Greece. The Minoan civilisation rediscovered at Knossos shows off an advanced palatial society from 2500 BC. As with other larger Islands in the region every power in the Eastern Mediterranean sought to make it their own: whether Roman, Byzantine, Arab, Venetian and Ottoman Turk. Fought over fiercely in WWII the island saw great loss of life whether of German paratroopers or New Zealand or British infantry. The island saw some of the memorable engagements of special forces in WWII with the SOE or SBS including the capture of a German General by Leigh Fermor and his associates. Olivia's grandfather survived to fight another day, and after the War was posted to Malta as the Flag Officer of the Mediterranean Fleet based at Malta, where briefly Prince Philip, recently married to Princess Elizabeth soon to be Queen, was under his command.

Malta, like Cyprus and Crete, has a many-layered history. Ruled from 800–218 BC by the Phoenicians, sea peoples of the eastern

Mediterranean, it then became a colony of the Carthaginians, Rome's great enemy. Carthage was defeated by Rome in the Second Punic War (218–201 BC) when Malta was taken by Rome. Rome would remain in charge until its fall to the Goths and Vandals in the fifth century AD. Then, with the invasion of North Africa by the Arabs in the seventh century, Malta's future once again became vulnerable. And in 890, both Malta and nearby Sicily fell to the Arabs.

For two hundred years Malta was ruled by the Arabs, until the Normans, those "attack dogs" of the Latin papacy, took the island in 1091. A succession of rulers followed: Normans, Angevins, Aragonese and Castilians. In fact, the island became a stepping-stone for Catholic Europe intervening in the Holy Land during and after the Crusades. With that cause in mind, the island was given by the Holy Roman Emperor, Charles V, to Knights of St John in 1530. They would rule it until the French under Napoleon invaded in 1798, and then, following the Napoleonic Wars in 1815, it was the turn of the British to rule the island until its independence in 1964.

On two occasions in its long and chequered history, the island's rulers and its inhabitants saw off its enemies: in 1565 against the Ottoman forces of Suleiman the Magnificent, and then against the Italian and German Forces in 1941. On both occasions they resisted courageously and successfully.

In 1565 Malta was governed by the Knights of St John, successors to the crusading Order of the Knights Hospitallers who had been ejected from Rhodes by the Ottomans in 1530. The Ottomans attacked with forty thousand troops and a host of ships, and although the Knights suffered many early losses, the stubborn resistance of the Grand Master, Jean Parisot de Valette, turned the tide, and the Ottomans were eventually repulsed. Valette gave his name to the new capital, Valetta, on the west side of the Grand Harbour.

Then, from June 1940 till November 1942, the people of Malta endured a second unrelenting assault, this time by air. Over three thousand bombing raids were made against Malta and British ships, including HMS Illustrious, by German and Italian air forces. With RAF support and re-supply convoys Malta's will to resist never failed. After the defeat of German forces at el-Alamein and the subsequent Torch landings in North Africa from December 1942, Malta's future was secured and it became the base for sustained and highly effective naval attacks against Axis shipping. In 1942 the island as an entity was awarded the George Cross for its resistance, and a plaque recording this is displayed in the main square outside the Prime Minister's house.

Valetta, the capital of Malta, encapsulates much of Malta's history. Our first day on the island was spent wandering its streets and absorbing its atmosphere. We went to the Grand Master's Palace and then the Pro-Cathedral, which in many ways is a chapel to the Order of St John. All the floor space is covered with memorials to Knights who were drawn from all over Catholic Europe. The decoration of this Pro-Cathedral is a frenzy of gilded baroque, with chapels commemorating knights from every territory in Europe: Provence, Aragon, Auvergne, Castille and Leon to name a few. And in the Oratory is the masterpiece of the Cathedral, the beheading of John the Baptist by Caravaggio, and alongside it a further painting of Saint Jerome writing.

Caravaggio's life (1571–1610) was as chequered as Malta's history. He was forced to flee Rome where some of his greatest works were completed (1600–1610) after killing Ranuccio Tomassoni in a brawl. He first went to Naples and then Malta where he was given protection by a member of the Columna family. He was commissioned to paint a work for the Knights, and chose the beheading of John the Baptist: one of his largest and most famous canvases. His use of *chiaroscuro*, through which he contrasts the darkness surrounding the figures with the light falling on the head of the to-be-executed Baptist is unsurpassed. Perhaps the work symbolises Caravaggio's own life: the brightness of his own brilliant talent surrounded by the darkness of his sometimes-violent behaviour. After another brawl and arrest in Malta, he escaped imprisonment by the Knights and fled to Sicily and then Naples where he died two years later. But he had left Malta a painting of incomparable drama and power.

In bright warm afternoon sunlight reaching 20 degrees Celsius in late February, we went to the firing of the Battery Canon over the Grand Harbour at four p.m. There are few greater harbours in Europe, and if someone has written a book on the great harbours of the world, surely Malta will be there, along with Lisbon, Sydney, San Francisco, Vancouver and Singapore. The sun began to set soon after five p.m., and in the evening, we went out to the Ambrosia restaurant in Archbishop Street for the ubiquitous Maltese dish of rabbit casserole.

On our second day we decided to take a bus to the central part of the island. We caught the No. 32 to Medina and Rabat in the central part of the island. Named by the Arabs in the ninth century, Medina is a walled city with narrow traffic-free streets that has been left behind by modern Malta to remain a haven for tourists seeking out the past. At its heart is the cathedral dedicated to St Paul, who came to the island in c. 60 AD when he was shipwrecked on its coast whilst travelling to Rome for trial under military escort (See Acts 27 and 28). After Paul arrived as a shipwrecked prisoner off the coast, he was taken along with his escort to the governor, Publius, where he prayed for the governor's father who had dysentery, and then recovered, and also for other sick people (Acts 28: 7–10). Paul seemed to have a particular ministry to Governors! The site of the cathedral is where the governor's house stood.

While waiting to go in we got talking to two women circling the entrance. They were Jewish sisters on holiday from Israel and they told us how in 1941 the British had refused their father entrance to Israel when fleeing Europe aged seventeen. He was interned by the British, but eventually must have been admitted, as the sisters were born in a kibbutz in Israel. But no, they would not be going into the cathedral: old memories die hard.

From Medina we walked to nearby Rabat and visited two catacombs. One was dedicated to St Paul and the other to St Agatha, perhaps two more contrasting stories one could not find, although the narratives of both lives are, in part, defined by suffering. Paul was under arrest and on his way to Jerusalem to face Roman justice in the imperial court when he was shipwrecked off Malta. For a brief interlude he was able to preach freely in the caves and open spaces in Malta before continuing his journey as a prisoner. St Agatha had fled from Sicily where she had been persecuted. Her breasts had been cut off, but she had been miraculously healed. She hid from her pursuers in these catacombs. In 1942 both sets of catacombs functioned as shelters for the population when the Axis powers bombed the island. Over the centuries these caves had afforded sanctuary and security.

We caught the No. 52 bus back to Valetta, arriving at six p.m., where it was back to Archbishop St, yes for more rabbit! The following day we decided to hire a car and drive to Gozo. Eventually finding our way out of Valetta with its narrow and very steep streets, we drove through a seemingly endless ribbon development around St Julian's and Silema. Along the coast are numerous places for snorkelling and scuba diving around coral reefs and wartime wrecks. Octopus, moray eels, damsel fish, lobsters and crabs can all be seen and there are underwater caves, fissures and near-vertical walls to explore. Eventually we reached the ferry that goes from Malta to Gozo and drove to the western end of the island. We passed close by the famous Azure Rock (like Durdle Door in Dorset) whose famous arch was destroyed in a storm in March 2017. We bathed in Xwejni Bay where salt is made through an ancient pan system in which the sea water dries leaving a residue of salt behind. It was a fitting way to end our short visit to the island, only one hundred and seven kilometres north lay the third of our islands in the sun: Sicily and the port of Syracuse.

Sicily

And so, to Sicily, the triangular-shaped island off the toe of Italy, which I first visited with Olivia at the end of February 2018. Sicily has figured in every age of European history from earliest times till the unification of Italy. Almost every conceivable regional power has governed it: the Phoenicians, Greeks, Carthaginians, Romans, Vandals, Ostrogoths, Byzantines, Arabs, Normans, Sicilians, Germans, French (Anjou), Spanish Hapsburgs, Bourbons and finally the Italians, when Garibaldi ended the feudal isolation of the island's rulers, as so graphically recorded in the famous historical novel, *The Leopard*. Almost all these rulers left their cultural footfall across the island and vestiges and legacies of their occupations. Furthermore, the greatest Greek philosopher, Plato, spent time in Syracuse vainly advising the Tyrant of Syracuse, Dionysius. And Cicero famously brought charges against the rapacious Roman Governor of Sicily Gaius Verres (120–43 BC) in 70 BC in a textbook piece of careful and devastating prosecution well written of in Robert Harris' book, Imperium.

Sicily is a large island, characterised by a mountainous interior, capped by the active volcano Etna at ten thousand feet and which covers four hundred and fifty-nine square miles and provides rich volcanic soil for vineyards and agriculture above Catánia. The island is also infamous for its Sicilian Mafia. We stayed in the north-west centred on Palermo and the surrounding region for our few days in Sicily. To see the island in any completeness would probably require at least three visits: one to the north-west and then a second to the north-east including Etna and Catania, and finally the south-east taking in Syracuse and the interior.

It is a large island of some ten thousand square miles. We spent five days in and around Palermo, the Arab, Norman, and Byzantine part and the writer John Julius Norwich's favourite part of the island.[180] It is Norwich who also writes that in Sicily there is an underlying sadness; a result of being unable to shake off the malevolent infestation of the Mafia, and the effects of interminable occupations by foreign powers.

On arrival you ate confronted by the legacy of the Mafia. The airport near Palermo is dedicated to two judges, Giovanni Falcone and Paolo Borsellino, who were assassinated by the Corleone Mafiosi, creating the awareness that, for all Palermo's history and faded charm, you are in bandit territory. Palermo, rather like Naples, has a dilapidated look. Beyond its tourist attractions it is the main commercial and industrial centre of the island and probably the centre of Mafia activity. Back in the eleventh century it was the centre of the new Norman government of the island.

Under Pope Alexander II and then Gregory VII (Hildebrand), a new papal policy was emerging: dependency on the Normans. Earlier, with the Byzantines, popes had opposed the Normans only to discover their effectiveness in battle, as in 1053 when they captured and imprisoned Pope Leo IX. Come the papacy of Alexander II (1061–1073) it was the Normans, sponsored by the papacy, who were to take Sicily and Puglia from the Arabs and Byzantines respectively. Using the de Hauteville family from Cotentin in Normandy, the papal conquest of Sicily took shape. By 1130, Roger II, a Norman, was King of Sicily. He was to consolidate what his father King Roger I and his uncle Simon had won. With Roger II a cultured, enlightened and powerful court came into

---

[180] John Julius Norwich *Sicily: A Short History from the Ancient Greeks to Cosa Nostra* (London: John Murray, 2016), p. x.

existence that transformed Sicily. Indeed, whether in Sicily or in England, the Normans now bestrode Europe and, in both places, melded enduring civilisations.

In Palermo, Monreal and Cefalù, this new blend of Norman chutzpah, Byzantine craftsmanship and Arab architecture was on show. In Palermo, the blend is easy to find. The church of the Martorana (St. Maria dell'Ammiurgalio) was built in 1143 by the greatest of Sicilian admirals, George of Antioch. Although subject to fearful redevelopments over the ages, enough of the original decorations remain to reveal the brilliance of the original mosaics. Among these are the Annunciation, the Nativity, the Presentation in the Temple and the Dormition of the Virgin.[181] Finally, a mosaic of Christ crowning Roger II represents the loyal devotion of Admiral John to his monarch.

The cream of Palermo's clutch of Norman-Byzantine-Arab buildings is the Palatine Chapel created by Roger II in 1140. It is exquisite. Little can prepare the visitor for this utterly sympathetic juxtaposition of styles. The chapel has three apses, with a single central dome decorated with a Christus Pantocrator. The nave has three pointed arches resting on classical columns, the walls on the lower part of the nave are of marble and are plain, but above on the arches are profuse cycles of brilliant gold mosaics, telling the stories of creation, of the life of Christ, of the Patriarchs and of Peter and Paul. You could say the entire biblical story is told in these depictions. Capping it all is a ceiling constructed in Muqarnas style by Arabic craftsmen from Fatimid Cairo. This creates a honeycomb or "stalactite" vaulting common in Islamic architecture. In the Palatine Chapel, set in an equally beautiful palace, these styles of Byzantine mosaics and structure, Latin or Norman form, and Arabic decoration, culminate in a unique blend.

We spent two days in Palermo enjoying this essentially working city, with its understated tourist attractions from the Norman period, plethora of churches, tasty street food, and dilapidated buildings of faded charm. Perhaps this is best represented by the Quattro Canti or Piazza Vigliena. We would call it the Four Seasons Square or perhaps more accurately, crossroads. On each side is a baroque building on three levels with statues recalling a Hapsburg King and a season of the year. It has all the

---

[181] J. J. Norwich, *Sicily* (London: John Murray, 2016), p. 79.

charm of an unobtrusive, decaying past which is so often the backdrop to busy contemporary Italian life.

After two days there we hired a car and drove via Monreale to stay in Cefalù, before a final night near the classical Greek site at Segesta. The car, which was a new Renault, had various unexplained features that needed a certain amount of working out: such as how to start it and a handbrake that was a button and fearsome to operate in the very steep streets of Monreale with its crowds of Sicilians coming out of church. It was a rather bulbous too, and driving down extremely narrow streets inches from houses on either side, with impatient Sicilian drivers behind who could see no difficulty, all made for a unique cocktail of motoring difficulties! On occasions Olivia had to walk ahead (as if with a warning flag, as in 1910) to see if we could turn left or right with any hope of getting through. In the end we found a way to park near the cathedral at Monreale, set as it is on the side of a steep hill, with its wonderful views over the bay of Palermo.

We had only had a short time in the cathedral as a service for the scout movement was about to begin. The cathedral of Monreale is a splendid anomaly, built as it is so close to the archdiocese of Palermo. Its building grew from the desire of William II of Sicily, the grandson of Roger II, to be free of the influence of Walter of the Mill, the Archbishop of Palermo. So, what do you do, being king he created a new archdiocese up the road at Monreale![182] William had recently married in Joanna, the daughter of Henry II and Eleanor of Aquitaine, (1177) and in penitence for the killing of Thomas Becket Monreale Cathedral recalls the martyred Becket, although it is dedicated to the Virgin Mary. Construction began in 1183, and was completed in six years. The result is a colossus in every sense, with mosaics recalling almost every miracle in the Old and New Testaments. We looked around before the scout service began, toured the cloister on the south side and then climbed up onto the roof with its magnificent views of Palermo and the coast.

From Monreale we drove to Cefalù on the north coast, where we spent two nights. The weather was cold and stormy, with something much worse brewing, in fact the so-called Beast from the East. Most of the restaurants were still closed for the winter season, and towering over

---

[182] Norwich, *Sicily*, pp. 99–102.

the old city was the other great cathedral church of Cefalù. The great Norman cathedral has a simple grand power: a long nave leading to an apse with an imposing and majestic mosaic of Christus Pantokrator. The solidity of the cathedral structure and the powerful simplicity of the Pantokrator leaves an indelible and imposing impression. Perhaps nowhere else does Norman strength and Byzantine beauty speak with such a single voice.

For the second day at Cefalù we went into the interior, visiting Castelbuono in the hills behind the city, but were not tempted to go west, and south of Monreale to Corleone, the base of the Cosa Nostra (Mafia) in the region. Then, whilst having a coffee in Castelbuono, we watched images of Rome under inches of snow and learned that all transport had ground to a halt in Italy. We began to wonder how easy our return journey would be. "The Beast from the East" had truly struck.

Our final night in Sicily would be in the west of the island near the Greek Temple of Segeste, so we drove back beyond Palermo to the western extremity of the island. As we did so we passed Termini Imerese, a commercial port of no particular significance, but it was from here in late 1943 that my father had embarked for Italy. The Allies invaded Sicily in Operation Husky in July 1943, as planned by Generals Eisenhower and Alexander in Malta. A hundred and fifty thousand Allied troops were involved with air cover and three thousand craft against two German Divisions. A diversionary tactic called Operation Mincemeat was conceived to deceive the Germans over where the Allies would be landing. In the face of superior odds, the Germans had withdrawn from Sicily to mainland Italy. The 24th Guards Brigade in which my father served as an Intelligence Officer, including the 5th Battalion Grenadiers, then embarked for Naples and Anzio from Termini.[183] In the fighting between 25 January and 10 February 1944, the Battalion lost twenty-nine officers out of thirty-five and five hundred and sixty soldiers of other ranks out of eight hundred. As my father in his Regimental History wrote, the fighting "was comparable to the battles of Ypres or the Somme in terms of doggedness and casualties".[184]

---

[183] Nigel Nicolson, *The Grenadier Guards 1939–1945, Vol II* (Aldershot: Gale and Polden, 1949), p. 357.

[184] R. H Whitworth, *The Grenadier Guards* (Barnsley: Leo Cooper, 1974), p. 103.

Such events, some seventy-four years earlier, seemed a long way off from our final quiet day in northern Sicily. We visited the Greek Temple at Segesta in a fold in the hills west of Palermo and close to the sea. To John Julius Norwich it is the loveliest of all the Greek temples on the island: "The general impression being of quiet perfection".[185] Situated beneath the nearby hill were the remains of a Greek theatre. It is everything a fifth century BC Doric monument ought to be, and stands simply, unobtrusively and gracefully.

We had our final night in a hotel in the nearby town of Alcamo, where an election meeting of the right-wing nationalist Five Star Movement was going on in the hotel foyer. The election was on 4 March, in three days' time and the populist Five Star party led by Guiseppe Conte won, and remained in power till 2021

. We managed our flight out from Palermo to Rome, with Rome still blanketed under snow. Soon after we arrived at Heathrow from Rome, they closed the airport, and by the next day we were under snow in West Berkshire. The "Beast from the East" had arrived in England too. It was good to remember the islands in the sun with all their varied history as we looked out on a wintry scene.

---

[185] Norwich, *Sicily*, p. 9.

Chapter XV
The Peloponnese

It was my final year in Bath Weston before retiring after forty years of Anglican ministry, twenty-one of which had been in Bath. In 2015 I had hoped to go with a group of ten to Tunisia. I had started writing early church history and had come to the great figure of Augustine of Hippo (354–430). Augustine was born in Thagaste in present-day Algeria, then the Roman Province of Numidia Proconsluaris, and had worked in Carthage as a Professor of Rhetoric before going to Rome and Milan, where he became a Christian. He returned to Hippo Regius, becoming its bishop, and remained so for the rest of his life. I was looking forward to going to Tunisia and seeing the remains of Carthage for myself. We had arranged a tour that took in Carthage, Cap Bon, the Garden of Tunisia, Dougga, Sfax, el Djem, Kairouan and Hammamet, eight of us were going. It looked a fascinating tour but it was not to be. On 18 March, just weeks before we were due to leave on 17 April there was a tragic terrorist attack in the Bardo Museum, Tunis, with twenty-one tourists gunned down inside by ISIL and fifty wounded. It was a massacre. There was no appetite to go, so soon after the attack, so we cancelled.

Instead, I used the time set aside to travel to Germany with Michael, to Trier, where the Roman Empire had its North European headquarters in the time of Augustine. Indeed, Augustine recalls in his *Confessions* meeting one Ponticianus from Trier who told him about an ascetic way of life he had discovered there.[186] Fine as the remains are, and the Museum of Antiquities at Trier also, it in no way compensated for not visiting Tunisia. Maybe another time. However, the following year the three of us decided to go to the Peloponnese.

A week to ten days in the Peloponnese makes for a wonderful holiday, and in April 2016 we set off for this famous peninsula. The

---

[186] Augustine, *The Confessions* tr. Henry Chadwick (Oxford: Oxford University Press, 2008), p. 143.

Peloponnese, or Morea as it was called for its resemblance to the leaf of a mulberry tree (*morea* is the transliteration of mulberry in Greek), boasts layer upon layer of Greek and Roman antiquities, a Byzantine past second to none, regional variations as in the Mani, a coast that affords innumerable bays and coves, and highlands which cover Arcadia. It is the way that this peninsula, detached from the mainland by the Gulf of Corinth and with its four fingers jutting into Mediterranean, encompasses such variety that makes it such an entity. Within its boundaries some of the greatest names of Ancient Greece can be found: Mycenae, Argos, Sparta, Epidaurus, and to cap it all, the site of the original Olympic games at Olympia. The Byzantine towns of Mistras and Monemvasia recall the long years of Byzantine rule before the coming of the Turks, and scattered throughout the peninsula are abandoned temples, and monasteries just about holding onto their lives.

Paul, Michael and I arrived at Athens airport at one p.m., having left home at three a.m., hired a car and drove along the coast road west to Old Corinth. We stopped at the Corinth canal and looked down the three hundred feet into its precipitous cutting. Although a canal had been envisaged since classical times, it was finally completed only in 1893, with several companies going broke trying to do so. Some four miles long and approximately seventy feet wide it can only accommodate small pleasure craft and narrow cruise ships, but it saves a voyage of four hundred kilometres around the Peloponnese from the west to Athens. We arrived at our guest house run by Anastasia in the late afternoon. It could not have been more cheerful, clean and refreshing after a long journey and then went out for a meal nearby. *En route* we were offered some oranges by a woman at her garden gate, and then stepped over a snake in its final death throes having had its rear end bitten off. All part of Greece!

The following day we went to Old Corinth and Epidavros. Classical Corinth is about three miles inland from the modern city of the same name. As so often happens, the shoreline advances as it did at Ephesus, so the old seaport town of Corinth now finds itself over three miles from the Gulf of Corinth. In classical times it was an affluent and powerful city on the Corinthian isthmus. On each side of the isthmus there was a port: on the Aegean side, Kenchreaia and on the Gulf of Corinth, Lecheon. It traded therefore equally to east and to west. And when it came to the Peloponnesian Wars between Athens and Sparta recorded by Thucydides (431- 404 BC), Corinth used diplomacy to chart a way through, although for the most part siding with Sparta against Athens. Later, it came under the control of Macedon until the arrival of the Romans in 146 BC. In 44 BC Julius Caesar rebuilt the port and expanded the city. By the first century AD, Corinth had a reputation for commerce, the arts, and a free and easy lifestyle.

The Apostle Paul came here after vising Athens in about 54 AD. It was here that he met Aquila and Priscilla. Aquila was a Jewish Christian from Pontus, on the Black Sea, who had been expelled from Rome in c. 53 AD by the Emperor Claudius, along with other Jewish Christians. Both were tentmakers and Paul supported himself with tentmaking to begin with while preaching in Corinth. His preaching met with success. Crispus, the synagogue ruler, believed, as did Titius Justus (Acts 18;1– 8) and a church was formed. It was a church characterised by two things: its vitality and the trouble it caused Paul! It appreciated style, eloquent Greek wisdom, human ability, and attention-getting spiritual gifts of prophecy and speaking in tongues. Its feasts could verge on orgies, and sexual temptation was never far away. In response, Paul wrote that true wisdom rested in the word of the Cross, power in weakness embraced by God, and that love was always more important than eye-catching gifts. There would be ongoing tension between the values of Corinth and the values of Paul, but the tension gave rise to some of Paul's greatest writing on wisdom (1 Corinthians 1:18–2:16), on love (1 Corinthians 13), and on the resurrection (1 Corinthians 15). Without the tensions in Corinth, we would never have received Paul's profound teaching.

The site of Old Corinth is extensive. The feature you notice immediately is a mound or limestone outcrop reaching five hundred and seventy-five feet, around which the city is built. On its summit was a temple to Aphrodite, whose priestesses were courtesans, and next to the temple a fortress. The remains at Old Corinth are extensive. There is a well-preserved Temple of Apollo, to the south of which is an extensive agora or forum, the site of fountains and baths. When we visited, a group of Roman Catholic nuns were taking it all in as part of their pilgrimage. We read the account of Paul's visit to Corinth, but did not linger too long as we had a full day ahead.

From Corinth we drove south-east to Epidavros, a place of extraordinary beauty and significance lying close to the Saronic Gulf, on the north side of which is Athens and the Island of Salamis, where the Persians were defeated in the great naval battle with the Athenian fleet led by Themistocles in 480 BC. The jewel of Epidavros is the theatre, which is beautifully preserved. Capable of holding fourteen thousand people in fifty-five rows (extended from thirty-three by the Romans) it looks over the surrounding wooded hills, which give it an eirenic and pastorral quality. We took our turns at declaiming from the central spot on the "stage", as even this could be heard high up into the seating. Paul sang *Amazing Grace;* I did some lines from Byron's *The Isles of Greece*. And then up stepped some Oxford University classics students to show how it is done, declaiming the opening lines of the *Iliad* in Greek, then translating (not that we needed that!). The Greek architect and sculptor, Polykleitos the Younger, had done his job well in the fourth century BC, the acoustics were faultless. Yet impressive though the theatre is, it is not the main purpose of this ancient site.

Epidavros is dedicated to the Greek god of medicine, Asclepius, the son of Apollo. Indeed, Socrates' final words as he died from hemlock was the ironic remark, "A cock for Asclepius", i.e., present a sacrifice of thanksgiving to the god of medicine! Typical of both the Greeks and Romans was that almost every aspect of medicine was given its own divinity. So, Asclepius's daughters are Hygieia (hygiene), Panacea (the goddess of universal health), Iaso (the goddess of recuperation from illness), Aceso (the goddess of the healing process) and Aglaea (the goddess of healthful beauty). Although we have carried only two of these siblings into our vocabulary—hygiene and panacea—it nevertheless demonstrates the Greeks' understanding of medicine and the healing process: the latent healing power of the body; the requirement for convalescence; the need for hygiene to prevent infection; the psychosomatic side to healing suggested by panacea; the importance of beauty and a place to inspire the healing process; the belief in prayer hence the religious setting of this healing centre at Epidavros; the intervention of a doctor operating under the Hippocratic Oath; and the enjoyment of a good play to raise or stimulate the spirits. All of these principles were to be developed by the medical profession and society over the centuries, but they were already present at Epidavros two thousand years ago and more. And what started as a classical healing centre in the fourth century BC had become a Christian healing centre by the sixth century AD.

In fact, the entire site was used as a healing centre. There was accommodation, baths, a gymnasium, a stadium for athletics, an odeon for musical and artistic shows, and most interesting of all, a museum of medical instruments used in the fourth century BC and later. Here were surgical instruments for incisions, stitching, holding and pulling, made from bone, metal and ivory. It was probably well over a thousand years before western medicine advanced beyond their understanding and ability then, perhaps not until the late nineteenth century. Stunned by the beauty of the surroundings and the origins of medicine in the west with its care of the whole person, we tore ourselves away to head south for an overnight stop at Nafplio.

Beauty upon beauty. Nafplio occupies a serene location on the Argolic Gulf and is now a well-known secret to travellers, tourists and day trippers. Nonetheless, situated on the water's edge of the Gulf and beneath the hills to the west beyond Argos, it cannot fail to charm. Its elegant Venetian houses, narrow streets, neo-classical mansions and flower-bedecked balconies lie beneath the great Palamidi fortress.

Nafplio had its brief moment in the political sun in 1831 when declared the capital of Greece after the Greek Wars of Independence, and when the first Governor of Greece, Ionnais Kapodistrias, resided there after the Ottomans left. A Greek from Corfu with a Cypriot mother, Kapodistrias trained as a doctor at Padua University, but in 1808 during the Napoleonic Wars was absorbed into the Russian Diplomatic service.[187] Having served as the Russian Ambassador to Switzerland and later as the Russian representative at the Congress of Vienna, he was chosen as the first leader of a new Greek state after the War of Independence. He lived in Nafplio, but was soon opposed by independent Greek regional rulers or merchants long used to ruling their own areas unmolested. Chief among these in Morea were the Maniots of Mani, to whom we will come. Their leader was Petrobey Mavromichalis, whose

---

[187] David Brewer, *The Greek War of Independence* (London: Overlook Duckworth, 2011).

son and brother Konstantis assassinated Kapodistrias outside the church of Saint Spyridon, Nafplio in 1831. Contrastingly and more peacefully, we had an excellent night in the Bonne Nuit guest house, after stuffed tomatoes and moussaka in town! We were all set to go to Mycenae and Arcadia the next day.

Mycenae, Arcadia, Sparta and Mystras

From Nafplio to Mycenae we passed through Argos, nothing to do with a supermarket chain in England, but the oldest city in Greece, said to have been continuously inhabited for six thousand years, and no doubt full of avid shoppers! Now it is a genuine local town, with its antiquities long since buried. It boasts a fine central square, Plateia Agiou Petrou, dedicated to St Peter. From Argos to Mycenae, it is only a few kilometres. We were there early enough in the morning not to be overrun by tourists. Mycenae is both the centre of one of the oldest Greek civilisations before the emergence of Athens and Sparta and after the Minoan in Crete, as well as the springboard of Greece's greatest legend, the war against Troy: part based in history, part story conjured by the fertile imagination of Homer, Greece's greatest poet.

The acropolis of Mycenae is peerless. Atop a hill of nearly a thousand feet it is approached by a single path up to its Lion Gates and its strong fortified position. With sweeping views across the plains below to the mountains of Arcadia, it occupies a wonderful defensive position. In the second millennium BC, Mycenae was the dominant force in the region, holding sway over the Cyclades, Crete and parts of the present Turkish coast. There are signs too of a high-level relationship with the Pharaohs of Egypt, particularly Amenhotep III. By 1200 BC the power of Mycenae was declining for manifold reasons: famine, the invasion of the Greek mainland by the sea peoples, and disruption of trade with the rise of the Hittite empire. But for at least two hundred years Mycenae had carried the torch of Greek culture and the arts and maybe for this reason became the chosen site for Greece's greatest epic poems: the *Iliad* and the *Odyssey* by Homer.

The Trojan war of around c1260–1180 BC occurred when Helen, the most beautiful woman in the world, wife of Menelaus, King of Sparta, was abducted by Paris, the son of the King of Troy, and taken to that city. Agamemnon, the husband of Helen's sister Clytemnestra, set sail with an army and the great warrior Achilles to defeat Troy and take back Helen. To obtain a fair wind for his fleet he sacrificed his daughter Iphigenia to the gods, so poisoning his relationship with Clytemnestra. A dispute broke out in the Greek camp over Agamemnon's jealousy of Achilles's concubine or sex slave, Briseis, captured from Troy in the fighting, and which almost spelt disaster. Troy was taken and Helen returned to Sparta, but Agamemnon was killed by Clytemnestra on his return. So concludes the *Iliad* with its sequel the *Odyssey* covering the lengthy journey home of Odysseus, who was fighting with the Greeks and the King of Ithaca, an island next to Cephalonia off western Greece. (The story of the *Iliad* has been powerfully retold from a feminist point of view by Pat Barker, in her haunting novel, *The Silence of the Girls.*) For the visitor to Mycenae there is much to ponder, and just a short walk below the acropolis brings you to the empty bee-hive tombs of Agamemnon and Clytemnestra, who are seemingly part-historical, part-legendary figures.

Around midday we left for Arcadia, stopping on the way for a picnic lunch, for ours was to be a comparatively short odyssey, without any sightings of one-eyed cyclops on the way!

The drive up into the highlands of Arcadia was dramatic and testing but our advanced rally driver Paul managed it with ease. When we left Mycenae, the temperature was thirty-two degrees Celsius, but by the time we reached the highlands it was ten degrees with an overnight frost to come. The Peloponnese is mostly mountainous, with a fertile undulating region in the north east. We were headed for Dimitsana in the heart of Arcadia and with surrounding mountains reaching six thousand feet. It was still early in the year, the second week of April, and the town, which in the season plays host to many hikers and walkers, was barely open. We found no hotel or bed and breakfast open yet, and asked around about accommodation. Eventually we found someone in the General Store who opened up a house in a back street that had at least four rooms and was more than adequate. We managed to find one restaurant open for an evening meal. You could well imagine how wars between Greek city-states or the movement of empires in former times could pass you by up here, but that was not the case in recent Greek history. Dimitsana spawned nationalist Greek leaders who took on the Turks. Its very remoteness did not breed indifference, but rather an unbowed patriotism, rugged like the mountains.

In the morning we went out foraging for breakfast, but finding nothing made do with a cup of coffee in a café near to our house. We met the local Orthodox priest who was doing his rounds. Although I didn't look like an Anglican priest, as I was wearing no insignia, I introduced myself as such. The height of our ecumenical exchange was: "You have wife?" he asked, "Yes", I replied. "And you have woman?" I asked. "Yes", he replied. At which we shook hands with a smile and toasted each other with coffee, thereby bringing Orthodoxy and Anglicanism as close as matrimonial bonds!

From Dimitsana we drove to Sparta, but to begin with we followed a small minor road that wove its way down the valley of the Lousios river. Never has a place lived up to its proverbial name as *this* idyllic valley in Arcadia. As we rounded a bend, we met a shepherd moving his flock of sheep and goats with their bells tinkling around their necks. We halted and turned off the engine to listen the sound of their bells, the scuffle of their feet and the occasional bleat of the sheep as they nosed past our car. A little further on we heard the rush of the river passing through some rapids before going beneath a bridge. We stopped again, and got out of the car and listened, and heard the birds singing with "full throated ease" in the trees now just coming into foliage. Nearby, there were poppies, oleander and lilac coming into bloom and high in the pine trees bees were working to produce their pure Arcadian honey. No honey is more memorable or delicious than this Greek variety drizzled over thick Greek yoghurt. Further down, on the far side of the road, we could see a monastery, perched on the side of the valley. We arrived there and went in; there was a cool and spacious entrance room where you could sit. Three older and kindly monks offered us water and *loukoumi* and we left the valley knowing we had been blessed.

The drive now took us over a high ridge out of Arcadia and into the plain below, where Sparta lies in the Eurotas valley beneath the highest mountain on the peninsula, the snow-clad Mount Elijah. On the way down the ridge, turning off the main road we came to a village taverna that looked over the plain below us. We all had a Greek salad: the local bread, the generous slice of féta cheese, and the olives and tomatoes could not have been more in keeping with the experience of the day: simple, honest, generous and completely satisfying. We headed on down to Sparta, into a modern town where virtually nothing survives of the ancient city.

Ancient Sparta was founded in about 900 BC and became renowned for its militaristic way of life. For most of the first millennium BC the Spartans were the rulers of the Peloponnese until defeated by Thebes in 371 BC. They did not leave behind great buildings—just simple villages as Thucydides said—but a reputation for war.[188] Male children were only kept if they were fit and healthy; others were exposed on the mountainside or the *Apothetae* or "dumping ground".[189] Boys from the age of seven were not brought up not by their families, but in a commune or military training school. They formed a mess, few in number but devoted in spirit, which became the core of the young Spartan's existence. Girls were likewise educated to be aggressive in throwing the javelin, to exercise in the nude, and to attract by their physical fitness and certainty of mind.[190] Their heads would be shaved in readiness for marriage, and they would be given at night as brides to their partner. Although virgins, many had been sodomised during their training. The boys meanwhile would be patronised by older men from the age of twelve, and not infrequently made their sexual partners subject to pederasty. They would be sent into the mountains and across the Taygetos range into Messenia armed only with a knife, and if necessary, would kill a Messinian or helot (a subservient population), and learn the art of survival in the wild. Nor would they be spared the whip, but were often thrashed to prove their toughness.[191] Trained in this cadre, called *agoge*, as laid down by the original Spartan leader and lawgiver, Lycurgus, of the ninth century BC, they were graded at their passing-out parade aged thirty. These graduates could then join the Crypteia, an elite cadre of

---

[188] Thucydides, Book 1:10, *The Peloponnesian War* (OUP World's Classics 2009), p. 7.
[189] Tom Holland *Persian Fire* (Abacus 2005), p. 81.
[190] Holland, *Persian Fire*, p. 85.
[191] Xenophon, The *Constitution of the Spartans* 2.9.

younger troops perhaps akin to the SAS. From the Crypteia, leaders and the two kings (Sparta having two) would be chosen. Such was Sparta: a fighting machine in which humanity was subjugated to prowess, tenderness to survival.

It was these fighters, combined with the Athenians and Thespians, who held off the Persians when they attacked Greece at Thermopylae in 480 BC. It was there that King Leonidas of Sparta held up a greatly superior Persian force with three hundred Spartans and seven hundred Thespians. It was probably the single greatest Spartan military achievement. After eventual sacking by the Persians, Athens was rebuilt in every sense by Pericles before the Peloponnesian Wars. Sparta's ascendency was tarnished but not overcome by the wars with Athens between 431 and 411 BC. Sparta came out the victor, but there were few benefits for the people.

The gradual decline of Sparta continued through its defeat by the Thebian general, Epaminondas, at Leuctra in 371 BC and through being overshadowed by the rise of Macedonia under Alexander the Great and his father, Philip of Macedon. With a new power in the region at Carthage, Sparta sided with Rome for protection, only to be absorbed into the Roman Empire by 150 BC. In time Sparta became a memory, and a byword for self-discipline, self-denial and endurance. A model no doubt to "special forces" around the world, but not one conducive to holistic human relationships.

"Nothing beside remains" of ancient Sparta or the famed past, except a suitably disciplined grid system of streets in the modern city and the wit of the modern Spartan: that laconic wit for which they are well known. We enjoyed our night there, looking out from the Maniatis Hotel towards the peak of Mount Elijah. We caught the scent of orange blossom on the warm evening, still twenty-six degrees, and watched the swallows and house-martins in their good location. We ate a simple kebab—three sausages—in a restaurant in the main Kentriki Square nearby, "and so to bed".

The following morning, we drove the short distance to Mystras on the slopes of the Taygetus mountains. Mystras is a Byzantine jewel in the landscape of Laconia (hence the word laconic). After the fall of Constantinople to the Ottoman Turks in 1453, Byzantium clung on in various locations: at Trebizond on the Black Sea and in Mystras and Monemvasia in Morea (the Peloponnese). Morea had already been ruled by Byzantine despots such as Theodore I Palaiologus (1383–1407) who had taken over from the great Kantakouzenos family. Byzantine rule would continue here until 1460, but its days were numbered, just as those of the Palaeologus dynasty (1259- 1453) had been in Constantinople. Morea was a land of fading Byzantine glory, but in its final years it shone brightly. Its scholars continued to influence the Italian Renaissance. Its greatest son, the syncretistic philosopher, Gemistus Plethon, encouraged Ficino to begin a Platonic philosophy school in Florence, thus founding the study of the humanities in Western Europe which inspired the Renaissance. The baton was passed from Morea to Florence in 1438, and in the museum in Mystras you can see the scholarship on show, in beautiful illuminated Gospels, prayer books and other manuscripts.

We wandered through this Byzantine town, lovingly preserved by present day Spartans. Nor was their contemporary life easy. We spoke to one guide who worked for the Department of Antiquities: she had taken a fifty per cent pay cut since the 2008 banking crash. There was high unemployment, and young people were emigrating for work, but with commendable spirit she had hope for the future. Like the hotelier in Cyprus, she was prepared to give it time.

Mystras exuded beauty. Built on the side of the mountain, it clung to the hill as it clung to its past. Old pink stones were covered by honey-suckle, jasmine and rambling roses. There were monasteries, churches, homes and courtyards all strung out along parallel streets in the lower and upper town, in various states of restoration. Arches, apses and half-deserted aisles made for poignant memories of a flourishing past; these buildings were the final vestiges of the eastern Byzantine Roman Empire in Morea.

The last Emperor of Byzantium was indeed crowned here when Constantinople was under pressure from the Ottomans. Constantine XI, the last Byzantine Emperor, was crowned in the Cathedral of Agios Dimitrios. The cathedral forms part of the Mitropolis, in which there is an attractive courtyard surrounded by a stoa (a covered shady walkway from which we get the word Stoics who philosophised in such a setting) and balconies. In the cathedral there is a wooden throne and on the floor is a marble slab on which is engraved a two-headed eagle, the symbol of

Byzantium, and the spot where the last emperor was crowned in 1449. He died on 29 May 1453 while fighting to save Constantinople from the troops of Mehmet II. Greece was later to fall under Venetian and then Ottoman control until 1831.

We left Mystras and Sparta conscious of the rise and fall of kingdoms, but aware that for all their present economic hardships and the strict economic conditions imposed by the EU for remission of debt, foreign occupations were a thing of the past. Since the war of 1939–45, fascism and Marxism had been seen off, the monarchy had been replaced by a republican government, the junta generals had long since left office, and now a long hard road of economic restoration had been painfully taken. With large numbers of refugees seeking entry into the country from Turkey, and now a pandemic to contend with (most effectively, in fact), the Spartan spirit of endurance and survival was much drawn upon, but it seemed to us that that their history, their faith, and their sense of optimism would see them through.

We now took the road over the Taygetus mountains towards Kalamata and then south into the Mani. The road was twisty and steep with signs of recent rock falls. From Kalamata, famous for its olives, we headed south to Kardamyli on the Mani peninsula. One of the reasons for going there was that Patrick Leigh Fermor, known for his famous walk to Constantinople begun in 1933 and his books thereon and his war exploits that included capturing a German General in Crete with the SOE, had ended up here with his wife Joan. They built a house just south of the village. I had recently finished Artemis Cooper's biography of him and was keen to see where he lived.

But first we needed a place to stay, and ended up being directed to a hotel just out of Kardamyli, only just completed. We settled in and then walked down through the village, passing several of the characteristic Mani towers on the way. The Maniots were a fierce and independent people. Secluded by geography from the rest of the Peloponnese, they pursued their independence from the Spartans, the Roman Byzantines, the Ottoman Turks and even from the newly-constituted Greek state and its first leader, Kapodistrias, whom they assassinated. Not only did they not get on with outsiders, but they pursued long held vendettas against each other, hence the towers, although these were not quite as tall as those in San Gimignano in Tuscany. They were sturdy nonetheless and with slits for guns. Indeed, Leigh Fermor describes them in his *Mani: Travels in the Southern Peloponnese* as follows, "On the other side of the valley rise a long saddle of rock on either end of which a village was gathered and each village was a long solid sheaf of towers. There were scores of them climbing into the sky in a rustic metropolis, each tower seeming to vie with the others in attaining a *more preposterous height*".[192]

We passed a few towers (not so tall) on the outskirts of the modern village of Kardamyli and went down to the beach where we had a somewhat overpriced meal and played scrabble. Paul thought he had cleaned up with interail until we noticed it should have been interrail (double r). A rematch at Olympia was planned for the following night: at least we all could get an Olympic medal, there being only three of us!

The following day we enquired at reception about the house of Patrick and Joan Leigh Fermor. We asked Vula, the hotel owner, if she knew them. "Yes". She knew them both. They were much loved in the village and had been quietly generous to many. Not only that, but she had taught Joan Greek.

Joan and Patrick had settled in Kalamitsi just south of Kardamyli. In her book, Artemis Cooper describes the site of this proposed house:

From Kalamitsi, the village of Kardamyli was a twenty-minute walk away. On their property, nothing could be heard but the sea and the almost deafening throb of the cicadas. Standing on the tip of the headland they could look out to an uninhabited island, on which stood the remains of a castle that was gradually being swallowed by trees. The island stood about half a mile offshore, while on the horizon rested the pale arm of the Messenian peninsula. To their right, the rock face tumbled down to a tiny cove. Turning to the left they could see the ground sloping off in terraces to a long-pebbled beach. Behind them, the coastal olive groves gave way to hillsides covered in pine myrtle, thorn and ilex, guarded by the slim lances of cypress trees; and hanging above them all were the grey flanks of the Taygetus mountains that glowed pink and orange at sunset".[193]

---

[192] Patrick Leigh Fermor, *Mani: Travels in the Southern Peloponnese* (London: John Murray 2004), p. 82.
[193] Artemis Cooper, *Patrick Leigh Fermor: An Adventure* (London: John Murray, 2012), 326.

Paradise indeed. A resting place in the long autumn of an adventurous life, and where Paddy's famous walk of 1933–5 was recalled, captured and painstakingly written over three books, the last of which, *The Broken Road,* was published posthumously.

We went down to the pebbled beach and swam in a place where you can look back at the house on the headland from the water. Then we walked up to the house, which although left to the Greek government, was in 2016 (five years after Patrick's death) still closed. We peered over the walls and into the unkempt garden and the rear of the house, and imagined the years of conversation, reflection and writing it had witnessed. We then went back into Kardamyli, bought some lunch for a picnic and headed for Olympia, without shaking off too quickly the slight sense of sadness following the sight of the abandoned house of the Leigh Fermors, which had once been so cherished, but I believe now is a smart hotel or retreat centre

In Olympia we found a place to stay called the Hermes Hotel, went into the town for supper and afterwards over the restaurant table played scrabble, and this time Paul won gold, with no appeals!

I was unprepared for the sheer beauty of Olympia, the birthplace of the Olympic games. Held there from 776 BC when first called by King Iphistos of Elis, the games were dedicated to Zeus, and took place every four years around the first full moon in August and were open to all Greek males. They reached the height of their prestige in 576 BC, but were ended by the Christian Emperor Theodosius I in 394 AD, presumably because of their associations with the gods. The games were then re-started in the modern era in 1896. But the setting for these early Hellenic games was pastoral and recreational, a festival of athletics and pagan piety. Although the competitive spirit was probably as sharp in the sixth century BC as it is today, the ambience was softer and blended in with its surroundings. The temple to Zeus was impressive, while other Hellenophile Roman emperors, such as Hadrian, had scattered their patronage through the site. Shrubs and flowers like the laurel, daphne, oleander, lavender and clematis abounded among the ruined buildings and temples. Wrestling, chariot racing, discus, javelin throwing and the pentathlon all took place, but the athletics was surely then, as now, the greatest draw. The stadium or running track measured at least two hundred metres with a parallel grass mound to accommodate the forty-five thousand spectators. Competitors were warned that should they cheat the wrath of the gods would catch up with them and visit afflictions upon them and their families. It was a "leave it to the gods" form of dope testing.

As we left the site to go back to Athens and fly home, we had an overwhelming awareness of the contribution that the Greeks have made to our way of life: in theatre, medicine, theology, philosophy, mathematics, politics, architecture, ethics, logic, rhetoric, athletics, military training and competition, literature, history and epic tales—much of it centred in and sprung from the Peloponnese. It is a legacy of which any nation would be proud; perhaps it is the greatest legacy that any country or culture has given to the world?

Chapter XVI
Saxony

What could be more different in atmosphere from Greece than Saxony! In 2017 Olivia and I went with a group to Saxony. Before leaving the parish of All Saints Weston, I had suggested a trip to Germany to mark the five-hundred-year anniversary of Martin Luther nailing his 95 Theses to the door of the castle church in the Saxon town of Wittenberg. A friend and member of the congregation at All Saints, Robert Groezinger, whose father was German and mother English, had agreed to co-ordinate the visit, using his many contacts. He came up with a wonderfully stimulating tour following, at least in part, the life of Martin Luther. Once in Germany, we became aware that we would learn not only about the life of Martin Luther, but also the effect of the bombing of WWII on Dresden and Leipzig and the effect of the division of Germany into East (GDR) and West in 1945, following the Potsdam Conference of that year. Far from there being a single focus to the visit, there would be three.

Six of us flew from Bristol to Berlin, and we met the other five, who had travelled by another route, the following day. For the third time since leaving in 1963, I found myself back, albeit briefly, in Berlin. We arrived in the evening in time to see *Nabucco* by Verdi at the Deutsch Opera. Although I had often heard the *Chorus of the Hebrews Slaves*, I had always wrongly thought that it referenced the period when the Jews were slaves in Egypt. In fact, it recalls the time when once again the Jews were threatened with slavery, only by Nebuchadnezzar, who had taken Jerusalem in 597 BC and was about to lead them into exile.

Nor was the famous *Chorus of the Hebrew Slaves* an inappropriate introduction to the life of Luther. The Chorus is a lament by the slaves over the homeland of Israel and the capital city of Jerusalem. The second stanza runs (in Italian), as follows:

Great the banks of the Jordan
And Zion's toppled towers

Oh, my homeland, so lovely and so lost
Of memory, so dear and so dead!
Rekindle the memories in our hearts
And speak of times gone by!

It is a lament expressing a longing for Jerusalem—its toppled towers and broken Temple—from a strange land. It recalls Psalm 137, where by the waters of Babylon the exiles sat down and wept. And the music is appealing, wistful, and moving. In fact, when Verdi's funeral cortège passed down the streets of Milan in 1901 the crowd spontaneously sung *this* chorus! Only in Italy could such a thing happen! And the link with Luther? Just as the Jewish exiles in Babylon longed for Jerusalem, Luther longed for a reformed church which far from being in exile in Babylon had become *like Babylon*—so he wrote passionately about the "Babylonian captivity of the church". But his respect for Jews and Judaism was sadly lacking, and his legacy on that score was used by the Nazis in the holocaust.

The following day we picked up the vehicle we were to use and left Berlin, driving south past Potsdam and Brandenburg, the centres of old Prussian power. The countryside is flat, with extensive forest and with road widening schemes seemingly everywhere. We stopped at Worlitz, a pretty town with its nearby Schloss east of Magdeburg, and on the river Elbe, which flows northwest to Hamburg and the North Sea, before arriving in the evening at our hotel near Erfurt airport.

Eisenach, Erfurt, Wittenberg and Wartburg Castle

Much of Luther's life was spent around these towns that we visited over the next three days. He was born in Eiselben, and his father worked in the copper mining business nearby, which was owned by the several Counts of Mansfeld.[194] His parents had high hopes for Martin of a legal career in the mining industry, so they paid for his education at a Grammar School at Eisenach and then University at Erfurt, after his early schooling, which was at Mansfeld and Magdeburg.

---

[194] Lyndal Roper, *Martin Luther: Renegade and Prophet* (London: Penguin 2016), pp. 18–19.

We visited Luther's birthplace at Eisleben, where the church caretaker expressed surprise at how few English people visited the town in this the five-hundred-year anniversary of Luther pinning his 95 Theses to the church door in Wittenberg, an act commonly regarded as the starting gun of the Reformation. Perhaps this lack of interest reflects ways the church in England has become disconnected from its Protestant roots in Germany, or how, given subsequent relations between the two countries, English Protestant churches are unwilling to acknowledge that strong link. Yet the fact remains that the main influence on the English Reformers came from the Germans and the Swiss (and arguably the French, as Calvin was French). Martin Luther was an influence on William Tyndale, and Martin Bucer, who was in turn a great influence on Thomas Cranmer, while Bullinger from Zurich was a real support to Elizabeth I. These men shaped the future of English thought in the sixteenth century, but there is scant awareness of that today as other things have come in the way.

We spent an afternoon in Eisenach where Luther went to grammar school. It is a town just out of Saxony in Thuringia, a small state in Germany bordered by Bavaria to the south, Saxony to the north, and Hesse to the west. Eisenach is famous now for two people: Martin Luther and Johann Sebastian Bach. For Luther it was a step up in terms of culture and sophistication from the mining town of Mansfeld, with its slag heaps and many bawdy mining taverns. It was also the town of his mother's relatives, who were doctors, academics, lawyers and administrators, and who mostly came from Eisenach.[195] It was full of churches then: seven monasteries, three parish churches and a seminary.[196] The town also boasts the memory of St Elizabeth of Hungary, who married Ludwig IV of Thuringia in 1221 and lived with him at the Wartburg castle nearby. Rather than live in splendid isolation in the castle, Elisabeth helped the poor and lived an ascetic life. She once invited a leper to sleep in her husband's bed when he was away! On hearing this he strongly objected, understandably annoyed at such liberties, he pulled back the sheets only to find the imprint of a cross!

For four years Luther stayed with his mother's relatives, the

---

[195] Roper, *Martin Luther*, pp. 38–39.
[196] Roper, *Martin Luther*, p. 39.

Schalbes, and attended school in Eisenach, learning Latin and becoming immersed in the classics, including Ovid, Cicero, Livy and Virgil. It was this exposure to language and literature, added to his own innate linguistic skills, that made him in time such a warrior with the pen. Not only would Luther translate the Bible from Latin into German, but his prose would also awaken a continent with its powerful directness and vivid metaphors. He sang in the church choir at St George's in the town where the Bach family would become organists and which Johann Sebastian Bach attended as a boy in 1690. Looking around the church I could not help noticing that the medieval rood screen featuring the crucifixion of Christ with Mary and St John had survived intact, while in England the iconoclasm under Edward VI and later Cromwell saw to the removal all such images. As so often happen, the originator of a movement can be less extreme than the followers!

From Eisenach, Luther continued his education at the University of Erfurt, the capital of Thuringia. In the Middle Ages, Erfurt was ruled by the Archbishop of Mainz, and the first Archbishop of Mainz was the Saxon missionary and martyr Boniface or Winfrid (c. 675–754) who came from Crediton in Devon. Mainz also hosted the first printing works, the Gutenberg Press, where in 1450 the Gutenberg Bible was produced from movable type-face, which was probably the greatest revolution in communication, arguably greater than the computer even, leading as it did to the advent of the printed book. Luther completed his education at Erfurt with the classic university *Trivium* (grammar, logic and rhetoric) and *Quadrivium* (arithmetic, geometry, music and astronomy). These courses were the same in outline all across Europe, and what is astonishing is how little they had changed since the fourth century AD. Other famous students at the University were Johann Pachelbel (1653–1706), famous for his Canon in D Major and the mystic Meister Eckhart (1260–1328). Luther was not only exposed to this ancient curriculum, he was also exposed to a more critical and modern form of learning called the *via moderna*, which followed the English thinker, William of Occam, and his famous "razor" (or dictum) of reducing things to their fundamental particulars, rather than holding to accepted universals.

Our guide in Erfurt, Brigid Messerschmitt, was keen to impress on us that throughout his training at Erfurt University, Luther would have seen only one Bible, printing not yet being common, and that was a manuscript copy held in the Cathedral church in the main square. No wonder that at the end of his university course, and having such an enquiring mind, Luther wanted to take his biblical studies further, a desire precipitated by three further events in his life.

First, a fellow student and close friend died, throwing Luther into melancholy. Second, he managed to cut himself severely with a knife in the upper leg. He prayed that the flow of blood would be staunched, and it was. Third, he was caught in a severe thunderstorm, and terrified, he once again prayed to an obscure saint called Anna. He was saved and decided to offer himself as a monk at the local Augustinian monastery in Erfurt. He knocked on the door and offered himself as a candidate, but not before he held a feast for all his university friends, revealing at the end, to their surprise, that he was taking monastic orders.[197] In 1505 he entered the Augustinian Priory, which still stands in delightful surroundings, but by 1520 he had been denounced by Pope Leo X, the second son of the great Lorenzo Medici in the Bull *Exsurge Domine* (Rise up O Lord). In the intervening years events in Luther's life and in Europe moved swiftly.

Luther found being, or training to be a monk a real struggle. He had risked much in going against the wishes of his father, who expected him to be a successful lawyer. He found no peace of mind, as he questioned the teaching of the church. He was ordained priest in 1507, and three years later he visited Rome, where he was shocked by the corruption, and the great building project of St Peter's, for which "indulgences" were sold. That same year the forward- looking, Renaissance influenced, Elector of Saxony Friedrich III invited him to teach at the new university he was setting up at Wittenberg. This began a vital relationship in which Luther was given protection by Friedrich, who would become a Protestant Prince.

It was at Wittenberg and in his lectures on the biblical text that Luther's understanding of the Christian faith crystallised. He lectured on the Psalms (1513–1515), and on Romans and Galatians in 1515–1516. What he understood was than an individual may be justified (put right

---

[197] Roper, *Martin Luther*, p. 47.

with God) through faith by the promise of undeserved grace found in Scripture and set forth in the words and deeds of Christ. There was no need for anything else: relics, masses, penances, indulgences, celibacy, works of supererogation or even the papacy. In other words, most of the panoply and rituals of the church were unnecessary. Indeed, more than that, they were actively a stumbling block, and the pope in maintaining their necessity was an "antichrist". All that was needed was *solus Christus* (Christ alone), *sola fide* (faith alone), *sola gratia* (grace alone) and *sola scriptura* (Scripture alone). This was Luther's creed. So, when a papal official called Johann Tezel came into the area preaching and selling indulgences, Luther was provoked to action. He considered the practice as crude as buying remission for your sins, or purchasing time off purgatory for your dead friends or relatives. A popular ditty went: "When a coin in the coffer rings, a soul from purgatory springs".

The balloon went up when on 31 October 1517, Luther nailed on the door of the Castle Church Wittenberg his 95 Theses or statements about Roman Catholic practice and doctrine, as if in an academic debate. Nevertheless "they have a cumulative rhetorical force that is far removed from dispassionate academic writing".[198] At the heart of Luther's indictment was the whole practice of selling indulgences, or to put it the other way, buying forgiveness for yourself or others already in purgatory, in which money supplanted faith. And at the very heart of Luther's discovery was Paul's quotation from the Old Testament Prophet Habakkuk, who said: "He who through faith is righteous shall live". Summarising his theology in 1545 Luther wrote, "That place in Paul was for me truly the gate of paradise".[199] Disputations followed with ever increasing intensity as Luther became the popular spokesman in Saxony for a much wider movement against the papacy.

In October 1518, Luther disputed with Cardinal Cajetan in Augsburg, then with Eck at Leipzig in 1519, and finally at Worms in front of the most powerful ruler in the western world, Charles V, the Hapsburg Holy Roman Emperor, nephew of Catharine of Aragon. Here, in a place that with a name that provokes every schoolboy's amusement, Luther

---

[198] Roper, *Martin Luther*, p. 95.
[199] Roper, *Martin Luther*, p. 100, citing *Luther's Works 34, 337*, 1545 (Philadelphia 1957).

was arraigned at the Diet of Worms in April 1521. Undoubtedly, it was the dramatic high point of the Reformation. Here, this brilliant, but very ordinary looking monk, was facing the young, athletic, immensely powerful ruler and lay defender of the Roman Catholic Church, Charles V, the most powerful man in the western world who in the west was taking on Protestantism and in the East the Ottoman Turks. It was, definitively, truth speaking to power.

The year 1520 had been the high point of Luther's writing, three immensely important works poured from his pen onto the printing presses: *To the Christian Nobility of the German Nation*, *On the Babylonian Captivity of the Church*, and *On the Freedom of a Christian*. The final work was like spring sunshine after a storm: clear, refreshing, profound and transformative. Yet for his works and theses he had been summoned to Worms to appear before the emperor, where he would be examined and given the opportunity to retract. After an eighteen-day walk from Wittenberg he appeared before the emperor, and after a short adjournment was asked to retract his theses and his books. He famously replied,

"Unless I am convinced by the testimony of the Scriptures or by clear reason (for I do not trust either in the Pope or in councils alone, since it is well known that they have often erred and contradicted themselves), I am bound by the Scriptures and my conscience is captive to the Word of God I have quoted. I cannot and will not retract anything, since it is neither safe nor right to go against conscience. I cannot do otherwise, here I stand, may God help me".[200]

Charles V wrote to Luther on 18 April 1521, declaring him a heretic, an outlaw and worthy of death, but out of courtesy would not renege on his promise of safe conduct to and from Worms, so Luther was allowed to return to Wittenberg freely. On the way home, he was kidnapped in Saxony and taken to Wartburg Castle, just outside Eisenach.

In fact, it was for his own security that Luther was kidnapped, and by his guardian the Elector of Saxony's men. He was spirited away to the Elector's castle in May 1521 where he lived secretly for the next few months. He grew out his tonsure into long hair and wore a knight's

---

[200] Roper, *Martin Luther*, p. 183.

clothes of hose and doublet.[201] On a more down to earth note he suffered severe constipation: "the Lord strikes me in the posterior with serious pain".[202] Nothing blocked his restless mind, however, and by October he had conceived of the project of translating the New Testament into German. In less than eleven weeks he completed the task. He was the Tyndale of the German language, finding direct and memorable phrases to convey spiritual truth to the ordinary German, although he was not above adding the odd word not found in the original, to emphasise a truth.[203] Luther was back in Wittenberg by March 1522, having completed this task of translation, and when it was deemed safe to return.

Luther's remaining years were spent at Wittenberg and when we visited the town and saw its layout, we could quickly appreciate why this relatively small town in northern Germany became the power house of the Reformation— at least in its early stages before its leadership dispersed, especially to Geneva, Zurich and then London by 1549. It quickly became clear that Wittenberg had everything necessary for the early stages of the Reformation to take root. Firstly, Luther had protection from a civil ruler, the Elector of Saxony, as symbolised by the castle. It was a university town, so ideas could be handed on, and hammered out. Philip Melancthon, probably the greatest linguist of the Reformation, and a more precise and sensitive character than Luther lived down the road on the High Street. Knowing both Hebrew and Greek, Melancthon pioneered the translation of the whole Bible into German. Further down the street was a printing works, where Luther's works and the works of others could be disseminated. Tens of thousands of copies were printed in the ever-moving presses. In the same street was the studio of one of Germany's greatest sixteenth century painters, Lucas Cranach the Elder. Cranach and his son would provide telling illustrations of Luther's campaign against corruption in the church and papacy, as well as illustrate his German Bible. The combination of writing, illustrations and printing would produce a campaign the like of which had not been seen before. And it was all there on the High Street.

---

[201] Roper, *Martin Luther*, p. 195.
[202] Roper, *Martin Luther*, p. 198.
[203] Roper, *Martin Luther*, p. 208.

Wittenberg also provided a haven for domestic life for Luther and his wife. In 1525 Luther had married Katherine von Bora, an ex-nun aged twenty-six, who had been smuggled out of her convent in a barrel. Between them they had six children, two dying in infancy. He was granted the old Augustinian Priory to live in with his family, along with a number of students. It was among this community that Luther's famous *Table Talk* was recorded: down to earth, vivid opinions of Luther, covering everything from tenets of the Reformation, the enjoyment of beer, to dealing with depression and the benefits of digging his allotment.

If Luther had much to be grateful for in his wife and family, the future after his break with Rome was fraught with difficulty. Back in 1520 he had publicly burnt the Pope's Bull excommunicating him. But now he must build a new church, with its own formulations of faith, as he did with Melanchthon in the Augsburg Confession in 1530. He must also contend with the humanist Erasmus about the true nature of humanity. He had to restrain the more radical forms of Reformation sometimes put forward by his friends, but also those put forward by his enemies, such as the extreme radical and heretic Thomas Müntzer. Luther also found himself at odds with other Reformers over his theology of the Eucharist, which he called the "Real Presence". He found that he could not support the peasants in their rebellion against the Elector and other landlords, despite their faith, "for nothing "he said "can be more poisonous, hurtful, or devilish than a rebel".[204] But his biggest blind spot was reserved for the Jews.

Although early in his career Luther sought the conversion of the Jews to Christianity, towards the end of his life he grew more vindictive. When he wrote *On the Jews and Their Lies* in 1543, he had turned against them: believing them obstinate, deceived by the devil, intent on gain and blasphemous when it came to their description of Christ as a bastard. His writings became both crude and cantankerous. The sculpture on the side of Wittenberg church that shows Jews clustered beneath a sow sucking her teats, and at the same time looking for the Talmud is deeply offensive, along with other such sculptures called *Judensau* which are amazingly, given recent history, still to be found across Germany. Luther's writings were used by the Nazi party to justify their attacks on the Jews, providing

---

[204] Roper, *Martin Luther*, p. 266.

ammunition for the eventual tragedy of *Kristallnacht* and the holocaust.

Our journey around Saxony and Thuringia had followed the story of Luther: his birth and death at Eisleben, his education and early years as a monk at Eisenach and Erfurt, and his challenge to the power structures of the Catholic Church that they forgo corrupt practices like indulgences and instead embrace the true grace and freedom of the Gospel. He was undoubtedly brave, exceptionally gifted as a theological writer and translator, but in some areas, like most of us, a prisoner of the attitudes of his age.

For three hundred years Germany would continue as a patchwork quilt of states, small and large, until the Prussian Chancellor Bismarck began the process of unification, One of my ancestors Lady Callum (neé Flood) was travelling in Germany and received a letter from the King of Hannover's Chamberlain, Count Linsingen, on May 17 1866 saying, "We, and in fact all Germany, are now in a sad state of anxiety owing to the pending warlike prospects so that we can scarcely venture to form a plan for the morrow with and degree of certainty" (Family Papers). This process of unification was ominously completed by an attack on France in 1870, with German troops and the Kaiser, Wilhelm I, reaching Paris in 1871.

There, in the Hall of Mirrors, Versailles, Wilhelm I declared himself German Emperor. France was humiliated by its losses at the battles of Metz and Sedan, and the capture of Napoleon III. Forty years later under Kaiser Wilhelm II, the grandson of Queen Victoria, the first World War began with catastrophic consequences. From the ruins of German defeat, the Nazi party rose in the 1930s led by Corporal Hitler, who vowed to reverse Germany's losses and create "living room" for German peoples in the east, and in the west along the Rhine. Further catastrophe followed. Following the defeat of Germany in 1945, the country was divided into sectors, with the Russians taking the largest Eastern Sector called East Germany or the Democratic Republic of Germany, which existed as part of the Iron Curtain bloc from 1945 to 1989. We were about to see and hear this story in the tale of two cities: Leipzig and Dresden, caught up in the tragedy of the past and hope for the future.

Leipzig and Dresden

To visit these two cities, we moved to stay just outside Halle, known to me for two reasons. It was here that Handel had a job as the cathedral organist in 1702–3 before he moved to England ahead of the arrival of the Elector of Hannover as the king who is known to us as George I. It is also the location of a grass-court championship that takes place every year in June, and where Roger Federer hones his grass skills before his assault on the Wimbledon title. For us it was the jumping off point for Leipzig and Dresden, the former renowned for music and re-unification, the latter for ruin and porcelain.

Leipzig is one of the fastest growing, and most progressive cities in Germany and has rebounded from great destruction in the Second World War and the years of drab rule under the GDR, when its population declined and it became a centre for heavy, polluting industry. During the war, the large and talented Jewish population was exterminated, with many perishing in Buchenwald near the town of Weimar. The city also suffered extensive bombing on the night of 3 December 1943, with nearly a thousand civilian casualties. Occupied by the Americans at the end of the war, it was handed over to the Russians and for the next forty-five years languished under Communist East German rule. Since then, a remarkable revival has come to the city. Pleasantly landscaped along the Elster River, it has a large out-of-town university with strong links to engineering. A university of music and theatre was founded in the city by Felix Mendelssohn in 1843, and it was also here that the poet Schiller wrote *Ode to Joy*, wonderfully set to music in Beethoven's Ninth Symphony. The centre is spacious, with plenty of room for cafés and parks, and running through the middle is a street joining two churches, both of which epitomise the life and soul of Leipzig.

Thomaskirche or St Thomas's is where Johann Sebastian Bach was organist and cantor for twenty-seven years from 1723. It was here that he wrote St Matthew and St John's Passion, as well as numerous cantatas based on the Bible readings for the Sunday in question—an extraordinary corpus of work unrivalled anywhere in the world. In later years others came here to perform and to remember and celebrate Bach's achievement, including Mozart, Richard Wagner, who trained here, and

Mendelssohn. It was therefore a special pleasure to hear a performance of Felix Mendelssohn's *Paulus,* considered by some to be his greatest work, in the church that evening. From a city that has seen so many ups and downs, such suffering and opportunity, this oratorio traces the life of St. Paul from standing by while the martyr Stephen was stoned (Acts 7: 58–8:1), to his own conversion on the road to Damascus. It is another example of transformation; from desolation to new horizons, and certainly spoke into the transformation of the city.

If one church in the city centre was all about wonderful music, the other was about peace. Earlier in the day we had spoken with a German couple in their forties from Leipzig about the end of the East German regime and the part Leipzig played in it in 1989. We asked about their memories of those days in the summer of 1989, after Austria had opened its borders with Hungary and before the fall of the Berlin Wall on 9 November 1989. Thousands of East Germans left via Hungary and Austria for West Germany, but thousands also gathered every night in the centre of Leipzig, seeking the re-unification of Germany. The German couple, who were then teenagers, remembered their parents going into the centre of Leipzig night after night for peaceful demonstrations and sometimes they were able to go with them. The crowds grew larger and larger, and they gathered around St Nicholas, the other church in the centre of town.

Initially, the meetings in Leipzig had been prayer meetings for peace, led by the minister of St Nicholas, but after the summer of 1989, these meetings grew spectacularly. By October the gatherings had grown to one hundred and fifty thousand people meeting peacefully and on October 23 this number reached three hundred and twenty thousand. The East German leader resigned and by March the following year a new united Germany with the same borders was recognised. In old East Berlin on Christmas Day 1989, Beethoven's Ninth Symphony was performed— what else? —the *Ode to Joy*, with an international orchestra conducted by Leonard Bernstein. The word "joy" was changed by Bernstein to "freedom", hence *Ode to Freedom*. A Jewish conductor was conducting a deaf composer's work. It was the last time Bernstein conducted the Ninth; he died six months later. Music and peace were Leipzig's special contribution.

The tale of the other city, Dresden, concerns porcelain and restoration. The drive from Halle to Dresden, which lies close to the Czech border and not far from Poland, is nearly two hundred kilometres through undulating fertile ground with abundant crops, not unlike Warwickshire in England. Near Leipzig we passed the site of the Battle of the Nations of October 1813. It was here that, after his devastating retreat from Moscow in 1812, Napoleon regrouped new forces to confront the nations of Russia, Prussia, Sweden and Austria. He was decisively defeated in the largest battle on European soil before WWI. There were over one hundred and twenty-five thousand casualties, and, soon after the defeat Napoleon abdicated and was imprisoned in Elba. It was a reminder that these fertile fields had been trampled over by armies for years. Some way past Leipzig we saw a notice to Colditz, the famous castle where high-value prisoners of war were interned during WWII, among them our former MP Airey Neave, who was the first officer to escape from Colditz in 1942, and later the leader of Margaret Thatcher's campaign to lead the Conservative Party and was assassinated by the IRA.

We arrived in Dresden in the late morning in what is a modern prosperous city and made for the centre of town. The controversial decision to bomb Dresden in February 1945 in four missions continues to divide opinion. There is no doubting the courage of Bomber Command, who lost huge numbers of crew over the war, but the choice of Dresden so late in the war, with three months remaining, must remain at best a controversial choice of target or at worst a stain on Britain's war reputation. The day after its bombing, Jack Colville, Churchill's Private Secretary and diarist met Sir Arthur Harris, C-in-C Bomber Command, in Downing Street and asked about the effect of the Dresden raid. "Dresden?" Harris replied. "There is no such place as Dresden".[205] A firestorm had developed in the city centre. Ninety-five per cent of the buildings were destroyed and there were about twenty-five thousand civilian casualties. Looking at the awful remnants of the city you would have to say that it was either the deleterious effect of warfare on our humanity, or just retribution on a nation with collective responsibility for camps like Auschwitz and other atrocities, or a descent by the coming

---

[205] Jack Colville, *Fringes of Power* (London: Weidenfeld and Nicolson, 2016), p. 533.

victors to the ways of their enemies. Perhaps there are elements of all three present.

We found our way first to the Kreuzkirche (the Cross Church) which is the main Lutheran church in the city. Badly destroyed, it has been restored very simply, so as not erase the evidence of the conflict that the church has come through, and its walls have a sober scratch-coat surface like rendered concrete. Being Germany, the organ is nevertheless first rate, so concerts can be properly held. When we arrived as an English group, we were told that there were prayers for reconciliation in a side chapel at midday. We went in, and learned that not many English came. The Cross of Nails on the Altar Table came from Coventry. It is one of many distributed around Germany with the bare, but sufficient, inscription "Father Forgive". We quickly realised that forgiveness here in Dresden was a two-way process: each nation forgiving the other. The destruction of their city was still a painful reality. Despite the restoration, there was still a kind of aching void in the middle.

In a thoughtful mood we walked into the central square, which was still being rebuilt well over seventy years later. The truth is that the GDR simply did not have the funds to rebuild Dresden, and it was only after unification that money was forthcoming for rebuilding. This was especially true for the great Baroque church called the Frauenkirche. Originally, the Catholic cathedral before the Reformation, it occupies a very prominent place in the city. Its restoration from almost nothing has been a remarkable feat costing 180 million Euros. Extraordinarily, two things did survive: a statue of Luther standing immediately outside the church as if he were preaching to the city and the altar relief of Christ's Agony in Gethsemane. Inside the church is a riot of baroque decoration, and the organ, over whose rebuilding there was a great dispute, is not a replacement of the old but a new one, yet still boasts 4,873 pipes. Atop the great dome is a gold cross made in London.

We had lunch in the main square and Robert had invited an Archdeacon of the Lutheran Church in Meissen to come and meet us. He spoke about falling congregations, older conservative members and declining revenues, despite Government assistance. It sounded familiar! We tried to encourage him.

If Dresden is well known for its destruction during the war, it is also well known for the indestructible reputation of its porcelain. In fact, Dresden, or to be precise Meissen, is porcelain mad. In 1704, an alchemist in the pay of Augustus the Strong, called Böttger, discovered the process of making porcelain; that fine white, fragile and brittle china that never lacks a market. Hitherto, all china had come from China. (It is not often that a country becomes synonymous with its finest product: we do not call Scotland "whisky", or Germany "sausage", but china is known by the nation that makes it!) Augustus the Strong developed a severe case of the *Maladie de Porcelaine*.[206] He had commissioned gargantuan and idiotic pieces of porcelain: a fox playing a piano, a drunken goat in glasses with a drunken Saxon official on his back, a dinner service to end all dinner services for Queen Sophia Dorothea of Prussia, and a whole menagerie of birds. Some of this and much more may be seen in the Elector's Palace on the banks of the Elbe, which thankfully survived the bombing.

The Electors of Saxony would prove flamboyant, but insufficiently single minded to survive with a neighbour like Prussia. At first stalwart supporters of Lutheranism, later Electors like Augustus the Strong would return to Catholicism and seek a future in alliance with Poland and Lithuania. But Poland would be partitioned by Russia, Austria-Hungary, and Prussia in 1772. After the Napoleonic Wars, Saxony would briefly become an independent kingdom until it was swallowed up by Bismarck and Prussia. Its fate was then tied to Germany, a partnership that would cost it dearly. Despite its preference for an alliance with Austria Hungary, it was forced by continual pressure into dependence on Prussia, and by 1871 was part of the new German Empire declared at Versailles after the defeat of the French. From then, Saxony's future was inextricably intertwined with the fate of Germany, and hence the destruction that came to Dresden.

Sobered by our visit to Dresden we returned to Halle for a final evening. A visiting group had arrived at the hotel that day, and began singing a hymn over the evening meal. Not to be outdone we sang one or two of our own! The following day we headed back to Berlin, and having some time before the flight called in at Potsdam to see the Sansoucci Palace, the delightful and modest (for a monarch) summer residence of

---

[206] Neil MacGregor, *Germany: Memories of a Nation* (London: Penguin, 2016), p. 319.

Frederick the Great (1712–1786). Frederick was one of a number of absolute monarchs in Europe at the time, and although a fine general he was more interested in music and philosophy. Hitler did him the grave disservice of idolising him. If only subsequent German kings and leaders had had his finesse and wide intellectual appeal, the treasures of Dresden and Leipzig would probably not have been caught up in the misfortunes of war.

Saxony for us recalled the tempestuous life of Martin Luther and the struggle he initiated with the old order, the sublime music of J.S. Bach and Mendelssohn, the romance of Meissen porcelain and the awful consequences of war. It certainly left its mark in its unusual, but all too human, combination of brilliance and tragedy.

Chapter XVII
A Velvet Revolution in Armenia

On 1 May 2018, we were about to board the plane from Paris to Yerevan, the capital of Armenia, when I got talking to a young Armenian in the queue. There is a large Armenian community in Paris and he was returning home to see his family. "It will be heaven or hell when we arrive in Yerevan", he said ominously. "How so?" I asked. He went on to explain there was to be a vote in the Armenian Parliament that evening in which some members, supported by most of the public were hoping to get rid of the "old guard" which had been in charge for years and replace them with a new government led by Nikol Pashinyan.

To be elected Prime Minister Pashinyan needed a number of votes from the "old guard" Republican Party. There were not enough, and consequently, when we arrived in Yerevan that night, the city and the country were very much on edge. Throughout the week we were there, and before another vote in Parliament could be taken a week later, it is fair to say the country was on tenterhooks. Thankfully, it was to be a velvet revolution. But again, I seemed to have arrived in a country at a time of critical change.

Armenia has an extraordinary and at times tragic history, and a people who are gifted, energetic, attractive and versatile; as well as passionate about their country. Although once occupying a much larger area in eastern Turkey and Syria, Armenia is now restricted to a mountainous and beautiful part of the Caucasus. They are bordered by much larger regional powers: Russia to the north (although not directly), Iran to the south east and Turkey to the south. They share the Caucasus with a number of smaller states, in particular Georgia to the north-west; beyond Georgia, the small state of Abkhazia on the Black Sea; and to the east Azerbaijan, with whom Armenia has a disputed border and regular flare-ups, including a recent costly war. In the northern part of Georgia are the small districts of South and North Ossetia and to the east is the troubled area of Chechnya in the Russian Federation. The Caucasus, like the Balkans, are a byword for tension, conflict and hatreds as deep and long-held as the ravines in the mountains.

For all the human tensions and conflicts of the region, there are few places more dramatic, compelling and beautiful than Armenia. It is landlocked, lying between the Black and Caspian Seas with mountainous scenery and peaks like Mt Ararat, just outside the country in Turkey, that go as high as five thousand metres. Everywhere you look there are breath-taking views and no more so than when looking south from the hills behind Yerevan to the twin peaks of Ararat, a mountain that is holy to the Armenian people, but kept by Turkey in the annexation of Armenian lands at the beginning of the twentieth century. It reaches over five thousand metres, higher that Mont Blanc and is the place where Noah's Ark is traditionally held to have come to rest at the end of the Biblical flood. In the north of the country is the stunning Lake Sevan, the highest lake in Europe (Armenia considers itself Eurasian), with a backdrop of high mountains to the north-east.

Armenia has a long and distinguished history, but because of its geography has been constantly squeezed by three larger neighbouring powers: Russia to the north, Turkey to the south and Iran to the south east. At one time or another Armenia has been occupied, ruled or decimated by one of these countries: most of all by Turkey between the years 1915–1921.[207] The high point of Armenia's history was under the rule of Tigranes the Great (140–55 BC). Brought up in the Parthian court in Ctesiphon, he was appointed King of Armenia by Mithridates II of Parthia. Tigranes began to expand his territory until it included most of eastern Turkey, and northern Iran, Iraq and Syria. By the time of Tigranes's death, Armenia was the largest kingdom to the east of the Roman Empire, and would become a client state of Rome. Thereafter, with flashes of independence Armenia would be frequently absorbed, firstly by the Byzantine and then the Ottoman, Iranian and Russian Empires. In 1922 Armenia was absorbed into the Soviet Union until its independence in 1990. Subsequently there was deep tension with its neighbour Azerbaijan and the disputed territory of Nagorno-Karabagh.

---

[207] Thomas de Waal, *The Caucasus: An Introduction* (Oxford: Oxford University Press, 2010), p. 53.

We stayed in Yerevan close to Republic Square in the Tigran Mets Hotel, and were well looked after by Georgiou our guide and Vera Mnatsahanyan in the hotel. A partner of my first cousin had been to Armenia and recommended a guide to take us around, but because he was busy, he in turn recommended his friend Georgiou. Given the political situation it was more important than usual to have someone who could take the four us around the country, our adventurous friends Richard and Sarah were travelling with us. We were dropped off at our hotel on the night of 1 May and told to be ready promptly in the morning, as there was no telling how easy or difficult it would be to travel around.

We set off the following day intending to visit an out-of-town Greek temple at Garni and the surrounding area. But this was not to be, for we quickly discovered that there were road blocks throughout the city. The protestors could not have been more friendly, but they were firm in their purpose. Their purpose of course was to bring pressure to bear on the government and parliament to vote for Pashinyan in the upcoming vote. At the first few road blocks I spoke to the protesters, saying "we had come a long way to see their wonderful country and could they let us through so we might enjoy it". The first two or three groups acceded but gradually this became more difficult, until we had to abandon the vehicle and walk. Georgiou said we should reconcile ourselves to a day's sightseeing in Yerevan and then make an early start out of town the following day.

We headed for the Matenadaran, a cathedral-like manuscript museum that is a source of enormous pride to the Armenians. The word Matenadaran literally means book depository. Armenian is a unique language, with some connection to Greek, Syriac and Phalavi, but having its own distinctive script. The alphabet was devised by Mesrop Mashtots in the fifth century AD, and he also set about establishing a grammar. Mashtots was a priest from a noble family and became a secretary of King Khosov IV. Having their own alphabet not only gave Armenians a strong national identity and a very individual cultural heritage, but also, over time, meant that the country built up a remarkable collection of ancient Christian manuscripts. Armenia was Christian from earliest times, as we shall see, and being close to the centres of the Eastern

Church in Constantinople, Caesarea and Antioch, had ready access to the writings of the early Church Fathers, in particular the Cappadocians and the leaders of the church in Jerusalem, where Armenian monks formed a community from the late fourth century. An Armenian Quarter still exists in Jerusalem today, as it did in Aleppo and Constantinople. In the Library there were many maps of Greater Armenia on display, as well as illuminated Gospels and Bibles.

From there we walked down towards the Armenian Opera House, passing the feature known as the Cascade, a garden stairway with water fountains leading to an arts centre at the top with a great view south towards Ararat. We stopped to have a coffee and learn more about everyday modern Armenia from Georgiou. Perhaps the first thing to understand is that more Armenians live in a diaspora abroad than in Armenia itself. There are approximately three million in Armenia, and seven million abroad, especially in the United States and France. An Armenian is readily identifiable by their surname, since nearly all end either in "an" or "ian". Thus, the Kardashians are Armenian, likewise the first oil magnate, Calouste Gulbenkian—Mr Five Per cent as he was called (having five per cent rights in the Iraq Petroleum Company later BP) and one of the richest men in the world — the composer Aram Khachaturian and the singer Charles Aznavour(ian).

We wandered through the city in the early afternoon. There seemed to be a festive atmosphere and a general buzz of anticipation, with no traffic because of the lockdown, and many young people on the streets waving red, blue and yellow Armenian flags. In a main shopping street, a group of young women were playing what looked like zithers, an ancient Persian and Chinese instrument. There were high hopes of pollical change They played *Sounds of Silence* by Simon and Garfunkel and the well-chosen, for the circumstances, *Bridge Over Troubled Waters*. In the late afternoon we headed back to our hotel and through the grand Republic Square, where a crowd was gathering for an evening rally of music and speeches.

We set out at seven a.m. the next day to avoid road blocks, but we need not have worried. Overnight Pashinyan called off the road blocks so as not to antagonise businesses and upset people's plans so we could now travel freely. We had a picnic breakfast in the warm sunlight overlooking Yerevan and further south, Ararat. Ahead was a vast expanse of rolling green plateau stretching as far as the eye could see, all pasture, without wall or fence. Richard and Sarah, both keen birdwatchers, spotted hoopoes and a skua. After breakfast we visited the classical Garni Temple, built in the first century AD in Armenia's pre-Christian days.

Garni is a reminder that Greek culture once stretched as far as Armenia. In fact, not so far away in Georgia the ancient Pontic Greek communities flourished for a thousand years until 1928 when they were ejected by Stalin, who came from neighbouring Georgia. These Pontic Greeks were turned into victims and deported to faraway Siberia and central Asian Soviet republics.[208] It has been estimated that as many as one hundred and seventy thousand Greeks were expelled to those places. In June 1949, in a single immense operation planned for many months, the entire Greek population was seized, packed into trains by NKVD (Russian Special Forces) operatives and scattered across Central Asia.[209] In Armenia the Greek population was never as large as on the Black Sea littoral, but the Temple at Garni was a reminder of their presence and influence, albeit mediated through the Roman Empire during which time this temple was built. Built in c.77 AD by the Armenian King Tiridates, who had visited Rome in 66 AD, its twenty-four Ionic columns, pediment and continuous frieze of acanthus, gives it elegance and proportion. But as with so much in Armenia, it is the setting that is the most arresting. Set on a small plateau, it is surrounded by typical Armenian uplands and below it, in the ravine, the fast-flowing Azat river.

From there we went down into the gorge made by the river and saw the balsamic rock formation which looks as if the cliff face is made from vertical stair roads of Brighton rock—an extraordinary geological feature, similar to the Giants Causeway in Northern Ireland. Leaving Garni to the south we travelled up the Azat valley, which grew narrower and narrower, to the beautiful location of Geghard Monastery. Said to have been founded in the fourth century, the buildings date from the thirteenth, and are, in part, carved out of the abutting cliff face. The monastery is based upon the legend that the spear that pierced the side of

---

[208] Neal Ascherson, *Black Sea: Coasts and Conquests from Pericles to Putin* (London: Vintage Books, 2007), p. 174).
[209] Ascherson, *Black Sea,* p. 174.

Christ during his crucifixion was brought here by the Apostle Thaddaeus. Built under the patronage of Queen Tamar of Georgia, who reclaimed Armenia from the Turks, there are two sanctuary areas with a large narthex or *gavit*, where people may assemble for teaching or worship. Four columns support four arches, on which rests a dome with an open skylight, as in the Parthenon in Rome. Light comes into the building through this skylight in the dome and through the open doors. While we were there a group of *a capella* Armenian singers came in dressed in black and sang a series of songs for us. Yearning, reflective and haunting, they perfectly matched the atmosphere of the place.

Outside there were two things to notice especially: the distinctive Armenian architecture and the *khachkars*. I was getting used to Armenian church architecture: the solid rectangular shapes, the small round octagonal drum towers with the conic pointed caps, like the peak of Ararat. It was vernacular church architecture, with echoes of both the Byzantine Romanesque and the Cappadocian cave churches. Tall arches were often well decorated with Christian motifs, and the stone was either volcanic tufa, as in Cappadocia, or grey balsamic rock.

The other feature that is so unusual and unique to Armenia is the *khachkars*, of which there were many around the monastery. *Khachkars* are free-standing stones with a carved cross surmounting a rosette on the face, about six feet tall and used to mark a grave or other significant place. They are to Armenia what the Celtic Cross is to the Celtic regions of Britain. Often intricately decorated with carved tracery, they also sometimes have biblical scenes depicted in the stone. Like Garni Temple, Geghard Monastery is set in unspoilt, wild Armenian scenery. At the end of the valley where the monastery is located, the ground quickly becomes mountainous, rising up to twelve thousand feet. We had a picnic in this compelling scenery with Mt Azdaak beyond, before returning to a still peaceful Yerevan, awaiting change.

The following day, before heading for the town of Goris, close to the disputed area of Nagorno-Karabagh, we visited possibly the most spectacular and historic of all the Armenian Monasteries at Khor Virap. We travelled south east from Yerevan towards the border with Turkey, and close to a small strip of land called Nakhichevan Azerbaijan. This area was Armenian in the sixteenth century, but had its entire Armenian population removed to Isfahan by Shah Abbas for their cultural and creative skills. There they created New Julfa near Isfahan, and one of their number, Harutiun Sayatian, became a great and celebrated composer of songs.[210] But now Nakhichevan was inhabited by one of the most powerful Azerbaijani clans, the Aliev family, and bordered Turkey and Iran.[211] Khor Virap is just short of this area, close to the Turkish border, which, incidentally, is patrolled by Russian soldiers, facing Mount Ararat across the Armenian plain. There are few more spectacular settings. It was here that Christianity first came to Armenia in the very early fourth century, making them the first nation as a whole to believe.

The origin of Christianity in Armenia revolves around a single individual, Gregory (or Grigor), a member of the royal family or nobility who grew up in exile in nearby Cappadocia. While there he became a Christian, and, on returning to Armenia, began proclaiming his new-found faith. For this he was thrown into a pit where he was kept alive by a local woman who fed him bread and water. During this time King Tiridates grew very ill and when no medicine could help, and as a last resort, Gregory was called for to pray for him. Needless to say, his health immediately improved, whereupon the king became a follower of Christ, and with him the court and nation (in much the same way King Edwin of Northumberland became a Christian at the preaching of Paulinus in 627 AD and the nation followed).

Gregory, who became known as "the Illuminator", was the first leader of the Armenian Church. One of his descendants, Isaac the Great (c.350–440), the tenth Catholicos of the Armenian church, ended its dependence on the Cappadocian church, and from then on it became autonomous or autocephalous (having its own head). At a similar time, St Mesrob Mashtots established the Armenian alphabet and translated the New Testament into Armenian, as well as the books of Proverbs and Isaiah from the Old Testament. Thus, by 440 AD, the Armenian church was well and truly established and would be especially linked with the Coptic church in Egypt, since both were monophysite churches subscribing to belief in the single divine will of Jesus in which his humanity was subsumed.

---

[210] De Waal, *The Caucasus*, p. 25.
[211] De Waal, *The Caucasus*, p. 14.

We enjoyed looking around Khor Virap and even descended the twenty-seven steps on a wall ladder into the dungeon or pit below, now a shrine to Gregory, and not a place in which anyone would want to spend much time. There were two small churches on the site, but its unique feature was its unforgettable setting, looking out towards Ararat.

From Khor Virap we drove south east towards the border with Iran and then towards Nagorno-Karabagh to arrive at Goris, which is on the edge of the disputed region. I have visited few places more out of the way or remote. There didn't seem to be anyone else staying in the hotel and there was a lot of military activity in the area. The town looked like a frontier town with its atypical uniformity of housing, unlike other parts of Armenia. We learned that a German architect who had been captured during the war had been isolated and detained here, whereupon he had designed the look-alike houses in a more Germanic style for the neighbourhood.

The region of Nagorno Karabagh (Nagorno being a transliteration of the Russian word for mountainous) is one of the tragedies of the Caucasus, along with Abkhazia, the Osettias in Georgia, and probably worst of all, Chechnya, to the north of Georgia. Nagorno Karabagh is a mountainous and remote region of Armenia lying next to Azerbaijan. It is so remote that although the inhabitants are Armenian by background, many speak Azeri, the language of the neighbouring Azerbaijanis and there is an intermingling of cultures. This was the case when both countries were part of the Safavid Persian Empire and it continued when they were both part of the Russian Empire (from 1805), and also during the period of the Soviet Union—at least up until 1988.

Shusha, now in ruins, was the capital of the region until 1905 when it was ravaged by communal violence. Further trouble was to come in 1920 and again in 1988, when it was seized by the Azerbaijanis, only to be taken back and burnt by the Armenians. When the Soviet Union disintegrated it seemed as though it supported the Azerbaijanis, and conflict flared again in 1992. Just up the road from where we were staying there had been fighting around Shusha and Stepanakert, and Khojali was attacked by the Armenians under Serzh Sarkisian (who later became Prime Minister until 2018). By 1994 Armenia had effectively won the war, showing greater unity of purpose than Azerbaijan, despite the greater oil wealth of the latter. Some three hundred and fifty thousand Azerbaijanis had been displaced and in 1994 the search for a settlement began. As neither side has been willing to compromise, little progress has been made and Karabagh remained an Armenian militarised zone, but in 2020 a through a further outbreak of violence precipitated by Turkey led to the loss of territory by the Armenians.

After a quiet night in Goris, a leisurely breakfast, and Georgiou getting one of the shock absorbers repaired, we set off for Tatel Monastery. In a fold of the hills and some way off the main road, the monastery is approached by what is reputedly the longest cable car in Eurasia at six kilometres in length. Before reaching the monastery, we saw a deserted hermitage far beneath the cable car, which looked as if it had once had a very good vegetable garden. And high above we could see eagles. Once at Tatel we walked the short distance to the monastery which stands on the side of a ridge with a spectacular view. The monastery is presently undergoing extensive renovations. It was once a significant theological centre of the Armenian church. But when we arrived there was no learned theological disputation going on, just a happy baptism conducted by Archimandrite Mikhail, who, I was told, was very popular in Armenia. He certainly had an enthusiastic and attentive crowd for the baptism and both the child and the congregation, who stood in the empty cavernous space of the church, were liberally sprayed with water from his branch of hyssop, confirming each person's baptismal vows.

We left the monastery and began the long journey back to Yerevan, stopping for a picnic by the rushing waters of the Vorotan River, which flows into the Aras, and then down into the Caspian Sea. Georgiou gave us a shot of some very powerful sixty-five per cent proof home-brewed vodka he kept in a large plastic bottle, looking for all it was worth like very innocuous water. It was undoubtedly Armenian firewater. Seemingly unaffected, Georgiou drove on to Sisian where we stopped at Carahunge, a stone circle, a little outside the town. It could have been Avebury, down the road from where we live, except for the panoramic view. The stones were set on a high plateau with the Garabagh Mountains to the north and the Zangezur Mountains to the south west. The highest peaks in each range are well over four thousand feet. The stone circle must have been used both for ritual religious gatherings, as in Stonehenge, but also for observing the stars since there were apertures which had been punched through the top of many of the stones. It was an extraordinarily atmospheric setting.

We continued to Yerevan along a minor road that took us through an Armenian pastoral idyll, another arcadian dream: streams, fields, mulberry trees, apricots, vegetable gardens, sheep and goats grazing, cows going home for milking. We arrived back in the city at night and ate pizza surrounded by lively Armenian families enjoying a Saturday night out with their children.

The following day we went to Echmiadzin Cathedral, the Canterbury of Armenia, for the main morning service of worship. It is just a few miles west of Yerevan and has since earliest times been the centre of the nation's spiritual and Christian life, and of the Armenian Apostolic Church. The original cathedral was built there in 303 AD, rebuilt in 480–483, and then had a major expansion in the seventeenth and eighteenth centuries.

The Cathedral is now set in a large compound which houses a theological college, the Catholicos' house and other administrative buildings. It was undergoing extensive repairs when we were there, so scaffolding prevented a decent view of the interior, but there were cycles of frescoes visible on the higher part of the walls. We found a place to stand in a side chapel for the cathedral was already fairly full, and soon the liturgy was underway. As with the Orthodox church in Kyiv, the sung liturgy felt like a sea of sound rising and fall in a rhythmic sequence. Behind the high altar were several priests wearing their distinctive hoods, while the celebrating priest, dressed in dazzling white, was wearing a crown. Penitential sections of the liturgy brought all those around us to their knees, with a priest blessing each individual penitent. Soon after that the Catholicos himself made an entrance, escorted by at least twenty priests on either side of him. He was taken to his chair at the east end and after the Gospel reading, he spoke while someone nearby translated. Speaking very much as father to his people he urged the government to resign and prepare for political change: the time was now. It was clear that the Catholicos has immense influence, and for all the antiquity of the liturgy, that the church has a significant voice in the nation's affairs. One could not imagine an English Archbishop encouraging the resignation of a prime minister however much he might want to, but here it seemed nothing exceptional. There was no dividing line between faith and politics. Having accompanied its people through all their ups and downs, the church was held in respect. Perhaps it was only fitting then that we were going to the Armenian Holocaust Museum that afternoon.

From their earliest days in the Ottoman Empire, Armenians were encouraged into and included in Ottoman life. In 1461 Sultan Mehmed II invited them to Constantinople, and an Armenian Patriarch was established there.[212] Armenians were the skilled craftsmen: the jewellers, carpenters, builders, bankers, architects and decorators of the empire, as well as its clerks and civil servants. Their skills were recognised, put to good use, and their communities grew in many of the larger Ottoman-controlled towns: Constantinople, Aleppo, Ephesus and Jerusalem. Then modern attacks against the Armenians began as early as 1896 when in August that year Turkish thugs went from house to house in the Pera, Hasskoy and Kassim Pasha districts of Constantinople, clubbing Armenians to death. The violence was provoked by ethnic hatred and the desire of Armenian revolutionaries to secure their own state in Turkey.[213] About six thousand people died, but apart from expressing concern, the Western powers did little, if anything, in support. Far worse was to come.

During the First World War the Ottoman Empire was on its final legs. It was about to lose to either the British or French most of its non-Turkish territories: Egypt, Syria, Lebanon, Palestine, and Iraq (as it would become)—all or most of the Levant, in fact. With the Sultan about to be toppled, power in Constantinople devolved to a Committee of Enver, Kemal and Talaat. This Triumvirate dictated policy, and it was they who sided with Germany in WWI. Constantinople became a war capital, as Turkey (or the Ottomans) took on the Allies and Russia. When news came that the Armenians in Anatolia, and particularly around Van, were actively supporting the Russians, Turkish reprisals began. In fact, the Committee decided on the extermination of Armenians and the removal of Kurds. In Anatolia some 6–800,000 Armenians died as a

---

[212] Mansel, *Constantinople*, p. 11.
[213] Mansel, *Constantinople*, p. 332.

result of deportations, disease, hunger, forced marches and massacres. Almost the entire Armenian community was deported from Constantinople, including 2,432 men.[214] The brutality went on and by the mid–1920s, deaths numbered well over a million.

It is these atrocities, this genocide, that the museum charts and that we saw that Sunday afternoon. Our Armenian guide Georgiou would not come in because he found it so upsetting. On a hill above Yerevan, in a sober concrete building, through a walkway that runs past all the exhibits of photographs, newspaper cuttings and personal accounts, we made our sad and shocked way round. In all, over a million lost their lives. Armenians were very nearly wiped out in Eastern Turkey, leaving behind their churches and communities, and are now confined to a small, beautiful, but restricted area in the region north of Ararat.

We went back to our hotel and saw the crowds assembling in Republic Square. The vote for a new government would be held on Tuesday. Would it be a new dawn for a country that carried a tragic back-story?

We had one more day in Armenia, and for that day we went north to Lake Sevan, which seems about the size of Lake Galilee and is the highest lake in Eurasia. The drive took about an hour and a half from Yerevan and we went first to Sevan Monastery, which is on a promontory overlooking the lake. First built in the fifth century AD in the time of Gregory the Illuminator, it was destroyed in an earthquake in 995 and then rebuilt by Princess Marian. It was then again destroyed by the Mongols in the thirteenth century and again rebuilt in 1441. Its main feature is its wonderful position looking out over the lake with high peaks rising to eight thousand metres feet beyond. There were a few other visitors, mostly from Russia, and in fact we met no other British tourists during our week there. We did get talking to the Russians (in English!). There were two younger Russians who were on motorbikes and had come down through Georgia for a holiday and an older couple. As an opener, I asked the older couple, "how is Russia going to repair its relationship with the UK after the Skripal poisonings in Salisbury?" (a very recent event), and "How long is Putin going on for?" They took it in good humour and joked about our Margaret Thatcher and Boris

---

[214] Mansel, *Constantinople*, p. 375.

Johnson, who was then Foreign Secretary. It seemed these Russians had a real fondness for Armenia, and weren't too badly informed about British politics either, but they held no brief for Putin: "Putin was Putin" they said with a shrug of the shoulders—just another Tsar! Calling leaders to account was not a concept with which they were familiar! The Skripals were probably traitors anyhow…

From there we went to our final monastery, called Haghartsin, which was in a forest, the Dilijan National Park, inland from the lake. We had a picnic in a clearing, and from there we could see the pointed roofs of the nearby monastery. When we arrived, we saw that it was in a perfect location on the edge of the forest, with a big courtyard in front of the main church dedicated to St Astvatsatsian. The church had a large central dome with sixteen sides, and beneath the dome were a number of arches and a clear open space for the worshippers. It had all been beautifully restored, with the stone work and pointing in great condition and a restored refractory on one side of the courtyard. Beyond the courtyard, were stylish accommodation blocks since the place was frequently and understandably used for retreats. Then a plaque caught my eye: the monastery had been restored by Sultan bin Muhammad Al-Quasimi, the ruler of Sharjar in the Gulf. That was a surprise! We enjoyed meandering through the grounds and absorbing the peaceful and spiritual atmosphere before making the journey back to Yerevan.

That evening was the last before the vote on the future of the government, so there were large crowds gathering in Republic Square. We went out to a typical Armenian restaurant where there were long communal tables with families and children dining with others. After the meal we joined in with the Armenian dancing, much to the amusement of the guests. It was a joyous and light hearted atmosphere. The following day, having said our goodbyes to Vera and Georgiou, we made for the airport to fly home via Paris. The next day we heard that Pashinyan had been voted in as the new Prime Minister, and I could imagine the rejoicing on the streets of Yerevan. A new day had indeed dawned for Armenia. And unlike Kyiv, it had been a bloodless coup.

Chapter XVIII
The Road to Romania

There were many reasons for visiting Romania in May 2019. It was another Black Sea country, and I have always been interested in the countries around The Black Sea. Romania has survived terrible suffering—especially that inflicted on children under the worst of the East European Communist dictators, Nicolae Ceauşescu. Sophia, one of our children, had been there to help with teenage summer camps. I had met a Baptist pastor called Josif Ton at Oxford in 1971. He had been persecuted badly, but had an extraordinary serenity about him. My parents visited the country in 1982 and stayed with the British Ambassador and his wife, Paul and Irene Holmer, whom they knew from Berlin days. On their way home they were turned off the train and made to walk to the nearest station in their night clothes, carrying their belongings! Transylvania was now becoming popular with the English, for its old-fashioned agriculture, its wild flowers and gentle, well-wooded countryside. The Prince of Wales had invested in its future and sought to preserve the harmony of its rural way of life particularly at a Transylvanian village called Viscri. I had also heard of the painted monasteries of Sucevita, and was very interested to see them and likewise the Saxon churches of Transylvania. In sum, it was a country whose complex history and culture was a real draw.

The plan was to drive from England in my Peugeot 206 with two co-drivers, Richard and Geoff, both lawyers—in case there were any difficulties! A third friend would fly out to drive back with me, and Olivia and Sarah would join us, swapping the slow progress of a car for the celerity of Wizz Air (Geoff's wife Debbie was detained by an impending new grandchild). We met to plan the details beforehand: the route out would-be Aachen, Passau, which I had visited in 2002, Budapest, and then Suceava, and the journey would be about two thousand five hundred kilometres each way. At Suceava we were almost in Moldova and the

Ukraine. Once in Romania we would not visit Bucharest or the Danube Delta for want of time, but restrict ourselves to the central and northern part of the country.

On 30 April 2019 we set off via EuroTunnel and made our way to Aachen or Aix-La-Chapelle. Aachen was the city of Charlemagne (748–814), the place from which he governed his vast empire in the ninth century. He was King of the Franks, King of the Lombards and the first Holy Roman Emperor, crowned on Christmas Day 800 by Pope Leo III. Thus, began one of those associations between pope and emperor that was to dominate central Europe until the arrival of Napoleon a thousand years later, after which came the gradual emergence of powerful nation states, especially Germany, leading to the catastrophic results of the twentieth century.

Charlemagne was a Christian emperor and his "evangelism" took place on a yearly basis in the shape of spring and summer military campaigns with the ultimatum to pagan tribes to the north and east, "be baptised or forfeit your life". He nevertheless sought to spread education and to this end employed the monk-scholar Alcuin from York as one of his chief educationalists and liturgists. The centre of his power—which stretched over all northern Europe: France, Germany, Northern Italy, and the Low Countries—was at Aachen; while to the south of his rule were the Moors in al-Andalus and to the east the Slavs and Bulgars.

Aachen Cathedral is home to Charlemagne's remains and vestiges of his rule. In this Gothic cathedral, with its soaring spires and dome, can be found the Palatine Chapel, which houses the symbols of Charlemagne's rule: the golden Karlsschrein where the emperor's remains repose, his simple stone throne, and the Barbarossa chandelier. All this is set beneath a dome covered with mosaics. The dome and first level gallery are supported by arches and columns of great strength and beauty and throughout there is an atmosphere of awe and reverence. German kings or emperors were crowned here between 936 and 1531, elected by the seven elector-states of Germany. As the secular arm of the papacy, these emperors became implacable opponents of Protestant Europe, leading eventually to the devastating Thirty Years War which concluded in 1648 and the Treaty of Westphalia.

Having met some friends of Richard's, who were also gazing at these cathedral wonders and likewise impressed, we walked out of the Cathedral to blink in the sunlight. We then visited the Rathaus or Town Hall, with its large upper reception room covered with romantic nineteenth century frescos of the life of Charlemagne by Alfred Rethel, and saw an exhibition depicting the extent of the destruction of Aachen in WWII when taken by American forces in October 1944. We bought some lunch at the thriving market nearby and by midday were on the road to Passau, arriving in the early evening after a long drive on the autobahn. We had supper overlooking the Danube, which has its confluence with the Inn at Passau, and ate the much-admired *spargel* or white asparagus. Apparently, Germans eat one hundred and twenty-five thousand tons of it a year, to which we added a few modest ounces!

The following morning, we walked along the towpath to the apex of the peninsula on which the city resides, and where the two great rivers meet and looked downstream. It would be just five hundred kilometres to Budapest, our next port of call.

There was no doubt that since my visit to Budapest seventeen years earlier on the way to Jordan, the city had grown in prosperity and confidence. Then Hungary was on the brink of joining the EU, but is now a full member, although showing signs of being an awkward one as it pursues strongly nationalist policies under present leader Viktor Orbán. Geoff joined us that first evening, having been detained by work. We had one full day in the city, staying in the citadel of Buda close to Saint Matthias' church with its lovely colourful tiled and patterned roof. We visited the Museum of Fine Art in Heroes Square with its excellent collection of antiquities and art. Out in the square I couldn't help noticing a sole protestor with a placard objecting to the Treaty of Trianon of 1920. I had no idea what this meant, but in Romania I would understand more.

The following day we left early for our longest drive—from Budapest to Suceava in north east Romania—about seven hundred kilometres and ten hours driving. It took all of that. Eastern Hungary is flat, and we did not linger, knowing in my case that I would stay there on my return journey. Having registered the car to travel on the motorway we took the motorway east, crossing the Tisza River, which is one of the main rivers in Hungary, running south to the Balkans, and joining the Danube at Novi Sad in Serbia before flowing out to the Black Sea.

Beyond the Tisza we passed Nyíregyháza to the north and Debrecen—the second city of Hungary—to the south, before coming to the border with Romania which took approximately an hour to negotiate; this was slow going for an EU border. But amazingly, it was the first border check since leaving England, a sign of the integration of the EU, whatever the challenges of the financial crash, the refugee crisis and the pandemic. An integration which it seems to me, however much Brexit politicians muse thar it cannot last, is unlikely to be reversed.

After crossing into Romania near Satu Mare and then heading south east to Dej, we were now in the Carpathians. The Carpathians are the great mountain range of eastern Europe and runs in an arc from south east Czech through southern Poland, southern Ukraine and Romania. There is an inner and an outer ring and include, in Czech and southern Poland, the High Tatras, rising to over ten thousand feet and likewise in Romania south of Transylvania. The Carpathians are one of the great wilderness areas of eastern Europe, with wolves, bears, lynx, red and roe deer and wild boar. We drove through the mountains, and over the Moldova river to Suceava where we had booked in for four nights, and from there we would explore the Bucovina-Suceava region, famed for its painted monasteries.

Before turning to the painted monasteries, it is worth spending a moment understanding the history of this part of the country. Romania, as such, is a relatively new country formed in 1861 by the merger of the two provinces of Wallachia and Moldova. Much had happened before that event. The Romans had occupied the region (which they called Dacia and which stretched from Hungary to the Black Sea), but they left in 270 AD, leaving the Roman or Romance language but also a power vacuum. Others, including Slavs, Bulgars, Avars and Magyars filled the vacuum, but soon larger regional powers shaped the country's future. The Hungarians took control of Transylvania in the thirteenth century and settled Germans there: first Catholics, some of whom later became Protestants. An elective monarchy resulted, with kings chosen by the ruling class and these *boyars* (rulers) founded the Basarab dynasty. It was a dynasty that would rule Transylvania, Wallachia, and at times Bessarabia or Moldova, and would last from 1310–1627, by which time the Turks had taken charge.

Romania would remain formally part of the Ottoman Empire until 1860, although the territory—including Transylvania—was already being carved up by Austria Hungary in the west, and by Russia in the north east in Moldova. Moreover, the Greek or Phanariot Princes from Constantinople were rewarded by the Ottomans with estates in Wallachia. Over the next ten days we would see three of these regions: Bessarabia or Bucovina in the north east; Transylvania in the centre and Marmures in the north west. We would not have time to go to Bucharest or the Danube Delta and the Black Sea region. That would have to wait for another time.

The region around Suceava is famed for the painted monasteries which we had come to see. The region is close to the border with Moldova, wherein lies another piece of the historical jigsaw. The whole region was once called Bessarabia and we found people in the hotel referring to it with this name. Then, in the nineteenth century two parts of Bessarabia were divided during the carve up at the end of the Ottoman Empire: Northern Bessarabia went to the Russians and formed a separate state within the Soviet Union called Moldova and the southern part was joined to Wallachia, forming Romania, and is also called Bucovina. This transfer of territory was confirmed in 1878 in the Treaty of Berlin. (Moldova in recent elections, like Ukraine, has been looking Westwards causing Russian government resentment).

On our first day in the region, we set out to the west and then to the north of Suceava to do a clockwise circuit of three monasteries. In no way could we cover all the monasteries in the region, there being forty-seven listed in our guide. We took a country road south west towards Gura Humorulu on the Moldova river. The pasture was lush green, and there were people working in the fields in groups, hoeing and planting seed potatoes by hand. Almost every village lamppost had a stork nesting on the top, where a metal frame, rather like a plant holder, had been placed to keep their voluminous nests intact. When the storks stood up, they could be clearly seen. We bought some apples (presumably last year's crop) from a road side stallholder who told me he had lived in Reading for eight years. He had liked it, but was pleased to be back! For me there seemed no comparison between Reading and this rural haven.

As we turned corners there were often horses pulling flat trailers with children and women on the back. As we passed Romanian homes, which seemed spacious and with good-sized gardens in this region, there was usually a well in the front garden with a highly decorated wheel-pump. These were the first weeks of spring, after the snow had melted, and everyone was busy making the most of the weather after what had no doubt been a hard winter.

The first monastery we visited, and one of the most famous, was Voronet. Many of these monasteries were founded by Stephen the Great of Moldavia, who reigned as Voivode or Prince from 1457–1504 (the same time as the beginning of the Tudor dynasty in England). Regarded as a saintly prince who fought for the Orthodox faith against his Catholic neighbours of Hungary and Poland and in the latter part of his reign against the Sultan Mehmed II, he was still honoured in the area. Although he initially defeated the Sultan's forces, in the end he was overwhelmed by the greatly superior Ottoman power in 1476 and had to pay them dues as overlords. This was not before making a treaty with the Voivode (Prince) of Transylvania one Vlad Dracula the Impaler, of whom we will hear more.

At the heart of Voronet Monastery is a church (katholicon), dedicated to St George, with an overhanging roof, below which are painted on the outer as well as the inside walls cycles of sumptuous frescoes in vivid colours, earning it the nickname "The Sistine Chapel of Romania". The church is set in the centre of a defensive courtyard with lodgings in the walls for the monks, and around the church at the centre of this quadrangle is a verdant green lawn. The cycles of frescoes are a mixture of history and faith; and are repeated on almost all the monasteries you see.

At Voronet there is a huge genealogy of Jesus painted as the tree of Jesse, showing Christ's ancestors as described in Matthew's Gospel. There is another fresco of the siege and fall of Constantinople, obviously a shattering event for Orthodox Christians in the region, which occurred just a few years before the monastery was built. On the west wall another massive fresco depicts the Last Judgement with a hierarchy of the just and a lower-archy of the damned. On the top, just beneath the Trinity, are the Apostles, then come the martyrs and saints. Below, being dragged off to hell by devils, are sinners of all kinds. On the west facade, whether it be Notre Dame or here at Voronet, there is a Last Judgement.

Inside in the Exonarthex (the outer lobby) there are frescoes showing the deaths of the martyrs in frightening detail. These were the faithful persecuted by the Turks: some are being boiled, others burnt, some broken like St Catherine on a wheel, others hung upside down, yet others pulled apart and some executed. Having entered the church past these ominous warnings there are more familiar and consoling cycles of frescoes of the nativity, the passion and resurrection of Christ in further rich and colourful detail.

The atmosphere was reverent, quiet and hushed. The monastery seemed active and well-staffed and the Romanian people, young and old, seemed closely connected to their church. We walked round this inner quadrangle with its church at the centre admiring the frescoes on the exterior. As is often the case, the frescoes on the north wall were weather-beaten and eroded, but to the south and west they were generally in much better shape. The winter winds from the Carpathians to the north and beyond that from the Ukraine and Russia had done their damage. Yet it was amazing how well the others had survived, and how vivid their colours still were. Painted around 1500 and founded by Stephen the Great, they had already lasted five hundred years. After Voronet we went to two further monasteries at Humorului and Moldovita before returning via Radauti to Suceava and our welcoming hotel.

The following day, a Sunday, we decided to go north west to some of the most important monasteries in the region of Suceava. We drove cross-country to a village called Arbore where we decided to go into a church with a number of cars parked nearby. We were in time, as it happened, for the last fifteen minutes of the liturgy, led by an orthodox Priest and a cantor singing the prayers. The congregation were standing in an open space around three tables laden with food. The women were dressed in black and the men in open-necked shirts, and there were a number of children also. There were saucepans decorated with pheasants of what was presumably a healthy stew. On top were loaves of bread and between them candles were burning. It was clearly some kind of thanksgiving. At the end of the service, we were given a large loaf of bread and a bottle of wine by the Priest, which we consumed reverently during our picnics over the next few days! The priest was very welcoming. How many visitors to an English church would be given a bottle of wine and a loaf of bread? Perhaps more would come! We were asked if we would like to see the bell tower. Two enthusiastic boys showed the way and demonstrated their bell ringing. Altogether, it was a very friendly visit.

We then went two hundred metres down the road to the monastery at Arbore. It was a very quiet spot, less visited than the more famous ones, but had a very friendly attendant who spoke good French. She told us that Prince Charles had been there two or three years before, and they were much honoured by his visit. She wondered if one of us might be another prince. We were sorry to disappoint her, but flattered to be so considered! In this place it was not so much about appreciating the cycles of frescoes, as enjoying the serenity and solitude. We said our goodbyes and thanks and moved on to Sucevița, a monastery at the other end of the scale.

Sucevița was about thirty kilometres north west, close to the border with the Ukraine and near a ridge of the Carpathians with outstanding views. Located in an alpine setting of hills covered in pine forest and firs, it stands peacefully in its semi-fortified surroundings. Once again there is a robust quadrangle of walls with attractive watchtowers set over the gates, and at the centre of the quad is the church. Well restored, it has an overhanging roof, a central spire, and a rich covering of frescoes on the outer wall. Founded in 1586 by a Prince of Moldova, Viovide Jeremia Movilă, the church is dedicated to the Resurrection. No monastery has better preserved or more remarkable frescoes. They include one of the Trinity (represented by the Angels at the Oaks of Mamre), one of the Last Supper preceded by a foot washing of the apostles, a Christ Pantocrator, and most daring of all a chalice containing a recumbent Christ, presumably signifying the true presence of Christ in the Communion. And in the porch where one enters is a depiction of the martyrdom of St John of Suceava, killed when the Turks pillaged the monastery.

We could only wonder at the skill, the dedication and the devotion of the artists in creating such a visual feast. Amazed by what we saw, we thought there might be time for one last visit, and so we went to Putna, the burial site of Stephen the Great at a monastery just miles from the border with the Ukraine, and further north from Suceviţa. Putna is a large, well-appointed monastery built along the same lines as the others, but with extensive outbuildings and a visitor centre for pilgrims. Like other monasteries, it is situated in dramatic scenery with a ridge to its south rising to about three thousand metres. We attempted to drive into Ukraine but the road was blocked. In what looked like wilderness territory on the other side of the border, the nearest town of significance on the map was Chernivtsi. It had once been the regional capital of Bukovina in the eighteenth century, but was now a cultural centre in southern Ukraine, and about 400 kms from Kyiv.

We returned to the hotel inspired by the majestic scenery, and the beauty of the monasteries and their settings, which were not just tourist attractions, but living centres of active faith among the Romanians. The following day continuous rain made it hard to fully appreciate a national park to the south of Suceava, and the day after that we headed south for Transylvania.

Transylvania

Transylvania is ever connected in the minds of many English with the fertile imagination of Irish writer Bram Stoker, and his gothic horror novel about Count Dracula. Although the Count existed, he was more of an Impaler than a vampire. Nevertheless, this beautiful region with its colourful history has certainly laboured under this fantasy.

Transylvania is a plateau surrounded by the Carpathians. Its enclosure has made it both a protected environment and a nurturer of old ways. We drove south from Suceava over the Carpathians in a snowstorm in early May, before descending into the serene scenery of Transylvania, with its wide-open spaces, gentle ridges and wild flowers.

We met Olivia and Sarah, who had flown in by Wizz Air to Cluj airport, the capital of the region well known for its cultural life and its fine universities. We made for the Black Lord Hotel at the edge of Târgu Mureş. That night we went to a local Romanian restaurant to enjoy spiced pork, cabbage rolls (*sarmale*) and the really sickly pudding of fried dough with sweetened curd cheese, jam and cream (*papanaşi*)! Not even the Black Lord could keep us awake. The next day would take us into the heart of Transylvania, and its history.

About fifty kilometres south of Târgu Mureş is the important Transylvanian town of Sighişoara. The old town provides a real window into the past. It was here that Count Dracul was born. His famous castle at Bran we would see later. Count Vlad Dracul, the Impaler (1428–1477), who was the Viovode of Wallachia—the region immediately to the south of Transylvania—sought to establish an independent kingdom. To do this he had to negotiate with the King of Hungary, Matthias Corvinus, the then ruler of Transylvania, and also gain the support of Stephen the Great of Moldova or Bessarabia in order to defeat the Turks. Although he did initially defeat the Turks—with brutal reprisals that no doubt involved impaling—and also the Bulgarians, he was more of a liability than an asset. He was imprisoned by Matthias in Hungary and later killed fighting for the Hungarians. His reputation for cruelty probably fuelled the idea of his being a vampire, but he was more a spiller of blood than blood-thirsty.

More instructive was a visit to a nearby Lutheran church in Sighişoara. Many descendants of the Germans who had first settled Transylvania from Hungary from the thirteenth century onwards became Lutheran at the time of the Reformation. Some sects even flourished, such as an anti-Trinitarian group led by Férenc David.[215] Transylvania was to the Protestant Germans what North America was to English Puritans on the Mayflower. Transylvania in the mid seventeenth century was seen as a possible kingdom of God on earth, with the great Protestant educationalist Comenius given refuge there by the Susanna Lorantffy, the Princess Consort of Transylvania in Sárospatak, now north-eastern Hungary. Transylvanian princes were Calvinist until 1688 when the Catholic Hapsburgs gained greater control following the Austrian defeat of the Turks. Gradually Turkish power diminished until the establishment, approved by the Romanian parliament, of the Romanian Monarchy in 1881.

The war memorials in the Lutheran Church underlined one fact: Romania had fought for different sides in the two world wars. The dynasty established in Romania in 1881 was Hohenzollern, therefore

---

[215] Diarmaid MacCulloch, *Reformation: Europe's House Divided* (London: Penguin, 2003), p 262.

German. Carol I was the first King of Romania and his son Ferdinand (Nando), a rather difficult character, married the granddaughter of Queen Victoria, the vivacious and beautiful Missy, daughter of the Duke of Edinburgh, Queen Victoria's second son. The *fin de siècle* years in Romania for the aristocracy were celebrated for their chic glamour, their sexual excess and their rounds of parties. It was in part due to Missy's influence that Romania was kept from joining the central powers of Germany, Austria Hungary and Turkey in WWI; instead, in August 1916, they entered the war on the side of the Russians, British and French. It was to be a brutally costly war for Romania—as for all nations—with an unprepared, mostly illiterate peasant army numbering six hundred and twenty thousand overwhelmed by Austrian/German forces.[216] Romanian military casualties would be three hundred and sixty thousand, not counting civilian casualties, and the country's allies failed to fulfil their promises of support.[217]

It was clear from the memorials in the church at Sighişoara how great the cost had been. However, at the Treaty of Versailles, and subsequently at Trianon, Romania was rewarded with generous terms and Transylvania, with its 1.6 million Hungarians, was transferred from Hungary to Romania. This was the explanation for the sole protester in Heroes Square, Budapest. He wanted a revoking of the Treaty.

Eighteen years later Romania had fatefully thrown in its lot with Germany. Politics in Romania became ever more complex in the interwar years. The young King Carol II, son of Missy and Nando, became unpredictable and erratic. The King had a Jewish Roman Catholic mistress Elena Lupescu, a sinister factotum called Colonel Ernest Urdărianu, who also was a lover of Lupescu,[218] and wanted to rule increasingly autocratically. In the meantime, Germany was busy fostering both fascism and anti-Semitism in Romania, while the traditional Francophile Romanian politician, Nicolae Titulescu, was eased out office by a king unable to see the destiny of his *ancient-regime* policies, even if they were not as extreme as those of the leader of the Fascist Iron Guard, Corneliu Codreanu.

---

[216] Norman Stone, *The Eastern Front* (London: Penguin Books, 1998), p. 264.
[217] Hannah Pakula, *The Last Romantic* (London: Phoenix, 1998), p. 256.
[218] Glenny, *The Balkans,* p. 454.

In March 1940 Romania was selling oil to Germany at low prices in exchange for armaments captured from the Polish army.[219] By March 1941 Romania had joined Germany in the invasion of Russia under the leadership of Marshal Ion Antonescu in the expectation of gaining territory in Bukovina and Bessarabia. The Jewish population of over one hundred and fifty thousand in that area was now mostly eradicated. Territory was gained, but with the defeat of German and Romanian forces at Stalingrad, in 1944 and under King Michal I (who had supplanted his father in 1940), Romania opened negotiations with Britain. In time Romania was occupied by Soviet forces, and, at the wartime Conference at Yalta in the Crimea, Churchill famously agreed, among other post-war carve ups, that Russia should have ninety per cent of Romania,[220] a proposal he had scribbled on a piece of paper. Stalin accepted the arrangement by placing a tick in blue crayon against the suggestion, thus opening the way for Communist Romania after 1945.

This was some of the background to the lives lost from Sighişoara in the First and Second World Wars, recorded on the plaques in the Reformed church there. They highlighted the dilemmas of a country only recently formed, and discovering in a most painful way where its allegiances lay. Many of the elite were Francophiles, very many ordinary Romanians were Orthodox Christians, hence the ties to both France and Russia. Yet between the wars, anti-Semitism and right-wing fascist movements created strong attachments to Germany. Romania was conflicted between these allegiances and, in the end, after Yalta, subservience to the Soviet Union would give way to an awful form of communism.

We walked to the top of the hill in Sighişoara, had a coffee in the square, and then drove south to Brasov, stopping at Viscri en route. By now the Transylvania countryside was opening up: wide open expanses of hillside stretching away to the horizon with no fences, walls or hedges, as in England, just pasture, cornfields and woodland, and room for shepherds to lead their flocks across the hillsides with their voices. The area stretched some one hundred kilometres east to the border with Moldova, and two hundred kilometres west to Timişoara, close to the

---

[219] Glenny, *The Balkans,* p. 459.
[220] Glenny, *The Balkans,* p. 522.

border with Serbia: a reminder that Romania is a Balkan country with all the challenges of that region.

Viscri is a typical Transylvanian Saxon village, and in British eyes, one that has been adopted by Prince Charles. With two main streets, it is an agricultural community where the blacksmith operates, cloth is dyed and cattle roam the dirt streets. When we turned the corner into the main street, a mare was being put to a stallion and horses and carts were parked outside people's homes. Undoubtedly the great attraction is the fortified Saxon church at the top end of the village. It stands inside a high castle wall with steep tiled roofs over the entrance, a church and other accommodation. You enter through a well-defended gateway into a walkway around the church. At the main entrance to the church there are white boards with the list of all who lost their lives in both world wars, and a roll of pastors going back to the thirteenth century. Inside the church the seating and décor is simple, with a baroque organ at the east end next to a pulpit and the minister's stall. At the west end you can climb the tower, which affords a fine view of the whole village and the region beyond. It could easily double up as both church belltower and defensive lookout.

The German community has long since dispersed. The church is rarely used for worship. As we left Viscri we wondered how long this mix of nostalgic old agricultural rhythms and tourist getaway for westerners would hold back the economic forces of change. For the present, a synergy had been created between the two that could just about preserve the old way of life. The relative remoteness of the village, and villages like it, meant that any change would come slowly and, in the meantime, could bring a livelihood for villagers and a refreshing experience for visitors.

From Viscri we took the road south to Brasov, once the capital city of German Transylvania in the southern Capathians and about one hundred and fifty kilometres from Bucharest. Up until WWI the city was forty per cent German, but now, with a population of almost four hundred thousand, making it Romania's seventh largest city, there are barely a thousand ethnic Germans left, and about sixteen thousand Hungarians. The Old Centre of the town is picturesque, with a fine square next to the Black Church (Protestant), which was darkened by a city fire in 1689.

Above it is a ridge reached by a cable car with excellent views over the region. Brasov was also our jumping off point for visits to two important castles: Bran Castle, once belonging to Vlad Dracul the Impaler, and the other at Peles, the seat of the Royal family.

Bran Castle is everything you could wish for in a Transylvanian castle. Set on an outcrop of rock above the town of Bran, its red roofs, pinnacles and turrets rise up above surrounding pines and larch. Built around an internal courtyard, its black and white galleries, staircases and rooms are attractive and cosy—a long way from the dread scenes of Bram Stoker who made it, on hearsay, the lair of *his* version of Dracul, the Impaler, who did once own the castle in the Middle Ages. Now it is owned by Dominic Hapsburg, the descendent of Queen Marie (Missy)'s fifth child Ileana, who married the Archduke of Austria and had six children, one of whom was the present owner. Ileana's mother Missy, the granddaughter of Queen Victoria, loved Bran Castle, and so did Ileana, who was close to her mother.

The life of Ileana (1909–1991) was hugely eventful and not unlike that of Princess Elizabeth of Hess and Prince Philip's mother, Princess Alice of Battenberg, both of whom, like Ileana, became nuns. Missy and Ileana could not be further removed in outlook or actions from the legendary associations of Dracula and the castle. For Missy (Queen Marie), Bran Castle was a welcome retreat from the formalities of the fractious royal court at Sinaia. It was a haven of quiet and beauty in her eleven years of widowhood while the country lurched towards the disaster of the Second World War.

The Royal castle of Peles, which we visited the following day, is everything that Bran is not. What they do have in common is a wonderful setting in the Carpathians. Peles was supposed to be a kind of Balmoral, a retreat for the Royal family from the summer heat of Bucharest. The nearby church and monastery of Sinaia enjoyed a spiritual and naturally beautiful location, next to a well-known fashionable resort. The monastery was founded in 1672 by Mihail Cantacuzino, who was fleeing the ruler of Wallachia, Grigore Ghica, and a beautiful church with frescoes by Pârvu Mutu resulted.

The Royal Palace of Peles further up the hill was designed by King Carol I (1839–1914) is a mixture of styles: German, Neo-Gothic,

Byzantine, Turkish and Transylvanian reflecting the diversity of the country's past. It seems to have been built by a royal family somewhat uncertain of its identity. Carol I's wife the German Elizabeth of Weid had no surviving children after the tragic death of her daughter Marie, and consequently she immersed herself in writing poetry, plays and novels under the pen name Carmen Sylva and in charitable work in Romania. Missy, the vivacious granddaughter of Queen Victorian, married to the adopted Crown Prince Ferdinand, escaped to the nearby Pelisor Castle (an *art noveau* alpine creation), whenever she could.

We returned to Brasov for a final night while Olivia, Sarah and Richard returned from Sibiu to the UK courtesy of Wizz Air. Geoff would fly home the following day, having just received the good news of the birth of new grandchild, Jude. Michael and I would start the long overland journey back to England, setting off the following day for the north west of the country.

Marmures

We were to travel the one thousand and seven hundred miles back to England via Hungary, Slovakia, the Czech Republic, Germany, Holland, Belgium and France. To begin with, we retraced our steps north through Transylvania, stopping at Sighişoara and Viscri, as Michael had not seen them.

As we drove through the beautiful Transylvanian countryside, we couldn't help noticing the occasional eyesore of an abandoned industrial plant, a symbol of the forced industrialisation during the communist era. Of all the Eastern communist bloc countries, Romania arguably had the worst of it. Two men are especially responsible for this: Georghe Gherorghiu-Dej (Dej for short) and Nicolae Ceausescu. "Dej was the worst thug of all"[221] —a home-grown, working-class communist who cultivated Stalin. Like Stalin, he set up prison and labour camps. The professions and traditional peasantry were his target. Eighty thousand peasants were arrested, and thirty thousand were tried in show trials. Church leaders were targeted also, and it was in this period from 1948 that the pastor Richard Wurmbrand suffered torture, solitary confinement and imprisonment for his faith, along with many others. In all,

---

[221] Glenny, *The Balkans*, p. 552.

Wurmbrand was to serve sixteen years in prison, coming through scarred but triumphant. Elsewhere a huge construction project called the Danube-Black Sea Canal, involving conscripted labour of eighteen thousand, was underway. The project was also used to "re-educate" the workforce, first by encouraging people to betray one another to the authorities, and then torturing them into submission.[222]

Ceauşescu succeeded Dej after manoeuvring through the ranks of the Communist party. His vision was to transform a peasant society into an industrialised nation, and he established his monopoly of power through the media. As so often with the implementation of communism, state directed industrialisation was a trojan horse for the advancement of personal power. Any opposition met harsh punishment from subservient courts. Alongside this was a policy of increasing the population: abortion was banned, contraception hard to obtain, and women were expected to have children regularly (and were regularly inspected to that end in a kind of industrialisation of the womb), ending up with countless children not cared for and housed in utterly inadequate orphanages. Indeed, it is thought that up to half a million children were kept in orphanages often with no clothes, little food, no running water or sanitation, with sewage running through dormitories in an atmosphere of brutal terror and a complete absence of love.

This terrible sight greeted the world at the end of communism; thirty years on many have been adopted and given new lives, but the healing of countless lives goes on. Ceauşescu maintained complete control, and indeed increased his own personality cult, by rotating party jobs and employing the feared secret police, the Securitate. He even managed to ride down the Mall in 1978 with the Queen (perhaps her most distasteful state visit), for Western governments believed he was an ally against the Soviet Union. By 1982 the economy was crashing with soaring debt and frequent power cuts. As late as 1988 Ceauşescu was seeking to destroy 8,000 villages and herd their inhabitants into agro-villages. Unable to read the signs of the times or Mikhail Gorbachev's new policy of *glasnost*, he was left unprotected when the revolution came and like many a dictator was strung up by his own people. Vestiges of his rule litter the most beautiful locations as decaying wrecks, symbols of the inhumanity and aesthetic blindness of the regime.

---

[222] Glenny, *The Balkans*, p. 555.

We drove north having spent another night at the Black Lord in Târgu Mures, where we were alone in the dining room and told it would be closing at eight p.m. when the staff went home. We took the road to Reghin (when we eventually found it) and headed into the Carpathians again and around the National Park of Muntii Rodnei in the Bistrita-Năsuăd. Once again in Maramures we were in a place of outstanding beauty and interest. Near Bistrita we stopped and listened: the cicadas were busy, a cuckoo called in the distance, and fertile rolling countryside swept away—some areas freshly ploughed and brown and others a vivid green. There was not a person to be seen. We proceeded up the valley, through ancient villages, wooden houses, and on street lampposts the familiar circle of stars denoting the European Union, as there were regional elections coming up. As it was Sunday, many villagers were sitting by the roadside, the women in black with head scarves and the men with smart jackets and open-necked shirts. In the fields hay was being dried on wooden frames like laundry, with white storks atop keeping vigilant watch. It was a day of rest, one in which to stop, stare and see the world go by.

At the top of the valley, and nearing the Ukrainian border we turned to the west and headed along a minor road towards the border town of Sighetu Marmației, very close to the Ukraine. Along this road were a number of wooden churches. The story behind these is that their Hungarian overlords, who were initially Catholic and then Reformed, refused to allow these Orthodox communities to build in stone. So, making a virtue out of a necessity the local people built wooden churches of unsurpassed beauty, displaying extraordinary versatility in their woodworking or carpentry. The result was a wonder to behold: and just as the Suceava region boasted the painted monasteries, not far away were these Orthodox wooden churches, quite distinct from the Saxon wooden churches of Transylvania.

We stopped to look at several. Some were wonderfully simple: a single room with a warm blue carpet, bench seats on either side, and an iconostasis behind which the priest celebrated. But undoubtedly the most impressive and active of the monastery churches in the region was the one at Barsana. Rebuilt in the 1990s it was buzzing with visitors and life.

Set out like a campus with several wooden buildings, at its centre was the Church of the Presentation of the Virgin in the Temple, with vivid frescoes and around it buildings for pilgrims to stay and meet. It had an alpine feel with its intense green grass and foliage. From there we made our way to Sighetu Marmaţiei, very close to the Ukraine border in search of the house of Elie Wiesel.

The town of Sighetu Marmaţiei was spacious and easy to get around and we soon saw a sign to Elie Wiesel's house. It was an ordinary home on a side street containing a memorial to the Jewish Holocaust in that part of Romania. Wiesel, who came from this town, was a Holocaust survivor, poet, human rights activist and Nobel Peace Prize Laureate. In 1940 Romania was forced to surrender half of Transylvania to Hungary and the regime of Admiral Horthy, following which one hundred thousand Jews living in the region were transported north west to Auschwitz. In May 1944, Elie, a fifteen-year-old boy, was taken there with the Jews of this town and survived until liberated by the Americans in 1945. The rest of his life he dedicated to researching and making known the events of those years. He died in 2016 and one of the final photographs in the exhibition was of him with President Obama in the White House, smiling, dignified and fulfilled. His was an extraordinary journey from this out-of-the-way place to the White House and the warm greeting of Barak Obama. We left the house with a heavy heart and decided we would enter the Ukraine for a coffee!

Crossing into the Ukraine was much slower than I had imagined. The border post was close to a bridge across the river Tysa (which we would pick up again in Hungary) and the border guards were surprised to see an English car. There was much inspecting of the car, my ownership documents, our passports and ourselves. The guards were burly and surly, and the process was quite different from crossing borders within the European Union, which for the most part, are barely marked. There is a distinct feeling that you are moving from one culture to another. We had our Ukrainian coffee and quickly returned; the border guards must have wondered what we were up to. We made our way out of town, picked up a woman and her son who were hitch-hiking home and took an evening drive of two hours down through the mountains to

Baia Mare, close to the Hungarian border.

Our hitch hikers kindly showed us where our hotel was and we dropped them off. It had been a long day since the Black Lord at Târgu Mures. Once again, we were the only ones in a huge dining room in the hotel, and once again we were encouraged not to take our time, nor did we mind too much for we were happy to go to bed.

The next day we had a relatively short drive to stay with friends from Bath—James, Virág and Sophie. Not knowing that Hungary was in a different time zone to Romania we arrived even earlier than they were expecting! They had been members of our congregation in Bath and in 2017 had tragically lost a son, Luke, from cancer. They were making a new life for themselves in Virág's home village of Tiszadob. They showed us the river and where, in straightening its many bends, a small part of the river was left behind as a lake. We also visited the castle in the village, which was more a chateau than castle, designed by the statesman Count Gyula Andrássy. We caught up on news and ate delicious pancakes for breakfast cooked by Virág's father. Then we said our goodbyes and headed north to Slovakia past Tokaj, where the famous Hungarian wine comes from.

There would be four days driving to get home. The first was in heavy rain, through which we could just make out the High Tatras, the highest peaks of the Carpathians in this region. The roadside cafés had a hunting lodge feel, as if everyone was off to the mountains in folk costume to bag some game. Indeed, aside from centres of population at Košice in the east and Bratislava in the west, the country is mountainous and sparsely populated. We stayed the night at Zilina which seemed to have no one about after eight p.m., and nowhere to eat, as if visitors never came. The next day we day we drove past Prague which I had visited with some of our family in December 2018. With the help of advice from Tereza Franclova and Venetia and Roger Dunlop we had a marvellous time, what with snow in the city and the Christmas Market in Old Town Square creating a memorable Czech mystique, a kind of Christmas Bohemian rhapsody! But now we headed to the famous Czech spa town of Karlovy Vary. The imperial grandeur of this Georgian and Edwardian spa resort and its hotels made Bath seem like a provincial bathhouse, but there was no time to bathe in the numerous spas with water temperature ranging from hot (48c) to hotter (62.4c) and hottest (73.4c). We set off for the final leg of our journey to Maastricht in Holland. Well known for the European Union Treaty which bears its name, and which caused parliamentary suspense in John Major's government, it is in fact a spacious, well organised city along the banks of the Maas River, with an animated night life, and plenty of pavement cafés to choose from, a real delight.

Chapter XIX
Back to Irish Roots

What drew me back to Ireland in 2020 was my grandmother Alice Whitworth (nee Hervey 1887–1974) who died when I was in my early twenties. Her family had strong connections with Ireland, her mother Mary Hervey (nee Hanford Flood) was the youngest of seven children of an Anglo-Irish family, but surprisingly, of these seven children (three brothers and four sisters) only her mother married and had one child: Alice, my grandmother.

 My other grandmother Daphne (née Butler) came from stock that numbered academics, head masters, and colonial administrators amongst their number, as well as the politician R.A. Butler. Her father Sir Cyril Kendall Butler of Bourton, founder of the Contemporary Art Society and patron of Artists like Rex Whistler, Henry Tonks, Ambrose McEvoy and Derwent Lees took her to Central Europe aged twenty, where she joined the Relief for Central Europe Commission in 1919 gaining an MBE. One of her several uncles had been the Governor of Burma (as it was) Sir Spencer Harcourt Butler, when George Orwell (Eric Blair) served in the Police there. Later he would write his blast against imperialism: *Burmese Days* and *Shooting an Elephant*.

Mary Hervey's (my great grandmother) father was a Flood, an old Irish family from Kilkenny, and her mother Frances Hanford Flood was the last of the Hanfords of Woollas Hall, Bredon Hill, Worcestershire. William Flood and Frances Hanford were married in 1847, and both having estates chose to be called Hanford Floods. The Floods were part of the so called "Protestant Ascendancy" in Ireland and the Hanfords were Worcestershire Roman Catholics with a chapel in their house who had lived in the county since the 16th century. In 1847 they were an unlikely combination, at a time when Catholicism was re-establishing itself precariously in England, but personal chemistry evidently surmounted religious differences!

Woollas Hall was built in 1611. You can go there today, but it is a sad pilgrimage, as the house is divided into several residences, and the occupants, whom I have met on occasional forays, had no interest in its history, and even less interest in who I was! So, there was a sense of *fin de siècle*: Alice, my grandmother, was the only heir of the Hanfords and the Floods. Both their properties in Ireland and Worcestershire were sold in the 1930s and 1940s; while her father, Constantine Hervey, was from a family with quite another story, to which we will come.

Both the Herveys and the Hanford Floods would figure in different ways in my Irish odyssey, which took two weeks in October 2020, and we will come to each family as we pass their respective stamping grounds in Ireland, north and south.

When I set off in early October 2020, England and Ireland (as indeed the world) were facing the second wave of the coronavirus pandemic. It was not a revolution unfolding, as in some of my previous travels, but instead the mounting ravages of a disease. In the next fortnight I would pass through areas with some of the highest numbers of cases in the UK, as in Strabane and Londonderry, where the case rate rose to nine hundred in every one hundred thousand while I was there. In fact, every time I moved from an area it went into a greater lockdown, giving further grist to my family and friends' rumour mill that everywhere I travel there is trouble!

My first port of call was Liverpool, from where I would take the Birkenhead-Belfast ferry for an opening week in Northern Ireland. I drove to Liverpool one Monday afternoon, arriving in the centre of the city where the water front and the grand Merseyside buildings were lit up, but the streets were deserted with a level 3 lockdown imminent. There was virtually no one in the hotel, and I had a snack on my own in the foyer. Early the following morning, I arrived, via the Mersey Tunnel, in Birkenhead where large spaces, cleared of old industrial buildings and warehouses, awaited redevelopment. The occasional old chimney stack thrust itself into the air in lonely isolation and redundancy. From here I would make the day crossing to Belfast on the Stena Line ferry.

I thought of the countless Irish who had arrived to seek a new future in Liverpool and England, as in Glasgow, following the Potato famine of 1846, and recalled also the transatlantic slave trade of which Liverpool and its docks had been so much a part. Across the Mersey I could see the Liver Building, with liver birds atop, and to the southeast the great bulk of the solid red brick Anglican Cathedral.

There was an unexpectedly large contingent of cars and passengers going to Belfast. We settled into the ship for the eight-hour crossing which took the northern route, north, that is, of the Isle of Man, past the offshore wind farm at Barrow and the Morecambe Bay gas field with its rigs. There was time to read, snooze and think of all that lay ahead and by five thirty p.m. we were passing the Mull of Galloway and turning west into the docks down Belfast Lough. By seven p.m. we had disembarked and an hour later I was searching in the dark for my bed and breakfast at Lisnacurran, near Hillsborough. I went into a local town, Dromore, for a bite to eat. I bought fish and chips in the Market Square and having bought a Guinness in the Mulholland Arms settled down to have them in a friendly, if near deserted, pub. In the morning I chatted over breakfast at the Bed and Breakfast with the landlady Lynn about present times. Covid–19 had decimated her bookings but she was amused to have found a new form of business: husbands taking a break from their wives or, very occasionally, vice versa! Breakfasted, I set off for Armagh, about thirty miles away.

Armagh is an important town for the whole of Ireland: lying in the North and giving its name to one of the six counties of Ulster. It has a fine open green at the foot of a hill on which are perched the two cathedrals: one Church of Ireland and the other Roman Catholic. On the day I went, the Roman Catholic Cathedral of St Patrick had a well-attended service, but the Church of Ireland's St Patrick's was closed. The Christian history of the town began when St Patrick built his first stone church on the hill of Ard Mhacha in 445 AD, and where the Anglicans much later built their cathedral. And St Patrick decreed that the Church in Armagh should have pre-eminence over all the churches in Ireland, and to this day the Archbishops of Armagh are the principal church leaders in Ireland. Having admired the view over the hills to the south and east, I headed west towards Tynan.

I had last been to Tynan in 1978, over forty years previously, on the way to a holiday in the south west of Ireland near Bantry. I had stayed at Tynan Abbey with the Stronge family, along with two friends, Claire Houston (as she was then) and Peter Daws. We enjoyed the stay with Sir Norman Stronge, who had been the speaker of the Parliament at Stormont, and his son Jim, ex-British Army and known to my father as a junior office in his regiment, the Grenadier Guards. For these two reasons they were targets for the IRA. In 1981, three years after our visit, an IRA unit came over the border, just a few miles away, and assassinated both of them on 21 January, before burning down Tynan Abbey, which remains a shell to this day, although the family still farm the land. To remember them I met with Thomas Marshall at the church in Tynan and he kindly showed me the memorials to the family and their graves. He recalled how every week Sir Norman would read the lesson in church, and how both father and son enjoyed banter at the door. The day of their killing was a devastating shock to the whole community, and Thomas suggested that the IRA unit was later identified and dealt with by special forces. What was clear then was that the border of Armagh was as unstable and violent a place as any in Northern Ireland, and the many Union Jacks I saw tied to telegraph posts on the roads around the village reveal those feelings are still not dormant today.

On the way back to Belfast, but not directly, I visited our son's in-laws, Maurice and Cherith McKeown at Ballygawley, where we had lunch outside in accordance with Covid rules: a delicious Irish stew and apple pie and then, well fed, I drove to Belfast, arriving in the early evening.

Belfast was quiet. St Anne's Cathedral, next to where I stayed, was closed because of Covid, as were many of the public buildings. I settled in, ate in their bar downstairs and prepared to spend all the next day in Belfast. The morning, I decided, would be for West Belfast, which I knew only from almost endless news reports during the troubles in the 1970s and 80s, and then the Titanic Exhibition Centre in the docklands in the afternoon.

In the morning I drove to the Falls Road and began with the huge Roman Catholic Milltown Cemetery overlooking the city. As a clergyman I am no stranger to cemeteries and believe they tell a story, in their way, of the communities they serve. This was certainly true of Milltown.

The names on gravestones stretched away: McBryan, Quinn, Conlon, O'Connor, Mckenna, Holland, Kennedy, McCullough, McCartney, Brennan, Donnelly, Mckenna, McKeown, giving away their Scottish and Irish roots. While many of their namesakes would have become Protestant or Presbyterian during the Reformation, these families most probably remained Roman Catholic, beginning the great divide of culture and religion in Northern Ireland. Some had names like Pat Finucane, the solicitor gunned down in 1989. There was a further feature to these graves of people whose families live in the area, for on the one hand there was a memorial for all who gave their lives in WWI, and on the other, there were military memorials to IRA members who died on what the IRA call "active service". It was yet another sign of the conflicted history of Ireland. Some died in hunger strikes, like Bobby Sands in May 1981. Nine more followed in the Maze prison, all wanting the status of political prisoners and not of mere criminals. I thought too of the occasion here in 1988 when the funerals of IRA volunteers shot by the SAS in Gibraltar were interrupted when a lone Protestant gunman fired into the crowd of mourners, killing three and wounding sixty. In turn this led to the killing of two British soldiers, Corporals David Howes and Derek Wood, who were tragically caught up in the funeral of the Catholics killed in Milltown. It was further killing in the endless cycle of violence from both sides, eventually brought to a kind of end by the Good Friday Agreement. I found it a sobering place, where deep convictions and yearnings confronted human frailty and, in the end, our common mortality. Yet it seemed like a real place to begin a brief visit to Belfast.

From there I drove down the Falls Road, where I called in at a post office to buy some writing paper and met a very cheery postmistress. I proceeded to the First Street intersection between the Falls Road and the Protestant Shankill area. There were steel gates separating the two communities, now open, but in the past closed in times of tension. Nearby was a mural of the head of Christ wearing a crown of thorns painted in red paint, and also words of the Roman Catholic South American martyr, Oscar Romero, which read: "There are many things that can only be seen through eyes that have cried". Although it was calm when I visited, I knew that sectarian organisations were still embedded in the communities and it might not take much to resurrect old antipathies or old ways. Indeed, the tensions over the Irish Sea Border, the Protocol in the Brexit Treaty, and the substantial funeral in time of Covid restrictions of former Maze prisoner Bobby Storey quickly exacerbated suspicions and in April 2021 there was renewed rioting where I stood. After pausing there I went on, coming down Crumlin Road into central Belfast, and from there towards the docks and the Titanic Exhibition Centre.

I had a sandwich near the Exhibition Centre looking out over some containers with lyrics painted on them, which were part of the Riverbox at the heart of the Maritime Mile. Recalling the many arrivals and departures of the port of Belfast, the words on the containers read "I sing for the inbound. I sing begin. I sing for all that we hold within. I sing the shore and the incoming tide. I sing for all that will become new." With those words of hope I went into the Titanic Exhibition, and the irony was not lost on me.

It is a magnificent exhibition, which seems to consist of three parts: the city of Belfast and its dynamic industrial and commercial past; the shipbuilding of Harland and Wolff, and the Olympic class of ships of which the Titanic was the prime example; and the final hours of the Titanic and its passengers, a human story of tragic loss, courage and endurance thar continues to appal and fascinate. The film *Titanic* with Canadian singer Celine Dion's rendition of *My Heart Will Go On* only adds to the emotional pull of the story.

In 1901 the population of Belfast was 349,180. Belfast was full of industries: linen mills, rope works, tobacco factories, such as Gallagher's, and whisky distilleries, such as Royal Irish Whisky. The largest and most celebrated employer was however Harland and Wolff, the shipbuilders who employed some ten thousand workers, and who built the Titanic.

In 1911 the Titanic was the largest ship in the world and its engines and fittings were second to none. Yet it was a vessel of contrasts: between the opulent and self-assured grandeur of the quarters of the richest passengers and the simplicity or spartan nature of the steerage accommodation; between the supposed unsinkability of the ship and the unknown dangers of the North Atlantic; and between the warmth and safety of privilege and the icy waters just feet away on the other side of the double skinned and powerfully riveted hull. As the Exhibition progresses into the real-life stories and memories of those final fraught hours, the full tragedy and deep ironies of the disaster take over. Of the two and half thousand passengers and crew, fifteen hundred perished in the icy waters.

That evening I was told by Robert and Ann McCullagh, friends of our second daughter, who live near Belfast, that normally some two hundred cruise ships visit the Exhibition every year, although not this year with Covid. If I were them, I would definitely check the readiness of the lifeboats on board afterwards! Again, it seemed an ironic statistic.

The following day I drove north from Belfast to Antrim. Along the coast from Larne, the road takes in wonderful scenery of flat-topped hills and a few delightful seaside towns and ports. At the pretty town of Carnlough I ran into a storm and a funeral with about eighty mourners walking behind the hearse. We waited for about ten minutes as the coffin, followed by the mourners, went into the church: a community funeral the like of which you rarely see in England now. Stopping in the town I noticed a plaque to Paddy the pigeon. Paddy was owned by Andrew Hughes of Cranlough, who trained him for use in air-sea rescue missions at RAF Ballykelly. He was subsequently handed over to RAF Hurn to be trained during the war. Paddy did proud service in Normandy and during the campaign of June 1944, carried coded messages from American forces about the Allied advance, reaching Hampshire in four hours fifty minutes. For his sterling work Paddy was awarded the Dickin Medal, the animal equivalent of the Victoria Cross, on 1 September 1944. What you could be sure of was that Paddy was well used to a storm. It was blowing a gale as I rounded the North Antrim Coast towards Bushmills and the Giants Causeway.

Bushmills is famous for its whisky and boasts the oldest distillery in the British Isles. The Scots, who came over in the early seventeenth century to settle in Ulster, could not last long without a wee dram, and Bushmills Distillery was founded in 1608. I noticed that the Presbyterian Church, founded in 1647, was well beaten by the distillery! There was no chance of enjoying a noggin, as the distillery was closed due to Covid, so I continued my journey along the coast towards the Giants Causeway past a very windswept and picturesque Ballintoy, which looks across the channel to Scotland.

The Giants Causeway, is the great geological feature of the Antrim Coast. Its interlocking basalt columns—mostly hexagonal in formation, numbering up to forty thousand—stretch out into the sea, as if a giant had made it his landing stage on the Irish coast. It was formed fifty-sixty million years ago when the area was subject to intense volcanic activity. Its chimney stacks, stones resembling giants' boots, and its basalt columns stir the imagination, and have spawned mythical folk tales in which an Irish giant, Fin MacCool takes on a Scottish opponent, Benandonner. The tales have various outcomes, but in the Irish version the Scottish giant is soundly defeated or craftily outwitted. Presumably in Scotland it is the other way around!

From the Causeway it is but a short way to Portrush, a popular seaside resort boasting the Royal Portrush Golf Club where the 2019 British Open was held. Here in Portrush, I was close to the stamping ground of my ancestor, the Earl Bishop.

Frederick Hervey: The Earl Bishop of Londonderry

My grandmother Alice (née Hervey) was the great-great-granddaughter of Frederick Hervey (1730–1803), the Earl Bishop of Londonderry. He was one of the great eccentrics of the late eighteenth century in Irish, and latterly English life, although he was rarely in England.

Bishop Frederick Hervey was appointed in 1786 to the very wealthy Diocese of Londonderry by his older brother George, who was briefly Lord Lieutenant of Ireland. Frederick was son of Lord Hervey, the diarist and gossip of the court of George II, of whom Lady Mary Montague said famously, "the world is made of men, women and Herveys", a saying sometimes also attributed to Voltaire. When Hervey heard the news of his appointment to Derry he was out leapfrogging, one of his enjoyable pastimes, with his curates in the Diocese of Cloyne where he was then bishop. "I have out jumped over you all", he declared "for I have jumped from Cloyne to Derry". He had indeed, for Derry was worth £20,000 a year, revenue not just for him personally, but for the running of the diocese. It was nevertheless a princely sum worth millions today, and made up of tithes and rents from the extensive diocesan property of seventy thousand acres.[223]

Frederick Hervey was exuberant (loving practical jokes), boisterous, a good linguist—speaking French, German and Italian—fascinated by volcanoes, and a traveller, especially in Germany and Italy. In theology he was a deist, although when visiting Londonderry, Wesley recorded his sermon as "useful" and commended him as being "a good writer and good speaker".[224] Above all, and this soon took centre stage, he was a builder, collector, philanthropist and politician.

Often referred to as "the edifying bishop" because of the amount he built for himself and others, he soon began building extensively in the diocese: many churches were adorned with spires, including St Columb's Cathedral. In Derry churches were built, not just for the Church of Ireland, but for Presbyterians and Roman Catholics alike. One of his guiding principles was to include all denominations in his philanthropy, an attitude well ahead of its time. He also built extensively for his family and to house his growing art collections.

On the headland overlooking the estuary of the River Foyle, he built Downhill, now a shell, but until 1930 a stately home and the Bishop's favourite residence. On the cliff nearby, the Mussenden Temple was dedicated to his second cousin, with whom he was besotted, but who died aged twenty-two. Now it stands on the edge of the cliff: a classical rotunda resembling the Temple of Tivoli, once housing the bishop's library. The Demesne of Downhill encloses an extraordinary collection of buildings in an unforgettable location.

Politics too was a sphere for his activity. He was actively involved in the Volunteer Movement: a defence force for Ireland against either invasion or any movement of Independence from the Crown, thus preventing any Irish imitation of the American War of Independence (1775–1783). In this force he became a Colonel of the Londonderry Volunteers with a uniform to boot. At the same time, in the Constitutional Convention of 1783, and as a member of the Irish House of Lords, he sought to extend the franchise to Roman Catholics. Yet in seeking to

---

[223] Brian Fothergill, *The Mitred Earl* (London: Faber and Faber 1974), p. 25.
[224] Fothergill, *The Mitred Earl*, pp. 37–38.

appoint the Protestant Ascendancy Parliamentarian Henry Flood as Chairman of the Convention, he chose someone who opposed this move toward Catholic emancipation. It would not be until 1830, and under the leadership of the Duke of Wellington, that Catholics would be included in the franchise. It was thus ironical that my great grandparents, descendants of Flood and Hervey, married at Eckington, Worcestershire in 1866, families previously in political variance had now been joined together!

A combination of events would serve to weaken Bishop Hervey's involvement with the diocese, although he retained until his death the episcopacy and its revenues, now mostly administered through his agent and heir in Ireland, Revd. Henry Hervey Bruce. On 22 December his brother Augustus (a rather philandering sailor who was married to Elizabeth Chudleigh, later Duchess of Kingston who was convicted of bigamy by the House of Lords) died without legitimate issue, and unexpectedly the title, lands and assets of the Earldom of Bristol passed to Frederick. It was "Christmas" indeed, and Frederick found himself heir to the estates in Ickworth, Suffolk, a town house in St James' London and a further £20,000 a year. He was now one of the richest men in Britain.

His family was growing up, and apart. His eldest daughter married Lord Erne, and later separated. His second daughter Elizabeth (Bess) married Thomas Foster an Irish MP, but despite two children the marriage did not last, and Lady Elizabeth Foster fell in with the Duke and Duchess of Devonshire forming a famous *ménage à trois,* bearing the Duke two illegitimate children, and briefly becoming the Duchess after the death of Georgiana. The story of these three has fascinated ever since. By 1780 Frederick was separated from his own wife Elizabeth, who left with their youngest daughter Louisa, (who would later marry the Prime Minister Lord Liverpool). Frederick never lived at Ickworth and he and Elizabeth scarcely met again. His oldest son died prematurely whilst Consul in Florence and his youngest son succeeded, becoming the first Marquess.

Frederick's inheritance and the disruption to his family life weakened his ties to Derry, although his memory was and is always cherished there on account of his generosity, philanthropy and inclusiveness. Still, the project of building a new house with his trademark rotunda at Ickworth, and collecting art for it consumed his interest. Periodic forays to the continent, and especially Italy and Pyrmont in Germany, turned into ever longer collecting tours, until in September 1792 he finally left his Diocese for good (or ill!), never to return. His circle in Italy was eclectic: English and Italian painters, members of the Curia, the British Ambassador to Naples, Sir William Hamilton and his beautiful wife Emma—soon to be the mistress of Nelson—and the mistress of the King of Prussia, Madame Ritz Countess von Lichtenau.[225] He took with him a cook, chaplain and an architect, and gave his name to numerous hotels throughout Europe. He collected, collected and collected, but in the end all it of it fell into the hands of Napoleon's forces, and he died by the roadside in 1803. His body was transported back to England in a naval frigate but since sailors were superstitious about having a corpse on board, the plain wooden packing case was labelled "A Classical Statue!" It seems like a very cautionary tale.

Having seen the remains of his house at Downhill, the beautiful demesne and the Mussenden Temple, I arrived in Londonderry. The following day, Sunday, I had arranged to go to the Cathedral, bearing a greeting, and was invited by the Dean, Raymond Stewart, to do the readings at the main service. And of course, we all wore masks, although not of the kind the Earl Bishop might have been used to in Venice and Italy.

Londonderry is a walled city above the River Foyle, over which Bishop Hervey built the first bridge. Established during the settlements of the seventeenth century, it had close links to the guilds of London, hence the name. During the campaign, which climaxed with the Battle of the Boyne on 30 June 1690, in which Catholic James II's forces were defeated by William of Orange, Derry was besieged by forces loyal to James. It was an attritional and iconic siege, with the Protestant population committed to the slogan of "No Surrender" which became a rallying cry for Unionism thereafter.

The city was to remain deeply divided, with Catholics occupying the Bogside area at the foot of the city walls to the south west, and

---

[225] Fothergill, *The Mitred Earl*, p. 179.

demonstrating their profound sense of discrimination from the late 1960s onwards. On 30 January 1972, a march against internment ended with British troops firing on the demonstrators and killing fourteen protestors and wounding others. I walked down to the memorial for Bloody Sunday near the Bogside Inn with its murals commemorating the massacre, and remembered those events quietly while the traffic swished by.

The following day I attended worship at the Cathedral, and was warmly greeted by the Dean and congregation as a descendent of their unusual, but much cherished bishop. Following the service, I left the city and made my way down towards Strabane, then recording the highest incidence of Covid in the British Isles! I kept my head down, picnicking in the lanes, spending the night in a bed and breakfast outside Castlederg where I was the only guest, and getting a takeaway from the very efficient El Grecos in the nearby town. In the morning, John, the owner, who had five sons mostly in the south, gave me breakfast and a parting box of chocolates! I set off with his words ringing in my ears, "Turn right at the T junction in sight of the Catholic church and take the bog road to Donegal". I did, and a beautiful road it was across the border into Donegal where there was little evidence that we had crossed into Eire, except a yellow road sign saying "Attention Achtung!" I did not think they would have a such a sign in Northern Ireland! And the border crossing, one of at least several hundred between North and the Republic, was unmarked, almost unknown, and in itself thus a symbol of the complexity of Irish politics and history.

Crossing Borders

It was a fine sunny day: breezy, with cotton-wool clouds scudding against a blue sky and a shower every half an hour with an accompanying rainbow. I hit the Ballybofey Donegal road, skirted Donegal and headed West to Killybegs, the principal fishing port on the west coast, with its large fishing fleet for catching herring and mackerel, tied up in in its deep-water harbour. From Killybegs I headed back towards to Dunkineely and St John's point and its lighthouse. There are few more scenic coastal views. While looking across Donegal Bay, with surf on the rocky shoreline, hills all around and the consciousness of that vast expanse of ocean before landfall in the United States, you are silent with awe at the grandeur. Then, to crown it all, another shower produced a complete rainbow that framed the view.

I pulled myself away to take the road along this wonderful coast south to Sligo, but on the way, I passed Mullaghmore. It was here that on 27 August 1979, Lord Mountbatten of Burma, Prince Philip's uncle, was killed by an IRA bomb, along with his grandson and a local boy. So ended a distinguished career, and at times controversial life, details of which are still much debated. I passed Mullaghmore Castle before reaching the small quiet harbour where the bombing occurred. The castle stood remote and a little foreboding in the soft green and blue colours of the day with its off-white clouds. The gates bearing the heraldic M denoting the Mountbatten residence were locked. In many ways the last few hours were typical of the country as a whole: beautiful, but with a deep streak of sadness that cried out from many of these places. I was to be reminded of this the following day especially.

I headed further south towards Sligo and Castle Dragan where I was staying and passed Drumcliffe. It is here that the great Irish poet, W.B. Yeats is buried. Sligo, its setting and inhabitants, were an inspiration to him. His mother came from Sligo. Her family, the Pollexfens, ran a successful shipping company, and many a childhood holiday was spent there. Yeats was part of the extraordinary flowering of Irish literature in the late nineteenth century, which included Bernard Shaw, Oscar Wilde, J. M. Synge and James Joyce. Often radical, unsettling and nationalist, they represented the upsurge of Irish culture against English dominance. Standing in Drumcliffe churchyard I read Yeats' lines, inspired by the nearby brooding flat-topped mountain, Ben Bulben.

Under Bare Bulben's head
In Drumcliff churchyard Yeats is laid
An ancestor was rector there
Long years ago; the church stands near,
By the road an ancient Cross.
No marble, no conventional phrase;
On limestone quarried near the spot
By his command these words are cut:

Cast a cold eye
On life, on death
Horseman, pass by!
Last Poems 1939

Arriving at Castle Dragan just outside the busy west coast port of Sligo, there was much to remember from a single day: the Bog Road to Donegal, the fishing fleet of Killybegs, the dramatic seascape of St John's point in Donegal Bay, the aloof and solitary castle at Mullaghmore with its sad associations, and the grave of W.B. Yeats. It had been a kaleidoscope of Irish life, beauty and conflict at one and the same time.

The following day I drove back to Belfast, crossing the border both ways to pick up Olivia from Belfast City Airport. Few people were flying, even less were at the airport, and the plane arrived forty minutes early! I drove through Enniskillen, past Omagh, Lurgan and Portadown: all places associated with troubles or massacres (Portadown in 1641). I was a little anxious about crossing the border, as I had heard that the Garda were turning back drivers if they did not have a good reason to enter Eire, but when it came to the crossing at Belcoo, there wasn't a Garda police car in sight!

The following day we set off for Connemara through Charlestown, Castlebar, to the delightful town of Westport. The day was once again bright and sunny with only a few clouds and the occasional shower. Beyond Westport the scenery became ever more dramatic as we entered Connemara, past Croagh Patrick, which I had climbed with my family years before, into the high upland with peaks either side. We were headed for Renvyle on a peninsular stretching out into the Atlantic and the hotel where my parents had stayed on their honeymoon in 1946. I often wondered what it must have been like for my father to be suddenly removed from the theatre of war in the 1940s, with all its mayhem, madness and killing, and find himself in the isolation of west coast Ireland. But for us this was not to be: the hotel was closed because of Covid and we had not received their message cancelling the booking. They recommended we stay at Abbeyglen Castle Hotel in Clifden. It was a good move if not quite such an arresting position.

The hotel owner's talk in the bar with Prosecco on the house was entertaining. It was to Clifden that Alcock and Brown had flown in the first trans-Atlantic flight in June 1919. The flight to Ireland took sixteen hours through fog, hail storms and darkness. Both men were knighted and Winston Churchill, Minister of State for Air presented them with £10,000 prize money from the Daily Mail. A little to the south Marconi had used fuel from the peat bogs of Galway to power wireless transmissions to Newfoundland after his breakthrough transmission of morse code from Cornwall in 1901. Suddenly, from being a sleepy fishing town on the west coast of Ireland, Clifden had become the breakthrough centre of global communications!

Much as we would like to linger, both the march of Covid and a rendezvous in Kilkenny kept us on the move. Once again, the hotel we were to stay at had just closed and we were redirected, fortuitously, to the Mount Juliet Estate nearby. It was to prove a cloud with a very big silver lining.

The Hanford Floods

If my grandmother provided the link to the Earl Bishop on her father's side, her mother, Mary Hanford Flood, was the youngest daughter of the Hanford Floods, a family that came into existence with marriage of Frances Hanford and William Lloyd Flood in 1848, and of which union my grandmother was the only grandchild. Our reason for going to Kilkenny was to deposit some papers inherited from my cousin Rodney Whitworth with the Kilkenny Archaeological Society, and to look over the land and properties that had once belonged to the Hanford Flood family.

When arriving at Mount Juliet, which is south of Kilkenny near Stoneyford, we were amazed to discover that we were only two miles from Flood Hall, one of the homes of the family before a fire mostly destroyed it in the 1940s. The next day we had a meeting at Rothe House in Kilkenny, once a prosperous Elizabethan merchant's house, now the home of the Kilkenny Archaeological Society, where we were to deposit the family papers. Here we met Ann Tierney and Patricia Bergin, adding to the records of the Hanford Floods they already had been given by my uncle Compton Whitworth. We spent nearly three socially distanced hours with masks on, handing over the papers and talking about their significance. And what were hitherto seemingly lifeless documents, took on meaning when Ann and Patricia recognised the names of people, whether tenants or landlords, who were still well known in the county.

The Floods were an old Kilkenny family, their presence dating back to at least 1372, when one Robert Flode served as Sovereign of Kilkenny and was MP for the city in Westminster, and a Commissioner for Ireland. In 1406 a subsequent Robert Flode of Kilkenny was pardoned for treason at the request of James, the 4th Earl of Ormond, the great feudal lord of the county and the King's Lord Lieutenant of Ireland (Family Papers).

But the Floods (as they became) had their real advancement through marriage, when in 1692 a Francis Flood married Ann Warden, who was heiress to the Warden lands in Kilkenny. Colonel Warden, Ann's ancestor, had been a Colonel in Cromwell's army and had been rewarded and paid for his military service in land. Cromwell had granted him 4,627 acres of the Burnchurch Estate, taken from the Fitzgeralds, who were the Earls of Desmond and one of the great Anglo-Norman feudal barons of southern Ireland along with the Ormondes (Butlers). Francis and Anne's heir was Warden Flood who became Chief Justice of Ireland and father of Henry Flood (1732–1791), the great Parliamentarian and orator.

Henry was an angular and singular character. Educated at Christ Church Oxford and called to the Bar in London, he returned to Ireland and began a career in politics, living at Farmley near Burnchurch on the family estate. He married Lady Anne Beresford, the fifth daughter of the Earl of Tyrone, but had no children. In 1768 he was involved in a duel with a political rival, Mr Agar, whom he shot through the heart. It was in fact his second duel with Agar, the first having taken place in Anglesey- for some reason there had been a re-match! Following an enquiry, Flood was cleared of wrongdoing.

Flood represented what was called the Protestant Ascendancy in the Irish House of Commons in Dublin, but at the same time he wanted greater independence from England. For a time, he was the greatest orator in the House, but by taking a post in the administration of Ireland offered by the Lord Lieutenant Lord Townshend he seemed to compromise his principles of Irish patriotism and independence. As a reformer, he wanted more frequent elections and to extend the franchise, yet he would not include Catholics. His younger rival Henry Grattan who wished to include Catholics in the franchise as well as strengthen Ireland's independence from the crown, surpassed him in the affections of the nation.

After the Constitutional Convention of 1781, in which he worked against the hopes of the Earl Bishop, he sought a future in the English House of Commons at Westminster, although he was less knowledgeable of the issues confronting parliament there. In a brilliant House of Commons, which boasted the likes of William Pitt the younger, Charles James Fox and Edmund Burke, he would find it less easy to shine. Plus, life was made more difficult for him because he refused to join a party.

He finally left England in 1790 and returned to Farmley, dying there a year later on 2 December 1791, just as the French Revolution was taking hold. Not close to his family, Henry settled his estate on Trinity College, Dublin, to found a chair of Irish Literature. This alienation of family assets was challenged by his cousin John Flood II of Flood Hall. John won the case on the grounds that Henry was illegitimate, which he was—his father Warden Flood had a common law wife Isabelle Whiteside to whom he was not married at the time of William's birth— and therefore he could not legally inherit. John Flood III succeeded his father and married Sarah Saurin, a Huguenot from Dublin, whose father was the Attorney General, but they had no children together. Nevertheless, John Flood III had two illegitimate children, William and Anne Lloyd, said to be born to the local blacksmith's daughter. However, forged, Ann and William became John's heirs as stated in a lengthy will of twenty-six A4 pages (Family papers). Anne married Reverend Sir Thomas Cullum of Hardwick, Bury St Edmonds and became a great traveller, even fraternising with the King of Hannover but had no children, while William, my great (x2) grandfather married Frances Hanford in 1848, creating the Hanford Floods.

Frances and William appear a resourceful, energetic and intellectually curious couple, living between Worcestershire and Kilkenny and raising seven children: three boys and four daughters, of whom only one married (my great grandmother). Frances was a friend of the Barrett Brownings and visited then in Florence. The two older boys went into the army, and Colonel John Hanford Flood of the Hussars reached the peak of his career at the battle of Tel-el-Kebir 1882 in Egypt. It was said that back in Kilkenny, the brothers were too busy hunting to get married. Two of the sisters, Annie and Alice, were accomplished artists, and after the death of her brothers, Annie became the chatelaine of Woollas Hall until 1939 and was godmother to the Poet Laureate, John Masefield.

Mary (nee Hanford Flood) Hervey died in 1937, and with her came to an end the family's living link with Kilkenny. From 1939 the lands and houses were sold, mostly to the Irish Land Commission. Those carefree holidays enjoyed by my father, uncle and aunts came to an end also in 1939, under the fog of war. Irish soldiers were billeted in Flood Hall during the war, and it later suffered a fire and much of it was pulled down.

Having completed our handover of documents to the Society, Olivia and I looked around Kilkenny, viewing Ormond Castle from the outside as it was closed. We then set off to Burnchurch, Farmley and Flood Hall to see what remained of the estate. We caught sight of the castle tower at Burnchurch from the main road between Kilkenny and Callan and were soon parked beneath the medieval fourteenth century tower. The tower, a kind of five story keep with a smaller round tower close by, was permanently closed. Great Aunt Annie had painted it many times, and I had with me her watercolour book to look at *in situ*. We went into the nearby churchyard with a plaque on its perimeter wall saying Henry Flood the Orator and Parliamentarian was buried here, but so overgrown was the churchyard and so eroded the lettering on the tombstones it was hard to find his tomb. We did find the family mausoleum or vault, also completely overgrown. Scraping off the ivy revealed the names of a host of great grandparents, great aunts and uncles buried there. I turned to look at the church nearby, and was in for shock. It was a ruin, with no roof, open to the skies, with weeds and ivy rife. It all took on a deserted and abandoned feel: with no living relatives nearby for nearly a hundred years to honour their dead and with no local support, the Church of Ireland having long since given up there.

In truth, it was more than that. It was the end of three hundred years in which an Anglo-Irish family had been part of the history of Ireland. They were part of that "ascendency" that was no more. The land which came to them through a Cromwellian soldier, in turn taken from a feudal Anglo-Norman family, the Fitzgeralds, had gone back to where it belonged. Indeed, from the late nineteenth century, Ireland had struggled to be free of England and its rule. Gladstone had tried to give it Home Rule and failed on two occasions, bringing down his government. The First World War postponed a solution, during which the Easter Rising took place in 1916. The Black and Tans, ex-soldiers from the British Army, visited terror on the population until eventually withdrawn. In the 1920s there was civil war, the emergence of the Republican Army, with many burnings of "English" property and the proposed partition of Ireland. It would not be until 1949 that the Irish Republic was fully declared. In all of this one family with insufficient funds, and insufficient heirs could not surf the changing tide. Standing in that churchyard it felt like something out of Thomas Hardy, in which for all these reasons an epoch and its way of life had come to an end.

For the rest of the afternoon, we visited the new owners of the old family properties. At Farmley down the road from Burnchurch we met Mr Woodcock recovering from a knee operation. We explained who we were, and showed him Aunt Annie's watercolours of Farmley, which he recognised. But those days were the distant past to him; life had moved on. From there we went to Flood Hall: once a fine regency mansion, but with little left except a small part of the old house. The outlying buildings are dilapidated. But we found members of the Cummins family who live nearby and intrigued by old photographs of how it once was they pressed us to come in for tea, which we did. Irish hospitality surmounted Covid restrictions.

We went back to Mount Juliet near Flood Hall, relieved to be staying there. It was an old estate that had made the transition to a new future much more elegantly. The original house was built by Somerset Butler, heir to the Earls of Carrick (of the Ormonde family) and his wife Juliet Boyle, the daughter of the Earl of Shannon. They built the present Manor House in 1760 on the banks of the Nore river and over time the estate was planted with beautiful specimen trees. It remained in the family until the McCalmonts bought it around 1900. A popular horse breeding and training family, and neighbours to the Hanford Floods, with whom they shared a passion for hunting, the McCalmonts survived the upheavals of the Irish civil war in the 1920s, caring for their employees and tenants. Then in 1987 the whole estate was sold and bought by Tim Mahony, the importer of Toyota cars, who developed it into a hotel and golf course designed by Jack Nicklaus!

The following day we left for Dublin. Because of Covid, travel by car without good reason was now almost non-existent. As we were leaving the country by ferry in two days' time, we proceeded to Dublin. We picnicked on the Curragh, well known for its racecourse and for the 1914 mutiny by British troops against the possibility of being used against Ulster.

We arrived in Dublin on a Saturday afternoon, and for the next twenty hours walked around the city centre. The bars were filled with pavement drinkers as the Irish made the most of the weekend before an anticipated complete lockdown on the Monday. All the galleries, public buildings, and dine-in restaurants were closed. We walked around St Patrick's Cathedral, Christ Church Cathedral, Dublin Castle, Trinity College, the National Gallery, St. Stephen's Green and Merrion Square, and promised ourselves we would return to see the inside of all these places another time. On Monday we left by ferry for Holyhead, Anglesey. Taking the road that skirts Snowdonia and passing many a slate mine and mound of scree, we made our way to Shrewsbury and England through valleys filled with ancient oak forest.

For all the poignancy of seeing where the family had once flourished and recalling the life of the Earl Bishop, only by going and seeing did I understand my grandmother and our family's connection with Ireland, and appreciate the context in which they waxed, and then waned. I also learned how my great grandmother, Mary Hervey (nee Hanford Flood), did her best to bring meaning and support to the community in the final years of her life. A tribute in a local paper after she died in 1937 held these words:

"In those troubled times sixteen years ago (during the Irish Civil War), in a period and at an age when less gallant spirits might have hesitated to shoulder their responsibilities, Colonel and Mrs Hervey left their home at Bury St Edmunds—a lovely peaceful spot—to come and live among us at Flood Hall and like the Happy Warrior (by William Wordsworth) 'who comprehends his trust, and to the same keeps faithful

with a singleness of aim' encouraged us with their warm and generous heart". The hymns characteristically chosen by Mrs Hervey herself included the triumphant hymn, "Jesus Lives".

So many of the places I have been privileged to visit, and that I have described in this book, have communities that have been, or are, struggling for their future. It was true for the German people and the Berliners struggling to come to terms with the war in the 1950s, and for those in the grip of communism in Eastern Europe and East Germany. Again, in the United States in the 1960s it was the black population that was struggling for freedom and civil rights, and still is. More than fifty years later, these same injustices have been re-ignited by the killing of George Floyd by police officers in Minneapolis, launching the Black Lives Matter Movement in 2020. In the Middle East, the struggle for self-determination and freedom continues: Israel struggles for security, the Palestinians and Kurds for self-determination and the Syrians for healing after a brutal and brutalising conflict, which has displaced five million as refugees, and killed over half a million people, including many children. Egypt continues with a repressive regime, with the Coptic Church suffering intermittent persecution. Most of these struggles have continued throughout my lifetime; some have grown worse. In Africa the church in Northern Nigerian looks for peace from Islamic extremists, represented by Boko Haram, and in South Sudan it addresses ethnic rivalry with the hope of reconciliation. In Eastern Europe a horrifying war has come to Ukraine catching the world off guard. For its part, Armenia has once again been subjected to attack by a resurgent Turkey arming the Azerbaijanis. To go, to listen, to see, and to try and understand is always a humbling and informative experience. It is a reminder that for many millions these painful struggles continue. All "a witness to struggle" can do is give evidence about what is going on and support the few he or she meets.

In November 2020 I came back from a short visit to Heliopolis in Egypt, just to the north of central Cairo, where I had been making some videos about the Cappadocian Fathers. An abiding image remains. I was worshipping in St Mark's Heliopolis on Cleopatra Street. It was during the pandemic and we were all wearing face masks. A man came in through the security fence, past two-armed policemen and through a metal detector and was given a temperature test and offered hand gel. Having done all that, he came into the church, stopped, remained motionless for a moment and then raised his hands in prayer! He reminded me of a saying from Ecclesiastes:

Who is like the wise person?

Who knows the explanation of things?

Wisdom brightens a person's face and changes its hard appearance. (Ecclesiastes 8:1)

In seeking the source of wisdom through prayer he was brightening his face in hope. Travel can also lead you into greater wisdom, and enriching, spontaneous encounters can wonderfully brighten your face. It has been my privilege to have been to many places and peoples. And it is not over yet! What about the Baltic States, Scandinavia, Southern Germany from Nurnberg to the Alps, and through Spain to Morocco? They are on the bucket list! Olivia, what do you think, shall we go?

Hooded matriarchs, Olivia and Mandy Falkus, at the Tombs of the Patriarchs in Hebron, The West Bank, 2011

Grandfather, Major Bartle Edwards MC, back row second from left, in the Palestine Campaign of 1917. They took Jerusalem by Christmas 1917

Patrick, the Bishop of Cairo and Michael. May 2011

The White Desert, Egypt

Desert foxes, The White Desert, Egypt

The author, The White Desert, 2011

A sea shell in the White Desert. The Desert was once all under sea-water

Three men in Cappadocia: Patrick, Tom and Paul.

The Three Magi: Mural in the Dark Church Göreme,
Cappadocia

The three not so wise men, ballooning

The Pechersk Lavra Monastery, Kiev. December, 2013

Three revolutionaries in Kriv, Maiden Square: Paul, Patrick and
Tom. December, 2013

Dormition Cathedral, Kyiv. December, 2013

Martin Luther, Dresden, 2017

The Reconciliation Chapel with Cross of Nails from Coventry
in the Kreuzkirche, Dresden

Playing Johann Sebastian Bach, near St Thomas Leipzig, 2017

Friendly revolutionaries May 2018, Yerevan Armenia

Mt Ararat overlooking the Khor Virap Monastery

Holocaust Memorial and Museum, Yerevan

Priest in the Cathedral in Echmiadzin Cathedral Church or
Armenian Orthodox Church

The painted monastery of Voronet, founded 1488, in the
Bukovina region, 2019

Richard and Patrick with an Orthodox Priest being given gifts of
bread and wine, 2019

The Elie Wiesel Memorial house in Sighetu Marmatiei in the Maramures
region of Romania (NW Romania – close to the Ukraine)

Family of Sir Norman Stronge and friends, 1978. Sir Norman (second
right) and James Stronge (second left) were murdered by the IRA in
1981, and the house Tynan Abbey burnt to the ground.

The Mussenden Temple, Downhill NI built by my Great x4 Grandfather,
The Earl Bishop of Derry

Appendix: Travel Time Line

1951–53	Krefeld, West Germany
1955–57	Hubblerath, West Germany
1957–1959	Milon-La Chapelle, France
1961–1963	Berlin, during which time the Berlin Wall was built
1968	Overland through France to Madrid
1969	Eight months in USA
1970	Overland France, Italy, Yugoslavia
1972	Overland Italy, Greece, Turkey and Iran
1973	Kenya, Tanzania, Zambia and Malawi
1974	Moscow and Leningrad (St Petersburg)
1975–1977	Tuscany summer holidays
1979	Israel: St George's Jerusalem, ten week course with Olivia
1991	Port Harcourt and Aba, Nigeria
1992	Washington: Parish Swop
1992	Katowice, Krakow, Auschwitz Poland
1993	Ludhiana, Amritsar, the Punjab India
1995	Kano, Bauchi Nigeria
2002	Overland to Amman Jordan, via Germany, Hungary, Turkey and Syria
2003	Family visit to Berlin
2008	Ephesus, Samos Patmos and the Seven Churches of Asia
2009	Athos and Macedonia
2011	February, to Israel
2011	May, overland to Egypt
2012	Maridi, South Sudan (March), Cappadocia (May)
2013	Paris, Berlin (again!), Warsaw and Kyiv (Dec)
2015	Cyprus

2016	Malta (February), Peloponnese (May)
2017	Saxony
2018	Sicily (March), Armenia (May)
2019	Overland to Romania: Germany, Hungary, Romania
2020	Ireland
2020	Heliopolis, Egypt
2021	Crete

Bibliography

Adams, R.J.Q. *Balfour The Last Grandee* (Thistle Publishing, London 2013)

Applebaum, Anne, *Twilight of Democracy: The Failure of Politics and the Parting of Friends* (Allen Lane 2020)

Applebaum, Anne, *Gulag: A History* (Penguin 2003)

Applebaum, Anne, *Iron Curtain: The Crushing of Eastern Europe* (Penguin Books 2013)

Applebaum, Anne, *Between East and West: Across the Borderlands* of *Europe* (Penguin 2015)

Ascherson, Neal, *Black Sea: Coasts and Conquests from Pericles to Putin* (Vintage 2015)

Asher, Michael, *Thesiger* (Penguin 1995)

Augustine, *The Confessions* tr. Henry Chadwick (OUP 2008)

Basil of Caesarea, *Letters 1–58* tr. by Roy Deferrari (Loeb Classical Library vol 190 Harvard University Press 1926)

Beaton, Roderick, *Greece: Biography of a Modern Nation* (Penguin 2020)

Bernieres Louis de, *Birds Without Wings* (Vintage 2005)

Binyon, T.J. Binyon *Pushkin: A Biography* (HarperCollins 2002)

Booth, Martin, *Opium: a History* (Simon and Schuster, London 1996)

Beevor, Antony, *Berlin: The Downfall 1945* (Penguin 2007)

Beevor, Antony, *Crete: The Battle and the Resistance* (John Murray 2015)

Bradley, Mark, *Too Many to Jail: The Story of Iran's Christians* (Lion Hudson 2014)

Brewin Don, *It will Emerge* (Self-Published 2008)

Calder Marshall, *The Two Duchesses* (Hutchinson & Co 1978)

Cameron, David, *For the Record* (William Collins 2019)

Camus, Albert, *The Outsider* (Penguin 1966)

Chadwick Henry, *East and West: The Making of a Rift in the Church* (OUP 2005)

Chapman, Caroline, *Elizabeth and Georgiana* (John Murray 2002)

Colville, John, The *Fringes of Power: Downing Street Diaries 1939–1955* (Weidenfeld & Nicolson 2016)

Connolly, *Airse and Go: W.B. Yeats — The People and Places that inspired him* (The O'Brien Press Dublin 2019)

Cooper, Artemis *Cairo: In the War 1939–1945* (John Murray 1989)

Cooper, Artemis, Antony Beevor *Paris: After the Liberation 1944–1949* (Penguin 2017)

Cooper, Artemis, *Patrick Leigh Fermor: An Adventure* (John Murray 2013)

Dalrymple, William, *From the Holy Mountain* (HarperCollins 1998)

Dannatt, Richard, *Leading from The Front* (Corgi Books 2010)

De-La-Noy, *The House of Hervey: A History of Tainted Talent* (Constable 2001)

Douglas Hume, Alec, *The Way the Wind Blows* (Collins 1976)

Eusebius, *The History of the Church* (Penguin Classics 1989)

Earle, John, *The Price of Patriotism* (The Book Guild 2005)

Ferriter, Diarmaid, *The Border: The Legacy of a Century of Anglo-Irish Politics* (Profile Books 2019 London)

Figes, Orlando, *Natasha's Dance* (Penguin 2003)

Figes Orlando, *The Whisperers: Private Life in Stalin's Russia* (Penguin 2008)

Flood, Warden, *Memoirs of the life and Correspondence of Right Hon. Henry Flood* (John Cummings Dublin 1838)

Fothergill, Brian, *The Mitred Earl: An Eighteenth Eccentric* (Faber and Faber 1974)

Frankopan Peter, *The Silk Roads: A New History of the World* (Bloomsbury 2016)

Gardiner, Brian, *Allenby* (Cassell 1965)

Glenny, Misha, *The Balkans: Nationalism, War and The Great Powers*

(Granta Books 2000)

Goodwin, Jason, *Lords of the Horizons* (Chatto and Windus 1998)

Grant, R.G. *The Berlin Wall* (Wayland Publishers 1998)

Hailsham, Lord, *The Door Wherein I Went* (Collins, Fount 1978)

Harman, Tim, *Poland* (Columbus Books 1988)

Harris, Robert, *Lustrum* (Arrow Books 2010)

Hegarty, Neil, The *Story of Ireland* (BBC Books Ebury Publishing, Random House 2011)

Herrin, Judith, *Byzantium: The Surprising Life of a Medieval Empire* (Penguin Books 2007)

Higgins, Fergus and Anne, *A Few Brief Hours: The Life of Charles Higgins* (Privately Published, Printed by W & J Mackay Ltd Chatham 1974)

Hislop, Victoria, *Those Who Are Loved* (Headline Review 2020)

Holland Tom, *Persian Fire* (Abacus 2009)

Howell, Georgina, *Queen of the Desert: The Extraordinary Life of Gertrude Bell* (Pan books Macmillan 2006)

Hughes, Bettany, *A Tale of Three Cities: Istanbul* (Weidenfeld & Nicholson 2017)

Hughes, Bettany, *Helen of Troy* (Pimlico 2013)

Hurndall Jocelyn, *Defy the Stars: The Life and Tragic Death of Tom Hurndall* (Bloomsbury 2007)

Josephus, *The Jewish War* (Penguin 1962)

Katouzian, Homa, *The Persians: Ancient, Medieval and Modern Iran* (Yale University Press 2010)

Kelly, John, *Henry Flood*

Kilkenny Moderator 1911 (Private Papers, Patrick Whitworth)

King, Charles, *Moldova: Romania, Russia, and Politics of Culture* (Hoover Institution Press 2000)

King Hall, Magdalen, *The Edifying Bishop* (Peter Davies 1951)

Lane Fox, Robin, *Alexander the Great* (Penguin Books, Allen Lane 1973)

Lane Fox, Robin, *Pagans and Christians* (Penguin 2006)

Lawrence John, *A History of Russia* (Meridian 1993)

Lawrence, T.E. *The Seven Pillars of Wisdom* (Penguin 2000)

Lee, Harper, *To Kill a Mockingbird* (Arrow Books, Penguin Random House 1969)

Le Carré, John *A Perfect Spy* (Hodders 1986)

Leigh Fermor, Patrick, *Mani: Travels in the Southern Peloponnese* (John Murray 2004)

Leigh Fermor Patrick, *The Broken Road: From the Iron Gates to Mount Athos* (John Murray 2013)

Leigh Fermor, Patrick, *Dashing for the Post: The Letters of Patrick Leigh*

Fermor ed. Adam Sisman (John Murray, 2017)

Lucas, Noah, *The Modern History of Israel* (Weidenfeld and Nicholson 1975)

MacCulloch, Diarmaid, *Reformation: Europe's House Divided 1490–1700* (Penguin 2004)

MacGregor Neil, *Germany* (Penguin 2016)

Mackintosh-Smith: *Arabs: A 3,000 Year History of Peoples, Tribes and Empires* (Yale University Press 2019)

Maclean, Fitzroy, *Eastern Approaches* (Penguin 2009)

Mansel, Philip, *Constantinople: City of the World's Desire 1453–1924* (John Murray 2006)

Mansel, Philip, *Aleppo* (I.B. Tauris 2016)

Mansel Philip, *Levant: Splendour and Catastrophe on the Mediterranean* (John Murray 2011)

Marshall Tim, *Prisoners of Geography* (Elliot and Thompson 2015)

Mazower, Mark, *Salonica: City of Ghosts* (Harper Perennial 2005)

McDowall, David *A Modern History of the Kurds* (I.B. Taurus 2004)

Molho M. *Monuments of Thessaloniki* (Molho Publications Thessaloniki 2006)

Moorey, Chris, *A History of Crete* (Haus Publishing Ltd 2019)

Morris, Jan, *Venice* (Faber and Faber 1993)

Muggeridge, Malcolm, *The Green Stick* (Collins Fontana, 1972)

Muggeridge, Malcolm, *The Infernal Grove* (Collins Fontana, 1973)

Neill Stephen, *A History of Christian Missions* (Penguin 1990)

Nicolson, Nigel, *The Grenadier Guards in the War of 1939–1945 Vol II The Mediterranean Campaigns* (Gale and Polden Aldershot 1949)

Nott, David, *War Doctor* (Picador 2019)

Norman, Edward, *A History of Modern Ireland* (Allen Land Penguin Press 1971)

Norwich, John Julius *Sicily: A short History from the Ancient Greeks to Cosa Nostra* (John Murray 2016)

Norwich John Julius, *The Popes: A History* (Chatto and Windus 2011)

O'Brien, Edna, *The Country Girls Trilogy* (Faber and Famer 2017)

Pakenham, Thomas, *The Scramble for Africa* (Abacus 2010)

Pakulah, Hannah, *The Last Romantic: A Biography of Queen Marie of Roumania* (Phoenix 1998)

Ratzer Beryl, *A Historical Tour of the Holy Land* (Gefen Publishing Jerusalem 2010)

Reid, Anna, *Borderland: A Journey through the History of the Ukraine* (Phoenix 2001)

Roper, Lyndal, *Martin Luther: Renegade and Prophet* (Bodley Head 2016)

Rousseau Philip, *Basil of Caesarea* (University of California 1998)

Runciman, Steven, *A Travellers Alphabet: Partial Memoirs* (Thames and Hudson 1991)

Sebag Montefiore, *Jerusalem* (Weidenfeld and Nicholson 2011)

Speake, Graham, *Mount Athos Renewal in Paradise* (Yale University Press 2002)

Stevenson, *1914–1918: History of the First World War* (Penguin 2005)

Stone, Norman, *The Eastern Front* (Penguin 1998)

Suetonius, *The Twelve Caesars* tr. Robert Graves (Penguin 2007)

Thesiger, Wilfrid, *Life of My Choice* (William Collins 1987)

Thubron, Colin, *Among the Russians: From the Baltic to the Caucuses* (Vintage 2004)

Thucydides, *The Peloponnesian War* tr. Martin Hammond (OUP 2009)

Tomlin, Graham, *Luther and His World* (Lion 2002)

Vassiltchikov, Missie, *The Berlin Diaries 1940–1945* (Pimlico 1999)

Ware, Bishop Kallistos, *The Orthodox Way* (St Vladimir's Press New York 1979)

Ware, (Timothy) Kallistos, *The Orthodox Church* (Penguin 1997)

Williams, Charles, *De Gaulle: The Last Great Frenchman* (John Wiley & Sons 1993)

Williams, Rowan, *The Wound of Knowledge* (Darton, Longman and Todd 2010)

Willner, Nina, *Forty Autumns* (Abacus 2016)

Winder, Simon, *Germania (*Picador 2011)

Woodham Smith, Cecil, *Florence Nightingale* (Constable & co 1952)

Wheeler, Andrew Ed. *Land of Promise: Church Growth in a Sudan at War* (Paulines Publications Nairobi 1997)

Whitworth, Patrick, The *Bible Inside Out* (Sovereign World Trust 2016)

Whitworth, Patrick, *Prepare for Exile* (SPCK 2009)

Whitworth, Patrick, *Becoming Fully Human* (Terra Nova 2003)

Whitworth, Patrick, Three *Wise Men from the East: The Cappadocian Fathers and The Struggle for Orthodoxy* (Sacristy Press 2015)

Whitworth Patrick, *From Constantinople to Chalcedon: Shaping the World to Come (*Sacristy Press 2017)

Whitworth, Patrick, *Suffering and Glory: The Church from the Apostles to Constantine* (Sacristy Press 2018)

(A.W. Whitworth) *Diary of a Tour in Greece Spring 1904* (Privately Published in the Papers of the Author)

Whitworth, Rex, *The Grenadier Guards* (Leo Cooper 1974)

Wilkinson, Toby, *The Rise and Fall of Ancient Egypt; The History of a Civilisation from 3000 BC to Cleopatra* (Bloomsbury 2010)

Yates, Timothy, *Christian Mission in the Twentieth Century* (CUP 1996)